Russia's First World War
A Social and
Economic History

Peter Gatrell

PEARSON
Longman

Harlow, England • London • New York • Boston • San Francisco • Toronto • Sydney • Singapore • Hong Kong
Tokyo • Seoul • Taipei • New Delhi • Cape Town • Madrid • Mexico City • Amsterdam • Munich • Paris • Milan

PEARSON EDUCATION LIMITED

Edinburgh Gate
Harlow CM20 2JE
United Kingdom
Tel: +44 (0)1279 623623
Fax: +44 (0)1279 431059
Website: www.pearsoned.co.uk

First edition published in Great Britain in 2005

ISBN-10: 0-582-32818-7
ISBN-13: 978-0-582-32818-1

British Library Cataloguing in Publication Data

Gatrell, Peter.
    Russia's First World War: a social and economic history / Peter Gatrell.– 1st ed.
    p. cm.
    Includes bibliographical references and index.
    ISBN 0–582–32818–7 (pbk.)
        1. Russia--Economic conditions–1861–1971. 2. Russia–Social conditions–1801–1917.
    3. World War, 1914–1918–Russia. 4. Russia–History–Nicholas II, 1894–1917. 5. Soviet
    Union–History–Revolution, 1917–1921. I. Title.

HC334.5.G378 2005
940.3'47--dc22   2004060071

Library of Congress Cataloging in Publication Data
A CIP catalog record for this book can be obtained from the Library of Congress

10 9 8 7 6 5 4 3 2
09 08 07 06 05

Set by 3
Printed and bound in Malaysia, PJB

To my brother

Contents

List of tables

Preface and acknowledgements

Intense interest in the history of the First World War shows no signs of abating. Major overviews are currently in progress, including Hew Strachan's comprehensive trilogy dealing with the global impact of the 1914–1918 war. A rich historiography now includes work on the cultural history of the war, on topics ranging from shell-shock and bodily dismemberment, to the myriad ways of commemorating the war and its victims. Important work also continues to be done on the economic history of the war, which is summarised in the new book edited by Stephen Broadberry and Mark Harrison, *The Economics of World War 1*.

In Russia the war has until recently been relatively neglected, as historians understandably skipped impatiently past the preliminaries of war to reach the revolution of 1917. Lest there be any misunderstanding, I have no wish to diminish the significance of the Russian revolution, but I seek to set the upheaval of revolution in the context of the preceding three years of debate, development and suffering – in other words to give the war its due. I have focused primarily on economic and social change, because these issues have been given insufficient attention in the English-language literature. Economic and social change cannot of course be divorced from political and military developments, to which I have alluded where appropriate. Interested readers are referred to thorough treatments of these topics by Bruce Lincoln, Norman Stone, Raymond Pearson and others, including Alexander Solzhenitsyn.

One of the challenges I faced was to decide when to bring the story of Russia's First World War to an end. To stop with the February revolution of 1917 makes no sense, because the Provisional Government kept Russia in the war. One option was to conclude with the abortive military offensive in the summer of 1917, but this would have prevented me from dealing with the October revolution. I decided that little would be gained by concluding with the Bolshevik revolution, because enemy troops remained on Russian soil and the Allies hoped that Russia would remain in the war. It seemed more appropriate to bring the book to a close at the beginning of March 1918, when Soviet Russia finally signed the treaty of Brest-Litovsk, although in practice I have taken the story through to the early summer, to take account of key decisions affecting industry and food supply. Thereafter the behaviour of the economy and the fortunes of society become more clearly bound up with the onset of the Civil War and Allied intervention than with the impact of the First World War.

I hope that this book will be of value to those interested in the history of the First World War and the history of modern Russia. If it encourages further attempts to give wartime developments the attention they deserve and to locate the Russian experience more firmly in a European perspective, as I have tried to do in my Conclusion, then it will have served its purpose.

I wish to thank the UK Arts and Humanities Research Board and the University of Manchester for research leave, and Stuart Jones, Raymond Pearson, Bob Service and Penny Summerfield for supporting my application for leave, without which it would have taken me even longer to bring this book to completion. At an earlier stage of my research I also received a travel grant from The Leverhulme Trust. Mark Harrison invited me to contribute to the collective volume on World War 1, commented on my draft chapter and saved me from several errors. My colleagues Theo Balderston, Bob Millward and Ruggero Ranieri also commented on work in progress and offered helpful advice, which I have tried to follow. At a later stage I received generous and timely advice from Daniel Orlovsky and Geoff Swain, both of whom read my manuscript carefully and made numerous suggestions for improvement. None of these scholars should be held responsible for any remaining errors or shortcomings in this book. Edward Acton, Mark Baker, Nick Baron, Richard Davies, Sarah Davies, Tony Heywood, Peter Holquist, Petra Kodalíková, Yanni Kotsonis, Eric Lohr, Karen Petrone, Pavel Polian and Josh Sanborn helped me in various ways, either by providing books, supplying references, allowing me to read unpublished work or offering encouragement. My debt to the work of other scholars who have explored aspects of Russia's First World War should be obvious. I am particularly grateful to Nikolai Smirnov for inviting me to contribute to a conference in St Petersburg on Russia's experience during the First World War. Some of my intellectual debts are noted in the guide to further reading at the end of each chapter.

I wish to thank the staff of the John Rylands University Library, Manchester; the Brotherton Library at Leeds University; Cambridge University Library; the British Library; the Library of the London School of Economics and Political Science; the Baykov Library, University of Birmingham; the Lenin Library, Moscow; the Russian National Library of St Petersburg; Helsinki University Library; and Columbia University Library. Staff at various Russian archives provided me with material during several research trips to Moscow and St Petersburg. Peter Shoenberg kindly offered accommodation in London. I would also like to express my appreciation to the staff at Pearson Education and to Helen MacFadyen, my copy editor, for their help in turning my manuscript into a book.

I am fortunate to have been able to write this book in happy circumstances, thanks to the love and support provided by close members of my family, above all Jane, Dave and Lizzy Gatrell.

Publisher's acknowledgements

We are grateful to the following for permission to reproduce copyright material:

Maps 1 and 3 adapted from Gatrell, Peter, *A Whole Empire Walking: Refugees in Russia During World War I*, Indiana University Press, 2000; map 2 adapted from Davies, R. W., Harrison, Mark and Wheatcroft, Stephen, *The Economic Transformation of the Soviet Union, 1913–1945*, Cambridge University Press, 1993; map 4 adapted from Pierce, Richard, *Russian Central Asia, 1867–1917. A Study in Colonial Rule*, copyright © 1960 The Regents of the University of California.

Table 5.3 from Davies, R. W., Harrison, Mark and Wheatcroft, Stephen, *The Economic Transformation of the Soviet Union, 1913–1945*, Cambridge University Press, 1993; tables 6.6, 6.8 and 11.4 from Gatrell, Peter, 'Poor Russia: poor show: mobilizing a backward economy for war, 1914–1917', in Harrison, Mark and Broadberry, Stephen, *The Economics of World War One*, Cambridge University Press, forthcoming; table 9.2 from Koenker, Diane P. and Rosenberg, William G., *Strikes and Revolution in Russia, 1917*, © 1989 Princeton University Press.

In some instances we have been unable to trace the owners of copyright material, and we would appreciate any information that would enable us to do so.

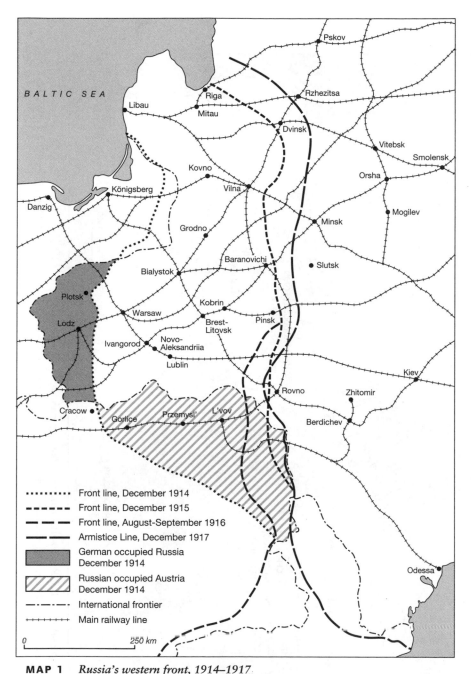

MAP 1   *Russia's western front, 1914–1917*

Source: Adapted from Gatrell, Peter, *A Whole Empire Walking: Refugees in Russia During World War I*, Indiana University Press, 2000.

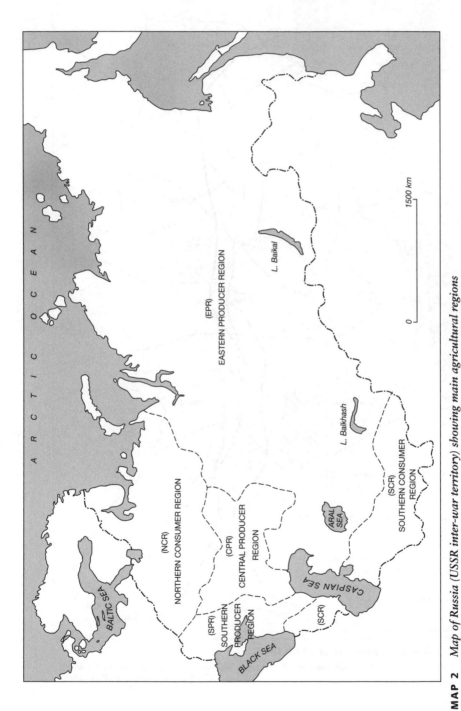

MAP 2   *Map of Russia (USSR inter-war territory) showing main agricultural regions*

Source: Adapted from Davies, R.W., Harrison, Mark, and Wheatcroft, Stephen, *The Economic Transformation of the Soviet Union, 1913–1945*, Cambridge University Press, 1993.

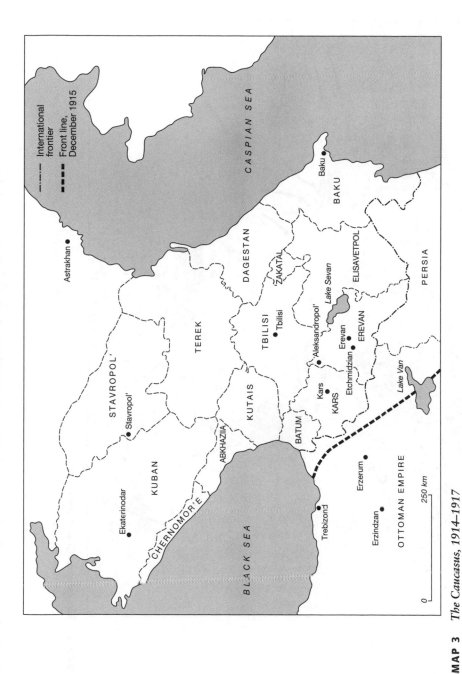

MAP 3 *The Caucasus, 1914–1917*

Source: Adapted from Gatrell, Peter, *A Whole Empire Walking: Refugees in Russia During World War I*, Indiana University Press, 2000.

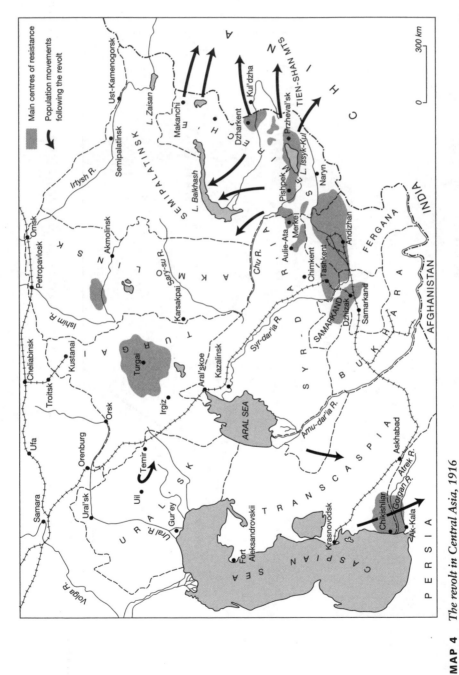

MAP 4   *The revolt in Central Asia, 1916*

Source: Adapted from Pierce, Richard, *Russian Central Asia, 1867–1917: A Study in Colonial Rule,* copyright © 1960 The Regents of the University of California.

Introduction

Russia's participation in the First World War lasted just over three and a quarter years, from 19 July 1914 to 26 October 1917 (Old style). During that time close on 15 million men passed through the 'grinding mill'.[1] Some 5 million Russian troops entered captivity and a further 2 million men died, either on the battlefield or as a result of wounds or infectious disease. In the first five months alone, military defeats left the tsarist army bloodied; 250,000 soldiers lost their lives before the year was out. The Russian High Command and those responsible for military procurement came under attack from parliamentary critics and from public opinion. Military losses, the involuntary displacement of civilians and the ensuing political turmoil in the summer of 1915 did nothing to improve the public mood. Confidence in the ruling elite quickly evaporated as stories emerged of 'dark forces' at the heart of the dynasty, compounding a popular belief that they had somehow exacerbated the food and fuel crisis. In February 1917 the 300-year old regime collapsed. In a fateful decision the ensuing Provisional Government kept Russia in the war, until it was overthrown in turn by the Bolsheviks in October 1917, whose platform famously identified 'peace, bread and land' as the key issues requiring an immediate resolution.

Most European powers betrayed unease about the strains that war would impose upon the social and political fabric, and for that reason governments as well as military planners initially demanded a speedy resolution to the conflict. Russia was no exception. Its size and reserves of manpower and food were believed capable of supporting a prolonged campaign, in the unlikely event that this happened. The eminent economist Tugan-Baranovskii anticipated that developed countries, such as Germany, would suffer most from a protracted war, whereas 'agricultural' Russia would be relatively unscathed. It did not take long for inflation and food shortages to make this assessment look excessively optimistic.[2]

Thus, as a direct result of the war a system of rule was established that endured until Soviet communism collapsed in the last decade of the twentieth century. This has inevitably coloured approaches to Russia's First World War. The tone of much of the debate was set by Lenin, for whom war created the preconditions for socialist revolution, by transforming the capitalist system and strengthening its contradictions. His analysis became the cue for successive generations of Soviet historians to conduct research on structural change and the class struggle. Western scholars also made a close connection between war and revolution, arguing that the prolonged conflict fatally undermined the progress made by tsarist Russia in the years beforehand.[3]

Of course we cannot discount what hindsight tells us about the outcome of war in Russia. Nor is it necessarily unhistorical to do so. Many contemporaries recalled the domestic turmoil that followed the Russo-Japanese War and were keenly attuned to the resurgence of social unrest in Russia after 1912. It makes little sense to overlook these anxieties, which helped to shape many of the decisions reached in the final years of the old regime. However, taking Russia's First World War seriously means regarding it as something more than a stepping stone on the path to revolution. Changes in the pattern of production or in economic and social policy are worth examining in their own right and as a means of making informed comparisons with other belligerents that grappled with the complexities of resource allocation and social and cultural mobilisation.

Another approach to 'locating' the First World War in Russian history is to concentrate upon what has been termed the 'continuum of crisis' between 1914 and 1921. In this interpretation, the revolution did not establish an absolute discontinuity; the Bolsheviks appropriated and extended wartime doctrines and techniques of rule from the old regime. The behaviour of economic variables also suggests continuities across the revolutionary divide, notably in the declining availability of food and the accelerating inflation. This stimulating body of work focuses attention on state practice rather than political ideology.[4]

Something of the challenge to the historian of Russia's First World War was well expressed by James Shotwell, the general editor of the Carnegie Endowment series on the social and economic history of the war:

In the case of Russia, civil war and revolution followed so closely upon the World War that it is almost impossible for history to measure with any degree of accuracy the effects of the World War itself upon the economic and social life of the country. Those effects were so distorted by the forces let loose in the post-war years and so confused with the disturbances of the revolutionary era that the attempt to isolate the phenomena of the War from the data of civil war has been a task of unparalleled difficulty . . .[5]

This book is in part an attempt to rise to Shotwell's challenge. I can best summarise my overall approach by saying that poverty, policy options and choices, and social faultlines are the threads that connect the narrative and constitute the underlying analytic framework. Due attention is given to structural shortcomings in Russia's economy and society. Economic backwardness limited many of the options available to decision makers, who could not remedy in a matter of months the constraints imposed by decades of under-development. I consider the decisions that were reached about the use of available resources. I make no glib assumptions about the stupidity or shortsightedness of Russia's leaders, although I show how some decisions had disastrous consequences. I also identify longstanding and unresolved conflicts that hindered the implementation of policy. The war introduced new divisions. They were intensified and reconfigured by the political transformation in February 1917, further complicating the conduct of the war effort.

Critics at home and abroad often described Russia as 'mighty but poor'. With a population of 169 million, the Russian empire was 2.5 times the size of its great continental rival Germany, and twice as big as France and Britain combined. By 1914 Russia had experienced more than a quarter century of rapid economic growth. This spurt was interrupted by a sharp downturn between 1900 and 1908, but the long-term trajectory was unmistakable. Total output grew by around 3.4 per cent per annum between 1885 and 1913, and by 5 per cent per annum between 1909 and 1913.[6] The industrialisation drive enabled Russia to begin to close the gap on western Europe. Other development indicators, too, suggest a more dynamic society. Literacy rates rose, infant mortality rates began to fall and new urban centres sprang up.[7] Yet, if this represented the 'mighty' part of the equation, poverty was implied by data on income per head. Here Russia was found wanting. In 1913 output per head stood at 42 per cent of German and French GDP; Britain enjoyed an even greater advantage. By all the normal criteria of economic development, Russia remained a backward country relative to its international competitors.[8]

Russian industry developed at a frantic pace before 1914. Its transformation took the form of a more modern fuel economy and a growing iron and steel sector, as well as the emergence of new industries such as chemicals and electrical engineering. The process of industrial and technological modernisation was sustained in part by direct and indirect foreign investment, primarily from Britain, France, Belgium and Germany.[9] However, new industrial enterprises coexisted alongside primitive work-shops, and even supposedly modern factories relied upon a mixture of new and traditional techniques. The manufacture of consumer goods, textiles in particular, relied quite heavily on imported raw materials. Labour pro-ductivity throughout the entire sector left much to be desired. Factory managers maintained a large labour force, so that they could offset the relative shortage of skilled labour with an abundance of cheap unskilled hands. (This helps to explain why many factories were located in rural Russia.) Typically, a Russian factory produced a bewildering array of product types, reflecting the small production runs and frequent changes demanded by capricious customers, including the government. Some attempts were made to impose control over the market, notably by the for-mation of controversial sales syndicates, but these were confined to a limited number of industries such as coal and steel.[10]

Russia's large and notoriously unstable agricultural sector developed at a less dizzying speed. Unpredictable meteorological conditions ensured that grain production remained volatile, but contemporaries focused on social relations in agriculture as a prime determinant of poverty. A vast literature dwelled upon the crisis in peasant farming, the decline of gentry farming and the reform of land tenure. The half-century since the emanci-pation of the serfs witnessed a steady transfer of land from the gentry to the peasantry. By the First World War, peasants owned 47 per cent of all land, including forests, meadows and arable land. Central and local gov-ernment authorities owned a further 37 per cent. Private proprietors made up the remainder. Peasants farmed nine-tenths of arable land.[11] Most allot-ments were cultivated by peasant households within a land commune, one of whose functions was to reallocate arable plots periodically in accor-dance with changes in family size and composition. (A German critic called periodic redistribution a device 'to ensure an equal right for everyone to die of starvation'.) The land reforms initiated by Stolypin between 1906 and 1910 encouraged more risk-taking peasants to embark upon the costly and fractious business of leaving the commune and privatising their plots. Continental observers lavished praise on government experts for having pursued this strategy, but it did not fundamentally alter the grip of the village community and the tightly knit households that underpinned it.[12]

All this activity was underpinned by an expanding transport network and by the growth of retail trade as well as a more sophisticated financial services sub-sector. As a large sprawling empire, much of whose popu-lation and natural resources were scattered in far-flung corners, Russia had developed a transport system appropriate to its size. The total length of railway track increased by around one-third between 1900 and 1913, and stood at 71,000 km on the eve of war. Total traffic grew at a much faster pace. However, the capital stock was ageing, with one in four Russian locomotives more than 20 years old; wagons were awkward to load and unload; locomotives had no automatic brakes; switching and signalling were carried out by hand; and many lines were single-track. Railways accounted for three-fifths of all freight transport in 1913, with river and sea transport making up all but a tiny fraction of the remainder. Russia had the equivalent of 42,000 km of navigable rivers and lakes, but not all were suitable for heavy traffic and many were frozen for months at a time.[13]

Organised retail trade was heavily concentrated in urban centres. It was supplemented by unlicensed trade at numerous bazaars and fairs, including the famous fair held annually at Nizhnii Novgorod which regularly attracted 400,000 visitors. Trade was increasingly dominated by major merchant houses whose owners built new warehouses, grain elevators and other facilities. During the war they would move into production as well as distribution. Co-operative societies accounted for a small but growing share of internal trade and played an important additional role in the cultural life of peasants and workers.[14]

War threatened a drastic curtailment of trade, much of it conducted across the western land frontier where fighting was expected to take place. Germany was an important trading partner as well as a source of foreign investment in utilities, electrical engineering, chemicals and the financial sector. In wartime these assets could be frozen or even seized. Trade posed more of a problem. Russia's trade with Germany amounted to 47 per cent of total foreign trade by value. Russia imported industrial equipment and precious metals (tin, nickel and aluminium were entirely imported) as well as dyestuffs and tanning materials. Substantial quantities of manufactured consumer goods, including foodstuffs such as tea and herring, were imported from China and western Europe. Alternative routes would have to be established with neutral partners and with the Allies.[15]

Imperial Russia had enjoyed more than a generation of monetary stability, the result of the momentous decision in 1897 to take the country on to the Gold Standard.[16] Even the Russo-Japanese War did not disturb fundamental confidence in the currency. This helped to underpin the surge in foreign investment before 1914. Most observers took the pre-war upsurge in prices as a sign of underlying economic wellbeing rather than crisis. Russian officials calculated that neither the currency nor Russia's credit-worthiness would be seriously damaged by war. In support they pointed to Russia's relatively painless recovery from the financial consequences of the war against Japan.[17]

Backwardness was deeply entrenched and a constraint on the adaptability of the Russian economy. A dearth of skilled labour made it hard to achieve rapid increases in labour productivity in the short run. Industries of crucial significance to modern war, such as chemicals and machine tools, remained weak. Backwardness implied difficulties in persuading subsistence farmers to apply themselves to the challenge of growing for non-farm consumption. It raised a question mark over the use of financial instruments to encourage the population to contribute to the war effort. The challenge was to remove adult men from agriculture and into the armed forces without damaging agricultural production, and to boost war production without depriving consumers of manufactured goods that they could purchase in exchange for food. These were tough objectives to meet. As one scholar rightly observed, 'poor countries lacked the commercial and administrative infrastructure which modern governments could use to foster the objectives of wartime economic policy'.[18]

Issues of economic potential cannot be divorced from questions of policy and the policymaking process. Which elements of Russian officialdom played a part in managing resources, what criteria governed their deliberations, and what were the consequences of the decisions they took? Who took the key decisions relating to foreign policy and defence planning, and what influence did parliament and the public exert?

One of the characteristics of pre-revolutionary Russia was the lack of institutional mechanisms to extend involvement in decision-making beyond a relatively narrow circle. The elected parliamentary assembly (the State Duma) was a recent innovation, deeply resented by Tsar Nicholas II, who appeared more at ease with political rituals that brought him face to face with his loyal subjects without the mediation of elected representatives. Re-forging that mystical bond could, in the Tsar's view, overcome the tensions that had culminated in full-blown revolution during 1905. Nicholas II demonstrated a very impoverished understanding of the complex forces unleashed by the revolution. Fortunately, many government ministers and civil servants had a more sophisticated grasp of politics. All the same, the hesitant and partial steps taken after 1905 towards liberalisation had not yielded profound changes in the political system as a whole. Unelected ministers and officials retained power and were rarely called to account except by the Tsar himself. Political debate instead crystallised outside parliament, for example in civic associations created in order to address this or that 'problem'.[19] How would the war sustain or undermine these hesitant steps in democratisation? Would it, rather, help to establish a new corporatist politics, conducive neither to traditional tsarist rule nor to democratic government?

The conduct of Russia's foreign and defence policy was entrusted to the Tsar. He alone could declare war and sign treaties. His advisers were drawn from a narrow circle. The establishment of the Duma did not alter that fundamental fact. Parliament voted on the defence budget, but it could only deny the government new resources and Nicholas could ultimately get his way by dismissing the Duma.[20] Public opinion played only a subordinate role in determining foreign policy. Growing criticism was directed at the secretive and often corrupt decision-making process.[21]

The Russo-Japanese War exposed differences of opinion, between those who wished to address Russia's weakness vis-à-vis the western powers (particularly Germany) and those who wanted to establish Russian domination in the Far East. For those who occupied the centre ground of Russian politics, the cornerstone of Russian foreign policy was support for Slav populations in the Balkans and the alliance with France. Centrist politicians expressed their opposition to Austrian and Ottoman rule over Slavs. A vocal lobby supported the idea of pan-Slavic unity. More troubling still was the growing power of Germany. German hopes of extending its influence threatened Russia's hopes of supplanting Ottoman predominance in the Near East. The liberal imperialist Petr Struve argued strongly in support of Russia's claim to pre-eminence in the Black Sea. In these circumstances few spokesmen embraced the idea of jettisoning the alliance with France and Britain in favour of a rapprochement with Germany.[22]

Nationalism and Slavophilism were the watchwords of government officials who wrestled with foreign policy before 1914. This meant support for Serbia in its struggle against Austria-Hungary. The chief political parties, namely the Kadets on the liberal left and the Octobrists to their right, shared this stance. The Kadet politician V.A. Maklakov calculated that espousing a nationalist platform would help undermine the regime's claim to be the sole arbiter of the public interest. Octobrists such as Aleksandr Guchkov and Mikhail Rodzianko drank at the well of Russian nationalism as the best guarantee of protecting Slav interests against the overweening ambitions of Austria and Turkey. This led them to support a more aggressive foreign policy. Yet they were playing with fire. The more Russia's political leaders sought to encourage disaffection among national minorities in Austria-Hungary, the greater the contrast appeared with tsarist Russia's conduct towards its own Polish or Ukrainian subjects.[23]

Russia spent around 965 million rubles on defence in 1913, compared with 640 million rubles in 1909, taking its share from 25 per cent to nearly 30 per cent of total government expenditure. Yet the overall growth in defence spending disguised the fact that Russia had not resolved fundamental strategic issues. Russia's imperialist ambitions in the Far East 'starved' the military of the resources needed to sustain a defence capability in the western borderlands, at the very time when the alliance with France imposed on Russia the need to contemplate military engagement with Germany as well as with Austria-Hungary. Whenever the 'Easterners' threatened to gain the upper hand, the 'Westerners' reminded them of the implications of the Franco-Russian alliance. The alliance confronted Russia with its own set of difficulties. In particular, it necessitated continued investment in fortresses in Russian Poland, from which salient Russia would be expected to launch troops into East Prussia. The Russian Minister of War, V.A. Sukhomlinov, argued that this strategy should be abandoned in favour of a concentration of troops further east. (In 1902 Nicholas II himself had contemplated a strategic withdrawal from Poland, in the event of war with Germany.) In 1912 Sukhomlinov was forced to back down, in favour of increased investment in fortresses in Russian Poland, but he delayed investing in new strategic railway lines that would have improved the prospect of mobilising troops to fight a war with Germany and Austria-Hungary. This investment did not get under way until 1913.[24]

Other measures were taken to remedy deficiencies in overall military preparedness after 1905. The Ministry of War secured resources for more generous officers' pay and pensions, and improved the system of regimental procurement under which peasant conscripts made their own uniforms and boots. Fresh resources were found not only to replenish the stock of weaponry and ships that had been lost, but also to modernise the material basis of both services. The most important measures were the so-called 'Small Programme' in 1910 and the 'Large Programme for Strengthening the Army', adopted in 1914 and due for completion in 1917. The former envisaged spending 700 million rubles on fortresses and railways but relatively modest amounts on heavy artillery. A similar amount was earmarked for the fleet, thanks to the strong personal support of the Tsar, who felt keenly its destruction in the waters of Japan. However, the rationale of maintaining an ocean-going navy was never fully justified, particularly when it diverted resources from other defence needs, including the defence of the Russian capital.[25] Partly as a result of these choices, the Russian army went to war with stocks of small arms, artillery and ammunition that fell short of the mobilisation norms, although only heavy artillery created grounds for concern by 1914. The prescribed norms were not revised upwards. Once they had been reached, orders to government arsenals turned into a trickle. Meanwhile other items, such as motorised vehicles, aircraft and communications equipment, got short shrift.[26]

The aftermath of the Russo-Japanese War encouraged other kinds of stocktaking. To judge from Russia's experience, little faith could be placed in the quality of military leadership. Russian generalship was lacklustre and unimaginative. Recent work has drawn attention to the professionalism with which the tsarist General Staff practised military manoeuvres, understood the need for military intelligence and planned the details of mobilisation. But they had a lot of ground to make up.[27] In an army that prized the soldier's fighting spirit, morale suffered. Reformers urged the inculcation of a much stronger sense of patriotic commitment. It was not sufficient to emphasise the spirit of advance and attack, without at the same time encouraging a 'moral regeneration'. Troops had to understand the goals that were set and enabled to take greater initiative. Accordingly, by 1911 the Ministry of War had espoused the cause of the 'militarisation of the population and the development of feelings of duty from childhood'. This left room for debate: did this mean unquestioning obedience to the Romanov dynasty? Hence the contacts between the Ministry and Octobrist politicians such as Guchkov, for whom professionalism mattered more than dynastic privilege. Russia's defence preparedness was a function of fundamental yet fluid political concerns and social mentalities.[28]

The relationship between government and business before 1914 was an uneasy one. Leading business figures came together in a pressure group called the Association of Industry and Trade. They complained of 'state socialism', including the subsidies given to outmoded and unprofitable enterprises in the state sector. Cumbersome government regulations on incorporation and on the exploitation of mineral wealth drew added criticism. Broadly speaking, there was a strong current of bureaucratic anti-capitalism, which did little to reduce public antipathy towards private enterprise.[29] Yet this critique overlooked the fact that the government supported the private sector with subsidies, tariffs and emergency financial assistance. Leading firms were linked to government by means of procurement agencies that purchased rails and other products, helping to stabilise market conditions. Entrepreneurs and government officials were joined together through a series of interlocking directorships.[30] This relationship tended to create a faultline between business magnates in St. Petersburg and the provincial minnows who were excluded from the councils of state. Moscow's merchant community, in particular, adopted a more critical stance towards government officialdom during the 1905 revolution and established a political forum in the Progressive Party.[31]

A gulf existed between plebeian social groups (workers and peasants) on the one hand, and propertied elements on the other. Such divisions were not unique to Russia, but they were especially acute in Russia because capitalism was still in its infancy and socially deprived groups did not recognise the legitimacy of private property in land or other assets. This tension erupted in a momentous social and political confrontation in 1905. Workers went on strike, soldiers and sailors mutinied and peasants engaged in mass trespass on privately owned land. In the event, the tsarist state and the propertied classes were able to stem the tide of revolution by a clever combination of repression and reform. Millions of the Tsar's subjects received the vote, albeit under a system of indirect franchise. Peasants were entitled to an internal passport, enabling them to travel more freely. The government legalised trade unions and extended the scheme of social insurance. Families of serving soldiers received an allowance from the state. Land reform was meant to establish a sense of the legitimacy of property among the peasantry. However, there was a limit to the concessions made by the state. Peasants failed in their attempt to secure a greater share of the land owned by private landlords. Only relatively small numbers of workers joined trade unions, which were liable to be closed down on the slightest pretext. Soldiers and sailors failed in their attempt to be treated as citizens. Repression meant the execution of hundreds of peasant activists, the punishment of mutineers and the incarceration of thousands of other dissidents.[32]

In the workplace the authority of owners and managers was ultimately underpinned by state power. Government officials rejected any suggestion that Russia should follow the lead of western Europe and introduce conciliation and arbitration procedures.[33] Along with basic material concerns relating to wages and conditions, the call for a more accountable regime in the workplace prompted labour protest after 1910. What counted in the first instance was the sheer growth in numbers of workers during the industrial spurt. Many were new to factory work; others had been laid off during the slump in 1906–1909. Metalworkers in particular faced intolerable pressures; this branch of industry accounted for more than one-half of all recorded strikes in 1912–1914. Managers sought to monitor workers' effort more closely, by introducing complex piece rates that linked payment to economy of effort. The overall strategy, as one employer put it, was 'to eliminate the dependence of production on the personality', without fundamentally altering the powers of the foreman to impose fines for lateness or slacking on the job.[34] Protest gathered momentum, notably in the aftermath of the appalling bloodshed at the remote Lena goldfields in 1912. The prevailing mood was well captured by the Bolshevik activist, Aleksandr Shliapnikov:

Enormous changes had taken place in the attitude of workers as compared with the time that I was last working illegally, in 1907 at the '1886' Power Station. The absence of the timidity and submissiveness which even then was very strong in the plants of St Petersburg, hit you in the eye. You sensed that the workers had matured considerably as individuals. However (he went on) the absence of trade union organisation was apparent.[35]

Industrialisation contributed to other kinds of foreboding. Migration aroused fears of social instability. Migrant labourers embodied poverty and disorder. They came into contact with men and women from different villages, and exchanged stories of displacement and dreams of economic betterment. New consumer wants were also thought to be destabilising, as peasant migrants acquired the taste for new manufactured goods and cultural products. Women began to shape their own lives in the city, unconstrained by traditional rules and patriarchal authority. The single woman often figured in the popular press as a purveyor of commercial sex. Liberal physicians and social commentators believed that the urban environment tended to deprave virtuous peasant in-migrants who forfeited the ties of community for the dubious privilege of individual licence.[36]

Memories of the cataclysmic social conflicts in 1905–1906 remained fresh in the public mind. It was widely believed that social and political divisions would be magnified if Russia went to war. Before his assassination in 1911, Stolypin asserted that war would wreck economic and social reform and, if not properly understood by Russia's people, would 'prove fatal for Russia and for the dynasty'.[37] In a famous Memorandum prepared in February 1914 a leading member of the ruling elite, Petr Durnovo, issued a stark warning about the dangers of war for Russia's future stability:

The peasant dreams of obtaining a gratuitous share of somebody else's land; the workman, of getting hold of the entire capital and profits of the manufacturer. Beyond this, they have no aspirations. If these slogans are scattered far and wide among the populace, and the Government permits agitation along these lines, Russia will be flung into anarchy, such as she suffered in the ever-memorable period of troubles in 1905–1906. War with Germany would create exceptionally favourable conditions for such agitation.'[38]

Such conflicts did not exhaust the potential for discord. Particular attention focused upon the corrosive division between the state and 'educated society', embracing progressive elements among the middle and upper classes. In essence this rift originated from the state's refusal to make government officials publicly accountable. Liberal social commentators found fault with government for having failed to address the consequences of rapid industrial and urban development and for having neglected the contribution of disinterested experts. This stance – which overlooked the fact that some officials were also committed to social improvement – translated into a critique of bureaucratic practice and, by implication, the authority of the Tsar. It helped to underpin the widespread movement for political reform. It explains the disillusionment that followed the conservative policies of the state, such as the restrictions imposed on public meetings and the closure of co-operatives. The First World War enabled professionals to discover fresh fields for expert intervention and to justify more aggressive political mobilisation.[39]

Given these conflicts, particular importance attached to the domestic role of the Russian army and the police. Relations between the military and civilian branches of the state were bedevilled by the growing insistence of military professionals that the primary duty of the army was to defend Russia's external borders, not to deter or pacify domestic unrest.[40] The war magnified rather than lessened the dilemma of civil–military relations. Florinsky termed this 'one of the most important causes undermining the position of the government'.[41] This was not the only issue at stake. The army reflected social division, but it could also be an instrument of social engineering. Properly organised and funded, the armed forces could help to create a sense of unity among hitherto disparate social and ethnic groups. Arguments in favour of creating ethnically-based units in the Russian army had circulated before 1914, but most military planners were reluctant to set an unwelcome precedent by approving such units. More compelling was the idea that non-Russians, particularly the 'foreigners' (*inorodtsy*) in Siberia and Central Asia, should demonstrate their loyalty by serving in the armed forces, rather than expecting the burden to be borne disproportionately by Slav soldiers. Exclusively ethnic units were not required; the issue was how to integrate non-Russians and Russians.[42]

Russian conservatives were unanimous that the state was not immune from further social instability of a kind evident in 1905 and 1906. The classic voice was that of Durnovo, but he was not alone in expressing alarm. Foreign diplomats shared his views. To that extent, the threat of renewed political turmoil may have encouraged German and Austrian military planners to believe that Russia would not risk war.[43] But not all supporters of the old regime could understand why this alarmist opinion held sway. In April 1914 Count V.V. Musin-Pushkin, a well-placed member of the imperial court, wrote to his father-in-law that:

the most bourgeois circles are becoming revolutionary, and it is worse in the provinces than in the capital. Absolutely everyone is discontented. What is most stupid and annoying is that there are no basic reasons for discontent. The country is becoming more prosperous ... but there is such hatred for the government that society is no longer guided by reason.[44]

This point is worth emphasising. Growing economic prosperity before the war did not translate into social stability and political harmony, but Russia's statesmen were prepared to risk war, counting on rearmament and Allied support to tip the balance against Germany and Austria-Hungary. For his part Nicholas II discounted the evidence of social unrest and pinned his hopes on the 'mystical union' between himself and the Russian narod that the tercentenary celebrations of the Romanov dynasty in 1913 appeared to confirm.[45]

Pre-war Russia had significant economic achievements to its credit: an expanding industrial base, a more modern financial sector and a growing communications network. By virtue of its size, the agricultural sector gave contemporaries little cause to anticipate shortages of food or fodder. Besides that inherent advantage, a period of hectic rearmament after 1905 had given Russia a more modern navy and a better-equipped army. Imperial Russia boasted impressive reserves of manpower, and its territorial extent gave it access to abundant raw materials. This demographic strength and the pre-1914 military modernisation, not to mention Russia's alliance with France and Britain, caused considerable alarm in Germany Military planners in Berlin also expressed doubts about Germany's own ability to fight a long war. They decided to strike first before Russia could do irreparable damage to Germany's own pretensions for mastery in Europe. The tsarist government could extend its influence in wartime without a radical departure in practice, since it already played an important role, directly and indirectly, in economic activity. The state boasted an impressive apparatus of social and political control, including a large army and police force that could be mobilised to suppress dissent or overt protest. Russia was not expected to fight alone. From an Allied point of view the tsarist empire brought immense resources to the coalition of forces ranged against Germany and Austria-Hungary. It combined reserves of manpower with impressive supplies of raw materials and a large agricultural sector.

These optimistic assessments disguised troubling features. Russia remained a poor country. Rapid growth did not suddenly eliminate the hallmarks of under-development, including traditional peasant agriculture and a low level of labour productivity. Tsarist society afforded few avenues for social advancement. The political system provided little opportunity to call officials and government ministers to account. Political sclerosis, social disadvantage and economic backwardness gave educated society plenty of good ammunition with which to attack the old regime. Experience hitherto suggested how difficult it was to turn numbers and size into effective military might. Optimists and pessimists alike were thus able to find support for their case at the outbreak of war.

Note on further reading

Foreign policy is best approached through the surveys provided by Geyer, 1987, and Lieven, 1983. On military doctrine and reform the essential work is Fuller, 1985. Rearmament, including its political and diplomatic context, is discussed by Gatrell, 1994. The best work in Russian is exemplified by Shatsillo, 1968. Important studies of social and political change include McDaniel, 1988, and Hogan, 1993, as well as Haimson, 2000. New work on urban culture and liberal anxieties is exemplified by Engelstein, 1992. The classic studies of the economy include Gerschenkron, 1962; Crisp, 1976; and Gregory, 1982.

References

1 Lobanov-Rostovsky, 1935.

2 Tugan-Baranovskii, ed., 1915, pp. 269–324. See too the remarks of Ivan Bloch, in Prokopovich, 1917, pp. 3–32.

3 Gerschenkron, 1962, pp. 138–42; Tarnovskii, 1964.

4 Holquist, 2002; Sanborn, 2003. Compare Lih, 1990. On economic change in 1914–1921 see Davies, Harrison and Wheatcroft, eds, 1994, pp. 216–37 (Gatrell).

5 James Shotwell, Preface to Struve et al., 1930: pp. ix–x.

6 Korelin, 1995, pp. 11–14; Gregory, 1982, pp. 56–7.

7 Gregory, 1982, pp. 172–3, pinpoints the high share of Russian government spending in total activity in 1913, relative to other leading economies, but notes that little went to improving educational opportunities.

8 Gatrell and Harrison, 1993, p. 430.

9 McKay, 1970, pp. 24–39.

10 Davies, ed., 1990, pp. 127–59 (Gatrell and Davies); Sidorov, 1973, pp. 379–81.

11 Antsiferov et al., 1930, pp. 22–3, 354; Koval'chenko et al., 1982, p. 111.

12 Pavlovsky, 1930, pp. 115–45, 245–6; Antsiferov et al., 1930, pp. 347–9 (quoting Wilhelm Preyer). Compare Yaney, 1982, p. 366.

13 Claus, 1922, p. 114; Vasil'ev, 1939, p. 15; Davies, ed., 1990, pp. 172–5 (Westwood).

14 Dikhtiar, 1960, pp. 145–6.

15 Khromov, 1950, pp. 491–3; Hardach, 1977, pp. 238–41; Davies, ed., 1990, pp. 212–18 (Dohan). Russia's trade with Germany included American goods that were re-exported in order to circumvent the tariff.

16 Crisp, 1976, chapter four.

17 Michelson et al., 1928, pp. 235–6.

18 Harrison, 1998, p. 18.

19 Bradley, 2002.

20 The first two Dumas were short-lived, because the assembled delegates brought forward radical proposals for reform. In June 1907 the electoral laws were revised to ensure a more compliant Duma. The Third Duma met between 1907 and 1912. The Fourth Duma was elected in 1912 and continued until the February revolution broke out in 1917.

21 Lieven, 1983, pp. 119, 122, for a more sceptical view.

22 Fuller, 1985, p. 206; Lieven, 1983, p. 127.

23 Lieven, 1983, pp. 126, 129.

24 Fuller, 1992, pp. 329, 377, 385, 440, 444.

25 This 'disproportion' is a major theme in Shatsillo, 1968; see also Mal'kov, ed., 1998, pp. 556, 565 (Shatsillo).

26 Gatrell, 1994; Fuller, 1985, pp. 159, 194–5; Rich, 1998, pp. 234, 273.

27 Coetzee and Shevin-Coetzee, eds, 1995, pp. 275–303 (Steinberg).

28 Fuller, 1985, pp. 197–8, 202–8. Fuller notes the participation of leading military professionals such as Gurko, Danilov, Polivanov and Lukomskii. Guchkov's mail was regularly intercepted by the police, who found only innocuous sentimental expressions of admiration sent by serving officers.

29 Gatrell, 1994, pp. 206–16; Clowes et al., eds, 1991, pp. 75–89 (Owen); Rieber, 1982, p. 339; Roosa, 1997.

30 Shepelev, 1987, pp. 231–44.

31 Rieber, 1982, pp. 324–31; Lohr, 2003, p. 27.

32 Bushnell, 1985; McDaniel, 1988; Ascher, 1988.

33 P&T, 1916, 7 (Vort); Izvestiia MVPK, 1916, 23–24 (Sirinov).

34 Hogan, 1993.

35 Shliapnikov, 1982, p. 3; Haimson, 2000.

36 Brower, 1990, p. 81; Engel, 1994; Engelstein, 1992.

37 Quoted in Mal'kov, ed., 1998, p. 238 (Tiutiukin).

38 Quoted in Golder, 1927, pp. 3–23. See also McDonald, 1992, pp. 199–201.

39 Clowes et al., eds, 1991, pp. 183–98 (Balzer); Neuberger, 1993; Bradley, 2002.

40 Fuller, 1985. This is not to diminish the harshness of the measures that were taken, for example by Vorontsov-Dashkov in the Caucasus.

41 Florinsky, 1931, p. 194.

42 Sanborn, 2003, pp. 65–74.

43 Lieven, 1983, p. 121.

44 V.V. Musin-Pushkin, 19 April 1914, quoted in Cherniavsky, ed., 1967, pp. 12–13.

45 Haimson, 2000; Wortman, 2000, pp. 439–80. Many historians argue that Russia was more stable in 1914 than in 1904. For an example see Mal'kov, ed., 1998, p. 241 (Tiutiukin).

CHAPTER 1

The front line, 1914–1916

From top to bottom, from the highest intellectual summits to the hardly civilised popular masses, the whole country is in a state of ferment. Everyone is anxiously waiting for some great cataclysm which shall bring in its train not only terrible destruction but also regeneration.
[M. Pospelov, August 1915, quoted in Odinetz and Novgorotsev, 1929, p. 163]

Most informed observers expected the war to last for weeks, rather than months. Mobilisation accordingly presented itself to all belligerents primarily as a technical matter of accessing pre-existing stocks of weaponry and ammunition, and of delivering them to the front line along with troops, foodstuffs and equipment. These tasks involved a relatively small number of military planners. So far as production was concerned, government-owned arsenals would continue to deliver artillery, small arms and ammunition, with some supplementary supplies from the private sector. No adjustments were made to production schedules. No thought was given to the impact of conscription on industrial production. Nor did the location of industrial enterprises close to Russia's external frontiers in the north-west give any cause for alarm.[1]

Even within this narrowly circumscribed scenario, however, much more was at stake than technical issues of supply. A small handful of radical socialist parliamentarians proclaimed their opposition to war credits, but even they expressed the hope that 'Russian culture could be defended against attacks from without and within'.[2] Leading Russian intellectuals and political leaders of virtually every hue proclaimed the legitimacy of war against the 'Teutonic foe'. On the political left, the leading social democratic critic Petr Maslov argued that all classes of society had a vested interest in a Russian victory: 'the murder of industry and agriculture in Ireland, inflicted by England, is a frightening foretaste of what would be in store', should Germany win the war.[3] In the provincial town of Iaroslavl' workers, professional people, merchants, shopkeepers, women and children attended patriotic meetings. An editorial in the local newspaper captured the mood by claiming that 'there are no longer political parties, disputes, no government, no opposition – there is just a united Russian people, reading to fight for months or years (sic) to the very last drop of blood. ... Here begins the second great patriotic war'. The entry of the Ottoman empire into the war on the side of Germany in October 1914 guaranteed a fresh outpouring of emotion that lasted until the beginning of 1915.[4]

Unhappily for Russia, the military campaigns failed for the most part to live up to expectations. At the apex of military command the tensions between the War Ministry and the Supreme Command in the field were accentuated by a personality clash between Sukhomlinov and Grand Duke Nicholas, contributing to a lack of co-operation over planning. Shortcomings also manifested themselves in terms of the supply and transportation of munitions. The scale of the task confronting the Russian army proved overwhelming. On the field of battle there was insufficient co-ordination between the generals. Far from dealing a decisive blow to German and Austrian ambition, the Russian army experienced a series of defeats that demoralised front-line troops and civilians alike. No less troubling were the first signs of involuntary population displacement, as the retreating columns of soldiers and the bedraggled ranks of refugees brought the war directly into the towns and villages of European Russia.

1.1   Tsarist military campaigns

Military misfortune meant the loss of territory to the German army in 1914. The pattern of defeat was established early on. Between August and December 1914, the German army repelled the Russian onslaught in east Prussia, by means of a brilliant manoeuvre that first crushed Samsonov's Second Army before turning its artillery on the First Army under the hesitant command of Rennenkampf (a Baltic German nobleman). German troops then advanced steadily along the Baltic coastal region and prepared to march on Warsaw. Following heavy losses at Tannenberg, Samsonov committed suicide, while Rennenkampf was accused of treason. A pattern quickly established itself comprising poor Russian generalship, weak military communications and intelligence and mutual recrimination. Supply difficulties and shortages of arms and equipment did not figure in the account at this stage.[5] By the end of the year, the Russian army had lost control of the major industrial town of Lodz, leaving the German army a mere 50 miles from the Polish capital, which had now become home to 100,000 Jewish and Polish refugees. To the north, the enemy advanced deep into the region of Kaunas (Kovno), capturing the Latvian port city of Liepaja (in German, Libau) and threatening the Russian capital.[6]

These defeats were offset by early victories over the Habsburg army. Russian troops attacked at great speed through Galicia and Bukovina, capturing L'vov only a month after the outbreak of war. Here, at least, was a success that could be exploited in propaganda terms.[7] Around 100,000 Austro-Hungarian troops were taken prisoner during this first offensive. A further 120,000 followed them into captivity when the Russians took the fortress of Przemysl' in March 1915.[8] Unfortunately, the Russian army proved unable to capitalise upon this victory. The new commander of Russian troops on the north-western front, Mikhail Alekseev, argued that he could only hold the line against the German army by reinforcing his own divisions; he was unwilling to see the front weakened in order to bolster Russian forces in the south-west. Disagreements and delays gave the Austrians time to regroup. Worse still, the Germans decided to deploy massive heavy artillery firepower in a narrow strip of land between Tarnow and Gorlice. The Russian army proved completely out-gunned, and its modest reserves of artillery ammunition evaporated. Some 240,000 Russian troops were taken prisoner. This was a moment of truth, exposing the lack of artillery and shell, as well as the modest quality of replacement troops and a shortage of rifles with which to send them into battle.[9]

Russian troops enjoyed greater success against the Ottoman empire, whose rulers had thrown in their lot with Germany. Turkish and German warships jointly bombarded Odessa and Sevastopol. This action led Russia to declare war on 18 October 1914, although the High Command hoped to commit the minimum number of troops and ships to the Caucasian front. However, the Russians were obliged to deal with a Turkish offensive in eastern Anatolia in November, which resulted in heavy casualties for the Ottoman army. After a protracted campaign, the Russian army entered Ottoman territory in the late summer of 1915.[10]

During 1915 the Russian army suffered a series of dreadful setbacks that put even the debacle of 1914 in the shade. After a series of carefully planned manoeuvres, the German army occupied all of Poland, Lithuania and large parts of Belorussia. In April, General Mackensen launched a fierce offensive against the Russian Third Army, stationed between Tarnow and Gorlice. During the next five months, the Russian army suffered losses of around one million war dead and wounded, while a further one million were taken prisoner.[11] Each month gave rise to fresh military catastrophes. Warsaw fell on 22 July. The fortresses of Ivangorod, Novo-Georgievsk and Brest-Litovsk succumbed as well. By mid-August no Russian troops remained on Polish territory. Further north, the German army consolidated the gains made during the previous year's offensive. Riga itself – the fourth largest city of the Russian empire – was threatened by troops who dug in no more than 25 miles from the city's outskirts. By the summer of 1915 the German army occupied Russian Poland, as well as the provinces of Grodno, Vilno, Kovno and Kurland. Substantial territory in Belorussia, including the provinces of Minsk and Volynia, also fell into enemy hands. Even Petrograd could not be regarded as immune from a German onslaught; plans were made in August for the evacuation of state archives, art treasures and gold reserves.[12]

Austrian troops re-conquered Galicia, capturing Przemysl' on 20 May and L'vov on 9 June, thereby enabling them to join up with the Germans in Russia's south-west. The enemy entered the province of Volynia on 13 August. General N.I. Ivanov, commander-in-chief of the south-western front, instructed his subordinates to prepare for the evacuation of Kiev, a proposal that sent government ministers into paroxysms of fury. Nor was Odessa immune from the panic induced by the succession of defeats suffered by the imperial army.[13]

Tens of thousands of tsarist soldiers were captured, some of them surrendering without a fight, in protest at what they saw as betrayal by their commanders. Certainly the enemy boasted superior forces and greater firepower. The Russian army was also let down by the failure to make adequate preparations for a phased withdrawal. Soldiers expressed outrage that famous fortresses such as at Brest-Litovsk could be abandoned without a fight.[14]

Russia's relations with its Allies came under strain. There was a widespread view that the Tsar's forces had tied up German troops during 1914 in sufficient numbers to give the French and British a significant advantage on the western front. The belief that the military burden fell disproportionately on Russia was further confirmed by events in 1915, when it was felt that the Allies were willing to contribute money but not men to relieve the pressure on Russia. A greater commitment of troops on the western front – so the argument went – might have enabled the Russians to launch a sustained offensive against Austrian forces following their withdrawal from Przemysl'.[15]

Russia's armed forces claimed greater success during the summer of 1916. Foreign observers such as the British general Alfred Knox and the

French military attaché Langlois testified that military supplies had begun to transform Russia's fighting potential. Under the imaginative generalship of Aleksei Brusilov, commander of the Eighth Army, the Russian army began to prepare for a surprise offensive along the south-western front. Brusilov believed that improvements in the delivery of artillery ammunition and small arms had improved the morale of the men under his command. Nor, in his view, did the relative shortage of heavy artillery dent their spirits. The Brusilov offensive was a resounding success, leading to the capture or death of half of the Austrian army on the eastern front. The Foreign Minister, Sergei Sazonov, declared that 'we have won the war, although the fighting will continue for several more years'.[16]

Sazonov was wrong on both counts. Other generals were unable or unwilling to match Brusilov's audacity, and his relatively heavy expenditure of troops, horses and artillery ammunition deprived him of the opportunity to press home his advantage by attacking the Carpathians and threatening Budapest and even Vienna. Military debacles elsewhere, including the fiasco of Romania's entry in the war and the diversion of Russian troops to bolster the faltering campaign of its new ally, darkened the mood.[17] It was not improved by Allied insistence that Russia should mount a fresh Russian offensive in the late spring or early summer of 1917.[18]

1.2   The initial phase of mobilisation: manpower, munitions and money

Mobilisation proceeded relatively smoothly. It was accompanied by state intervention to maintain sobriety and public order. The declaration of prohibition in August 1914 was designed in part to avoid a repetition of the drunkenness in the armed forces and on city streets during 1905, although it did not stop soldiers and reservists from looting alcohol stores. The Tsar's decision was hailed as a step towards reconfirming his position as the 'father' of his people and the guardian of their interests. Peasants (including children) wrote letters thanking the Tsar for ridding Russia of the 'green serpent', the popular term describing the menace of drink. But this needs to be interpreted carefully.[19] The overriding mood was one of resignation and 'muffled, submissive, sullen discontent'. Seasoned observers understood that the villages gave a send-off in support of soldiers, not the war.[20]

Shliapnikov observed that 'a wave of chauvinism seized a significant part of the labour force which is making collections on behalf of the war effort', equivalent to one or two per cent of wages, to create a fund to support conscripts' families. There were few protesting voices when Bolshevik deputies in the Fourth Duma were arrested; in any case radical political parties were in disarray.[21] Strikers faced hostility from fellow workers, many of whom had only recently returned to work, who felt that the withdrawal of labour jeopardised the prospects of their comrades in uniform. Skilled workers hoped that the war would bring a big influx of government orders and thus boost their earning power.[22]

Yet there were signs of dissent and disturbance. Peasant radicals demanded land as a condition of their being asked to shed blood. Revolutionaries called upon the troops to defend Russia from the German and Austrian onslaught and then return to 'free the Slavs in Russia itself'.[23] It took firm action by the authorities to prevent crowds from attacking the Austrian embassy in Petrograd, as they had earlier attacked the German embassy. Even more troubling to government officials preoccupied with public order were the reports of looting and rape by Russian conscripts in the front zone, behaviour that was encouraged by army pamphlets warning troops to be on their guard against spies and other 'subversives'.[24]

Technically speaking there was much to applaud in mobilisation, given that upwards of 4 million men were conscripted on schedule. In the real 'war by timetable', Russia's railways worked ahead of schedule, helped by the hectic attempts made before the war to construct or complete lines in Russian Poland, where French and Russian generals anticipated intense military activity. There were, however, signs of problems to come. Ensuring that customers had sufficient wagons at their disposal when needed, and that the wagons actually carried the freight they were supposed to carry, presented an enormous challenge.[25]

Around 18.6 million men served in the Russian army during the First World War, including 1.4 million already in uniform at the outbreak of war.[26] The annual intake of men thereafter was as shown in Table 1.1.

TABLE 1.1 *Dynamics of conscription into Russia's armed forces (millions per annum)*

Year	Total number mobilised	Regular troops	Internal defence forces
1914	7.17	6.40	0.78
1915	5.64	5.01	0.63
1916	3.09	2.76	0.34
1917	2.70	2.43	0.26

Source and notes: Volkov, 1930, p. 50. Totals exclude Finland, Khiva and Bukhara. The 1914 figures include those in uniform at the outbreak of war.

Around 5.1 million men were drafted during the second half of 1914. In the first half of 1915 a further 2.33 million men were called up, and in the second half of 1915 a further 2.88 million.[27] Raw statistics do not tell the whole story. Conscription badly depleted Russia's farms and factories. Half of all primary school teachers were called up.[28] Yet by the winter of 1914 military planners were already complaining that the army suffered a *shortage* of able-bodied manpower. The only options were to draft conscripts ahead of schedule, to recruit only sons in the second tier of the militia or to look to the men who had been retired to the first-tier militia. The planners opted for the first, but in September 1915 they had to concede the need to supplement their number with a draft of only sons. This measure provoked a fresh wave of civil disturbance. Peasants complained that the Tsar had made inadequate preparations for war, and that he was no better than 'an old woman' (*baba*), an 'idiot', and a 'drunkard'.[29]

Potential conscripts made use of a range of tactics in order to evade the draft, such as making claims about disability, inflicting wounds on their arms or legs, or resorting to outright bribery of members of the draft board. Others claimed exemption on spurious grounds or enlisted in reserved occupations to avoid being conscripted. Officials reported that evasion had generated an 'enormous' correspondence. The main theme of the letters of protest was not conscription as such, but rather the manner in which some occupations had been exempted. The draft disclosed an underlying mood, not of anti-patriotism but of contempt for the privilege that allowed well-connected individuals to avoid patriotic duty. A collective letter from soldiers' wives expressed outrage at the abuse of social connections:

The whole Russian narod will stand in the ranks of the army, not even excluding cripples, to defend itself against the enemy, but only when fairness is seen in everything.[30]

Paradoxically, the very success of conscription caused great difficulty, because industry quickly found itself deprived of skilled workers. Complaints by factory owners fell on deaf ears. General Mikhail Beliaev, Chief of the General Staff, refused to consider exemptions, let alone to return conscripts to their civilian jobs, on the grounds that it would have a 'deleterious impact on morale' at the front.[31]

The severe losses during the 1914 campaigns quickly depleted the officer corps. Reservists were quickly called up and, as a result, the officer corps increasingly acquired a less aristocratic profile. Infantry regiments in particular became even more socially heterogeneous than they had been before the war. Educated peasants entered the ranks of the officer class as NCOs. Hurriedly trained, many of them struggled to form a positive relationship with the men under their command. Their relations with the professional soldiers in the higher echelons were even worse.[32] The scale and intensity of the conflict brought about other changes, including a demand for extra military chaplains, to assist doctors in tending the wounded and removing corpses from the battlefield.[33]

The army in the field could only function if men had supplies of food, uniforms and footwear, as well as weaponry, transport equipment, fodder for their horses, and so forth. In the first months of the war Russian manufacturers, co-operatives and public organisations stepped in to supply grain, hay, knitwear, coats, footwear, canvas and sacks. Russian firms began to manufacture barbed wire, surgical instruments and other products. Orders for drugs, bandages and chloroform were hurriedly placed with foreign suppliers.[34]

Particular anxiety surfaced over munitions. All observers agreed that the performance of the tsarist army was badly limited by a shortage of shell. Before 1914 the procurement agencies had expected to rely primarily on state arsenals and ironworks in order to meet supply norms. This created great difficulties, once the scale of military consumption made itself apparent. General Beliaev, representing Military Headquarters, attended a meeting in mid-September between the Main Artillery Administration (GAU) and Russian industrialists, and threw a tantrum once he learned that Russian industry could promise only half a million shell per month, one-third of estimated consumption. In his view output should be trebled 'whatever the cost'. The GAU sought out American firms to manufacture additional quantities of rifles, machine guns, shrapnel and explosives.[35]

Some reorganisation of procurement and production was clearly required. 'We have no factories equipped to transfer rapidly to the task of satisfying the burgeoning demand for military materiel', wrote an official in the Ministry of Trade and Industry with mounting despair, as he watched orders being despatched unsystematically to overseas suppliers.[36] With the advent of the 'shell shortage', the government sought the assistance of the biggest engineering firms in Petrograd and the Central Industrial Region. Arguing that 'only large factories can give the best results', in September 1914 the GAU placed an order for five million rounds of artillery ammunition from Putilov, Parviainen, Briansk and Lessner.[37] Putilov agreed that 'the mobilisation of private industry will yield a favourable outcome only when large private firms are in charge of things, working for state defence as organisers and leaders of new suppliers'. He urged other leading industrialists to sing the same tune. A 'Special Preliminary Commission for Artillery', established by the GAU in February 1915 and dominated by Manikovskii (chief of the GAU) and his subordinates, dealt with private contractors in an attempt to address the 'gross defects' in munitions supply. However, Manikovskii continued to believe that the chief source was likely to remain the state sector. State factories were placed 'on a special footing', subordinating workers to army discipline and preventing their unauthorised departure.[38]

It made little sense to increase the output of munitions (or take deliveries from overseas suppliers) without addressing problems of transport. During the early phase of the war, the transport system coped reasonably well with the demands placed upon it. Improvements to the carrying capacity of railways were made during 1914 and the first half of 1915, increasing wagon loads and cutting back on maintenance. New lines were opened, additional track laid and junctions improved.[39] In the medium term, problems loomed. Russia was forced to rely upon Vladivostok as the major port of entry for foreign supplies, placing strain on the Trans-Siberian railway. The other main point of access during the war was Archangel, but its narrow gauge rail link with the centres of industry and population in European Russia was wholly unsuitable. Had the planners contemplated the likely consequences of blockade, they might have pursued these options more seriously before the war.

Problems became acute during 1915 when a huge increase in railway traffic subjected the entire system to unprecedented strain. More people (including refugees) and more goods – military munitions and equipment, food and fodder – were transported, although not necessarily over a longer average distance. The number of civilian passenger journeys increased from 237 million in 1913 to 344 million in 1916. Several key lines could not cope with the extra strain that the war imposed. They included the North–South trunk route, particularly the connection between Petrograd and the central industrial region, the Trans-Siberian and the Archangel–Vologda line. The latter could accommodate just three freight trains per day, equivalent to 0.25 per cent of the goods, mostly coal, awaiting collection from the port.[40] In order to cope with the cessation of imports from Britain and Poland, coal from the Donbass was diverted to consumers in the north-west.[41]

Early assessments of the war painted a relatively rosy picture. One optimistic commentator believed that Russia would be able to live off accumulated stocks of materials, leaving its fixed capital untouched.[42] Yet, in addition to the railways there were other troubling signs. Activity in the stock market came to a virtual standstill, with transactions largely confined to government bonds. Credit dried up. Iron and steel firms lost business and bemoaned their prospects.[43] During the first three months of the war, around 47,000 workers (excluding those in Poland) lost their jobs and a further 114,000 were laid off, owing to difficulties in obtaining raw materials and working capital.[44] Shortages of skilled labour were soon being reported in key sectors, and the Main Artillery Administration had to take special powers, preventing workers from leaving its arsenals to bring in the harvest.[45] Although government contractors tapped reserves of unemployed labour, private employers suffered a haemorrhage of labour. In the Donbass the number of coal miners fell from 203,000 to 138,000 in July 1914 alone, exacerbating fears of a fuel crisis. Industrialists in the Urals feared that they had lost workers for good. The Goujon metalworks in Moscow lost one-fifth of its workforce in the space of a single month. The situation at the giant Kolomna works was no better.[46]

Fiscal and monetary policy was conducted against this disturbed economic background. The Russian Ministry of Finances underwent a change of leadership. Kokovtsov's dismissal by Tsar Nicholas II in January 1914 brought P.L. Bark to the fore. Bark was originally asked to find ways of reducing the country's dependence on revenue from the sale of vodka, by taxing business and property receipts. The advent of war curtailed his room for manoeuvre. Bark's options were narrowed by prohibition and by military defeats, which deprived the Treasury of income from Poland and the western territories. He soon realised that the additional costs of fighting the war could not be financed out of taxation.[47]

The vodka monopoly raised the enormous sum of 665 million rubles in 1913, equivalent to around 26 per cent of all government revenue. Shingarev, one of the leaders of the Kadet fraction, spoke of the financial risks of taking this step:

From time immemorial countries waging war have been in want of funds. Revenue has always been sought either by good or by bad measures, by voluntary contributions, by obligatory levies, or by the open confiscation of private property. But never since the dawn of human history has a single country in time of war renounced the principal source of its revenue.[48]

Broader considerations were also at stake, such as the need to stem drunkenness. Bark spoke of a 'deliberate calculation' to extend prohibition until the war came to an end, and to deal with the consequences for the state budget; 'better that brewers and tavern keepers suffer than the whole country'.[49]

At the outbreak of war Russia suspended the convertibility of currency, in order to prevent the leakage of gold abroad. Gold quickly disappeared from circulation. The same decree permitted the State Bank to issue additional notes far in excess of the pre-war maximum, up to 1,500 million rubles, and to discount short-term Treasury bills in accordance with wartime need. The government availed itself of the opportunity to increase the note issue, legislating further increases in the right of emission in March 1915, August 1915, August 1916 and December 1916. A foreign loan agreed in October 1915 also enabled the government to relax the restrictions on note issue.

Thanks to the support of the State Bank, commercial banks survived an initial run on funds in the summer of 1914, as customers demanded to withdraw their deposits. Soon afterwards, a reverse tendency set in. The banks, including state savings banks, witnessed a sharp increase in their business during the first year of the war, as customers deposited additional savings in their accounts. Bark attributed this to the ban on the sale of vodka, although critics believed that the state's coffers were swelled as a result of peasants' decisions to dispose of their inventories.

As Russia entered the sixth month of war signs of strain began to be registered on the money markets. By December 1914 the ruble lost a fifth of its value on the foreign exchanges. This was not yet a full-blown crisis of confidence, but it did reflect the strains imposed on Russia by the growing trade deficit, which was expected to get worse as the war dragged on.

1.3   Military administration and civilian life at the front

The Russian High Command controlled much of civilian life as well as military activity at the front. Two new military districts were created for Dvinsk and Minsk, adding to the existing districts in Petrograd, Kiev, Odessa and the Caucasus, all of which were answerable to the Supreme Military Headquarters (Stavka). Regulations introduced in 1914 ensured that the normal writ of tsarist government did not run across a broad swathe of territory stretching from Poland and the Baltic provinces to the Caucasus, as well as to parts of Central Asia and Siberia. Here military officials dictated economic arrangements and policies. At the front, army commanders requisitioned supplies and prevented the removal of goods.[50]

Military procurement disrupted existing commercial relations. It created unnecessary waste. For example, the army calculated its total meat requirements and ordered its agents to procure sufficient quantities but, since storage facilities were inadequate, much of the meat had to be discarded. Nor was the disturbance in local economic networks confined to the front.[51] According to regulations imposed in February 1915, embargoes were placed on the export of grain beyond provincial boundaries, in order to allow procurement agents a free hand to requisition food and fodder crops at a cut price.[52] These ad hoc decisions provoked angry exchanges between the army and the central government, whose relations were already frosty as a result of Stavka giving the Ministry of War only the most hazy and unhelpful information about stocks of munitions and their depletion.

The division of Russia into a rear and a front zone had deleterious consequences for transport. The railway network was divided into an eastern and western region, the latter (around one-third of the total track) coming under military control. Russian generals moved quickly to commandeer rolling stock, but no overall agency existed in order to resolve conflicting demands and to establish priorities for civilian and military use. By the beginning of 1916 government ministers were being bombarded with complaints. The network's ability to meet competing claims was not helped by the severe winter: coal shipments were down to 1.8 million tons a month in early 1916, 20 per cent below estimated requirements. Freight accumulated at railway stations and sidings. In peacetime, this was not necessarily a sign of neglect or maladministration, because managers did not wish to send trains on their way if they were half empty. In wartime, however, it was easier to make the charge stick. Military chiefs jealously held on to wagons rather than release them to civilian authorities in the rear. In the midst of the worsening transport crisis during 1916 lines in the north-west became clogged with wagons that the military commandeered. Nor did the situation improve with the Russian offensive that took place later that year. Leading parliamentarians, such as Rodzianko, the Octobrist chairman of the Duma, maintained that the transport crisis could best be addressed by unifying the administration of the network in the front and the rear.[53]

Even more striking was the extent to which Stavka appropriated political control, something that the lack of co-ordination among cabinet ministers made much easier to accomplish. Goremykin, the hapless premier, categorically declared that 'the government will administer the rear, but all matters relating to the war are not my business'. The generals and their civilian subordinates had the power to dismiss government officials, to impose censorship, to close schools and universities, and to seize private property. By 1915 Stavka was even running its own diplomatic chancery.[54]

Tsarist military administration reached its apogee in the Russian army's occupation of Galicia during 1914–1915. Galicia was seen as a 'Slav' land that suffered from the Austrian yoke. Backed by this belief, the occupying powers took scant notice of legal niceties. Russia's obnoxious occupation became a licence to rape, rob and kill local Jewish inhabitants, who were accused of subversion, sabotage and espionage. Jewish, Polish and Ukrainian officials were dismissed and their property seized. Local notables were taken hostage. One hallmark of the conquest was an adjustment in the exchange rate of the ruble against the Austrian crown, to the immediate benefit of the occupying army. At the same time, Galicia became the site of an aggressive 'Russification' campaign, with the aim of bringing the territory fully into the imperial fold. Virulent attacks were made on the Ukrainian language, on the Uniate church and on the flourishing Ukrainian press, in the hope of 'assimilating' Ukrainians with Russia. Jews were another matter; expropriating them meant currying favour with Ukrainians and Poles.[55]

1.4   Retreat and evacuation

Military misfortune meant the loss of valuable resources and capacity. Total losses corresponded to 15.4 per cent of the territory and 23.3 per cent of the pre-war population of European Russia. The loss of territory in 1915 equated to 12.4 per cent of pre-war national income (this followed a 3.7 per cent loss in 1914). Russia was deprived of around one-third of its factories, contributing the equivalent of 20 per cent of annual industrial output in peacetime. Before the war Poland produced 10 per cent of the empire's total output of iron and steel. Two-fifths of the chemical industry was based in Poland and the Baltic. Poland had also been an important source of textiles for the Russian market.[56]

Some of this capital stock was evacuated and eventually re-established further east.[57] Around 650 enterprises were evacuated from Poland and the Baltic provinces during the war. Manufacturers of rolling stock suffered particularly badly. Phoenix Engineering and Russo-Baltic were both evacuated and production was interrupted for several months. The situation was slightly better in the north-west, although valuable reserves of zinc were lost when German troops occupied Libau. According to one scholar, goods and materials to the value of 78 million rubles were evacuated from Riga, as well as a further 108 million rubles' worth of machinery and equipment. Riga was an important engineering centre, probably accounting for around 5 per cent of total industrial production before 1914. From a sample of industrial enterprises evacuated from Riga, 40 per cent were relocated in the Central Industrial Region, 35 per cent in Khar'kov, 10 per cent in Petrograd, 10 per cent in the Volga region, and 5 per cent in Kiev.[58]

To set this in context, total investment in industrial stocks (inventories) and structures amounted to 400 million rubles in the last year of peace. Thus the value of capital evacuated from Riga was equivalent to around half of total annual investment in industry in the Russian empire. The authorities concentrated on evacuating precious machine tools and instruments, as well as equipment in chemicals, rubber, leather and garment factories. Perhaps two-fifths of Riga's moveable industrial assets were removed by Russian officials between 1914 and 1917. This may have been the most successful case of evacuation. The story elsewhere was more depressing. Most of the industrial assets in Lodz, a major textile town, fell into enemy hands.[59] News of the evacuation spurred some local authorities in the Russian interior to bid against one another in order to entice Baltic and Polish firms to relocate in their area.[60]

The great retreat swelled the number of civilian refugees. 'As soon as our troops withdraw, the entire population becomes confused and runs away', wrote one leading official.[61] Sometimes civilians fled, lest they lose contact with relatives on Russian territory, including fathers and sons who currently served in the tsarist army. Many peasants despaired of continuing to farm when horses and livestock had been badly depleted by requisitioning. They expressed a wish to seek a better life 'in the depths of Russia'.[62] Other motives also came to the surface. Civilians were warned that 'voluntary' departure was the only alternative to being conscripted or terrorised by the enemy. Tsarist officials abandoned their posts. Civilians – mostly farmers, craftsmen and factory workers – fearful of enemy brutality, joined them in the journey eastwards.[63]

Yet displacement was by no means solely dictated by a fearful civilian response to punitive action by the enemy. The actions of the Russian general staff provided one of the main impulses to population displacement. Ianushkevich singled out Jews for special treatment, encouraging 'a pogrom mood' in the army. These crude and desperate measures extended also to Poles, Lithuanians, Germans, Gypsies and others, who were deported from the vicinity of the front in July and August 1915.[64]

Population displacement also characterised the conduct of war on the southern borderlands of the empire. Turkish radicals blamed Armenians for the defeats already suffered by the Ottoman army in the winter of 1914 and early 1915, and charged them with having instigated uprisings against Turkish rule. Those Armenians who remained on Ottoman-controlled territory suffered a terrible fate. Hundreds of thousands of Ottoman Armenians were disarmed, arrested and deported, being forced to endure long and humiliating marches to the south from which many never recovered. Many were simply butchered. A quarter of a million Armenians managed to flee across the Russian border during August 1915. Perhaps as many as one-fifth of them died en route. By the beginning of 1916, 105,000 ex-Ottoman Armenians sought refuge in Erevan, whose population in 1914 barely reached 30,000.[65]

Population movement on this scale placed a heavy burden on the overstretched Russian railway network. Government officials attempted to 'plan' the shipment of refugees, but were frustrated by the competing demands of other agencies for scarce rolling stock. In order to cope with the strain, the government prohibited all non-military passenger traffic between Moscow and Petrograd for one week in November 1915.[66] None the less, tens of thousands of refugees slowly made their way eastwards by train. In all, some 115,000 wagons – equivalent to one-fifth of the total stock in 1915 – were involved in the evacuation of refugees (and industrial equipment) from the western borders in just two months.[67] Conditions on board the refugee trains were squalid and demoralising. Trains arrived and departed unsystematically. Carriages were coupled and uncoupled without any advance warning to passengers. Many families were separated. There were other hazards as well. Refugees sometimes installed boilers in unheated railway wagons, creating a fire hazard. When the authorities warned of the dangers refugees replied that 'it's all the same to us, whether we die of frostbite or from fire'.[68]

This brings us to the question of what belongings refugees could take with them. Most of them were farmers, craftsmen or petty traders. Some peasants drove horses ahead of them and thus saved their most valuable assets, but they were the fortunate ones. Moreover, horses had to be grazed and fed, and an unknown number of draught animals perished en route. Other refugees were forced to sell horses at a fraction of their pre-war market value. Thousands of horses were simply abandoned. In the course of one and a half months, around 50,000 horses were placed at the

disposal of the regional refugee commissioner. Cattle herds were also decimated. Farmers were told they could buy replacements in Russia at a
reasonable price.[69]

We can make a rough approximation of the value of moveable assets
that peasant refugees could salvage. The heaviest farm equipment had to
be left behind, along with the basic immovable element of the peasant
household, namely the stove. But smaller items – work tools, clothing and
bedding, utensils, perhaps spinning wheels and small looms – might be sal-
vaged. Refugees were probably deprived of around two-fifths of their
assets. If they were unable to rescue or retain any of their livestock – a fair
assumption – this figure would rise to three-quarters. Assuming that
500,000 peasant households were caught up in the process of displacement, the value of assets that were lost during the war amounted – at a
conservative estimate – to at least 500 million rubles. This was equivalent
to around five per cent of all peasant property (other than land) in 1914.[70]

The mass movement of refugees was invested with profound political,
social and cultural anxieties. One illustration of this was the widespread
tendency in Russia to identify refugeedom with natural calamity: thus,
'flood', 'deluge', 'wave', 'avalanche', 'lava flow' and 'plague' (as in plague
of locusts). Government officials regularly denounced the 'spontaneous'
and chaotic movement of refugees, who refused to follow the directives of
local authorities. Such choice of language encouraged the belief that Russia
faced a battle on at least two fronts, against invasion by enemy troops and
by newly displaced populations, whose loss of self-control and self-respect
was deemed to contribute to the collapse of social order and economic
stability. It was consistent with a view that no refugee could be a good
citizen if he or she had to beg, thieve or engage in prostitution in order to
survive.[71]

Military events led to huge increases in budgetary expenditure. In the
words of one authority:

*A series of unsuccessful military operations on the western front involved
simultaneously the retreat of the army and larger credits to meet the
resulting situation. In addition to the loss of territory with valuable
fields, forests, towns and villages, industrial plant, natural wealth in the
soil and in the working population, every retreat meant either the
relinquishment or the destruction of vast military stores, which had to be
replaced at great cost by new purchases. These losses produced an effect
almost as pronounced upon the home market as upon the Treasury.
Retreat meant also heavy expenditure on the requisition of the necessary*

supplies for the retiring army, for the support of refugees and for compensation for destroyed property.[72]

In this way military defeat, population displacement and financial perturbation were closely intertwined.

Conclusions

Men went to war in the Russian empire with the same mixture of emotions as their counterparts in other countries. They continued to fight because of a commitment to comrades, not to the Tsar. The desire to see enemy troops driven from their land also played an important part. Government propaganda exploited that motive. In Russia's towns and villages new forms of cultural expression connected the front and the rear by popularising sentimental images of heroism and steadfastness. However, in due course, the patriotic message gave way to a more direct preoccupation with loss and sacrifice, which the tsarist government found difficult to allay. Russians now glimpsed a world no longer dominated by fixed points of reference such as the Tsar, the Church and the propertied elite.

The first phase of the war presented an uneven picture. Conscription proceeded relatively smoothly, but the first months were dominated by stories of shortages of weaponry and munitions as well as strains on available capacity. The shell shortage gave rise to rumours of backroom deals with shadowy entrepreneurs, as well as reports of more purposeful activity by leading private firms. As shortages became apparent, the emphasis shifted from stocks to production, from reserves of manpower to issues of labour productivity, from grand gestures such as prohibition to graver issues of state credit.

We should not exaggerate the depth of crisis in the spring of 1915, when an eminent economist could safely assert that 'our national economic organism not only is not being destroyed by the war, as we are already seeing in Germany, but is hardly affected by it'.[73] However, there was little room left for such optimism as the first year of war came to an end. Defeats exposed Russia to the charge that its leaders had been far too complacent. The campaigns of 1914 and 1915 dented the public reputation of the Russian army commanders, and only Brusilov's brilliance in 1916 allowed the High Command to recover some of their credibility as they basked in his glow.

Mounting public criticism reflected an understandable anger at having ceded control of territory to the enemy. Resources were tied up in moving troops, civilians and physical assets from the front to the relative safety of the interior. Considerable disquiet surfaced about the extent and consequences of population displacement, in great part the product of a militarised, 'atavistic regime untouched by the momentous political changes which had grown out of the 1905 revolution'.[74] A specific issue was the cost of compensating those whose property had been lost or destroyed by the army's 'scorched earth' policy, of meeting the immediate needs of desperate and deprived refugees, and of replacing military stores and other items that had been lost or destroyed during the retreat. There was also a political symbolism in the loss of famous cities and in facing the prospect of having to abandon Kiev or even Petrograd. The immediate political ramifications were profound. Kerenskii expressed this in a neat encapsulation: 'Przemysl' fell – Maklakov went. L'vov fell – Sukhomlinov went. When Warsaw goes – Goremykin will go too'.[75]

Note on further reading

An old but still valuable survey of wartime political developments is Florinsky, 1931, which should be supplemented with the highly informative account by Lincoln, 1986. More specialist works include Pearson, 1977, and the masterful discussion in Diakin, 1967. Those seeking a survey of developments on the battlefield can consult Stone, 1975, and the excellent overview in Jones, 1988. Sanborn, 2003, is essential reading on conscription into the army. The origins of forced migration are traced by Gatrell, 1999, and Lohr, 2003, Chapter 5.

References

1 Mikhailov, 1927, pp. 495–7. For a careful and nuanced discussion of 'shell shortage' on both fronts in 1914, stressing its relationship to prevailing military tactics, see Strachan, 2001, pp. 993–1005.

2 Quoted in Mal'kov, ed., 1998, p. 241 (Tiutiukin).

3 Maslov, 1918, pp. 9–10, from a letter published in *Russkie vedomosti*, 10 September 1914.

4 *Golos* (Iaroslavl'), 22 July 1914.

5 Lincoln, 1986, pp. 64–76.

6 *Izvestiia VSG*, 1915, 9, pp. 76–7.

7 Petrone, 1998, p. 116.

8 Rachamimov, 2002, p. 38; Lincoln, 1986, p. 121. The prolonged siege cost the Austrian army an additional 50,000 casualties.

9 Lincoln, 1986, p. 125; Stone, 1975, pp. 136–43.

10 Lincoln, 1986, pp. 167–8.

11 Wildman, 1980, p. 89; Lincoln, 1986, pp. 125–9.

12 RGVIA f.369, op.1, d.39, ll.28–33ob. German occupation policy is discussed by Liulevicius, 2000.

13 Cherniavsky, ed., 1967, pp. 95, 147–8, 168–72, 228–30.

14 Buldakov, 1997, p. 62; Wildman, 1980, pp. 89–94, recounting the tale told by the disillusioned soldier Dmitrii Os'kin.

15 Neilson, 1984, p. 59; Lincoln, 1986, pp. 176–7.

16 Rachamimov, 2002, p. 38. Sazonov, speaking in May 1916, is quoted in McReynolds, 1993, p. 171.

17 Romania declared war on Austria–Hungary in August 1916. Lincoln, 1986, pp. 240–41, 250–51, 258; Jones, 1988, pp. 306–8. For a more sceptical assessment of Brusilov see Mal'kov, ed., 1998, pp. 632–4 (Nelipovich). Alekseev's expenditure of artillery ammunition was comparatively modest.

18 Mal'kov, ed., 1998, p. 590 (Zhilin).

19 Berkevich, 1947. Sukhomlinov feared a repeat of stories that reached the Ministry of War in 1904, when troops made the 'long journey to the theatre of battle in an alcoholic haze'. Peasant conscripts traditionally received a vodka-rich send-off. Buldakov, 1997, p. 56.

20 Gurko, 1939, p. 538 (quotation); Smirnov, ed., 1999, pp. 147–59 (McKee); Senin, 1993, p. 46; Mal'kov, ed., 1998, pp. 464–5 (Porshneva); Sanborn, 2003, p. 30.

21 Shliapnikov, 1982, p. 221; Kir'ianov, 1994.

22 Tiutiukin, 1972, pp. 78, 83; Trotsky, 1934, pp. 58–9.

23 Tiutiukin, 1972, p. 79.

24 Lohr, 2003, pp. 14–20.

25 Stone, 1975, p. 49.

26 Volkov, 1930, p. 50.

27 Prokopovich, 1918, p. 151.

28 Odinetz and Novgorotsev, 1929, p. 63.

29 Sanborn, 2003, pp. 34–5; Porshneva, 2000, p. 121.

30 Sanborn, 2003, pp. 37–8.

31 Beliaev's report was dated 22 February 1915. Golovin, 2001, pp. 227–8.

32 Kenez, 1973; Jones, 1976.

33 Senin, 1993.

34 Kayden and Antsiferov, 1929, p. 308; Zagorsky, 1928, pp. 29–30; Saul, 2001, p. 21.

35 Barsukov, 1948, pp. 26–7; Saul, 2001, pp. 23–4.

36 Litvinov-Falinskii, quoted in Manikovskii, 1930, volume 2, pp. 293–7.

37 Manikovskii, 1930, volume 1, p. 357; Sidorov, 1973, p. 29.

38 RGIA f.1276, op.11, d. 814, ll. 1–3, 5–16 (Memo from Association of Industry and Trade to Council of Ministers, 12 January 1915). Its paperwork was enormous: one overseas order alone generated 1,800 pages of correspondence. Bukshpan, 1929, pp. 241, 274–6; Manikovskii, 1930, volume 2, pp. 14–17; Sidorov, 1973, pp. 36–8.

39 Vasil'ev, 1939, p. 268.

40 Grinevetskii, 1919, p. 108; Bukin, 1926, pp. 105–6.

41 Supplies of coal from the Donbass to Russia's north-west increased tenfold between 1913 and 1915, reaching 2.15 million tons. Maevskii, 1957, pp. 215–16. The railway system accounted for nearly half the total consumption of fuel in 1916. Grinevetskii, 1919, p. 90.

42 P&T, 1914, 21 (Raffalovich).

43 Tarnovskii, 1958, pp. 18–19.

44 Claus, 1922, p. 50; Khoziaistvennaia zhizn', 1916, p. 32. The net loss was slightly smaller.

45 P&T, 1916, 18 (Polupanov); Anon., Materialy, 1916–1917, volume 2; Vasil'ev, 1939, p. 268; Struve et al., eds, 1930, pp. 3–8; Golovin, 1931, pp. 164–6.

46 Sheliakin, 1930, p. 36; Gaponenko, 1970, pp. 75–6; Efremtsev, 1973, p. 105; Markevich, 2001.

47 Gatrell, 1994, pp. 150, 368; Beliaev, 2002.

48 Michelson et al., 1928, p. 87.

49 Sabler, quoted in Gal'perina, ed., 1999, p. 76, cabinet meeting on 25 September 1914. See also Prokopovich, 1917, p. 87; Michelson et al., 1928, pp. 80–89.

50 Graf, 1974, p. 392.

51 Bukshpan, 1929, pp. 253–4.

52 Struve et al., eds, 1930, pp. 443–52; Porshneva, 2000, p. 121.

53 Bukshpan, 1929, p. 268; Pokrovskii, 1925, pp. 69-81; EPR, 1957, volume 2, pp. 18–32.

54 Graf, 1974, p. 393; Florinskii, 1988, pp. 164, 166; Kitanina, 1985, pp. 62–3.

55 Graf, 1974, p. 397; Bakhturina, 2000, pp. 57–69; Prusin, 2002; Lohr, 2003, pp. 96–7. Recent scholarship emphasises the conflict between the Russian High Command, particularly Ianushkevich, and the civilian administration, led by Count G.A. Bobrinskii.

56 Zagorsky, 1928, p. 17.

57 Prokopovich, 1917, pp. 69, 129; Kohn and Meyendorff, 1932, p. 166; Vainshtein, 1960, pp. 368–9.

58 RGVIA f.369, op.1, d.307, ll.195–7ob.

59 The standard Soviet account is Sidorov, 1973, pp. 213–51 (first published 1945). Netesin, 1974, pp. 206–7, is less dismissive of tsarist efforts.

60 *Izvestiia VSG*, 1915, 20, pp. 207–10.

61 S.I. Zubchaninov, speaking to the Special Council for Refugees, 10 September 1915, RGIA f.1322, op.1, d.1, ll.1ob.–2.

62 RGVIA f.2020, op.1, d.131, l.184, Beliaev to Danilov, 24 July 1915.

63 Memorandum by Prince N.L. Obolenskii, 30 August 1915, RGVIA f.2003, op.2, d.945, ll.10.

64 Lohr, 2003, pp. 137–45; chapter 8 below.

65 Gatrell, 1999, pp. 18–19, 52–3.

66 Vasil'ev, 1939, p. 206.

67 Sidorov, 1973, pp. 590–92.

68 *Bezhenets*, 4, 1 November 1915.

69 Gatrell, 1999, p. 30.

70 The total value of peasants' assets in January 1914 was 9.9 billion rubles. Vainshtein, 1960, p. 403.

71 Gatrell, 1999, pp. 78–83, 200.

72 Michelson et al., 1928, pp. 192–3.

73 Tugan-Baranovskii, 1915, p. 319.

74 Graf, 1974, p. 394.

75 Cited in Diakin, 1967, p. 81.

CHAPTER 2

'Educated society' and the Russian elite

The problem of organisation in the rear – this is at one and the same time the problem of the organisation of power
[A.I. Konovalov, quoted in Laverychev, 1967, p. 134]

In July 1914 most members of 'educated society' (*tsenzovoe obshchestvo*) supported the declaration of war, seeing in it an opportunity to dent the enemy's claims to supremacy. With the exception of the five Bolshevik deputies in the State Duma, Russia's elected representatives held out an olive branch to the Tsar. Parliament reconvened briefly in January 1915 and reiterated its support for the war. However, the relationship between state and 'society' already showed signs of strain. In March 1915 leaders of the Progressive Party proposed changes to the cabinet, on the grounds that government ministers lacked the ability to take the necessary steps to ensure a Russian victory. A month later the Kadets, having hitherto adopted a more cautious stance, followed suit. Military setbacks and munitions shortages encouraged this political assertiveness.

Beyond the Duma, progressive opinion directed a steady barrage of criticism at government officials. Bolder spirits claimed the right to become involved in war work by creating new 'public organisations'. Subsequently, influential elements within these new organisations – the Union of Zemstvos and the Union of Towns, and the war industry committees – raised the banner of 'a government of public confidence'. In other words, they capitalised upon difficulties in dealing with wounded soldiers and displaced persons, as well as problems in munitions supply, in order to advance the case for political concessions.[1]

By whom would mobilisation be realised and given practical expression? For the war industry committees, the answer was provided by patriotic businessmen whose potential contribution had been neglected. They believed in 'getting things done'. However, mobilisation also invited the active participation of a professional intelligentsia that comprised disinterested experts, capable of providing accurate information about social and economic trends, bringing enlightenment to the Russian people (narod) and generating solutions to pressing 'questions' on the basis of scientific knowledge.[2] Crucially, in terms of the evolution of this body of experts, the organisational setting in which they operated was quite fluid. The war rendered less secure the pre-existing framework, in which the state imposed limits upon professional autonomy.[3]

The mobilisation of educated society carried particular connotations for elite social groups, traditionally regarded as the mainstay of the political and economic order, which accounted for more than half of Russia's national wealth in 1913.[4] The leading social estate (soslovie) was the nobility (dvorianstvo), a complex amalgam of wealthy landowners and minor gentry whose members struggled to maintain their standard of living. It included a large element of privileged people (and their dependants) who had been ennobled as a reward for state service in the armed forces or the bureaucracy. At the outbreak of war only one-third of all noble families actually owned land, compared with one-half in the 1890s; many families had sold part of their property and diversified their sources of income. Landowners complained that the state did little to protect their interests from families that lacked a connection with the soil.[5]

The counterpart to the 'crisis of the gentry' was the business elite, a portmanteau term that disguises the fact that Russia's commercial middle class was neither economically secure nor socially homogeneous. Officially constituted as the mercantile estate (kupechestvo), merchants in the Russian empire bemoaned the bureaucratic regulations that hampered the conduct of business, such as the complicated procedures for registering one's firm or maintaining the right to trade. But this estate concealed internal divisions. The largest group, dispersed throughout Russia's provincial towns and cities, complained of upstart entrepreneurs who had more in common with European corporate leaders and bankers than with the Orthodox Russians who ran a family business. Social fragmentation rather than unity characterised the merchantry. Most merchants also had little time for the emerging technical intelligentsia, such as engineers and accountants, who found a role in modern business enterprise. These tensions, too, underlay the politics of industrial mobilisation.[6]

2.1 Field work: the Union of Zemstvos and the Union of Towns

Initially the voluntary organisations trod carefully. Zemstvo leaders dis-
avowed any overt political ambitions. They couched the call for public
participation in the war effort in terms of personal obligation, humanitar-
ianism and technical efficiency. All the same, it was difficult to maintain
the stance that the public organisations stood above the political fray. The
new watchword was 'mobilisation'. An editorial in the Progressive newspaper *Utro Rossii* in May 1915 made this clear when it appealed for the
reallocation of labour and capital to the war effort. Workers should be
placed on a war footing, since 'at the present time work at the lathe is as
vital as sentry duty at the front line'.[7] Other commentators made more
explicit the political implications of mobilisation: 'He who knows how to
work will also become the master of the country ... The public forces
(*obshchestvennye sily*) aim to make transparent the difference between the
bureaucracy and people from society'.[8]

Established by statute in 1864, as part of the package of 'great reforms'
launched by Alexander II, provincial and district zemstvos supported a
broad range of activities relating in particular to public health, primary
education and veterinary care.[9] Generally speaking, the leadership of
provincial zemstvos was vested in local dignitaries, such as the landed
gentry, who controlled elections to the zemstvo assemblies. However, the
gentry had no option but to delegate responsibility for the implementation
of policy to professional employees who became known as the 'third
element'.[10] During the Russo-Japanese War local zemstvos engaged in
relief work, assisting invalids, families of servicemen and prisoners. Prince
G.E. L'vov was even allowed to create an 'all-zemstvo organisation' for the
relief of sick and injured soldiers. Municipal authorities similarly
expanded their operations prior to the war, after a prolonged period in
which their resources failed to keep pace with the growing needs of the
urban population. All this practical work gave rise to a great deal of
official suspicion, in so far as the third element claimed a moral superiority
vis-à-vis the existing bureaucracy.[11]

When war broke out the government set aside its misgivings about collective action and approved the formation of two umbrella organisations,
an All-Russian Union of Zemstvos (VZS) and an equivalent Union of
Towns (VSG). L'vov, regarded in conservative quarters as a dangerous
progressive, became chairman of the VZS, a post he held until 1917.[12]
Their task was 'exclusively (*sic*) to aid the war wounded and sick for the

duration of the present conflict', and to this end the two agencies were formally placed 'under the flag' of the Russian Red Cross. Theoretically, the Red Cross was responsible for the care of sick and wounded in the vicinity of the front, leaving the unions to concentrate on relief operations in the Russian interior. But this distinction was not rigidly maintained. The VSG also went further than the government wished, by deciding to support the families of municipal employees who had been called up. It breathed fresh life into the most moribund municipalities.[13] The VZS, which financed its activities from voluntary contributions, made an impressive start. By November 1914 it had responsibility for 1,700 hospitals, staffed by doctors and nurses who had been exempted from military service.[14]

Conservative members of the government argued that the public organisations constituted a thinly disguised attempt by Russia's liberals to hijack the state. Nikolai Maklakov (1871–1918), Minister of the Interior, lost no time in denouncing their 'conference' activity that would end in 'revolution'. Even the call for a reform of the zemstvo statute, to add a lower tier of local administration, fell on deaf ears. Other like-minded ministers hoped to curb the activities of the public organisations, deeming them a flag of convenience for the Kadets. But this tactic foundered on the support they received from the army and the realisation that official bodies were simply overwhelmed by the effort required to sustain wounded soldiers and refugees.[15]

The situation in the Russian interior was another matter entirely. Here the voluntary organisations challenged the civilian government on its own turf. It was difficult to maintain the fiction that they were wholly non-political.[16] Population displacement provided the pretext for public action. In a bold move designed to facilitate the resettlement and relief of refugees, the leaders of the public organisations began to co-ordinate action in the rear. Not only did the zemstvo union leadership draw attention to the broad scope of refugee relief, it also asserted, more radically, that the needs of refugees could not be distinguished from those of the settled population with whom they increasingly came into contact. Only the public organisations could organise the supply and distribution of the means to inspect and disinfect the refugee population; only the unions of zemstvos and towns could adequately implement a 'rational' plan for refugee resettlement and thereby prevent a national calamity.[17]

The war revived claims on the part of the unions' leaders to assume greater executive responsibilities. Evident deficiencies of existing bureaucratic methods for administering defence production and procurement had brought Russia to the brink of catastrophe. The zemstvo union ventured beyond social welfare and the procurement of uniforms and painkillers. Rodzianko, the chairman of the State Duma, spoke of his 'plan', which entailed taking charge of orders for footwear: 'if we succeed with boots, then half the battle is won; we can then proceed to add rifles and shell'.[18] On behalf of the VSG, Teslenko observed that the voluntary organisations were in effect becoming substitutes for official agencies.[19]

In June 1915 the two unions formed a joint supply committee, Zemgor, headed by L'vov and M.V. Chelnokov, the mayor of Moscow and a leading member of the Progressive Party.[20] The two unions began to accept orders for munitions and, amid some fanfare, they presented the Duma on 12 June with the first shell turned out by a Zemgor workshop. Other orders quickly followed, from the Main Artillery Administration (GAU) and the Main Intendance Administration. By March 1916 Zemgor had received orders worth 72 million rubles. The advances on these orders enabled Zemgor to plan ahead. This mattered a great deal, because the financial position of the unions remained precarious; their tax receipts declined and they struggled to raise loans from overseas.[21]

Zemgor and individual unions of towns and zemstvos purchased materials on the open market. They sub-contracted some orders to private firms. One contemptuous critic described Zemgor as 'a kind of Muir and Mirrelees', a sarcastic reference to Moscow's fashionable department store. The unions also manufactured on their own account dyestuffs, pharmaceuticals, spirits, foodstuffs, uniforms (outerwear and underwear, boots, gloves, stockings, caps and belts), as well as such vital items as basic transport equipment, shell, grenades and mines. By November 1915 the Moscow municipality alone had repaired 400,000 pairs of boots, 800,000 trench coats, 220,000 felt boots, and manufactured 1.4 million caps and 2.1 million gas masks. This activity involved the public organisations in the acquisition of raw materials from domestic suppliers and in importing drugs and medical equipment.[22]

The growing ambition of the unions in the sphere of military procurement exposed a division between those members who espoused a non-political stance and those who argued that the public organisations could hardly escape political involvement. The leadership of the VSG included politically more radical elements associated with the Progressive Party, whereas the leaders of the VZS aligned themselves with the Octobrist Party, although the distinction was probably lost on conservative figures such as Maklakov.[23] None of the leaders of the public organisation shed any tears when he was dismissed in July 1915, paving the way for the Duma to be reconvened.[24]

Government ministers asserted that the zemstvos lacked business acumen,[25] but the Zemgor leadership felt that it made the best of limited funds. Zemgor received orders worth a total of 286 million rubles from the army and managed to fulfil around three-fifths by 1 January 1918. This record compares favourably with the war industry committees, which had a more complex product mix to administer, and did nothing to undermine the 'fantastic myth' generated by the zemstvos' publicity machine.[26]

2.2   Shell shock: the war industry committees

Russian businessmen expressed concern at the slow pace and limited scale of mobilisation. The most serious assault on the prevailing pattern of industrial mobilisation was led by a group of merchants and entrepreneurs, largely Moscow-based, who proclaimed their readiness to work for state defence. They were not, however, politically disengaged. On the contrary, their spokesmen included Pavel Riabushinskii and Aleksandr Guchkov, both of whom had accumulated years of political experience, in the Progressive and Octobrist parties respectively. They believed that the government (in particular the Ministry of War) was in thrall to big business. Under this arrangement, the Ministry of War acted as both principal and agent. That dependent relationship only reinforced their belief that the task of industrial mobilisation could not be entrusted to tsarist officialdom.[27] The war industry committees attacked the traditional organisation of the defence industry: 'Why should small businessmen not be showered with money, or is it only going to feed big business?' asked one journal.[28] There was no shortage of factories and workshops capable of manufacturing shell. The dilemma for the war industry committees was that their claim to fill a gap in armaments production could most easily be met by delivering large quantities of shell, but the government insisted that existing suppliers could do the job instead.[29]

These difficulties lay in the future. The war industry committees were founded in a climate of ebullient confidence. At the Ninth Congress of the Association of Representatives of Industry and Trade on 27 May 1915, Riabushinskii denounced the domination of munitions supply by a Petrograd financial and industrial oligarchy, supported by southern industrialists. This was a remarkable intervention, given that the Congress itself was the voice of big business. Other speakers supported the call for an overall 'directorate of military supply', whose job it would be to administer all defence establishments, whether state or privately owned. The congress agreed to establish a Central War Industry Committee (TsVPK), on the grounds that the state lacked a sufficient grasp of the scale or type of industrial mobilisation now required. Delegates maintained that it was essential to organise the 'unutilised power of Russian industry'.[30] For some of the delegates, this meant marginalising state arsenals in favour of the private sector. For others, it meant allocating orders to factories that the government's procurement agencies had so far overlooked, particularly in the provinces.[31]

War industry committees quickly sprouted up throughout the country. Regional committees – more than 30 – were not confined to European Russia but operated in Siberia, the Urals and the Caucasus as well. Never shy of publicity, they advertised their achievements in an impressive statistical compendium, which stated that (as of March 1916) 78 local committees had established contact with around 230 enterprises in towns and cities. The number continued to grow. A regional war industry committee in Moscow became their chief power base. It co-ordinated the affairs of other provincial committees in the hope of displacing the TsVPK. Riabushinskii and Tereshchenko (the millionaire sugar magnate who chaired the Kiev committee) lost no time in proclaiming Moscow as the heart of the war effort – far from the front line and 'authentically Russian', unlike the capital, where 'German influence' made itself felt. Here, in essence, was reproduced the longstanding cultural faultline between 'patriotic' Moscow and 'cosmopolitan' Petrograd. At the first congress of the TsVPK, on 25–27 July, Guchkov and Konovalov, both of them closely involved in Moscow's public life, became respectively the chairman and vice-chairman of the central committee, winning it for the Muscovite cause.[32]

The war industry committees demanded that fuller use be made of existing manufacturing capacity and clamoured themselves for a 'fairer' distribution of orders for 3" shell.[33] The government obliged instead with orders for rifles and for heavier calibres of shell, products that posed a much greater technical challenge.[34] By the spring of 1916 the war industry committees had agreed 800 contracts for items required by the War Ministry worth a total of 195 million rubles, including 118 million rubles from the GAU and 56 million rubles from the Main Intendance Administration. For an organisation that had proclaimed the need to challenge the predominance of Petrograd, it came as something of a shock to realise that one-third of all orders had gone to firms in the capital and its environs. The Moscow region managed only 16 per cent of the total, equivalent to 32 million rubles' worth of business. This hardly amounted to a major redistribution of industrial capacity, and it reflected the continued importance of enterprises in Russia's north-west. Overall the war industry committees garnered no more than five per cent of all defence orders.[35]

Crucial to the success or otherwise of the war industry, committees were the resources at their disposal. Other public organisations could draw upon tax revenues, at least to some extent. The Association of Industry and Trade offered only limited financial support, its leaders feeling little sympathy with their provincial cousins. The TsVPK siphoned off 1 per cent of the value of orders, in order to cover its operating expenses. Much was expected from government credit, in the form of advances on new contracts to be concluded with the war industry committees.[36] Yet this exposed the weakness of their position; if the government refused to place orders, the committees could achieve little in practical terms. So it proved. By January 1917 the government concluded contracts worth a total of 400 million rubles, but officials used the low rate of completion to justify its refusal to commit to new orders on the same scale. For their part the war industry committees complained of difficulties in obtaining sufficient raw materials to keep their operations afloat.[37]

The committees were dedicated not simply to the production of munitions, as well as to 'cabbages and sheepskins', but also to the principle of a morally superior form of mobilisation.[38] Enterprises established by the committees had to agree to accept orders at cost price. The committees derided the close links that big business enjoyed with tsarist officials and commercial banks, and the consequent complacency and sense of routine to which that relationship had given rise. They eschewed autocratic principles of management, as embodied in government arsenals. They claimed to be able to monitor the fulfilment of contracts in a rigorous and transparent manner. They purported to unleash the energies of local businessmen and technical specialists. One writer went so far as to say that the committees were 'schools of industry, in which people who hitherto were remote from and even hostile to industry could learn to understand it'. This made it imperative that the committees would survive into peacetime, where they could 'direct, unite and inspire our industry'. Few of these claims stood up to detailed scrutiny. But this was less important than the belief that bureaucracy should be made accountable to the educated public.[39]

The alternative vision of mobilisation came to be embodied in the labour policy adopted by the war industry committees. Their leaders supported the idea that organised labour should be allowed a role in the mobilisation of industry, because experienced organisers would be able to exercise 'responsibility' over the rank and file. In 1915 Guchkov, Konovalov and Tereshchenko came out in favour of the establishment of workers' groups. They secured a positive response from labour leaders such as the Menshevik K.A. Gvozdev, who sought to improve the conditions of the working class.[40] Not surprisingly, this issue proved particularly contentious. Guchkov advocated 'social peace' and supported the formation of conciliation chambers. Konovalov (Guchkov's deputy) maintained that the working class 'represented the element on which depends ultimate victory over the enemy'.[41] According to this doctrine, capital should collaborate with labour in modern economic life and patriotic labour leaders should be involved in the war effort. By contrast, the business elite in Petrograd articulated a more technocratic view of labour as one input, rather than as one half of a dynamic partnership in industry. Hence their support for labour militarisation, something that the war industry committee leadership never endorsed. The experiment came unstuck as a result of working-class militancy in early 1916, rather like the government's own venture with police socialism in 1903.[42]

More broadly still, the war industry committees regarded themselves as educators of public opinion and as organisers of industry in peacetime. They could inspire Russia's economic regeneration.[43] Sometimes this stance seemed to be quite partisan. Von Ditmar, a member of the TsVPK and himself a leading southern industrialist, called for economic reform, including a liberalisation of the laws on company formation and better technical education. He also promoted the idea of import substitution and railway construction on a massive scale. Other voices were more radical and demanded greater intervention in the affairs of private enterprise. The industrial elite felt threatened by the emergence of the heavily politicised voluntary organisations, which they believed to be superfluous in terms of industrial mobilisation, and an amateurish experiment to boot. They were determined not to relinquish their primacy. Nor did the Russian government relish the intervention of the war industry committees, which thus found powerful forces ranged against them.[44]

2.3   Expert knowledge and professional expertise in wartime

The war greatly expanded employment opportunities for statisticians, accountants, engineers, agronomists, doctors, fel'dshers (medical auxiliaries), psychiatrists and social workers. The 'third element' numbered around 60,000 (employees of the VSG), 170,000 (VZS), and 105,000 (Red Cross). If we add to their number those engaged on other technical activities, for example on behalf of port authorities, railways, waterways and forestry work, the total number rises to more than 1.5 million. Nor was this merely a matter of recruiting qualified personnel. New staff also received training. The purpose was to establish the basis from which professional expertise could be deployed in the interests of the Russian public.[45]

In the workplace, the number of engineers and technical staff increased by more than a third between 1913 and 1917. In machine-building the numbers virtually doubled.[46] At a higher level of economic administration, engineers and economists employed in local or even central government hoped to organise production in a way that corresponded to social need rather than private profit. The men who came to the fore were different in social origins and outlook from the products of the traditional elite institutions. The new technical intelligentsia received their practical and theoretical training in Russia's expanding polytechnics, such as the St Petersburg Technical Institute, the Moscow Higher Technical School and the Khar'kov Technical Institute, which sponsored a number of specialist engineering societies. The most important figures included Piotr Pal'chinskii, Vasilii Grinevetskii, Nikolai Savvin, Vladimir Ipatiev, Piotr S. Osadchii and Karl Kirsh, all of whom affirmed the importance of professional expertise and authority. Grinevetskii (1871–1919), director of the Moscow Higher Technical School, played an important part in bringing together the Society of Technologists (St Petersburg) and the Moscow Polytechnic Society, although his attempt to create an independent national organisation of engineers fell foul of the government. In addition to founding a new journal (*Vestnik inzhenerov*) in 1915, he and his colleagues established a Committee of Military–Technical Assistance, which conducted experimental work and trained students. The war gave them a public platform and an opportunity to establish their expertise in addressing the need for improved technical education, developing links between polytechnics and factories, and promoting 'scientific administration' at the level of the individual enterprise. These initiatives were intended to bring long-term benefits. Thus electrical engineers hoped that the spread of electricity would transform the prospects of rural consumers, revolutionise municipal transport and enable small-scale industry to compete with large-scale enterprise.[47]

The specialists advocated drawing an accurate statistical picture of the various branches of Russia's economy, in order to arrive at an overall

assessment of its potential and of the constraints that needed to be overcome. The fuel section of the Committee of Military–Technical Assistance
analysed costs of production, assessed the quality of alternative fossil fuels
and eventually worked out a fuel balance, which later became the basis for
planning at a national level.[48] Other specialists, too, demanded to be
heard. They argued that trained statisticians and economists should be
brought on to the new Special Council for State Defence.[49] Indeed the
Special Council took on dozens of engineers as factory inspectors
(although there were never sufficient), monitoring the activity of firms
under its control and checking on the quality of output. Economists produced countless bulletins summarising data on output, productivity and
prices.[50]

Russia's technical schools and universities also provided a platform for
experimental work in the preparation of new drugs, vaccines, iodine and
dyestuffs. Their workshops manufactured medical equipment, surgical
instruments and artificial limbs, items that had largely been imported from
Germany before the war. At Moscow University, leading scientists such as
Chelintsev, Kablukov and Shpital'skii carried out research in the properties of explosives, mines and gases. Scientific and technical institutes
engaged in meteorological and aeronautical research, sponsored by the
Ministry of War. These developments continued after the Bolshevik
revolution.[51]

One far-reaching example of the mobilisation of expertise was the
decision taken by the Academy of Sciences in early 1915 to establish a
'Commission for the Study of Natural Productive Forces' (KEPS).[52]
According to Vladimir Vernadskii, its chief architect, the war confronted
Russia with the need to develop its own natural resources, partly because
of the need to emancipate itself from reliance upon German imports and
partly in order to establish knowledge of national assets for its own sake.
Vernadskii cleverly used the rhetoric of national defence to extract support
from the Academy of Sciences in the task of 'mobilising chemistry' and
enhancing the status of scientific research. For a relatively modest outlay –
'the cost of one super-dreadnought' – Russia could get all the research
institutes it needed. Originally conceived as a means of supporting research
in military–technical activity, KEPS brought together Russian natural scientists and technical specialists in a project designed specifically to
formulate and co-ordinate applied research. Key problems included the
expansion of hydroelectric power, the development of new mineral wealth,
scientific investigation of the properties of materials and research into
plant and animal breeding. Research institutes were planned in fields such

as hydrology, petroleum, pharmaceuticals, coal and ferrous and non-ferrous metals. KEPS continued to meet and publish its findings throughout the revolution and Civil War. In the post-war years it made a major contribution to the development of Soviet 'big science'.[53]

Professional expertise was not confined to industrial administration and research, but extended into agriculture and social welfare. In agriculture the food specialists employed by the Ministry of Agriculture trained at the Moscow Agricultural Institute, the Mining Institute and at various academies that specialised in horticulture, stock-breeding and forestry. Many more served in the Special Council for Food Supply.[54] The Stolypin land reforms had created openings for around 5,000 agronomists and 7,500 land surveyors. In 1914–1915 many of them continued this work, although the great retreat brought land settlement to an end in the border-lands. Activity elsewhere was gradually wound down, not least because of the absence of adult male villagers who were expected to approve schemes for the re-organisation of land tenure. Perhaps one quarter of the agricultural specialists had also enlisted by 1915. Most staff in the Ministry of Agriculture remained in post but were expected to devote their time to matters of food supply rather than land tenure. Thus no real depletion took place in the existing body of purely agricultural expertise – Antsiferov called it 'a single family [bound by] true comradeship'. Its members were entrusted with fresh responsibilities after February 1917.[55]

Efforts were also made to train students ('youthful friends of the peasantry', in the words of one observer) to serve as accountants, bookkeepers and statisticians in rural co-operatives. Leading figures in the co-operative movement saw the war as an opportunity to create a more systematic programme of agronomic research and assistance. The zemstvos employed graduates of agricultural institutes to instruct peasants in the use of new farm equipment. Others hoped to continue the reform of peasant land tenure or to exert greater influence over government policy by taking charge of the collection of statistical data. By these means the zemstvos were able 'to watch the life of the peasantry very closely'.[56]

The unions of towns and zemstvos created a joint section for refugee welfare. Sub-sections dealt with employment, refugees' property and child welfare, and the collection of statistics. Many of its staff were young, radical professionals, with a background in medicine, law and the humanities, motivated by a firm sense of public duty towards the displaced and by a strong aversion to bureaucratic practice. More generally, humanitarian initiatives provided additional evidence of a newly emerging professional ethos in late imperial Russia, giving social workers, doctors, psychiatrists, lawyers and others extensive practice in observing, counting, examining and managing the Tsar's subjects.[57] This expertise was not confined to refugee relief. Traumatised soldiers required treatment, and this increased the profile of psychiatrists, neurologists and zemstvo hospital doctors who threw themselves into the care and rehabilitation of soldiers scarred by the experience of battle.[58]

2.4   The landed elite

The landed elite inhabited a very different milieu. The gentry might have been expected to operate at the heart of the war effort, by rallying public support and promoting productive activity, but their prestige and economic standing had suffered before the war. To be sure, the largest landowners wielded influence at Court and through the upper chamber of parliament, the State Council. Others dominated the system of rural administration, partly by directing the provincial and district zemstvos but also in their capacity as land captains (*zemskie nachal'niki*). Yet holding these posts could not disguise the fact that the landed gentry were something of a spent force. The noble estate (*dvorianstvo*) had been diluted by new entrants from the upper reaches of the civil service and the army. By 1914 around half of the pre-revolutionary officer corps was of non-noble origin. Landed estates were being mortgaged and sold to merchants and peasants. Thus, even before the war, economic difficulties and declining political influence had combined to create a crisis among the Russian landed elite.[59]

At the outbreak of war around 200 large landowning families held estates in excess of 50,000 hectares apiece, but they were the exception. In European Russia as a whole the average size of gentry estates did not exceed 73 hectares.[60] This figure disguised significant regional variations. In the south-west, the centre of sugar cultivation, some enormous properties were run on factory lines. In the mid-Volga and New Russia, where the average property exceeded 100 hectares, the landowners concentrated upon cereal crops. Most estates were modest in size. Some farms bore a closer resemblance to prosperous peasant households than to large latifundia. We should also bear in mind that many landowners leased part of their estates to peasants. In 1913 around one-quarter of arable land owned by the gentry was leased to peasant farmers, providing them with a regular unearned income, but it, too, was vulnerable to changes in market conditions.[61]

Gentry farmers who relied on hired labour suffered particularly badly from conscription. True, the largest landowners persuaded the government to assign them prisoners of war, and some 227,000 refugees also found work in the agricultural sector. However, each successive draft removed able-bodied men from the villages in the tens of thousands. The war brought to a virtual standstill the long established pattern of temporary migration (*otkhod*) in search of farm work, because the men were now in uniform and the other family members devoted effort to their own farms instead of going 'abroad' (*na storonu*). Difficulties in labour supply on the large estates were compounded by reductions in the supply of agricultural equipment and draught animals. The consequent decline in the area under crops on larger farms was bound to have an adverse effect on grain marketings and thus on gentry incomes.[62]

Where landowners had other sources of income, for example from processing industrial crops such as sugar, they did manage to make a reasonable living, but even so they had to reckon with rising costs of production. The gentry also lost out because of falling rental income, the result of declining peasant demand for land. In addition, many members of the nobility had invested in securities that offered a fixed return, which became less and less rewarding as inflation gathered momentum.[63]

It is difficult to ascertain if the nobility trimmed their expenditure, so as to live within their means. What is known of spending patterns before the war suggests that some gentry probably failed to reduce outlays on the upkeep of noble households, sinking further into debt. For all these reasons the war brought the landed elite no prosperity and reinforced the sense of crisis.[64]

One brief episode suggests that some members of the landed nobility were prepared to defend their interests in these difficult times. In November 1916 a group of large landowners headed by Count V.P. Orlov-Denisov and Prince N.V. Shcherbatov established an All-Russian Union of Landowners. The organisers asserted that only by addressing the needs of private landowners could the emerging crisis in food supply be stemmed, something they described as their 'patriotic goal'. It was a sign of the times that they extended membership to anyone who owned more than 50 hectares of land, regardless of the estate to which they were ascribed. Many of the Union's most active members were in fact wealthy peasants. It made only a limited impact. The first congress did not take place until the end of July 1917, by which time the issue was not how to sustain their income but how to stop the encroachment of poor peasants on privately held land, which brought back painful memories of 1905. Together, therefore, war and revolution set the seal on the economic and political enfeeblement of the landed elite.[65]

2.5   The middle classes

What conclusions can be reached about the social and economic position
of the Russian middle classes? This was a very diverse category. On the eve
of the war the business elite amounted to around 200,000 individuals comprising industrialists, bankers, merchants and their dependants. However,
sheer size did not translate into a unified social stratum. The business elite
bore the hallmarks of regional, ethnic and confessional fragmentation.
Moscow's businessmen, as we have seen, challenged the pretensions of
their counterparts in Petrograd. Both groups scarcely disguised their
antipathy towards rival entrepreneurs in south Russia and central Asia or
their loathing of Jewish merchants. This is a marked contrast with the situation in Germany, where employers forged a common alliance to negotiate
with the state and the army.[66]

We know virtually nothing about the impact of war on the personal
wealth of Russia's business leaders. Radical economists suggested that a
tiny elite (perhaps between 3,000 and 5,000 thousand individuals,
including landlords) were sitting on fabulous fortunes, with a total worth
of up to 50,000 million rubles by 1917, including 15,000 million rubles in
cash reserves, stocks and shares.[67]

We are on slightly firmer ground in discussing incomes. The annual
income of company directors and managers increased from 5,720 rubles in
1913 to 8,825 rubles in 1916 (when a worker would be earning around 573
rubles on average). In 1917 the average salary climbed to 13,050 rubles.
However, the increase was progressively eroded by inflation. Although
company directors managed to maintain their real income through 1915,
by the following year their salaries had fallen by 15 per cent compared with
the pre-war average. In 1917 the salary of a company director and manager
was worth only one-third of the pre-war figure. White-collar workers,
including factory engineers, fared little better during 1917. These figures
are illustrated in Table 2.1. However, they take no account of other payments that were made to management, which nearly trebled during the war,
but these did not compensate for the real decline in basic salaries.[68]

The behaviour of profits sheds some indirect light on bourgeois
incomes. Profits and dividends in corporate industry were hard to come by
during 1914, but they picked up in the following two years. Among the
mercantile elite enormous gains were to be had from dealing in scarce commodities. Companies reported good dividends for their shareholders in
1916, running at around 15 per cent of share capital compared with
9.5 per cent in 1913 and 7.7 per cent in 1914. Sectors such as cotton

TABLE 2.1   *Salaries of directors and white-collar employees in large-scale industry, 1913–1918*

Year	Directors and administrative staff		Technical staff		Other white-collar employees	
	Rubles, 1913 prices	1913 = 100	Rubles, 1913 prices	1913 = 100	Rubles, 1913 prices	1913 = 100
1913	5718	100	1464	100	690	100
1914	6017	105	1467	100	685	99
1915	5584	98	1322	90	598	87
1916	4884	85	1143	78	534	77
1917	1683	29	567	39	323	47
1918, 1st half	1280	22	550	38	350	51

Source: *Promyshlennaia perepis'*, 1926, volume 2, pp. 102–3.

textiles, engineering and utilities performed exceptionally well, with machine-building firms reporting dividends of 22 per cent in 1915 and 25 per cent in 1916, compared with 7 per cent in 1913.[69]

Net profits were passed on to shareholders, reinvested in the enterprise and handed over to the Treasury. Businessmen who succeeded in making a profit also invested in new enterprises or speculated in commodities. There is some evidence to suggest that companies put their money in other ventures, such as charitable or artistic activity. Total corporate contributions to charities increased three- or fourfold in real terms.[70] Social democratic economists believed that profits supported excessive consumption by the wealthy rather than productive investment, and on that basis called for a redistribution of income. What can be said with certainty is that the increased profits, regularly reported in the press, antagonised working-class consumers who felt the pinch by 1916–1917.[71]

Small business managed to survive to some extent thanks to the Union of Zemstvos. Although total output in small-scale enterprise fell by around 12 per cent between 1913 and 1916, many craftsmen and artisans remained in business supplying gloves, boots, belts, knapsacks, harness, tents and surgical instruments. The zemstvos contributed supplies of yarn, leather and metal, as well as knitting frames and other equipment, by-passing merchant intermediaries. Some contemporaries believed that the war revived trades that had all but died out, such as the cutlery trade in the Urals. Presumably this activity helped sustain the money incomes of small businessmen, although inflation must have eroded their real income by 1917.[72]

The chief losers, as in other belligerent economies, were those on fixed incomes, such as bondholders who had no means of cushioning themselves against the falling value of the ruble.[73] The same applies to teachers, lawyers and doctors. Those who lived in the countryside probably relied upon payments in kind from their clients; others sought charitable assistance. Students, public servants, bank employees and actors relied on supplies of essential goods from the 'closed co-operatives' that were specially created during the war. In 1916 students reportedly spent the night at railway stations or on the street. Faced with higher rents and increased tuition fees, some of them abandoned their studies altogether. Pensioners were doubtless hardest hit.[74]

The lower middle class comprised a complex category, which included white-collar workers in industry and the tertiary sector (such as clerical workers, postal and telegraph workers, book-keepers and sales-clerks, occupations in which women now made an inroad) as well as those in longstanding occupations such as tradesmen and independent craftsmen. Employment opportunities as a whole expanded as a result of the war effort, including the growth of the voluntary organisations. In factory industry, the number of white-collar workers increased by around 50 per cent. However, many clerical workers would have struggled to make ends meet and their relative position vis-à-vis factory workers deteriorated. By the winter of 1916 their difficult personal financial circumstances helped persuade many of these 'lower middle strata' that their interests coincided with those of lower social origin, such as domestic servants, apprentices and factory workers, for whom watchwords such as the eight-hour day, government regulation and 'democratisation' held great appeal. These groups all pursued the path of unionisation of labour after February 1917.[75]

Professional expertise also implied an expanded sphere for middle-class women. Some middle-class feminists argued that their present contribution underscored the extent to which patriarchal authority had failed Russia in the past, and that the war gave their talents belated yet important recognition. Nursing is the obvious example. Thousands of nursing personnel volunteered for service at the front and in the rear, where they looked for 'adventure' and found themselves idealised as 'sisters of mercy'. Women placed themselves at risk, by virtue of their direct exposure to shrapnel or to liability to gangrene, and undertook tasks that challenged accepted norms of gentility and modesty. Other women enlisted in the war effort as drivers, couriers and firefighters. Some managed to enlist in the armed forces, such as the redoubtable Princess Shakhovskaia who became a pilot.

According to Alfred Meyer, their patriotic narratives 'follow a persistent pattern. Singly or with a companion, a young woman cut off her long hair, perhaps darkened her complexion, smoked cigarettes to roughen her voice, acquired a uniform, and then tried to enlist in an army unit. In some cases the woman tried to serve in the same unit as her husband'.[76]

Charitable work with refugees also illustrated women's contribution to society. The war inspired a multitude of 'ladies' committees' and 'maidens' societies' whose members arranged programmes of welfare and work. Yet, for all their commitment, Russia's women were unable to achieve much prominence. Although they figure in the historical record as clerical staff, actively engaged in registering refugees or handling requests to trace missing persons, they remain in the shadows, dutiful yet anonymous assistants to male officials.[77]

Conclusions

Russia's First World War confirmed the lack of common ground between the tsarist state and 'educated society'. This point should not be laboured to excess. To some extent, a division of labour was established between the state, whose agents assumed responsibility for munitions, and the unions of zemstvos and towns, which took charge of civilian relief and the care of wounded soldiers, as well as contributing substantially to the supply of military necessities such as uniforms and boots. Other kinds of accommodation were also reached. In respect of refugee relief, government officials, the voluntary organisations and private welfare agencies all became involved, with some staff moving between them. Finally, it should be remembered that many professionals embarked on careers in the civil service, as statisticians, doctors and legal advisers. Naturally enough, few of them adopted a hostile stance towards tsarist authority.

All the same, zemstvo and municipal activists drew a contrast between the broadly positive relationship they enjoyed with the military authorities at the front and the sour attitude of central government, which sought to curb attempts by the public organisations to assume overall responsibility for refugee relief. Political issues were never far from the surface, as in the zemstvos' critique of government inaction in respect of civilian population displacement. This constituted one important area of activity in which the voluntary organisations could establish a degree of legitimacy in the public mind. Yet they proved unable to capitalise upon their efforts and to mount an effective political challenge to the regime. In the event, they became the beneficiaries rather than the instigators of the crisis of tsarist authority in the winter of 1916.

The provincial war industry committees had in their sights the long-standing association between big business and the state. They did not see their role as supplementing the private and state sectors but as making an independent contribution to the war effort. They constituted a self-conscious alternative to official efforts at industrial mobilisation, to unlock untapped potential among small businessmen, technical specialists and workers. From their point of view, mobilisation was too important a matter to be entrusted to bureaucrats. It embraced all sections of society and transcended considerations of private interest or class affiliation. However, as we shall see, the close association between the state and big business survived this onslaught. Their relative lack of concrete achievement left the war industry committees to assert a grand, but much less tangible, 'creative stimulus'.[78]

The war also witnessed the mobilisation of expert knowledge. Experts defined themselves in opposition to older corporate bodies of knowledge. Expertise was couched in traditional terms of service to the 'people', combined with deep-seated mistrust of government officials. Ministers found it difficult to accept the broader claims being advanced by Russia's professional experts. However, the war enabled scientists, engineers and other members of the emerging technocratic stratum to assert their right to deliberate and resolve 'questions'. Increasingly the rhetoric of expertise was deployed to advocate technocratic supervision or intervention in market transactions. In the words of Alessandro Stanziani, 'the dreams of Russian radical economists turned from the pre-war apocalyptic utopia (the collapse of the capitalist system) into a rational-technocratic utopia, a well-ordered world made by the specialist'.[79]

Among the privileged strata, Russia's landowners experienced the war as a time of trial. Only belatedly did they create an organisation to defend their interests, and this was something of a last-ditch attempt to salvage something from the war. Even tsarist victory would not in itself have contributed to a revival of their economic fortunes or their political influence, both of which were on the wane before 1914. Certainly the landed elite could not be counted upon to underpin an effective propaganda offensive in the countryside. Russia's commercial bourgeoisie remained equally fragmented. Prominent entrepreneurs and bankers threw in their lot with the government. A more adventurous element among those of lesser means opted for the war industry committees. But the commercial middle class did not unite; regional and ethnic differences remained too deeply entrenched. The cultural and political distance between the moneyed middle class and the lower strata remained unbridgeable. Professionals among the large urban middle class did not disguise their distaste for the world of commerce. In emphasising disinterested service rather than profit, the war afforded these men and women an opportunity to proclaim the moral high ground and eventually to negotiate the change of political regime.

Note on further reading

The standard works in English on the voluntary organisations are by Polner, 1930, Gronsky and Astrov, 1929, and Siegelbaum, 1983. A modern, full-scale history of the unions of towns and zemstvos remains to be written. The otherwise informative volumes edited by Balzer, 1996, and Clowes et al., 1991, have little to say about the war. The best book on the commercial middle classes is by Rieber, 1982, but his treatment of the war years is also quite brief. The landed elite in wartime has been almost entirely neglected, with the exception of a chapter (in Russian) in Anfimov, 1962. On women and gender relations the reader may consult work by Engel, 1997, Petrone, 1998, and Stockdale, 2004.

References

1 Laverychev, 1967, pp. 109–23.

2 George Yaney expresses this as follows: 'military mobilisation was not a breaking away from specialist ideals but a fulfilment of them'. Yaney, 1982, p. 443.

3 Bradley, 2002.

4 Vainshtein, 1960, p. 403; Gross, 1981, pp. 220–21.

5 Gatrell, 1986, pp. 38–9, 112–14.

6 Rieber, 1982, pp. xxiii–xxv, 418–27.

7 Laverychev, 1967, p. 113.

8 N.V. Teslenko, 5 June 1915, quoted in Grave, 1927, p. 20.

9 Emmons and Vucinich, 1982, pp. 133–75; Polner, 1930, p. 36.

10 The landed gentry and the zemstvo executive comprised the first and second element.

11 Gronsky and Astrov, 1929, pp. 154–65; Polner, 1930, pp. 53–4; Miliukov, 1967, pp. 313–14; Gross, 1981, pp. 206–7, 222.

12 Polner, 1930, pp. 54–8; Gross, 1981, p. 219. There was no obligation on any zemstvo to join the new union, but only the notoriously conservative Kursk zemstvo refused to participate.

13 Gronsky and Astrov, 1929, p. 253; Polner, 1930, pp. 59–60.

14 Gleason, 1982, p. 369; Polner, 1930, p. 109; Bukshpan, 1929, p. 287.

15 Gurko, 1939, p. 540; Miliukov, 1967, pp. 313–15; Gleason, 1982, pp. 369–70.

16 Gross, 1981, pp. 236–7.

17 *B. Ved.*, 15037, 20 August 1915, quoting K.N. Anufriev; *Izvestiia VSG*, 1915, 17, pp. 16, 34–7; *Izvestiia VZS*, 28, 1 December 1915, pp. 68–9.

18 *Padenie tsarskogo rezhima*, 1927, volume 7, p. 123.

19 Startsev, 1977, p. 136. For a contemporary critique of their 'revolutionary' pretensions see Gurko, 1939, p. 541.

20 Gronsky and Astrov, 1929, p. 255; Polner, 1930, p. 88. In May 1916, Boris Stürmer, then Minister of the Interior, charged that the Unions 'began work before the limits and actual permissibility of such work attracted the attention of the government.' *Izvestiia VSG*, 1916, 33, pp. 6–13.

21 Tverdokhlebov, 1915, pp. 450–51.

22 Belevsky and Voronoff, 1917; Gronsky and Astrov, 1929, pp. 256–7; Polner, 1930, pp. 62–5.

23 Gross, 1981, pp. 218–19.

24 Semennikov, 1927, p. 96.

25 Krupina, 1969, p. 59, quoting Maklakov.

26 Polner, 1930, p. xi (James Shotwell). *Statisticheskaia razrabotka dannykh*, 1917, pp. 5–6, 83–7; Bukshpan, 1929, p. 293; Maevskii, 1957, p. 97.

27 *P&T*, 1915, 12 (Fridman).

28 *Promyshlennaia Rossiia*, 1915, 10–11, quoted in Diakin, 1967, p. 92.

29 P. I. Pal'chinskii, as reported in *Izvestiia MVPK*, 1916, 31–32, p. 141; *Vestnik inzhenerov*, 1916, 1 (Savvin).

30 *Trudy s"ezda predstavitelei*, 1915, pp. 92–6. Tsarist approval for the TsVPK did not follow until 4 August.

31 *P&T*, 1915, 11 (Fridman). See also *Novyi ekonomist*, 24, 13 June 1915 (Fridman).

32 *Trudy s"ezda predstavitelei*, 1915, p. 115; Rieber, 1982, pp. 376–7; Diakin, 1967, pp. 94–5.

33 *Trudy Vtorogo s"ezda*, 1916, volume 2, pp. 440–43; *Izvestiia Obshchestva zavodchikov i fabrikantov Moskovskogo promyshlennogo raiona*, 1917, 1–2 (Charnovskii).

34 *ZhOSO*, 13 June 1915; 24 June 1915.

35 *Statisticheskaia razrabotka dannykh*, 1917, pp. 14, 17. Of the 195 million rubles' worth of contracts, delivery had been taken of goods to the value of 33 million rubles.

36 *Vestnik inzhenerov*, 1916, 3 (Zhukovskii); Siegelbaum, 1983, pp. 115–16.

37 When allowance was made for the complexity of work undertaken (the war industry committees taking on more complex work than Zemgor), the unions of towns and zemstvos had a better track record of completion. *RVMV*, 1925, pp. 57–8; Sidorov, 1973, pp. 203–4. On the war industry committees' relationship with Prodamet, see RGIA f.1276, op.12, d.1083, ll.58–84ob.

38 *Izvestiia MVPK*, 1915, 1 (Bogolepov).

39 *Vestnik inzhenerov*, 1916, 3 (Zhukovskii); Siegelbaum, 1983, p. 80.

40 Kir"ianov, ed., 1999, pp. 43–4; McKean, 1990, pp. 437–43.

41 RGVIA f.369, op.1, d.124, ll.8–9, dated 4 January 1916.

42 *Izvestiia MVPK*, 1916, 23–24 (Charnovskii); Korelin, 1964; Siegelbaum, 1983, pp. 159–82.

43 *Izvestiia MVPK*, 1915, 1 (Bogolepov).

44 Pogrebinskii, 1941, pp. 183–6.

45 *RVMV*, 1925, p. 25. Of these, 346,000 worked on the Northern Front, 359,000 on the Western Front, 351,000 on the South-Western Front. For background see Balzer, ed., 1996, pp. 117–42 (Ramer).

46 *Sbornik statisticheskikh svedenii*, 1924, table 14; *Promyshlennaia perepis'*, 1926, volume 1, p. 57.

47 Bailes, 1978, pp. 38–43; Coopersmith, 1992, pp. 88–9, 99–120. For contemporary analyses, see *P&T*, 1915, 2 (Dembovskii); *Vestnik inzhenerov*, 1915, no.1 (Bezprozvannyi); *Izvestiia MVPK*, 1916, 31–32 (Pal'chinskii). Dembovskii urged engineering students to spend their holidays visiting factories. Pal'chinskii wanted invalids to retrain as engineers.

48 Coopersmith, 1992, p. 109; Rieber, 1982, pp. 402–3; Balzer, ed. 1996, pp. 55–88 (Balzer).

49 *P&T*, 1915, 12 (Fridman). The young economist Lev Kafengauz (1885–1940) joined the Special Council for Fuel Supply, being promoted to Assistant Minister of Trade and Industry under the Provisional Government.

50 Bukshpan, 1929, p. 324; Odinetz and Novogorotsev, 1929, p. 189.

51 Odinetz and Novgorotsev, 1929, pp. 173–83.

52 Kol'tsov, 1995.

53 *P&T*, 1916, 21 (Avtonomov); Fersman, 1917; Bailes, 1978, p. 41; Kojevnikov, 2002.

54 Balzer, ed., 1996, pp. 276–8 (Orlovsky).

55 Antsiferov et al., 1930, pp. 355, 360; Yaney, 1982, pp. 398–9, 537.

56 Polner, 1930, pp. 149, 153 (both quotations). See also Kayden and Antsiferov, 1929, pp. 406–7; Stanziani, 1995, pp. 175–7.

57 Gatrell, 1999, pp. 45, 82–4, 90–91.

58 Tereshkovich, 1924; Solomon and Hutchinson, eds, 1990, pp. 227–44 (Brown).

59 Acton et al. eds, 1997, pp. 482–3 (Lieven); p. 534 (Kenez).

60 Pavlovsky, 1930, pp. 210–11, citing the 1916 Agricultural Census. In the south-west the figure reached 186 hectares, and in the mid-Volga and New Russia the mean size was over 100 hectares.

61 Anfimov, 1962, p. 89; Koval'chenko et al., 1982, pp. 113–16. The proportion was highest in the Black-Earth provinces.

62 Anfimov, 1962, pp. 95–7, 107; Polner, 1930, pp. 154–5.

63 Anfimov, 1962, pp. 177–83, describes an estate in Tula where the owner kept his starch-making factory in business by employing women and children.

64 Koval'chenko et al., 1982, pp. 122–5. The scale of landlords' indebtedness and the burden of debt payments are difficult to establish.

65 EPR, 1967, volume 3, p. 505; Osipova, 1976.

66 Acton et al., eds, 1997, pp. 572–83 (Gatrell); Rieber, 1982, pp. 421–22; Kocka, 1984, pp. 73–5; Bokhanov, 1994, pp. 18–26, 41–9.

67 Volobuev, 1962, pp. 313–14.

68 Promyshlennaia perepis', 1926, volume 2, pp. 114–15.

69 Sharyi, 1917; Cohen, 1943; Strumilin, 1958, p. 247.

70 Promyshlennaia perepis', 1926, volume 2, pp. 114–15, adjusted for inflation.

71 Maslov, 1918, p. 223; Danilov, 1922, p. 52. Reported profits must be treated with caution.

72 Adamov, ed., 1972, pp. 333–45 (Ol'khovaia); Tarnovskii, 1995; Polner, 1930, pp. 61–5, 186–7.

73 Katsenelenbaum, 1917, pp. 74–6; Maslov, 1918, p. 223.

74 Kayden and Antsiferov, 1929, p. 74; Odinetz and Novgorotsev, 1929, pp. 17, 87, 206–9. Refugee teachers suffered most.

75 Orlovsky, 1989.

76 Thurstan, 1915, pp. 153, 175; Meyer, 1991, pp. 209, 219–20; Sanborn, 2003, pp. 147–8.

77 Polner, 1930, p. 109; Lindenmeyr, 1996, pp. 13–16, 125–9; Gatrell, 1999, pp. 123–6.

78 *Vestnik inzhenerov*, 1916, 1 (Zernov); *Trudy Vtorogo s"ezda*, 1916, volume 2, pp. 466–7.

79 Stanziani, 1995.

CHAPTER 3

Narod: plebeian society during the war

The purposes of the war were not clear and the government did nothing to explain to the narod the real meaning and significance of the struggle or to show to what extent the welfare of the country and the people would depend on its favourable outcome

[Gurko, 1939, p. 544]

The focus in this chapter switches to Russia's lower orders, particularly workers and peasants in their capacity as civilians and as members of the armed forces. In 1914 these 'people of lesser means' accounted for 90 per cent of Russia's population but only 24 per cent of its national wealth.[1] At issue here is the impact of war upon plebeian men and women and the inducements used in order to sustain their commitment to the war. What of other non-privileged groups who stood on the margins? Village priests and schoolteachers, for example, were customarily treated with scant respect by their social superiors and peasants alike. How were they affected by the war? Similar questions relate to refugees, whose marginal status was a direct consequence of the war.

As the numerically largest *soslovie*, the Russian peasantry was expected to cultivate the land and supply food under the watchful eyes of landlords and rural officials. The peasantry also made up the bulk of army conscripts. In wartime peasants would be obliged immediately to provide large numbers of men and then keep them supplied with food and fodder. Peasants were not defined exclusively in terms of their economic function or military obligation. They retained a strong element of social solidarity, rooted in shared material conditions and expressed in common cultural forms. These distinctive characteristics caused thoughtful contemporaries to ponder whether peasants could ever be integrated into 'modern' society.[2]

Only in rare instances did peasants come into direct contact with social superiors such as landlords, merchants or the police. They were more likely to rub shoulders with the village teacher and the parish clergyman. The onset of war carried an expectation that peasants' social superiors would help promote Russia's cause in the village. But the relationship between the 'rural intelligentsia', priests and their parishioners was a frosty one. The war did nothing to improve it.[3]

Workers too were expected to obey their social superiors, in order to ensure that the wheels of industry and commerce turned smoothly. In practice, Russian workers had already acquired sharp political instincts and an appetite for collective protest. In a rapidly industrialising country, such as Russia, social reality was also complex and unsettled. There was no clear dividing line between the world of the factory and the village: peasants left their farms in search of additional sources of income; workers left the bench to join family members in the countryside and help bring in the annual harvest. Contemporaries expressed concern about the social, economic and cultural consequences. Urban society replicated patterns of village organisation, as in the *zemliachestva* or brotherhoods that supported migrants in the factory who shared a common point of origin. The war did nothing to reverse these processes.[4]

Millions of raw recruits entered the ranks of the tsarist army during the war, posing vital questions about provisioning them with food, uniforms and weaponry. Given the scale and uncertainty of the conflict peasant soldiers could no longer cultivate the land or supply their own uniforms, as they often did before the war. Nor was it simply a question of military supply. Conscripts had to be inducted rapidly into the armed forces and taught whom to obey and how to fight. Issues of discipline and obedience arose much more acutely than they did in the world of the factory and the farm. But soldiers could not be expected to forget the town or village where they had left loved ones, or to abandon hope of a better life when the war ended.[5]

The war also gave rise to unfamiliar and unexpected social disturbances. The most significant of these was mass civilian population displacement. As one journalist put it, 'refugeedom is an unprecedented phenomenon ... a new form of civic status'. Most refugees had lost their property, jobs and income, surrendering whatever social standing they possessed before the war. Other losses were still more perceptible. Established family ties had been ruptured. Refugees needed as a matter of urgency to be found somewhere to live and to secure the means of subsistence. In due course they were expected to return to their homes and assume their former role in society. In the meantime, however, 'their social position has not been resolved. The result has been a kind of nomadic group and a highly unusual one at that'.[6]

3.1   Soldiers and soldiering

As we saw earlier, conscription proceeded relatively painlessly. Some soldiers avoided the military draft, although fewer than pre-war rates of evasion might lead one to expect. More troubling was the sluggish supply of uniforms and footwear, which contributed to a loss of morale. Military defeat, coupled with the death or capture of soldiers, reinforced the sombre mood. How did these tribulations affect the people most directly involved?

Service in the Tsar's armed forces was accompanied by various inducements. Under a law passed in 1912, each soldier's family received an allowance from the state. This could only be withdrawn in the event that he deserted or 'voluntarily' entered captivity.[7] Substantial sums were involved. In 1914 these transfer payments amounted to 191 million rubles, rising in the following year to 624 million rubles, an increase that reflected the large numbers of men who were conscripted. This was also a useful, if blunt, instrument in the hands of the authorities, struggling to cope with desertion; they simply withdrew the allowance from the offending households.[8] The allowance was an important lifeline, but its value did not keep pace with inflation. Rumours of the profits made by shopkeepers and military contractors also invested it with a new meaning, emphasising the gulf between those who risked their lives and those who enjoyed a comfortable standard of living.[9]

Other means of encouraging military enthusiasm and commitment were contemplated. Chief of Staff Ianushkevich proposed to grant Russian soldiers who had shown conspicuous valour land that had been seized from German settlers. Leading right-wingers supported Ianushkevich, but most government ministers treated his proposal with contempt. Yet the principle of offering land in return for gallantry persisted – the government earmarked land in order to reward soldiers who had distinguished themselves in battle, such as those who won the Cross of St George. Meanwhile the Tsar established a new medal for women who had made a vital contribution to the war effort.[10]

Some troops needed little inducement to fight. Officers as well as army chaplains continually reminded them that this was a 'holy war' and that Wilhelm II was 'Satan'.[11] It was but a short step to demonise German or

Austrian civilians, or to suspect non-Russian subjects of the Tsar of espionage and other crimes. Russian troops were thus quite capable of inflicting death and destruction, both upon the enemy (as in Galicia) and upon selected 'elements' in Russia itself. Stories of rape and the maltreatment of civilians were hushed up.[12]

Military action on Russia's various fronts exposed soldiers to great danger. How, to put it crudely, did Russia pick up the pieces? Public organisations arranged for the evacuation of war wounded to hospitals in the rear and took over the clearing hospitals administered by the Ministry of War. Students assisted by helping wounded men to detrain and giving them meals. Workers and peasants donated food, soap and linen to local hospitals.[13] During the course of the war nearly 5.2 million men were hospitalised in the rear, usually for an average of three or four weeks. Around 2.8 million of them required treatment for war wounds, particularly injuries to arms and legs, and 2.3 million received attention for infectious diseases, frostbite and rheumatism. Around six per cent of those who were discharged as sick subsequently died from their illness. A much larger proportion – 36 per cent – died from the wounds they received.[14]

The war led to massive trauma on the battlefield and thus to the need to consider psychiatric care. Shell shock had already been diagnosed among veterans of the Russo-Japanese War.[15] By 1915 the Red Cross reported 12,000 cases of mental illness, directly attributable to the war,[16] but medical opinion could not agree whether shell shock afflicted only those who were already psychologically predisposed to be vulnerable, such as 'alcoholics and syphilitics'. Mentally disturbed soldiers were usually transferred to the rear by the Red Cross. The Ministry of the Interior arranged for local authorities to reserve beds for soldiers in mental hospitals. Other hospitals sent patients home in order to create space for injured troops. Some in the unions of towns and zemstvos resented the role claimed by the Red Cross and the army, whose own staff sought to keep control of the process of scrutinising and examining individual soldiers.[17]

Other afflictions required different kinds of medical intervention. The most common infectious diseases were typhoid and dysentery; the most lethal were typhus (relapsing fever) and cholera. New hospitals were built as a result of local initiative. Not surprisingly bitter turf wars erupted between the public organisations and the government, whose chief official (Prince Aleksandr Oldenburgskii) was viewed by liberals as an archetypal member of the old elite. The Special Council for State Defence established a 'commission for medical-sanitary supply' under the chairmanship of Guchkov. It supported the creation of a special bacteriological and vaccination institute and discussed measures to improve field hospitals.[18]

Apart from susceptibility to death or wounds on the battlefield, the other catastrophe that affected all soldiers was to become a prisoner of war. This fate befell more than five million men in the Russian army. Nearly half of the total number of Russian POWs entered captivity during the campaigns in 1914 and 1915. A further third were captured in the fighting that took place in 1916. The remaining 918,000 men were captured in 1917.[19] Some 3.41 million men remained in captivity by 1 January 1918. They had different perspectives on their experience, depending on whether they had been incarcerated in POW camps or engaged as agricultural labourers. The former were radicalised by their experience, having been exposed to Bolshevik propaganda, whereas the latter were impressed by the superior economic methods employed by central European farmers.[20]

Troops in the rear (some 2.3 million by early 1917) likewise experienced the war in terms of boredom. Changes in the size and social composition of Russia's garrisons turned them into hotbeds of subversion. The civilian authorities punished striking workers and other 'undesirables' by distributing them in garrisons throughout the empire. Their numbers were swelled by new recruits and by battle-hardened men who had been evacuated to the rear in order to recover from illness or wounds. There they languished until called upon to suppress demonstrations. Notoriously, in Petrograd in February 1917, they conspicuously failed to do so.[21]

The Tsarist navy was something of a world unto itself. The social world of the ship replicated social divisions in Russian society between officers – largely an aristocratic elite – and the ratings, who were drawn predominantly from a plebeian (and literate) milieu. Inequality was inscribed in the numerous regulations that demeaned the common sailors. Mistreatment was commonplace. Naval bases such as Kronstadt enjoyed a relatively quiet war, because the blockade confined most men to shoreline duty, routine maintenance and incessant training. Yet Kronstadt proved to be a tinderbox, because of the harsh regime that the officers inflicted on the young trainees under their command.[22]

Soldiers and sailors suffered the consequences of declining food availability. Army meat rations were reduced from 0.4 kg to 0.3 kg per day in the middle of 1916, and to just 0.2 kg at the end of the year. Unwilling to blame impersonal forces or to target peasants, soldiers in garrisons in the rear turned their anger instead on merchants whom they accused of withholding grain for speculative purposes. As in other instances, direct action stemmed from a breakdown in trust and a deep-seated resentment that those who were better off could always get by.[23]

Given these difficulties – the experience of defeat, the danger of battle, the shortages of uniforms and food – why did the tsarist army not disintegrate? One explanation is that tough sanctions applied to soldiers who disobeyed or deserted. Another is that mutual solidarity and comradeship overcame misgivings about the war. Finally soldiers were joined in a common code of duty to the Tsar. While the Tsar's authority remained intact, so too did the Russian army. Nicholas II may have been more astute than he realised when he became Commander-in-Chief. But after the overthrow of the Romanov dynasty in February 1917 it did not take long for deep-seated antagonisms to surface, with catastrophic consequences.[24]

3.2   Workers and the urban milieu

The labour force in large-scale industry increased by around 20 per cent between 1914 and 1916. During the first 12 months of the war such an increase would have been regarded as unthinkable – the slump in business confidence led to an immediate upsurge in unemployment in the autumn of 1914. The labour market was badly disrupted. The Russian High Command resisted attempts to return conscripted workers to civilian jobs, arguing that this would have a 'dispiriting effect' on those who remained in uniform. Individual factories were entitled to petition for the return of workers, but the procedure was cumbersome.[25] In principle the bargaining power of skilled labour improved, because employers competed for experienced workers to replace those who had been called up. The situation was less promising for unskilled workers, since the early onset of unemployment ensured that employers had access to a ready supply of labour.[26]

Demand for labour picked up during the second half of 1915 as the mobilisation of industry got into full swing. Unemployed men and women found work in factory industry. Legal restrictions on the employment of women in underground work were lifted in 1915. In 1913 women made up around 30 per cent of the labour force in manufacturing industry, but by 1916 this proportion had risen to around 40 per cent. Most of the gains were in metal-working and machine-building, where female employment increased from six to 18 per cent of the total labour force. Around 98,000 women were employed in the engineering trades by 1916, compared with fewer than 23,000 in 1913. Women also increased their presence in chemicals, textiles and other occupations.[27] Employment in large-scale manufacturing industry is summarised in Table 3.1.

The labour force in the Moscow region remained stable until the end of 1915, but in the following year increased by around 15 per cent, most of

TABLE 3.1 *Employment in large-scale manufacturing industry, 1913–1918 (USSR territory)*

	1913	1914	1915	1916	1917	1918, 1st half
Shopfloor workers, 000s	1,844	1,876	1,988	2,193	2,274	1,798
Index, 1913 = 100	100	102	108	119	123	98
Per cent female	30.7	31.8	36.0	39.6	40.2	41.2
Per cent juvenile (male & female)	10.6	11.0	12.5	14.4	12.6	12.2
Technical staff, 000s	11.34	12.46	13.23	14.36	15.33	12.87
Ratio of shopfloor to technical staff	146	138	133	125	115	103

Sources and notes: Rows 1–4 are derived from Mints, 1975, p. 79. Rows 5 and 6, data from 2,029 enterprises working continuously, as reported in *Promyshlennaia perepis'*, 1926, volume 1, p. 101. These data are not directly comparable with those in Row 1.

it the result of a sharp rise in the number of women employed. The change was even more marked in Petrograd and its environs, the heart of the metal-working and engineering trades. Here total industrial employment rose by more than 150,000 between 1914 and 1917 and the number of women in industry almost doubled. Other regions that noticed an increase were Ekaterinoslav and Khar'kov, both centres of iron- and steel-making where employment jumped in 1916.[28]

The tsarist authorities and employers alike sought to obtain additional effort from the workforce. Workers were encouraged to take fewer holidays and festivals were cancelled. (At the Kolomna engineering works 108 days fell into the category of 'rest days'.[29]) In the Moscow region the average length of the working day increased only marginally, from 9.2 in 1914 to 9.7 in 1916, reflecting the cutbacks in non-defence industry. Overtime increased in defence plants, where workers found it impossible to refuse to work longer hours, because they needed the extra income. In any case, men who refused might find themselves before the draft board. As the war dragged on and households had to devote additional hours searching for food, time spent at work became less and less tolerable.[30]

The bargaining power of labour increased as a result of the intensive mobilisation of industry in the second half of 1915. It had nothing to do with the role of organised labour, which remained weak as a result of government intransigence. If employers were to secure labour (and labour effort), they had to offer a monetary inducement. In order to counteract the widespread turnover of labour, employers were obliged to pay higher wages, passing on the increased costs to the state.[31] Nominal wages in the defence industry increased from 393 rubles in 1913 and 442 rubles in 1914 to 594 rubles in 1915 and 912 rubles in 1916. This helped to bring workers back into state arsenals and steelworks.[32] Throughout the second half of 1915 skilled workers in the defence industry made greater gains than unskilled workers, reflecting the premium that many employers placed upon skill. However, the relative position of skilled workers was vulnerable to changes in the labour process, particularly in engineering where management introduced new methods of manufacturing. By 1916 'deskilling' had begun to be reflected in relative rates of remuneration. Unskilled workers also improved their relative position because many employers paid cost of living allowances as a lump sum.[33]

Trends in nominal wages do not take account of the rapid changes in the cost of living. Real wages improved in 1914 and 1915, although they fell back slightly during 1916, except for key branches of industry such as metal-working, iron and steel and chemicals, where workers could use their leverage to secure wage rises. Hence real wages in munitions were some 24 per cent higher in 1916 than at the outbreak of war, whereas in non-defence industry they declined by around 15 per cent over the same period.[34] Trends in real wages in Russian manufacturing industry are illustrated in Table 3.2.

The number of supervisors and clerical workers increased by around 50 per cent during the war, as employers took on staff in order to monitor unskilled workers. However, they fared less well than people on the shopfloor, recording an increase of 18 per cent in their average salaries between 1913 and 1915, at the same time as factory workers secured an average rise in money wages of 42 per cent. By 1916 nominal salaries stood 61 per cent higher than in 1913, but this compared with 120 per cent for factory workers. In real terms, salaries fell by 22 per cent, whereas wages had risen by 8 per cent between 1913 and 1916. In 1917 the gap

TABLE 3.2   *Real wages in Russian industry, 1913–1917 (1913 = 100)*

Year	White-collar workers	All shopfloor workers	Workers in munitions	Workers in military equipment	Workers in other defence enterprises	Workers in non-defence enterprises
1913	100	100	100	100	100	100
1914	99.2	105.0	110.9	106.7	97.4	100.3
1915	90.9	105.7	115.3	103.7	96.2	86.8
1916	78.0	107.1	122.8	102.1	93.6	84.8
1917	38.0	83.3	74.7	76.2	85.9	53.9

Source: Promyshlennaia perepis', 1926, volume 1, p. 57.

narrowed still further. The decline in the relative position of clerical and other employees was certainly a factor in their radicalisation.[35]

In defence-related occupations the war witnessed an increase in the size of the factory. An average metal-working factory might have 160 workers in 1913, but this increased to 234 by 1916. More workers competed for access to basic facilities such as washrooms, canteens and infirmaries, provision for which did not keep pace with the growth of factory employment. Overcrowding in the workplace added to workers' sense of frustration with their conditions.[36]

The war failed to bring an end to protest in the workplace. Fewer than 10,000 workers downed tools between August and December 1914, but in the following year the strike wave revived. Workers thought carefully before taking strike action, both because of the risks involved and because they wished to support their comrades in uniform. Around 540,000 workers went on strike during 1915, and a further 880,000 in 1916. The average number of days lost to strikes amounted to 1.4 in 1915 (the same as in the last full year of peace) but increased to 2.2 in 1916.[37] Some of these stoppages – such as those in the Central Industrial Region in the late spring of 1915 – coincided with attacks on German businesses whose owners were accused of poisoning the workforce.[38] Other stoppages were more symbolic and short-lived, as in Petrograd in October 1915, the tenth anniversary of the strike that forced the Tsar to grant a reform manifesto, and on 1 May 1916, when a joint appeal by Bolsheviks and Socialist Revolutionaries (SR) brought workers out on strike. Workers also protested in November 1916 at the closure of the State Duma. Similarly, workers downed tools in large numbers in Petrograd on 9 January 1917, the twelfth anniversary of Bloody Sunday.[39]

Throughout the war, workers in metal-working and machine-building, often in medium-sized enterprises, took the lead in political strike action. The disputes often ended in victory for organised labour, indicating employers' readiness to settle rather than risk a prolonged interruption to defence production. One scholar speaks of 'pressure from the military, the Okhrana (secret police) and bureaucrats to avoid unnecessary interruptions'.[40] The history of the strike movement between 1909 and 1917 is shown in Table 3.3.

Strikes elsewhere were often prolonged and bitter. Deputy Minister of Trade and Industry A.I. Konovalov was despatched in March 1915 to investigate the reasons for a strike in the Donbass. He concluded that the chief explanation for the stoppage was the rising cost of living, and that employers alone had it in their power to address this issue.[41] Other strikes

TABLE 3.3   *The strike movement in Russia, 1909–1917*

Year	Strikes recorded	Numbers on strike	Total days lost, million	Days lost per striker
1909	340	64,160	0.418	6.5
1910	222	46,600	0.256	5.5
1911	466	105,100	0.791	7.5
1912	2,032	725,500	2.378	3.3
1913	2,404	887,100	3.483	3.9
1914	3,534	1,337,548	5.795	4.3
Jan–July	3,493	1,327,897	5.662	4.2
Aug–Dec	41	9,561	0.133	14.0
1915	928	539,528	1.863	3.5
Jan–July	523	231,794	0.920	4.0
Aug–Dec	420	292,282	0.963	3.3
1916	1,161	878,347	3.369	3.8
Jan–June	676	518,501	2.317	4.5
July–Dec	485	359,846	1.052	2.9
1917				
Jan	389	264,928	0.670	2.5

Source: Derived from Haimson and Sapelli, eds, 1992, pp. 389–451 (Haimson and Brian).

too were prompted by the failure of wages to keep pace with rising prices, as at the Naval' shipyards in Nikolaev in January and February 1916. This was not a wildcat strike. The local strike committee adopted a careful strategy, publishing the factory accounts as well as backing a decision by workers in the shell shop to continue to work, thereby denying officials a propaganda victory. Factory inspectors concluded that the workforce, which had grown by 5,000 during the course of the war, had been infiltrated by social-democratic 'troublemakers'. In vain did more sympathetic observers suggest that labour be offered a share of increased profits in exchange for abandoning the strike weapon.[42] The strike ended when the government intervened, threatening strikers with dismissal and conscription or exile to Siberia. Cossack troops remained on hand to prevent further trouble.[43] Yet the fundamental issue did not disappear. In June 1916 General Alekseev recommended to the Tsar that measures be taken to guarantee workers cheap food and other necessities, if they were to be kept in check. His appeal fell on deaf ears.[44]

In what ways did the remuneration of Russian workers affect their behaviour as consumers? Patterns of consumption changed in complex ways, according to branch of industry and locality. In Moscow food and rent normally absorbed 70 per cent of the wages of metal-workers, but by 1915 this rose slightly to 74 per cent. In the textile trade, where wages were more sluggish, spending on food and housing rose to 106 per cent of income compared with 67 per cent before the war.[45] Working-class households cut back on the consumption of sugar, meat and dairy products. Studies of household budgets demonstrated the impact on the working class of increases in the cost of clothing, footwear, lighting and heating. In 1916 64 per cent of workers' outgoings in Ufa went on food (compared with 77 per cent in 1913), 16 per cent on heating and lighting (9 per cent) and 20 per cent on clothing and shoes (14 per cent).[46]

Where the chief breadwinner was conscripted, households suffered extreme deprivation. Women who earned more cash provided one lifeline. Another option was to pin one's hope on charity.[47] We should not be surprised that Russia's workers protested against the rising cost of subsistence. Tsarist officials acknowledged their growing radicalism but – betraying a common establishment view of plebeian incapacity – blamed outsiders for leading peasants and workers astray. In truth, however, the war created opportunities for activists to emerge from within the ranks of the working class – in labour groups, co-operatives and other institutions – rather than from without. The role of these activists in leading the demonstrations and strikes in February 1917 is well attested.[48]

Workers did of course come into contact with other elements of plebeian society. Many Russian workers had only recently arrived from the village. At the Obukhov plant, for example, 5,000 newly engaged workers retained an allotment.[49] Of the 990,000 factory workers enumerated in the 1918 census of industry, 32 per cent owned up to having a plot of land. This was particularly marked in the Central Industrial Region. Rural women established closer contact with the world of the factory, taking temporary employment in order to boost the family income. In the short term these affiliations enabled some workers to gain access to reserves of food when circumstances permitted. From a political perspective, the continued ties between town and country meant that the urban poor and the peasantry together understood that the tsarist regime failed to satisfy the demands of the propertyless.[50]

3.3   Peasant society during the war

Conscription changed the social complexion of the countryside. The military draft deprived peasant households in general of every other able-bodied rural male. In some provinces, such as Khar'kov, nearly four in ten peasant households lacked adult male hands by 1917. However, not all provinces were affected equally. Conscription had serious consequences for peasant farmers in New Russia, the lower Volga region and the north

Caucasus, as well as in provinces close to the front where the army conscripted men (and women) for construction work and transport. In the
Central Agricultural Region and parts of Ukraine, by contrast, peasant
farms encountered fewer problems.[51]

Peasant farms were often sufficiently flexible to replace conscripts with
young or elderly household members. The local community also rallied
round households that otherwise found it impossible to cultivate their
plots.[52] However, conscription had more far-reaching consequences,
giving peasant women an opportunity to play a more prominent part in
rural life. By 1916 they outnumbered men in the Russian village by 60 per
cent. Peasant women gained new skills.[53] According to Tikhon Polner, the
female peasant 'found herself acquiring a new importance in the eyes of the
community and was getting for the first time (sic) in her life into personal
contact with the authorities.' Polner also acknowledged the 'surprising dis-
covery ... that the peasant women were less conservative than the men;
spurred on by necessity, they showed themselves quite ready to welcome
new methods of farming (and) saved the farms of the peasantry from total
collapse' during the war.[54]

The war brought about an increase in cash at the disposal of the peasantry. They received various transfer payments as well as money from the
sale of livestock to the Russian army. Peasants who had a surplus took
advantage of the sharp increase in agricultural prices brought about by the
army's initial spending spree. Others played a waiting game, seeking to
evade the controls that local authorities began to impose on prices and
anticipating further price rises.[55] Peasants had additional cash as a result
of prohibition, the reduction in expenses associated with migration and the
curtailment of celebrations linked to births and marriages, whose incidence declined during the war. Prohibition alone may have saved peasants
at least one billion rubles per annum, equivalent to around one-third of
their annual outlays. The estimated increase in peasant incomes during the
war years is illustrated in Table 3.4.

According to Antsiferov, peasants secured an extra 18 per cent over
and above their normal peacetime income, receipts that were 'in no way
dependent upon the peasants' own efforts'. Peasants themselves commented that 'cash is as easy to come by as wood shavings'.[56]

This additional windfall was placed on deposit in co-operative banks or
held at home: peasant deposits in co-operative credit associations
increased from 199 million rubles in 1915 and 219 million in 1916 to 420
million rubles in 1917.[57] These accumulated balances meant that peasants
no longer had to sell their produce at the earliest opportunity and therefore

TABLE 3.4 *Estimated increase in peasants' money income, 1914–1917, million rubles, current prices*

	1914	1915	1916	1917
Transfer payments to soldiers' families	442	760	1,107	3,000
Peasants' share	340	585	852	2,310
Sale of horses to the army	300	150	n.a.	
Other sales to the army	146	526	n.a.	
Assumed gains from prohibition	600	600	600	600
Additional disposable income (rows 2+3+4+5)	1,386	1,861	1,076	
Peasants' estimated cash income in 1913	1,500	1,500	1,500	
Nominal increase in disposable income relative to 1913	92%	124%	72%	

Sources and notes: Columns 1 and 2 from Danilov, 1922, pp. 44–5; other sales to army from Dikhtiar, 1960, pp. 215–16. Danilov assumed that the peasants' share of transfer payments was 77 per cent. He followed Prokopovich, 1918, in estimating total national income at 12.8 billion rubles in 1913, and assumed that the peasants' share was 4.6 billion rubles, including 1.5 billion in a monetised form. Columns 3 and 4 are derived from Michelson et al., 1928, p. 216, and Dikhtiar, 1960, pp. 215–16, with similar assumptions.

at a disadvantageous price. Countervailing pressures, the result of declining opportunities to obtain off-farm employment on large estates or to gain income from handicrafts (*promysly*), do not seem to have affected the overall picture.[58] An illustration of changes to peasant household budgets is provided in Table 3.5.

Peasant wellbeing was reflected in their purchases of more varied food, thereby enjoying a qualitative improvement in nutritional standards. In 1915 peasant consumption of grain increased by as much as ten per cent. Peasants used disposable cash to buy meat, milk, butter, sugar, wheat flour, fish, vegetable oil and other products on a larger scale than hitherto. Some zemstvos detected a two- or threefold increase in meat consumption, albeit from a low base.[59]

TABLE 3.5 *Peasant household budgets, 1912–1916 (rubles per household)*

Year	Simbirsk				Volokolamsk			
	Income	Expen-diture	Surplus	As per cent of income	Income	Expen-diture	Surplus	As per cent of income
1912	475	427	+ 48	10%	542	500	+ 42	8%
1915	707	528	+ 179	25%	830	756	+ 74	9%
1916	1277	787	+ 489	38%	1731	1344	+ 387	22%

Source: Kondrat'ev, 1991, pp. 131, 427.

Later on, the incentive for peasant farmers to enter the market suffered as a result of the creeping shortage of manufactured goods. In 1916 peasants could only obtain textiles, shoes and other items at uncontrolled prices that rose faster than the price of most agricultural products. By the end of that year the cash they held at home or in savings banks took on the character of forced saving. One peasant correspondent wrote that 'the richness caused by the money is like the money itself: it is of paper, and has no weight, and good only to be counted. It goes like water, and leaves no trace'.[60]

What of peasants' access to land? Russian peasants had less opportunity to buy land during the war, because landowners were reluctant to sell in exchange for a depreciating currency.[61] But the widely held belief that Russian peasants were short of land needs to be treated with caution. A norm of 2.5 hectares per household was sufficient to provide for the basic needs of the average peasant farm. In 1916 the actual amount cultivated fell not far short of 4.5 hectares. Considerable scope existed for peasants to extend the area under cultivation still further. Half of all arable land lay fallow or was used to mark the boundaries between neighbouring strips.[62]

The resurgence of peasant anger during the war was associated with prices and privilege rather than land as such. A police report in July 1916 suggested that:

Revolutionary work has originated out of the campaign against the high cost of living and has then been artificially expanded to enormous dimensions by the efforts of the most active and prominent leaders of the revolutionary parties

The atmosphere was aptly described as 'poisonous'.[63] Yet to suggest that the poison was spread by outsiders overlooks the undercurrent of anger against the Tsar, who was responsible for taking their menfolk, livestock and crops.[64]

There was an important age and gender dimension to rural protest. Peasant youths were thought to have become 'hooligans' as a result of the absence of firm parental control; this was an old refrain. Some observers believed that the peasantry had too much time on its hands, and that it was incumbent upon educated society to organise 'rational recreation'. Others called for 'yet another mobilisation', advocating the inclusion of more women in the co-operative movement, as a means of creating a stronger counterweight to the merchants who used their market power to speculate and force up the price of food.[65]

The war turned several million women into soldiers' wives whose 'more modern sense of entitlement derived from their connection to men at the front.' Soldiers' wives complained to local officials about land surveys and restrictions on petty trade. Recent work on food riots has drawn attention to their participation in subsistence struggles that expressed a powerful longing for social justice and equality of entitlement. In the short term peasant women's actions had explosive implications for the old regime, because Russian troops were reluctant to suppress riots in which the wives and mothers of fellow soldiers were prominent participants.[66]

Changing gender relations were associated not only with overt forms of protest but also with shifts in consumption. Prohibition meant that women claimed cash that had hitherto been spent on vodka by their menfolk. Some women reportedly began to subscribe to illustrated journals such as 'The Twentieth Century', 'World of Fashion', 'Woman', 'Dragonfly'. The author of an article who asked, 'Is the village getting poorer or richer?' commented that 'money is now going from Peter to Dar'ia, from Ivan to Mariia'.[67]

Newer forms of cultural expression also evolved during the war. Rival attractions such as the cinema proved extremely popular, particularly in the towns and cities, but also in the countryside, where the zemstvos organised screenings of information films. This reinforced peasants' awareness of the world beyond the village, but the death or dismemberment of their menfolk and the shortages of manufactured goods had already brought home to them the terrible impact of war.[68]

3.4   On the margins

To speak of plebeian society is also to take account of hard-pressed and often downtrodden individuals such as the village clergy and schoolteachers who traditionally maintained a close but uneasy contact with peasantry. They were directly affected by the war, both because of their responsibilities and because of changes in their status and wealth. Orthodox priests were expected to deliver sermons that enjoined the congregation to support the war effort, and to report on the mood of the population. The Church authorities played a part in publicising war loans and encouraging the population to subscribe. Yet the grip of the established church should not be exaggerated. Peasants showed little respect or affection for the parish priest, who relied upon his equally impoverished parishioners for a fee in cash or in kind to supplement his earnings. Priests complained that attendance plummeted during the war, as otherwise devout peasant women spent more time on economic tasks.[69] Some Church leaders did not help their cause. The foolish Bishop Varnava of Tobol'sk diocese came close to arguing the death of Russian soldiers was divine retribution for abortion, a stance that was hardly likely to endear him to his peasant flock.[70]

It cannot by any means be assumed that priests peddled a conservative agenda or supported the war without question. (A leading government minister felt that poverty made them likely candidates for the 'socialist gospel'.) Before the war many priests supported a more liberal dispensation designed to weaken the bonds between Church and state, in the hope that a closer relationship between the priest and his flock might result. But the lurid stories that emanated from Petrograd during the third year of the war only served to undermine the claims of the Orthodox establishment to represent the interests of 'Holy Russia', and they do not appear to have brought peasants and priests any closer.[71] Village priests pinned their hopes on charitable donations from their peasant parishioners.[72]

Even though they appear to have been supportive of the war to begin with, Russian schoolteachers were not a reliable instrument of the establishment. Village teachers, of whom there were 90,000 in European Russia alone by 1915, criticised an undemocratic political system that kept the population, including themselves, in a state of poverty. Many sympathised with the Socialist Revolutionary Party. During the war their salaries were pegged and they became still more impoverished and dependent upon intermittent and haphazard cost of living increases awarded by their employers. Rising class sizes and impoverishment made it difficult for teachers to maintain a close eye on their pupils and did little to sustain morale. They bemoaned the lack of professional respect accorded them by the state and by the peasants they were employed to serve.[73]

Refugees too stood on the margins of wartime society, numbering at least 3.3 million at the end of 1915. These figures certainly under-estimate the size of the refugee population. One careful calculation, taking account of under-registration, put the total number at just over six million by the beginning of 1917, including 367,000 refugees in the Caucasus. As a result, refugees probably accounted for something like five per cent of the total population.[74] Although not all of them were of plebeian origin, refugees were marked by a tendency towards downward social mobility.

To be sure, contemporaries did not depict the displacement of civilians wholly in sombre colours. Some observers set great store by the influx of farmers who were expected to introduce superior methods of cultivation to the Russian peasantry.[75] The Russian village also stood in sore need of craftsmen whose numbers had been depleted by conscription.[76] However, such optimistic visions of economic and cultural interaction proved somewhat premature. One provincial governor observed that refugees contributed to the peasant economy to a limited extent: 'they feel themselves to be temporary residents, and are unlikely to become accustomed to the special conditions of local life and work, for which in any case their state of mind renders them of doubtful use'.[77]

Refugee women were often obliged to travel with their dependants and their primary obligation was towards them. Refugeedom did not reinforce the sense of liberation associated with geographical mobility; rather, it served to remind women of their 'domestic' responsibilities. The contemporary portrayal of the refugee catastrophe tended to emphasise conventional motherhood. Refugee women were persuaded instead to join sewing circles or to spin and weave at home. Women from a working-class background expressed a preference for paid work in factories producing confectionery, matches or tobacco, where they hoped to socialise more freely.[78] More frequently, female refugees were deemed to stand in need of protection from unscrupulous and mercenary or lustful individuals. The hazards began at the moment refugees left their homes and travelled to the Russian interior. Predatory brothel keepers reportedly scoured the ranks of refugees in Petrograd for potential prostitutes. Violetta Thurstan applauded the intervention of female students in Petrograd who 'have done admirable work in keeping the young girls straight and out of temptation.' Not all contemporaries pinned the blame on those who organised commercial sex. There was also some suspicion that young women offered themselves all too willingly to prospective customers, choosing 'debauchery' as a means of economic survival.[79]

The war was widely seen as having disrupted family relations and given rise to an epidemic of juvenile crime. Sergei Bakhrushin attributed this to an absence of parental control. Some youngsters in Moscow looted German shops in 1914 or took part in pogroms in Baku in May 1915. Neither the courts nor orphanages could deal with the causes of crime. Only a greater attentiveness to the impact of war on impressionable young minds, a good dose of extra-curricular activity and recreation and the restoration of family relations would make inroads into this social 'problem'.[80]

Conclusions

Social upheaval manifested itself in population displacement. Soldiers were wrenched in huge numbers from the fields and the factory in order to serve in the Tsar's army, where they were exposed to personal risk. Industrial enterprises recruited migrant workers and employed them in defence production where the tempo of work never ceased. Military defeats in 1914 and 1915 generated several million internally displaced civilians, who moved into European Russia from the western borderlands, where they needed to be fed, housed and if possible restored to health.

Although different elements of non-privileged society have been discussed in turn, it must be remembered that plebeian and marginal groups interacted with one another. Some of the factory workers who were conscripted in 1914 returned to the shop floor in 1915 or 1916. Peasants entered the industrial labour force. Soldiers corresponded with their families in the village. Garrison troops mingled with workers in Petrograd and other cities. Peasants encountered refugees, many of whom spoke a different language and brought a contrasting culture to the Russian village. The encounters were not always benign. Anger erupted when the urban poor pinned the blame on peasants for the shortages of food or when refugees appeared to be getting favourable treatment.

As one example of this social interaction, consider how women correspondents sought (in Alfred Meyer's words) to 'reassure the warrior in the field that the home front was well taken care of and that the domestic hearth he was protecting was in good shape'. However, 'by the end of 1916, if not before, such morale-building letters had been replaced by letters in which women complained about their difficult lives, their loneliness, their tiredness, and their despair.'[81] Thus the war encouraged communication across social and occupational boundaries, giving rise to expressions of bewilderment and outrage at the endless deprivation it inflicted. The fact that it yielded temporary gains for segments of the workforce and peasantry did not alter the common experience of senseless sacrifice.

The plebeian population also interacted with their social superiors. Of course not all such encounters were novel. Workers encountered the factory foreman before the war, and peasants were familiar with the village shopkeeper and the merchant, but the wartime terrain facilitated more such encounters. Middle-class nurses and orderlies looked after soldiers who had been scarred in battle. Peasants – men and women – negotiated with food procurement officials. Workers came face to face with middle-class members of the co-operatives. Peasants met zemstvo employees and volunteers who provided agronomic advice and laid on entertainment in the village. Social workers from relatively comfortable backgrounds mobilised themselves in order to look after bedraggled and dispossessed refugees. Forging such relations could have a profound personal meaning for those involved. Middle-class women discovered the means to escape from existing constraints, while the recipients of relief derived comfort from the realisation that they had not been forgotten. These encounters also had the potential to create a political explosion, as plebeian and educated society discovered a common dislike of the old regime and its privileged segments.

War meant more than the physical transfer of men from the factory into the armed forces. Mass conscription implied a different relationship between the state and its subjects. An important change had been flagged in 1912 by the decision to make transfer payments to the wives and children of serving men. A degree of reciprocity now entered into the equation whereby, in return for service, soldiers and the *soldatki* expected support from the state. When it was not forthcoming, they protested. Other changes were also brought about by the war. As wartime opportunities for employment expanded, women mounted a challenge to male dominated economic spheres. Nor was this the only form of 'dilution'. The mass mobilisation of men enabled women to enter negotiations with officialdom in a manner that had scarcely been possible hitherto. Thus for some women the war opened up new possibilities for self-realisation. Yet existing gender hierarchies were difficult to subvert, and gains in employment or civic involvement proved difficult to defend as war came to a close.

For all belligerents war was a moment of truth in which underlying assumptions were sorely tested. This was nowhere more apparent than in the boundaries of gender. At first sight, no such difficulty arose at the front, where fighting and killing 'belonged' to men.[82] Yet the image of a fixed front, conceived as a masculine domain, became increasingly difficult to sustain during the First World War. Neatly gendered dichotomies tended to dissolve on closer inspection. As we have seen, important changes also took place in the peasant family as women began to challenge the primacy of the male head of the household. Changing military fortunes ensured that 'front' could become 'rear' and vice-versa. Occupation by the enemy brought the front into spaces hitherto occupied by civilians, forcing civilian women (and men) to confront warfare at close quarter.

It is also important to make the obvious point that the experience of war was bound up with personal risk. Soldiers were exposed to mortal danger, whether death on the battlefield or subsequent death from wounds or infectious disease. Displaced civilians ran the risk of violence from enemy bombardment and – particularly if they were Jewish or German – from the Tsar's own troops. Factory workers, particularly those working in munitions, handled dangerous substances and occasionally suffered collective catastrophe. Their health suffered from working in confined conditions. The faster pace of work also carried the risk of industrial injury. Whatever their background or occupation, plebeian Russians asked themselves if the risk and the sacrifice made sense, and when the war would end.

Note on further reading

There are no full-length studies in English of Russian workers and peasants during the war. An outline is provided by Keep, 1976. Wildman, 1980, and Sanborn, 2003, are thought-provoking books on soldiers and soldiering, the latter covering the years before, during and after the First World War. The chief work on refugees is Gatrell, 1999. On women and gender relations the reader may consult Engelstein, 1992, and Goldman, 1993, although little of this impressive body of work touches directly on the war. An exception is the article by Engel, 1997.

References

1 Vainshtein, 1960, p. 403.

2 Lewin, 1985, pp. 72–87; Eklof and Frank, eds, 1988, pp. 7–43 (Mironov).

3 Clowes et al., eds, 1991, pp. 199–211 (Ruane and Eklof).

4 White, 1994, pp. 14–15.

5 Sanborn, 2003, pp. 23–5.

6 Gatrell, 1999, pp. 197–8.

7 Polner, 1930, pp. 134–6; Porshneva, 2000, p. 238.

8 In all the government transferred 4,920 million rubles to the families of conscripts during the war. Michelson et al., 1928, p. 216.

9 Porshneva, 2000, p. 247.

10 The Foreign Minister called Ianushkevich a 'narcissistic nincompoop', and the Minister of the Interior posed the rhetorical question, 'How does the Chief of Staff plan to buy the heroism of non-landowners?' Cherniavsky, ed., 1967,

pp. 22–6; Gurko, 1939, p. 561; Lohr, 2003, p. 103; Antsiferov et al., 1930, pp. 364–6, and Meyer, 1991, p. 222.

11 Senin, 1993, p. 47.

12 Sanborn, 2003, p. 172; Lohr, 2003, pp. 145–50.

13 Polner, 1930, pp. 89–90, 101; Odinetz and Novgorotsev, 1929, pp. 160–62.

14 *RVMV*, 1925, pp. 4, 25. Occupancy rates in zemstvo hospitals and disability relief are discussed by Polner, 1930, pp. 104–8, 127–33.

15 Seniavskaia, 1999, pp. 357–62 mentions a questionnaire reported by M. Kutanin to a congress of psychiatrists in March 1916.

16 Binshtok and Kaminskii, 1929, pp. 61–2.

17 Smirnov, 1999 (Friedlander). The quotation belongs to Kutanin, reported in *Golos* (Iaroslavl'), 12 October 1914. See also Polner, 1930, pp. 121–2.

18 Polner, 1930, pp. 101–3; Voronkova, 1975, p. 43; Solomon and Hutchinson, eds, 1990, p. 107 (Weissman).

19 Volkov, 1930, pp. 63, 68 for a discussion of rival estimates.

20 Okninskii, 1998, p. 49.

21 White, 1992; Wade, 2000, p. 27.

22 Mawdsley, 1978.

23 Bukshpan, 1929, p. 164.

24 This point owes a great deal to Bushnell, 1985; see also Service, ed., 1992, p. 107 (Mawdsley).

25 Golovin, 2001, p. 227, referring to a report by General Beliaev dated 22 February 1915.

26 *Khoziaistvennaia zhizn'*, 1916.

27 *Nar.khoz. v 1916g.*, 1922, volume 7, pp. 128–9.

28 *Nar.khoz. v 1916g.*, 1922, volume 7, pp. 130–31; Sidorov, 1973, p. 415.

29 RGVIA f.369, op.1, d.98, ll.58–62; *Sbornik statisticheskikh svedenii*, 1924, pp. 170–71; Grinevetskii, 1919, pp. 163–4. Strumilin, 1964a, p. 365 reports different figures.

30 *Statistika truda*, 1919, 8–10 (Mindlin); Zagorsky, 1928, p. 56.

31 Sidorov, 1973, p. 48; Markevich, 2001.

32 Gaponenko, 1961, p. 160; Strumilin, 1964a, p. 334. Total numbers employed in state enterprises reached 311,000 by January 1917, compared with around 92,000 in 1913. The figure continued to grow in 1917.

33 Strumilin, 1964a, p. 370, from a survey of daily wage rates at the Parviainen metal works in Petrograd. The same pattern was detected at Putilov,

according to *Vestnik metallista*, 1918, 1, p. 13, and in the Moscow engineering firm Goujon, according to Markevich, 2001.

34 *Promyshlennaia perepis'*, 1926, volume 1, p. 57; Zagorsky, 1928, pp. 51–8.

35 Grinevetskii, 1919, p. 151. On differentials between shopfloor and clerical staff see *Promyshlennaia perepis'*, 1926, volume 1, p. 57.

36 *Nar.khoz. v 1916g*, volume 7, 1922, pp. 128–9; Meyer, 1991, p. 215; Markevich, 2001.

37 Fleer, ed., 1925, pp. 6–7. These figures exclude state enterprises.

38 Mal'kov, ed., 1998, p. 434 (Kir"ianov).

39 Koenker and Rosenberg, 1989, pp. 59–60.

40 Haimson and Sapelli, 1992, pp. 399–451 (Haimson and Brian); McKean, 1990, pp. 406–29 (quotation on p. 419).

41 Sidorov, 1973, p. 515.

42 *Gornozavodskoe delo*, 1916, 45 (Dimanshtein).

43 Liudkovskii, 1955; Koshik, 1965, pp. 144–76. See also Kir"ianov, 1971, p. 241, and Mal'kov, ed., 1998, p. 245 (Tiutiukin).

44 Manikovskii, 1930, volume 2, pp. 342–3.

45 Kayden and Antsiferov, 1929, p. 96.

46 *Izvestiia VSG*, 1916, 38, pp. 79–85.

47 Danilov, 1922, p. 51.

48 Wade, 2000, p. 32.

49 *Materialy k uchetu*, 1916, volume 1, pp. 25, 53–4; Gaponenko, 1970, pp. 84–5.

50 *Promyshlennaia perepis'*, 1926, volume 2, pp. 120–21, 130–33.

51 Antsiferov et al., 1930, p. 117 gives the data from the 1917 census. See also Baker, 2001. The difficulties were not confined to cereal farming.

52 Polner, 1930, p. 148. For co-operation among farmers in Khar'kov and Kiev see *Izvestiia VZS*, 16, 1 June 1915, p. 7.

53 *Izvestiia Kostromskogo gubernskogo zemstva*, 7, July 1915, p. 74.

54 Polner, 1930, pp. 157–8; Meyer, 1991, p. 218; Pallot, ed., 1998, pp. 189–90 (Stanziani).

55 *Dvizhenie tsen*, 1916, p. 13; Struve et al., 1930, pp. 233–9, 247–62. Less wealthy farmers were more cautious. In Iaroslavl' peasants reportedly said that 'we are afraid to sell – if you sell you may find yourself left with not enough for your animals or your seed, and then you find yourself paying three times as much to buy grain'. *Golos* (Iaroslavl'), 13 December 1915.

56 Quoted in *Pskovskie eparkhial'nye vedomosti*, 1916, 8, pp. 172–4; Antsiferov et al., 1930, pp. 133–8.

57 Kayden and Antsiferov, 1929, p. 273. Figures are for 1 January, in current prices.

58 Antsiferov et al., 1930, p. 137; Kondrat'ev, 1991, pp. 130–33. For a contrary view, see Anfimov, 1962, pp. 243–69 and the critical discussion in Fallows, 1978, p. 89fn.

59 Kondrat'ev, 1991, pp. 129–30, 132–33, for estimates of the per capita consumption of rye by peasants in 1911–1915; Struve et al., 1930, pp. 347–8.

60 Kayden and Antsiferov, 1929, p. 282.

61 Antsiferov et al., 1930, p. 353, notes that some peasants, having accumulated large cash balances, had no need of credit to finance their land transactions.

62 Antsiferov et al., 1930, pp. 16, 23, 31–2.

63 Quoted in Kayden and Antsiferov, 1929, pp. 98–9.

64 Porshneva, 2000, pp. 121, 129–30.

65 *Teatr' i iskusstvo* (1915), quoted in Porshneva, 2000, pp. 114–15; *Golos* (Iaroslavl'), 10 July 1915 (A. Izgoev).

66 Engel, 1994, p. 707; Baker, 2001.

67 *Vestnik Penzenskogo zemstva*, 1916, 13–14, pp. 196–7 (Belianin).

68 Porshneva, 2000, p. 115.

69 Michelson et al., 1928, pp. 269, 271; Porshneva, 2000, p. 133.

70 'We often ask whether this war will end soon. But it is appropriate to raise this question: Does the number of our dead sons equal the number of innocent babies killed in the womb by foolish mothers?' Curtiss, 1940, p. 390, quoting from a speech given to the Duma's budget commission by Sukhanov. Bishop Varnava was one of Rasputin's protegés.

71 Curtiss, 1940, p. 406, quoting Kokovstev; see Lewin, 1985, Chapter 2.

72 *Pskovskie eparkhial'nye vedomosti*, 1916, 8, pp. 172–4 (Ladinskii).

73 Emmons and Vucinich, eds, 1982, p. 255 (Brooks); Seregny, 2000; Odinetz and Novgorotsev, 1929, p. 91; Horne ed., 1997, pp. 39–69 (Audoin-Rouzeau and Fava).

74 Gatrell, 1999, pp. 211–13.

75 *Vestnik Riazanskogo gubernskogo zemstva*, April–May 1916, 4–5, pp. 98–9.

76 *Utro Rossii*, 223, 14 August 1915.

77 RGIA f.1284, op.194, d. 43–1916, ll.10–13.

78 Gatrell, 1999, Chapter 5.

79 Thurstan, 1916, pp. 64, 69–72.

80 *Izvestiia VSG*, 1916, 29–30, pp. 54–65.

81 Meyer, 1991, p. 224.

82 In one famous exception, the Tsar permitted Maria Bochkareva to create a 'women's battalion of death'. Lincoln, 1986, p. 406.

CHAPTER 4

Tsarist authority in question, 1915–1916

*Each war of ours ends in a victory for society and the fall of autocracy,
as witness the history of Russia. Remember 1812, the Decembrists,
Sevastopol' and the war against Japan. Now the decisive moment is
beginning. For the sacred future we need just one more energetic push
and we will achieve what the best Russians have dreamed.*
    [A.I. Shingarev, 7 September 1915, quoted in Grave, ed., 1927, p. 51]

The summer of 1915 inflicted a series of heavy blows on tsarist
Russia. Its armed forces suffered defeats on every front, territory was abandoned to the enemy and the Russian interior became a place
of refuge for people from the western borderlands of all ages, ranks and
occupation. Military catastrophes were echoed in the parliamentary and
extra-parliamentary spheres. In June 1915 Sukhomlinov, the Minister of
War, was forced out of office, his humiliation compounded by the 'dis-
covery' in spring 1915 that one of his lieutenants had been a traitor. Other
ministers followed soon afterwards.[1]

The great retreat appeared to validate the gloomy reports of shell
shortage. A shortage of munitions – and a surfeit of displaced civilians –
emboldened critics of the old regime to demand a greater say in the administration of the war effort. The Tsar was compelled to reconvene the
Duma. In August 1915 moderate parliamentarians set aside their political
differences to create a 'Progressive Bloc' which commanded a huge
majority in parliament. The Bloc backed extensive political reform,
including the creation of a 'united government enjoying the country's confidence'. Nicholas II's more liberal-minded ministers urged the need for
dialogue with the reformers. However, they did not have things all their
own way. The Tsar – 'you are the Autocrat', his wife had to remind him –

hit back, in a bold manoeuvre designed to neutralise his critics in the Russian High Command, the Duma and the public organisations.[2] He dismissed most of the ministers who had tried to stand up to him. He took over as supreme commander of the armed forces. He kept the Duma at arm's length. Finally Nicholas established four special councils for defence, food supply, fuel and transport, giving the voluntary organisations the semblance of power but keeping control of economic management firmly in the hands of his own ministers.

Patriotic fervour was promoted by means of propaganda methods, including the use of the new medium of film, as well as traditional benefit concerts and staged pageants. These efforts were underpinned by more stringent methods of control, such as surveillance, censorship and martial law. Traditionally the tsarist state monitored and pursued its enemies, whether they operated on the territory of the Russian empire or abroad. Surveillance techniques were employed by the tsarist police, who had powers to authorise the imposition of 'reinforced protection' (*usilennaia okhrana*) which excluded named individuals from taking up residence in a specified area, and entitled provincial governors to ban public meetings deemed contrary to public order. In appropriate circumstances they could impose 'extraordinary protection' (*chrezvychainaia okhrana*) under which a 'commander' could additionally dismiss elected members of local authorities as well as government officials. Other kinds of surveillance were also deployed. Policemen, janitors and others were all mobilised in the task of scrutinising the behaviour of suspicious individuals and known revolutionaries. During the war these familiar forms of surveillance were extended and developed in new directions. Now the entire population, not just dissident groups, came under the lens of government scrutiny, not because they had done anything wrong but because their attitudes were a matter of concern to the state.

4.1   Propaganda, tsarist institutions and state surveillance

The prolonged duration of the war necessitated a commitment on the part of officialdom to propaganda efforts. Propaganda had of course been invoked when Russia went to war against Japan. It belongs in an account of economy and society in the world war for two reasons: first, propaganda (like surveillance) absorbed financial and personnel resources on a significant scale; second, propaganda was calculated to have an effect upon society's commitment to war.

As in other belligerent societies, the Russian public was desperate for news from the front. A small number of hand-picked journalists were allowed to visit military headquarters and speak with senior officers.[3] Newsreels and documentary films went some way towards satisfying that demand, conveying an impression of the war without risking too 'realistic' a version. Sometimes battle scenes were staged for the benefit of cameras; on occasions, old footage (for example, of the Balkan wars in 1912–1913) was presented as fresh material. The one significant exception was the capture of Erzerum, where authentic footage tended to dominate, and where the documentary style conveyed the bravery of Russian troops and the desolate state of the city.[4]

The tsarist government had, to begin with, only a limited grasp of the potential of official propaganda. It looked on while private publishing houses issued cheap broadsides (*lubki*) in a traditional format, as well as short stories and posters that depicted individual acts of bravery and the 'deep bond' between soldier and officer. Right-wing monarchists created patriotic *tableaux vivants* in which actors took the part of military heroes from the distant past. Semi-official bodies, such as the Skobelev Committee, encouraged the population to donate to charities in support of war wounded, orphans and refugees. The Skobelev Committee issued patriotic films and other propaganda material, and the army allowed it to screen newsreel films close to the front line. Mobile projection facilities anticipated Bolshevik techniques. Much of its wartime output emphasised the use of new military technology, the threat posed by Germany to Russian female virtue and the need for goodness and courage to triumph over evil and cowardice.[5]

By 1916, however, the patriotic emphasis upon adventure and bravery had given way to a more troubling preoccupation with loss, suffering and the depressing endlessness of war. The government issued two million posters and ten million pamphlets, in order to promote war bonds. But the invitation to the Russian public to dig deep into its own pockets only emphasised the extent of personal sacrifice and loss. In the words of one historian, 'that charity replaced heroism on posters and postcards reflected a war-weary nation's longing for peace'.[6]

What kind of resonance did patriotic initiatives have in the sphere of popular culture? The national anthem, 'God Save the Tsar', was played at every opportunity, but over-use meant that it was a 'patriotic prop without much specific meaning'. Traditional *lubki*, issued in their thousands, depicted in a simple and direct manner the brashness and brutality of the enemy. More common still were images that established the heroism of the ordinary Russian soldier in repelling the invader. These images, familiar to generations of peasants, connected the front-line soldiers with families in the Russian village. However, in reinforcing the sacrifices that peasants had made in the past for the sake of the Emperor, these woodcuts may have fostered a belief that patriotic sentiment and support for the monarchy did not necessarily go hand in hand. Nor did other popular cultural forms convey a jingoistic message. Postcards, for example, were much more likely to depict sentimental images of the soldier parting from his family or of the nurse attending to the wounded soldier. These were 'sober and compassionate' images, which reinforced a sense of loss and of longing to be reunited with loved ones. The emphasis was on personal sacrifice and danger, not on 'aggressive patriotism'. Few images focused upon Russia's leaders as a means of rallying support; more common were images of medieval knights and other heroic symbols of Russia's past 'glory'.[7]

The war fostered new forms of surveillance, reflecting a keenness to gauge the mood of the entire population. This meant an extension and development of traditional techniques of rule. By 1912 more than 63 million people were subject to 'reinforced protection', more than twice as many as on the eve of the first revolution. A further 2.3 million people lived in areas subject to martial law imposed in 1905. At the outbreak of war, therefore, two-fifths of the Tsar's subjects lived under some kind of special administrative regime. The Russian army gathered information on the number and location of foreign residents in the western borderlands.[8] These measures continued in force, but government officials and the military now began to take a more active interest in public opinion and how it might be managed. Like its counterparts elsewhere, the Russian High Command busied itself with establishing the mood of the armed forces, intercepting and censoring the postal traffic between front and rear, as well as employing staff to report on public opinion. From spring 1915 onwards, the Ministry of the Interior and provincial governors collated monthly reports on the attitude of Jews to such issues as military service and the enemy. Similarly, police agents submitted monthly reports on public meetings at which critical speeches were made. Correspondents knew that their post was being intercepted and read. Those who attended public meetings knew that they were likely to be spied upon; the Okhrana regularly reported on party political assemblies.[9]

Surveillance was not the sole preserve of tsarist police officials. Traditional instruments, such as the Church, the gentry and schools, were weakened by the war. (However, army chaplains were on hand to sustain 'loyalty and devotion to the Tsar to the point of self-sacrifice'.[10]) The government accordingly resorted to more modern methods. Local authorities regularly enquired into public opinion, as a basis for taking decisions about the appropriate allocation of resources. Zemstvos regularly asked peasant correspondents to comment on attitudes in the village ('Is agriculture getting better or worse in this locality?' was a typical question), although they complained when the answers 'deviated from reality'. But, as the Khar'kov zemstvo put it, it was 'better to provide no answer than to provide an inexact or incorrect one'.[11] In Peter Holquist's words, 'surveillance had begun to shape how people thought they could express themselves, while at the same time suggesting to them that their views – whatever they might be – were of significance'.[12]

4.2   Tsarism fights back: the formation of the special councils

The emergence of the voluntary organisations and the challenge they posed to the existing framework of economic mobilisation need to be related to the broader political crisis in the summer of 1915. Liberal politicians maintained the pressure on the Council of Ministers; Kadet and Octobrist politicians forged a new consensus over the need for further political reform, above all the establishment of a government that enjoyed 'public confidence'. The resignation of reactionary ministers at the end of June encouraged them to press for the greater participation of 'society' in the tasks of economic mobilisation.

The tsarist establishment confronted the liberal challenge head on by reasserting state control over the war effort. The chosen instrument was a 'Special Commission for State Defence'. This body originated in the decision by Grand Duke Nicholas, following concerted lobbying at Stavka by Rodzianko and leading businessmen in May 1915, to set up a special council 'to strengthen munitions supplies', by bringing together Russia's major arms suppliers and members of the Duma under the aegis of the Main Artillery Administration (GAU).[13] Apart from the War Minister, who chaired it and was answerable only to the Tsar, the special commission comprised four members apiece from the Duma and the State Council, as well as five officials from the War Ministry and two from the Navy. Three leading businessmen, Putilov, Vyshnegradskii and Litvinov-Falinskii, completed the membership. Others soon joined them, but Moscow merchants and other provincial businessmen, as well as other members of 'educated society', were conspicuous by their absence. They lost no time in complaining about the conflict of interest that arose in the commission, some of whose members stood to gain directly from its decisions.[14] Government ministers briefly discussed the possibility of including workers' representatives, but they rejected the suggestion as being 'impractical'.[15]

Progressive politicians proposed replacing the special commission with a much more wide-ranging 'Committee of State Defence' that would bypass the Council of Ministers and report directly to the Tsar. In their version a single committee would be responsible for military supplies, the regulation of the transport system and food supply. It would have powers to sequester enterprises, to requisition goods and materials and to compel workers and technical staff to take up particular jobs. Members would be drawn from parliament, from the military and from nominations made by the voluntary organisations and organised labour. Other parties were much more circumspect, not wishing to provoke a confrontation with government ministers who stood to lose control of the process of economic administration. The Kadets favoured a Ministry of Supply, a scheme that would allow parliament to scrutinise its affairs but not to participate directly in issues relating to economic mobilisation. Rival candidates included Guchkov, sponsored by the Octobrists, and Riabushinskii, the favourite of the Progressists.[16]

The emergence of the voluntary organisations and the enforced departure of Sukhomlinov on 12 June eclipsed these proposals. The Central War Industry Committee (TsVPK) and the key Moscow regional committee were permitted to join the special commission in July 1915. They lost no time in stirring up complaints about a cartel, dominated by the Putilov group and the Russo-Asiatic Bank, whose members sat alongside them. The inaugural congress of the TsVPK on 25 July called (more in hope than expectation) for one of its number to chair the special commission, in order to bring the voluntary organisations into the heart of the decision-making process. The new Minister of War, Polivanov, argued in favour of an extension of the commission's powers, for example integrating artillery and other supplies, and co-ordinating the supply of inputs according to agreed production schedules. This proposal highlighted the clash between those who espoused the idea of a supreme body for the war effort and those who backed the existing bureaucratic machinery.[17]

On 17 August 1915 the Tsar used his emergency powers to establish four new special councils, for transport, fuel, food supply and (*primus inter pares*) state defence.[18] The inaugural meeting of the new Special Council for State Defence (*Osoboe soveshchanie po oborone gosudarstva*, or OSO) took place on 22 August, in the presence of the Tsar and his entire cabinet. Nicholas welcomed the prospect of 'united and collegial work'.[19] The membership was drawn from government departments, the Duma, the State Council and the voluntary organisations. Given that they had been in existence for less than six months, the invitation extended to the war industry committees and Zemgor was highly significant. This appeared to represent a victory for the voluntary organisations and something of a setback to big business. Business leaders not only forfeited institutional access to procurement agencies, but now found themselves at the mercy of a body which combined bureaucracy and 'educated opinion' (obshch-estvennoe mnenie) in an unholy alliance. Petrograd's leading engineering employers complained that, 'looking through the lists of members (i.e. of the special council) we see that they include many worthy figures, but very few of them are actually industrialists, still less do they represent the largest enterprises that are working for defence'.[20] The bureaucratic principles that had governed Russia's mobilisation thus far continued to apply. The chairmanship of the OSO was entrusted to the Ministry of War, not – as liberal opinion had hoped – to a new 'minister of supply'. Other councils, too, were chaired by the relevant government ministers.

The OSO did not, however, become an all-encompassing body. Polivanov, who chaired it between August 1915 and March 1916, tried without much success to intervene in issues relating to transport and food supply, on the grounds that no rational programme for economic mobilisation could detach these from each other or consider them separate from 'state defence'. However, fuel, food and transport continued to come under the aegis of dedicated special councils, whose ministerial chairmen resented the War Minister's interference and successfully claimed jurisdiction of their own fiefdoms. Besides this, the arrangement of the special councils left no obvious role for the Minister of the Interior (MVD) who might be expected to chair a special council for labour, should it have been established. Part of the reason for the failure to create a supreme economic body was that the Ministry hampered attempts to transform the OSO into a body with wider powers of economic administration. It also jealously guarded its power to intervene in matters relating to food supply and the cost of living. Thus, the Minister of the Interior, A.N. Khvostov, who was appointed in September 1915, insisted that the provincial governors (who answered to the MVD) should retain responsibility for calculating food stocks and requirements, not the special councils. By the end of 1915 Khvostov cannily established an informal working party of five ministers – Interior, Agriculture, War, Transport and Industry – virtually sidelining the Special Council apparatus.[21]

4.3   Economic management: the special councils in action

Much of the business of the special councils was taken up with detailed questions of economic administration. To that extent, a brief account of their activities is essential for a proper understanding of the course of economic mobilisation. Further details will be given as appropriate in later chapters.

In the sphere of defence procurement and military production, the OSO occupied the most important place. The OSO had primary responsibility for approving and allocating defence contracts among domestic and foreign suppliers. It had powers to remove factory managers, to sequester or close under-performing factories, to build new enterprises, to prescribe the schedule of work at defence establishments, and to determine wage rates.[22] Litvinov-Falinskii believed that it presented Russia with the first serious opportunity to rationalise defence procurement, by linking contracts to available capacity and by ensuring that orders for finished goods went abroad only in case of absolute necessity. Much remained to be done. Litvinov-Falinskii complained that no one had a clear idea of the extent to which government contracts were being processed. To that end existing institutions, such as the Military Council and the heads of the main administrations (for artillery, intendance and so forth) were subordinated to the OSO, whose executive officers monitored the allocation and completion of orders.[23]

The OSO played a key part in the Russian war effort. It directly controlled some 4,900 enterprises with a total of nearly 2 million workers. Millions of rubles' worth of orders passed through its hands and it controlled the allocation of foreign currency. By January 1916 Manikovskii (chief of the GAU) concluded that it had successfully organised the productive resources of the country. Under Manikovskii's guidance, the Special Council launched a programme for the construction of new armaments factories.[24]

The OSO divided the Russian empire into regions, each of them headed by a commissioner, not unlike the system in France and Britain. At a regional and local level the OSO delegated its powers to new factory boards (*zavodskie soveshchaniia*), which were entrusted with the task of promoting 'co-operation between factories in the production of military goods'. The voluntary organisations were again represented, although the boards were chaired by military officers. The boards could instruct factory managers to give priority to specific orders and were empowered to inspect factories (including having access to accounts and inventories) to ensure that work was being carried out properly. If it was not, materials and equipment could be reassigned to other enterprises. A separate committee intervened in the day-to-day supply of ferrous and non-ferrous metals, reinforcing the system of regulation by checking production costs and imposing price controls. Infractions of the rules – for example, attempting to sell above the maximum price – were ultimately punishable by closure or sequestration. However, the quid pro quo was that enterprises could count upon state support in accessing inputs.[25] By 1916 there were 12 regional boards, of which Moscow was far and away the most important, with responsibility for more than two-fifths of the labour force under OSO control.[26]

Government largesse was carefully monitored. Kolomna Engineering, employing more than 15,000 workers, endured a government inspection in the autumn of 1915, headed by the right-wing Petr Durnovo and two technical specialists, V.I. Grinevetskii and N.F. Charnovskii. The inspectors made a scathing indictment of delays in delivery and appalling labour productivity, the result in part of poor management practices: 'whenever workers succeed in raising their productivity, the factory administration immediately reduces their piece rates'. Other evidence supports the view that the firm suffered low rates of labour productivity compared with other engineering factories in the Moscow region. The Special Council recommended that the managing director A.P. Meshcherskii be dismissed, although it later reversed the decision. Investigations of leading shipyards (Nevskii, Russo-Baltic and Becker) also highlighted financial irregularities and delays in the completion of military contracts.[27]

One of the most notorious decisions taken by the OSO was to proceed with the sequestration of Putilov, Russia's nearest equivalent to Krupp or Schneider. Sequestration had been on the agenda as early as spring 1915, but the government retreated for the time being, offering instead a multi-million ruble loan at 6.5 per cent, in return for participation in board meetings. The company was accused of using these funds to discharge obligations to the commercial banks. A minority of OSO members was opposed to sequestration (including Konovalov and some officials in the Ministry of War and the Ministry of Trade and Industry), but the majority – including Guchkov and Manikovskii – secured the takeover of Putilov. In itself this measure did not shift the balance of power from big business to the state, but rather reflected a sense of official frustration over the fortunes of a poorly managed company. But this did not stop Putilov from blaming the voluntary organisations as a whole for the fate of his company. The shareholders were offered compensation and the firm's creditors were relieved of an unprofitable albatross, until such time as it could be returned to the private sector. In addition, responsibility for handling Putilov's militant workforce now rested with the government. All the same, many tsarist officials had mixed feelings about the OSO, regarding it as a soft touch for Russian industrialists and bankers who were unlikely to demonstrate a 'prudent regard for the state's resources'.[28]

The Special Council on Transport (*Osoboe soveshchanie po perevozkam*), which had responsibility for the shipment of grain, fuel and military material, drew up regular plans for the use of rolling stock and monitored the overall performance of the network. Grain for the army received priority over other grain shipments and the council also allocated wagons for the transport of available fuel products. However, it faced an uphill battle; a report submitted by a leading railway official to the special council in November 1915 spoke of competing claims for rolling stock, and drew attention to the arbitrary claims made by individual customers, who tended to demand more than they needed. Yet another committee was established in December 1915 – a 'temporary regulatory authority' (*Vremennyi rasporiaditel'nyi komitet po perevozkam voennogo vremeni*), meeting several times a month in order to draw up detailed plans for the shipment of freight, particularly coal. Much of its time was spent on measures to improve the supply of food and fuel to Petrograd, but it also devised impressive estimates of the capacity of the entire railway network to handle claims for available space. The work of these various committees revealed serious shortcomings in the management of the rolling stock.[29]

The size and quality of the stock also left much to be desired. In 1914 the total number of locomotives amounted to 19,760 units (20,000 at the end of the year), an increase of 1,000 on the previous year. This figure remained static during 1915 and fell to 16,800 during 1916. The average stock of locomotives during 1917 plummeted to just over 10,200. At the end of the year it stood at 9,200. Normally, around 15 or 16 per cent of locomotives were out of service at any given time, and this proportion does not appear to have increased until the spring of 1917.[30] Some of these were being repaired – or supposedly so – but others were scrapped and not replaced at a sufficient rate to maintain the stock. Already in the spring of 1915, the Association of Industry and Trade complained that the shortage of wagons was creating a shortfall in deliveries of fuel to iron and steel producers, threatening some of them with closure. One problem was a shortage of sufficient goods wagons to create an adequate reserve and allow goods to be shifted from the factory or bulkhead.[31]

A general transport plan never materialised. As a consequence, much of the day-to-day operation of the railway network took on a 'spontaneous' (*stikhiinii*) character. In practice, government officials managed around 15,000 daily wagonloads of freight, equivalent to half the country's total shipments, but much of the country was left to its own devices. In October 1916 Rodzianko called for a unified transport authority, but his appeal fell on deaf ears.[32] During the war, military and civilian personnel operated Russian railways, a competing jurisdiction that did nothing to improve the performance of the network. The system improved its productivity in 1915, but increasing pressure thereafter on available rolling stock took its toll. Late in 1916, an attempt was made to rectify the anomaly. Gurko wrote to Trepov on 2 December outlining a plan for the militarisation of labour on the entire railway system. No Ministry of Transport employee would be able to look for other work without official sanction.[33]

Transport was closely linked to questions of fuel supply, which became the responsibility of a separate special council. The chairman of the Special Council for Fuel Supply could, like his colleagues on other special councils, impose his will on suppliers, inspect their books, requisition fuel, sequester enterprises, remove management and fix prices and wages throughout the industry. In the short term, the main aim was to improve the rate of despatch of coal from the pithead. No attempt was made to intervene directly in the sphere of production.[34] In the second half of 1915 the commissioners engaged by the special council began to requisition stocks of coal, at a price that was supposed to deter profiteering but also to take account of increased costs of production (that is, to compensate suppliers for losses incurred on pre-war contracts). Consumers came to look upon these as a ceiling, which they were never intended to be. So far as oil prices were concerned, the council imposed a maximum price, but this was undermined by a lack of regulation of shipping costs. There was a vocal lobby in support of closer regulation of the entire sector. In part this reflected disillusionment with the early actions of the Special Council for Fuel Supply, whose attempts to control fuel prices had met with little success. More aggressive intervention was required.[35]

By the beginning of 1916 the pattern for government intervention had been set. Fuel consumers were categorised according to their importance for the war effort, and the council stipulated the quantity to which each category of consumer was entitled. A fairly sophisticated system of planning began to take shape, with an embryonic 'fuel balance' that established output and supply norms by region. This was not yet the instrument of economic planning that was later associated with Soviet practice, but it paved the way for a more systematic assessment of production and consumption. In other respects, wartime planning conformed to that of other belligerents whose officials limited the freedom of manoeuvre of the industrial and household consumer. In Russia, for example, the government purchased any coal from the Donbass that remained at the pithead; a large team of inspectors had the job of visiting the mines and examining the quality and quantity of coal. However, the disorganisation of transport made it difficult to adhere to the schedules that the commissioners had drawn up, and there remained plenty of scope for speculation and for interference by third parties.[36]

In September 1916 the Special Council decided to concentrate all transactions in coal from the Donbass in a single body, *Tsentrougol'*. Mine owners protested, arguing that they had been made scapegoats for the failure of the transport sector to perform its allotted role. *Tsentrougol'* took over responsibility for the acquisition of coal, at prices fixed for six months in advance, and for its onward sale to consumers, in accordance with the agreed schedule of categories. Its membership included government officials but – to mollify the industry – there was a preponderance of mine owners, an indication that the state had concluded that there was no alternative but to involve entrepreneurs in the business of economic regulation. Arrangements were made to support mine owners whose business was thought likely to be damaged by the imposition of fixed prices. The system essentially required the industry to police itself, under the watchful eye of the state.[37] In the meantime, municipal authorities were left to cope as best they could with the shortage of fuel for urban households. By the winter of 1916 reports appeared in the press about shivering citizens and unlit thoroughfares, adding to the sense of political incapacity.[38]

The fourth government agency, the Special Council for Food Supply, also failed to live up to expectations.[39] The Special Council appointed staff in each province (and in eight major cities) whose task was to improve food supply, if necessary by regulating and controlling prices. It employed a team of brilliant economists and statisticians including the young Vladimir Groman and M.V. Ptukha. These arrangements did not resolve many of the outstanding difficulties. Other agencies, locally and at the centre, pursued their own interests, preventing the Special Council from imposing any overall authority over food supply. The more freedom of manoeuvre was enjoyed by a provincial official, for example to set a ceiling on the price at which grain could be traded, the more this was likely to encourage speculative activity. Peter Struve and Groman argued that successful administration required a more systematic control over production as well as distribution.[40]

The council painted a depressing picture of shortages, which its officials seemed powerless to address. It also suffered from the same kind of
bureaucratic rivalries that beset other councils. Khvostov planned to circumvent the Special Council, by resolving to bring food supply under his
aegis, since his ministry's interests were not – he said – adequately represented in the arrangements agreed in August 1915. Khvostov established
a 'Society for the Campaign against the High Cost of Living', under whose
auspices a number of consumer co-operatives were opened in Petrograd
and elsewhere. (At the same time he refused to tolerate a national committee of co-operatives, seeing this as an instrument of potential
subversion.) Ministry of Transport officials were asked to expedite deliveries of food to the Russian capital. Khvostov hoped thereby to nip in the
bud growing working-class consumer discontent, by demonstrating the
solicitude and efficiency of the tsarist police. But all he succeeded in doing
was to alienate other members of the government, notably Krivoshein in
agriculture and Rukhlov in transport, and to draw attention to the fact
that anti-commercial sentiment was alive and well in the corridors of
power.[41]

4.4   The personal rule of Nicholas II and the crisis of high politics

Tsarist rule faced a series of challenges during the summer of 1915. Defeat
and evacuation severely damaged the authority of the Tsar's generals and
ministers. War industry committees embarked on a campaign for the
'mobilisation of industry', although the outcome hardly gave them the
influence they craved. A fresh outbreak of labour protest in June, July and
August culminated in police shootings of strikers in Ivanovo-
Voznesensk.[42] In the broader political sphere the omens for the tsarist
regime seemed no better. A leading Octobrist politician, speaking at the
end of July, observed that 'if events continue to develop as tragically as
they have hitherto, then the time will fast approach when we can demand
everything and be confident of getting it too'.[43]

Within the Duma the Progressive Bloc fashioned an ambitious policy
agenda, which embraced autonomy for the Kingdom of Poland, the abolition of civil disabilities for Russian Jews, the release of political prisoners
and freedom of association for trade unionists. These reforms were linked
to the fundamental demand for a 'united government' that enjoyed public
confidence and whose leaders were committed to working with parlia-

ment. The Bloc also committed itself to a new compact between government and the public.[44] Some of the Tsar's ministers recognised in this
movement the potential for a new kind of co-operation between state and
'society'. Krivoshein, for instance, believed that the hostility between the
'warring camps' could give way to harmonious and productive collaboration. Other ministers shared his view, but the elderly prime minister,
Goremykin – 'an evil witch', according to the public organisations –
refused to accept the need for any change and called off further discussions
at the end of August. He persuaded Nicholas II to bring the current sitting
of the Duma to an end. In the event, the Progressive Bloc foundered
because of internal disagreement over the extent to which it should or
could put real pressure on the Tsar. Some right-wing Kadets believed that
there was a risk of a conservative backlash. In the short term they were
proved correct by the Tsar's decision to put the reactionary A.A. Khvostov
in charge of 'pacifying' the country.[45]

One manifestation of tsarist initiative was Nicholas's decision – the day
after chairing the first session of the OSO – to replace his cousin as commander-in-chief and to take charge himself of the armed forces. This was
a momentous move. Grand-Duke Nicholas had appeared to enjoy popu-
larity with the rank and file, but he was unceremoniously packed off to the
Caucasus. Other changes included the installation of General Alekseev as
chief of staff in place of Ianushkevich. Nicholas II relished the opportunity
to become commander-in-chief and took some pleasure in refusing to
accede to the objections voiced by most of this cabinet. He discovered (in
his words) a world of 'beauty', 'health' and authenticity, far removed from
what he described as political intrigue and backstabbing. As commander-
in-chief he could distance himself from the 'chatter' in Petrograd and
exploit the 'bond' that he fondly believed existed between the monarch
and his people.[46]

This did not bring to an end the political in-fighting over the process of
economic mobilisation. At the beginning of February 1916 Prince L'vov
told the Tsar that 'the internal national economy has been completely
destroyed, and threatens to undermine the armed forces'. He called upon
Nicholas to entrust the burden of mobilisation to persons 'enjoying the
country's confidence'.[47] Nicholas II responded by backing Khvostov's
public campaign against the rising cost of living and against the 'German
menace' inside Russia. This was certainly not what L'vov had in mind, nor
did it convince the military.[48]

Liberal politicians intensified their critical stance. The actions of the
Tsar had done nothing to assuage the sense of impending catastrophe.

Konovalov and Guchkov, as well as Chelnokov, the liberal Mayor of Moscow, remained in close touch with Alekseev and with sympathetic diplomats, such as the French ambassador Maurice Paléologue and his British counterpart Sir George Buchanan. There was even private talk (endorsed by Konovalov and Riabushinskii) of persuading the Allies to demand internal political reform in Russia as the price of extending fresh credit. Konovalov met with members of the socialist intelligentsia, including S.N. Prokopovich and his wife E.D. Kuskova.[49] However, they faced a dilemma, neatly put by the Kadet politician Nikolai Astrov in January 1916: 'it is the tragedy of Russian society that while we do not believe in those who hold power, at the same time we cannot but acknowledge that only powerful authority can save the situation'.[50]

Nicholas and his entourage rejected any closer involvement by the voluntary organisations in the management of the economy. At a cabinet meeting on 17 June 1916 the chairman Boris Stürmer grandly announced that 'I am not against *glasnost*'. The more light, the better. But it is impossible to deprive the government of its initiative. It is out of the question for power to be handed to the voluntary organisations'.[51] It was symptomatic of this constellation of forces that Nicholas approved the appointment of the financial magnate A.D. Protopopov to the post of Minister of the Interior. Protopopov was no friend of the voluntary organisations, believing them to be a kind of political fifth column.[52]

Bolder spirits among the military leadership sought to intervene more decisively in the politics of mobilisation. Alekseev presented a memorandum to the Tsar in June 1916 in which he called for 'extraordinary measures', in order to overcome shortages of skilled labour, coal and metal and to expedite the delivery of greater quantities of shell for heavy artillery. Other priorities included the imposition of order over the chaotic transport system. Alekseev recommended that 'authority should be concentrated in the hands of one responsible person', having power over all government departments as well as the public organisations: in other words a 'supreme minister of state defence'. The chosen minister would be responsible for the militarisation of all defence industry in return for a guarantee that the workforce would receive cheap food and other basic necessities. In its call for an economic dictator Alekseev's report anticipated the famous Hindenburg programme in Germany.[53] As Minister of the Interior Boris Stürmer seemed the most likely candidate, but he declined to take on these additional responsibilities. In the end Nicholas II confined himself to the creation of a smaller cabinet of ministers, which Stürmer was eventually persuaded to chair, handing his portfolio to

Khvostov. This decision succeeded in alienating most members of the Council of Ministers, whilst doing little to convince Alekseev and other military leaders that the politicians had established proper authority. It was widely believed that the Empress took advantage of her husband's extended absence at the front to exercise influence over appointments and other key decisions. Thus in the political realm too it appeared that the tsarist elite had snatched defeat from the jaws of victory.[54]

Against this uncompromising background the Tsar's commanders embarked upon what amounted to a military coup. During the winter of 1916 they endorsed the assassination of Rasputin and conspired with Grand Duke Nicholas. Their contemplation of regime change reflected not only months of dissatisfaction with the drift of Nicholas's policy but also years of accumulated commitment to a professional-cum-technocratic ethos. Talk of a separate peace with Germany outraged them. They maintained that Russian troops had sufficient morale, ability and weaponry to hold the line and avoid further catastrophe on the battlefield. The front was holding, but the war effort was being undermined by knowledge of economic chaos in the rear, to which ministers and bureaucrats had no solution. Stavka's military professionalism, patriotism and contempt for the pen-pushers proved to be a powerful cocktail.[55]

Russia's armed forces regrouped and embarked upon a successful military offensive during the summer of 1916. However, this only reinforced the sense among the military leadership that the political establishment had exhausted its claims upon their loyalty. They were attracted to the idea of a new political dispensation. Whether this would take the form of a military dictatorship or a system maintained by the public organisations remained unclear. Among the troops, too, morale had generally plummeted. The majority did not want to lay down their arms, but they felt betrayed by the courtly elite. By 1916 the Russian royal family itself attracted more opprobrium than at any time in the history of the Romanov dynasty. The prestige it had garnered at the outbreak of war proved to be transitory. The Romanovs, too, were victims of war.[56]

Nicholas II perfected the art of personal rule by reaffirming his control over ministerial appointments and by assuming control of the armed forces. His resolve showed no signs of weakening. Whenever it faltered, his closest confidants were on hand to remind him of his obligation to his predecessors and to 'Holy Russia', now embodied in the person of Grigorii Rasputin. Government ministers, the beneficiaries of ministerial 'leapfrogging', remained faithful to a traditional conception of tsarist authority, but even the loyal Minister of the Interior later acknowledged the 'lack of direction and leadership'. The assertion of personal rule did nothing to lessen this confusion.[57]

It is remarkable how much the revival of patriotic discourse was deployed to inflict maximum damage on the dynasty. At its peak, the liberal critique allowed parliamentarians such as the normally cautious historian and leading Kadet Paul Miliukov to denounce the court clique. In a speech delivered at a new session of the Duma on 1 November 1916, he catalogued the regime's failures and asked 'Is this stupidity or treason?' Miliukov's speech was disseminated in a pirated version across provincial Russia. As it seeped into public consciousness, his rhetoric helped in the medium term to seal the fate of the Romanovs, the more so as it was followed soon after by a similar denunciation by the right-wing maverick V.M. Purishkevich.[58] Rasputin symbolised the cancer of corruption, sexual depravity and superstition that was the very opposite of the virtuous self-discipline and rationality upon which liberal opinion prided itself. Religious dignitaries also bemoaned his influence: 'this ulcer is frightful [and] may cause great harm, not only to the Church but even to Orthodox people in general'.[59] His opponents deployed the same language – 'poison', 'ulcer', 'gangrene' – that was the stock of trade of those who denounced imperial Germany. Their rhetoric cemented the connection between the Rasputin clique and German intrigue.

Street literature depicted the royal family and its entourage in a deeply unflattering light. *Lubki* and other popular cultural forms poked fun at the Russian monarchy. In the weeks leading up to the February revolution, semi-pornographic images circulated in large numbers, suggesting a liaison between the Tsarina and the 'mad monk', whose self-seeking lasciviousness seemed to mock the personal sacrifices that ordinary people had made.[60] Even rumours of the young Tsarevich's medical condition, haemophilia, served as a metaphor for the ceaseless flow of blood on the battlefield.[61] Popular opinion tapped into the language of patriotism, claiming that Russia had been betrayed by the Tsar and his courtiers. Peasants denounced the pro-German sentiments of the Tsar's wife. According to D. Khozova, a 47-year-old peasant from Iaroslavl', 'she corresponds with the Germans, and when Russian soldiers are killed she is happy, when our boys kill German soldiers she cries.' Others accused her of siphoning off funds to Germany. Troops condemned the influential 'German party'.[62]

Conclusions

The changing fortunes of war had profound consequences for imperial Russia. Defeat encouraged and emboldened critics of the old regime, since they could point to the capture and imprisonment of Russian men and the abandonment of territory to the enemy. However, more than national pride was at stake. By unleashing an unstoppable displacement of civilians, defeat helped bring the war into the daily lives of provincial Russia. In these ways the war changed the contours and conduct of Russian politics.

Paradoxically, the overt and intensive methods used by the state to promote public support – the pamphlets and sermons, the public spectacles, the new medium of film and so on – helped to erode public sympathy for the Tsar's war. Propaganda enabled the reading public to reflect on the meaning of battle and on the sacrifices being made at the front and in the rear. Perhaps, too, ordinary churchgoers grew tired of the Orthodox Church's close connection to the state. Hoping for comfort and reassurance, they were fed instead a diet of bellicose propaganda. The resources of the political police were also over-stretched, nor were matters helped by a lack of co-ordination between government ministers and their officials.[63]

In the sphere of business, merchants and industrialists harnessed private interest to public duty, suggesting that the war provided an opportunity to press the claims of 'national' industry. Army chiefs, in private at least, questioned the wisdom of entrusting military leadership to the Tsar; from their perspective the national cause could best be served by promoting professionalism rather than espousing dynastic duty. For his part the Tsar attached huge importance to being in the 'authentic' world close to the front rather than in his effete and intrigue-ridden capital. Yet the remaining reserves of loyalty were gradually depleted. Put another way, the close association between the empire and the old regime damaged the prospects for Russia's 'national' survival. Patriots looked to other kinds of leadership to save the country from further humiliation.

The tsarist bureaucracy opposed any attempt to create a nation-wide body for economic mobilisation, fearing that this would provide a platform for educated society to intervene in the decision-making process. Some members of the OSO envisaged that it would become the supreme decision-making body; there was talk of an embryonic 'economic general staff'.[64] This vision never materialised under the old regime. Instead, the OSO became a forum for ascertaining the capacity of defence industry and distributing government contracts. At the same time, its regional agencies, as well as the other special councils, gave Russia's technical specialists an opportunity to gain experience in economic administration that they could put to use after the revolution.

By 1916 the drama of shell shortage had receded, thanks to a successful campaign to develop the productive capacity of Russian factories as well as the supplies from overseas that began to reach Russian shores. The front stabilised, the only significant breach being Brusilov's dramatic offensive against the Austrians. Even the beleaguered Tsar appeared to have bought himself extra time, having neutralised the Duma as a political forum and installed a clever conservative politician to 'pacify' the country. But Nicholas's military commanders, headed by Alekseev, betrayed their impatience with the tsarist political elite, believing that Russia's troops deserved better support. Unhappily for the Tsar and his protégé A. A. Khvostov, there were also troubling signs of economic mismanagement, in the shape of fuel supply problems and a looming food supply crisis in the rear. Problems such as these, reflected in tales of shortage and in the behaviour of retail prices, could not be contained within the confines of the special councils. These difficulties form the subject of the following chapters.

Note on further reading

An old but still valuable survey of wartime political developments is Florinsky, 1931. This is brought up to date by Lincoln, 1986. Specialist works include an informative study by Pearson, 1977, and the unsurpassed discussion (in Russian) by Diakin, 1967. Some of the discussions in the Council of Ministers have been translated into English in Cherniavsky, ed., 1967. Patriotic culture receives a nuanced treatment in Jahn, 1995. The role of the Church and schools has yet to attract the attention of modern historians. The standard source on the special councils remains Bukshpan, 1929 (he edited the bulletins issued by the special councils for food supply and fuel), but his work now needs to be supplemented by Sidorov, 1973. All these books are available only in Russian.

References

1 Colonel Miasoedov, the person concerned, was executed in March 1915. Diakin, 1967, p. 78; Gurko, 1939, pp. 550–54. Sukhomlinov's departure was followed by those of N.A. Maklakov (Minister of the Interior), I.G. Shcheglovitov (Minister of Justice), and V.K. Sabler (Procurator of the Holy Synod), at the end of June 1915. Maklakov and Shcheglovitov were executed by the Bolsheviks.

2 Lincoln, 1986, p. 200. Alexandra urged her husband to run Rasputin's comb through his hair before meeting his ministers.

3 Berezhnoi, 1975, pp. 21–2.

4 Petrone, 1998. Around 1,200 films were made in Russia during the war.

5 Jahn, 1995, pp. 155, 167, describing the 1916 film *The Poor Chap Died in an Army Hospital*; Petrone, 1998, pp. 100–02; McReynolds, 1993; Acton et al., eds, 1997, p. 566 (Stites).

6 Michelson et al., 1928, p. 263; Strakhov, 2003, p. 34; Jahn, 1995, pp. 63, 68–72, 156–7 (quotation on p. 83).

7 Odinetz and Novgorotsev, 1929, pp. 57–62, 75–6; Jahn, 1995, pp. 47, 147.

8 Waldron, 1995; Coetzee and Shevin-Coetzee, eds, 1995, pp. 29–56 (Zuckerman); Lohr, 2003, p. 18.

9 Pearson, 1977, pp. 121–2; Berezhnoi, 1975, pp. 14–74; Smirnov, ed., 1999, pp. 160–70 (Izmozik).

10 Senin, 1993, pp. 45–6.

11 Quotation courtesy of Mark Baker; see also Baker, 2001, pp. 153–4.

12 Hoffmann and Kotsonis, eds, 2000, p. 94 (Holquist).

13 Sidorov, 1973, pp. 36–46. This body replaced the 'Special Preliminary Commission for Artillery'.

14 *P&T*, 1915, no.12 (Fridman); Somov, 1973; Krupina, 1969, p. 67. The Duma members were Rodzianko, Protopopov, Dmitriukov and Savich, all linked to the Octobrists.

15 Gal'perina, ed., 1999, pp. 189–93, meeting on 26 June 1915.

16 Diakin, 1967, pp. 87–8; Laverychev, 1967, pp. 116, 119; Dumova, 1988.

17 Diakin, 1967, pp. 87–102.

18 Krupina, 1969; Bukshpan, 1929, pp. 309–14.

19 Bukshpan, 1929, p. 314.

20 GIASPb, f.2145 op.1, d.361, ll.237–242ob.

21 Laverychev, 1988, pp. 98–102; Bukshpan, 1929, p. 317. Aleksei N. Khvostov is not to be confused with his uncle, A.A. Khvostov, who served as Minister of Justice between July 1915 and July 1916, when he became Minister of the Interior.

22 Bukshpan, 1929, p. 318; Zagorsky, 1928, p. 98.

23 *ZhOSO*, 29 July 1915; Manikovskii, 1930, volume 2, pp. 293–7; Bukshpan, 1929, p. 321. This sub-committee was chaired by a deputy minister of war.

24 Sidorov, 1973, p. 119; *ZhOSO*, 20 January 1916.

25 RGVIA f.369, op.1, d.29, ll.26–29; d.96, l.352.

26 One quarter of all enterprises under the authority of the OSO were based in Moscow, and a further fifth in Siberia, but Siberia accounted for a mere two per cent of the workforce. Petrograd's share was 14 and 16 per cent respectively. Bukshpan, 1929, pp. 325–6.

27 RGVIA f.369, op.16, d.59, ll.2–3, 8–10; op.1, d.568, ll.1–212; *ZhOSO*, 9 December 1915; 3 February 1916. For Meshcherskii's riposte, see *Trudy Pervogo s"ezda*, 1916, p. 26 and GIASPb f.2145, op.1, d.163, ll.58–63.

28 Beliaev, 2002, p. 269; Shatsillo, 1963.

29 Vasil'ev, 1939, pp. 185–209; Sidorov, 1973, pp. 615–28.

30 January 1917 the stock of locomotives in working order stood at 17,010, but six months later the number had dropped to 15,930, according to *Narodnoe khoziaistvo*, 5–6, 1920, p. 5 (Mikhailov). There were almost 1,000 more locomotives in service on 1 January 1917 than there had been a year earlier. After April each month saw a net loss of between 200 and 400 locomotives. See *EPR*, 1957, volume 2, p. 259.

31 RGIA f.32, op.2, d.10, ll.27-29ob., memorandum dated 13 March 1915.

32 Sidorov, 1973, p. 624; Maevskii, 1957, p. 237.

33 Bukin, 1915; Bukshpan, 1929, p. 269.

34 Sidorov, 1973, pp. 544–64; Zagorsky, 1928, pp. 114–26; Bukshpan, 1929, pp. 401–22.

35 'Sindikaty i gosudarstvo', editorial, *B. ved.*, 15400, 23 February 1916; Bukshpan, 1929, pp. 258–9; Sidorov, 1973, pp. 529–30.

36 Zagorsky, 1928, pp. 118, 124; Sidorov, 1973, p. 531; Hardach, 1977, pp. 58–62.

37 Bukshpan, 1929, pp. 401–22; Zagorsky, 1928, pp. 125–6. Sidorov, 1973, pp. 557–8, discusses the battle over the introduction of the coal monopoly, but fails to draw any conclusions about the new agency.

38 *Izvestiia VSG*, 1917, 40, pp. 318–32.

39 Lih, 1990, pp. 16-19 and Struve et al., eds, 1930, pp. 9–13. A.N. Naumov replaced Krivoshein in October 1915.

40 Stanziani, 1998, p. 176.

41 Diakin, 1967, pp. 132–4; Zagorsky, 1928, pp. 166–7; Kayden and Antsiferov, 1929, p. 98.

42 Fleer, ed., 1925, pp. 211–5.

43 N.V. Savich, quoted in Diakin, 1967, p. 96.

44 Miliukov, 1967, pp. 319–27; Gurko, 1939, pp. 572–5; Kir"ianov, ed., 1999, pp. 89–117; Diakin, 1967, pp. 96–109; Pearson, 1977, p. 51.

45 Diakin, 1967, pp. 95, 129; Rieber, 1982, p. 394.

46 Jones, 1988. Krivoshein acknowledged (6 August 1915) that Nicholas's decision was 'fully in keeping with his spiritual make-up and his mystical understanding of his imperial calling'. Quoted in Lincoln, 1986, p. 160.

47 Grave, ed., 1927, pp. 59–60.

48 Gal'perina, ed., 1999, p. 322, Council of Ministers, 4 March 1916. See also Chapter 7.

49 Laverychev, 1967, pp. 132, 140–42, 152; Grave, ed., 1927, p. 80.

50 Quoted in Siegelbaum, 1983, p. 122. Guchkov urged 'state power to grant the demands of society ... in order to defend our homeland from revolution and anarchy'. Lincoln, 1986, p. 203.

51 Gal'perina, ed., 1999, p. 342.

52 Laverychev, 1967, p. 148; Lih, 1990, p. 47.

53 The report was dated 15 June. Quoted in Manikovskii, 1930, volume 2, pp. 342–3. For the text and accompanying discussion see Semennikov, 1927, pp. 255–66.

54 Manikovskii, 1930, volume 2, pp. 337–41; Pearson, 1977, pp. 105–6.

55 Pearson, 1977, pp. 124–39.

56 Soldiers' songs and letters reflect their disillusionment with the tsarist regime as early as 1915. See Porshneva, 2000, pp. 247–9.

57 Protopopov, cited in Lincoln, 1986, p. 281; Balzer, ed., 1996, pp. 267–92 (Orlovsky).

58 Ironically Miliukov quoted in German from enemy newspapers to catalogue the behaviour of the Empress and of Stürmer. Pearson, 1977, pp. 115–17, 119.

59 Quoted in Curtiss, 1940, p. 402.

60 See the example in Figes and Kolonitskii, 1999, and Porshneva, 2000, pp. 129, 250.

61 The Russian 'Workers' Marseillaise', first composed in 1875 and widely sung during the February revolution along with other revolutionary hymns, spoke of the 'vampire Tsar'. Kolonitskii, 2001, pp. 17, 23–4.

62 Porshneva, 2000, pp. 122, 128, 248–9 for this and other expressions of outrage on the part of peasants and soldiers.

63 Coetzee and Shevin-Coetzee, eds, 1995, pp. 38–9 (Zuckerman).

64 Bogolepov, 1916.

CHAPTER 5

Mobilising industry: Russia's war economy at full stretch

We need all factories and workshops at the present time to become one gigantic factory, working only for the Army.
        [P.A. Riabushinskii, July 1915, reported in P&T, 1915, no. 11]

Tsarist Russia embarked on an orgy of armaments production during the war. This served two purposes, to sustain the war effort and to improve the credibility of the state in the teeth of criticism from educated society. Considered in these terms, there is nothing very remarkable about the sharp increase in the output of defence items. The government paid huge advances and granted loans to Russian firms, which in turn purchased raw materials, acquired new equipment and took on additional labour, passing on the increased costs to the Treasury. Yet this bald summary fails to do justice to important aspects of the tsarist war economy and the productive effort. First, the government intervened to smooth out disruptions in the supply of raw materials to its defence contractors, thereby helping to cement the close relationship between tsarist officialdom and big business. Second, acute bottlenecks in the supply of machine tools placed Russian arms suppliers at a disadvantage. One means of resolving shortages was to concentrate available stocks at a relatively small number of enterprises. This policy hastened the process of industrial concentration already under way before 1914. Individual firms were re-organised into new conglomerates. Third, the war enabled some branches of industry to modernise their capital stock; it also launched newer industries such as dyestuffs, electrical engineering and aircraft manufacture. Fourth, Russian management re-organised the labour process in the factory work, simplifying manufacturing methods and encouraging the standardisation of output.

The war also encouraged rival visions of industrial organisation. Military procurement agencies allocated orders between private and state-owned enterprise. An orchestrated campaign to establish a greater role for state-owned enterprise threatened to diminish the claims of the private sector. The war industry committees portrayed themselves as an alternative to private enterprise, and the conventional autonomy of private enterprise was called into question, as firms found themselves subject to investigation. Long before the Bolshevik revolution, Russian entrepreneurs were confronted by challenges to their economic position, not by organised labour but by the tsarist state and educated society.

The government made little direct attempt to intervene in the labour market, leaving monetary inducements as the main instrument of directing and motivating labour. Women entered the industrial labour force in greater numbers than hitherto. The composition of the workforce also changed as a result of substituting prisoners of war and refugees for conscripted workers. Disruption of the labour force, combined with difficulties in sustaining supplies of fuel and raw materials, were reflected in an overall decline in labour productivity.

5.1 Key inputs: fuel and raw materials

Russia was rich in fuel reserves and in the basic raw materials vital for a modern war economy, such as ferrous and non-ferrous metals. However, it proved difficult to translate these advantages into an effective system of supply. One factor was the location of deposits. Copper, lead, zinc and other metals were found only in the Urals, Caucasus or western Siberia, far from the major centres of manufacturing industry. Dealing with these problems in turn raised important questions about industrial organisation, the responsibilities of capital and labour and the appropriate role of government.

By 1915 the supply of fuel and raw materials became a matter of serious concern to industrialists, officials and politicians. Factory managers had exhausted their stocks. Industrialists complained that their normal suppliers were reneging on contracts in order to impose new and disadvantageous terms on customers. Government officials expressed anxiety about the ability of defence firms to process munitions orders. Politicians drew the lesson that greater controls needed to be imposed over big business, since 'monopolists' had cornered the market in copper, zinc, instrument steel and other items. This analysis also found favour in sections of the press.[1]

The productive effort demonstrated a mixed picture. Output from the Polish Dombrowa fields had to be written off following the German invasion, but since Polish coal mostly went to local customers this loss did not have drastic consequences. Elsewhere, production of coal fell slightly during 1914 and 1915, but increased in the following year before falling back to below peacetime levels during 1917. Oil production followed exactly the same trend. Even the revolutionary upheaval in the Donbass merely brought total output back down to pre-war levels.[2] Smaller deposits of coal were worked more intensively than hitherto. Newer fields in the Moscow basin, the Urals and Siberia were developed; their share of total coal output increased from 12 per cent to 21 per cent between 1913 and 1917. There were constraints on the expansion of coal output, including a dearth of pumps, winches and other equipment, as well as explosives. Attempts were made to compensate for the shortage of coal by increasing the output of timber, but these fell foul of a shortage of transport, including horses commandeered by the army.[3]

Significant shifts took place in the pattern of consumption. Railways absorbed an increasing proportion of total coal output, rising from 30 per cent in 1914 to nearly 50 per cent in 1917. Steel makers and engineering factories took a larger share of output than in peacetime, in accordance with the faster tempo of industrial mobilisation, depriving civilian consumers and non-defence sectors of sufficient coal to meet their needs.[4] Imports of coal to supply Petrograd declined drastically and only the diversion of coal from the Donbass helped keep the city's defence factories afloat.[5] Against this background it became necessary to impose restrictions on non-essential use. Steps were taken to substitute wood, oil and peat, but the oil industry struggled to meet the demands placed upon it.[6]

Supplies of fuel were vulnerable to the general deterioration in transport. Russia's railways did not serve the coal producers well – in October 1915 1.1 million tons of coal awaited despatch from the pit head and six months later this figure had risen to 3.5 million tons. Firms in the Central Industrial Region and in the south were starved of fuel. The Special Council for Fuel Supply did little to improve this situation.[7]

The war produced far-reaching proposals for the fuel economy, including plans to develop hydroelectric power stations and to invest in long-distance transmission of electricity, reducing the reliance on coal transportation. In the meantime, the war enabled the main power stations in Moscow, Petrograd and Baku to increase their output substantially.

Projects for the expansion of capacity included the construction of new state-owned oil refineries. A proposed new facility costing 53 million rubles at Maikop in the northern Caucasus was expected to supply 820,000 tons per annum, at a price 25 per cent below that charged by the private sector.[8]

The war transformed the market for iron and steel and for non-ferrous metals such as copper and zinc. Cemented steel, used in the manufacture of shell and shrapnel, accounted for 13 per cent of all production in 1916, compared with less than two per cent in 1913. Rails and related items accounted for 15 per cent, down from 20 per cent in 1913. Construction items fell from 20 per cent to 9 per cent. General purpose rolled iron and steel maintained its share at around 35 per cent. Government demand for iron and steel in peacetime did not exceed 30 per cent (and more normally 10 per cent) of the total, but during the war the state absorbed virtually the entire output. Foundries struggled to maintain production in the face of shortages of labour, iron ore and coking coal, which by the middle of 1916 had reached serious proportions, 'threatening state defence' according to the November congress of the southern metallurgical industry. Iron and steel producers retained a greater proportion of their output for themselves, in order to manufacture shell casings and other products that gave a better profit margin. As a result, fewer supplies reached the market and the price of steel rose.[9]

In November 1915 the government created a Metals Committee to purchase ferrous and non-ferrous metals from domestic and overseas sources and to supply the domestic defence industry with the necessary quantities of metal. A month later a more systematic attempt was made to ascertain aggregate demand for metal, to establish the productive capacity of Russian enterprises, to supply inputs to Russian blast furnaces and foundries and to supply metal to nominated factories. The committee was headed by a Special Commissioner and backed by a series of regional boards which determined the schedule for supplying metal to approved firms, ascertained the prices being charged and implemented the arrangements for transporting metal. By 1916 most of the industry was being regulated by government, with the assistance of leading industrialists from the metals syndicate Prodamet. The Metals Committee began to stipulate the price at which different products could be sold, giving manufacturers a reasonable mark-up on the manufacture of shell. One leading firm assured its shareholders that these prices not only covered the costs of re-equipment but also gave a 'sufficient commercial rate of return'.[10]

Attempts to calculate a balance of metal production and consumption are very instructive. In September 1915 the Metals Committee put total demand from government, industry and private households at 3.77 million tons per annum. This corresponded precisely to estimates of likely output in 1916, leaving no room for manoeuvre in the event of a fall in output or a sudden rise in consumption. In April 1916 these calculations were revised to take account of burgeoning demand, giving a shortfall of up to 1.15 million tons; by October the estimated deficit had crept up to around 1.37 million tons.[11] Non-essential users were the first to feel the pinch. Local and regional war industry committees, not on the list of approved customers for metal, complained that Prodamet stifled attempts to boost the output of iron and steel, but this cut no ice with government officials who interpreted the complaint as a cry for favourable treatment. The administration of metal supply thus became a political as well as an economic instrument.[12]

The chairman of the Metals Committee spoke in aggressive terms of establishing 'the principle that all metal ... is at the sole disposal of the government ... without whose agreement and organisation no one should be able to produce a single ton.' He boasted of clipping the wings of the metals syndicate. In practice Prodamet continued to arrange orders and shipments, because neither the Metals Committee nor government had the necessary staff. The major private firms were, however, treated to examples of official disquiet at the power they wielded. The Ministry of Transport advocated new state-owned enterprises with a planned capacity amounting to 0.65 million tons of pig iron (equivalent to 15 per cent of pre-war output); the explicit aim was to force down the prices charged by private firms. However, with construction costs at 40 million rubles this initiative remained on the drawing board.[13]

In other extractive industries, the need to find fresh sources of supply was even more urgent. Copper was vital for the war effort, being used in the manufacture of fuses, shell casings and driving rings, as well as wire and other products. The output of ore fell continuously during the war, notably in the Caucasus. Imports assumed far greater significance, increasing from 70,000 tons or less than 20 per cent of Russia's copper requirements before the war to 786,000 tons (meeting 75 per cent of Russia's needs) by 1916. As with non-ferrous metals, suppliers reneged on old contracts in order to take advantage of the surge in prices. In 1916 the Metals Committee fixed copper prices and brought in the long-established trading company Wogau and Co. to help allocate supplies to a handful of approved manufacturers.[14]

Generally speaking the difficulties referred to above had a number of consequences. First, the war exposed the need for investment to develop new deposits of coal, iron ore and especially non-ferrous metal in Siberia, the Urals and the Caucasus. Second, manufacturers themselves sought greater control over the supply of essential inputs. Although key firms could count on government intervention, they took steps to secure control by acquiring a controlling stake in extractive enterprises. Third, the government intervened to plan the allocation of inputs into the metallurgical industry, creating an elaborate quota system that worked to the advantage of the leading steel works. Regulation established close relationships between tsarist officials and industrialists, thereby inflaming opinion among those manufacturers who remained outside this charmed circle.

5.2   The labour force: recruitment, retention and motivation

As mobilisation intensified, employers complained that the best-qualified workers had been poached. A military specialist put the problem succinctly: 'cadres cannot be improvised' in wartime. Russian manufacturing industry had to deploy unskilled workers in greater numbers, making adjustments to the production process accordingly.[15]

The draft led to the withdrawal of significant numbers of workers from the labour force. Its consequences lasted well into 1915. The Moscow industrialist Goujon complained that 'if the issue (returning conscripts to their place of work) is not resolved, then there is little point in our buying machinery'.[16] Only in 1916 did exemption become more widespread, with a committee established by the Ministry of War on which employers and war industry committees were represented.[17] By October some 300,000 workers had received certificates. When the system was extended in March 1917, the figure climbed to 1.86 million, including 433,000 reservists assigned to government enterprises. These arrangements effectively meant the designation of work in state arsenals as a reserved occupation.[18]

Apart from measures relating to exemption, the Russian state did not intervene actively in the labour market. Ministers were nervous about using compulsion as a weapon to tie workers to particular enterprises (except in the case of state arsenals and dockyards), even where management urged this course of action. Early on, government officials refused to countenance the militarisation of labour in the private sector, 'relying upon the complete loyalty and acquiescence of the workforce, and taking into account the possibility of occasioning unwelcome rumours and unrest' among the working class.[19] In mid-1915 a proposal for the militarisation of labour, drafted by officials in the Ministry of Trade and Industry, reached the cabinet. It stipulated that munitions workers in the private sector could not hand in their notice without prior approval. Employers could also insist on overtime work. The Ministry was to arbitrate in the case of disputes.[20] The proposal was sent to the Special Council for State Defence (OSO), and Nikolai Savich, a leading Kadet politician and member of the OSO, suggested that militarisation would only be acceptable to workers if they received an assurance that 'more intensive labour input did not simply produce extra profits for entrepreneurs'. The public organisations were also resolutely opposed. Others felt that it was only fair to impose militarisation, given that the government was now inspecting the behaviour of factory owners closely.[21] The discussions led nowhere and the only restrictions were imposed upon workers in the reserves, who could not transfer from one job to another without official permission.[22]

The chief sources of labour were unemployed workers, new and unskilled entrants to industry, refugees, prisoners of war and invalids, dismissed by one historian as 'a rabble, new to the work and taken on at haphazard'.[23] Labour exchanges in Petrograd and Moscow channelled builders, domestic servants and shop assistants towards jobs in the industrial economy.[24] The age structure of the labour force changed, with a declining proportion of workers aged between 20 and 39 years and an increase in the proportion aged over 40.[25] Female participation increased, from around 30 per cent in 1913 to 40 per cent in 1916. Juveniles (those aged under 17) comprised 14 per cent of the industrial workforce in 1916, compared with less than 11 per cent on the eve of the war.[26]

Prisoners of war were employed in back-breaking occupations, whether in the coal and iron ore mines of south Russia, in agriculture and forestry, or in construction. The iron mines of Krivoi Rog employed 2,000 prisoners in August 1915, but by January 1917 their numbers had risen to more than 15,000, three-fifths of the total. In the Donbass POW labour increased from 15,000 in October 1915 to 76,000 in March 1917, or more than one quarter of the total labour force. Others were put to work in iron and steel works in Ukraine and the Urals. Around half a million men worked on road building projects and fortifications close to the front.[27]

During the early months of 1916, when the situation in the labour market became critical, the potential role of refugee labour commanded more attention. A leading Petrograd newspaper stated that it would be 'criminal' to continue to employ Chinese and Korean workers in Russia's Far East when there were 'fit, healthy, energetic and enthusiastic' Slavic refugees to take their place.[28] However, the use of refugees as a source of labour met with a number of difficulties. Some employers doubted their commitment and suitability for industrial work. In the south Russian iron and steel industry, only 3 per cent were refugees, the authorities having prevented them from entering mining districts, in order to reduce the risk of infectious disease. Armaments firms made some use of refugees; nearly 1,000 refugees were employed at the Samara fuse factory.[29]

Did the overall quality of the labour force improve? At a general level this question is difficult to answer. The army claimed many skilled workers in their prime of life and only reluctantly discharged them back into civilian occupations. Many of those who replaced experienced workers found it tough to adjust to factory life, especially with the added pressures imposed by the wartime emergency. According to one eyewitness the performance of women compared favourably with that of men, but juveniles of both sexes were 'careless and irresponsible'. Little improvement in productivity was expected from the employment of prisoners of war.[30]

In terms of educational attainment we have a snapshot taken in 1918 of basic literacy, which serves as a crude proxy for the educational attainment of workers. The census conducted in that year painted a picture of a labour force that was characterised by high overall rates of illiteracy. One-third of all workers lacked basic literacy. Among male workers the proportion of illiterates was around 21 per cent but it rose to 56 per cent among females. In the engineering and metal-working trades the overall rate was lower, at around 16 per cent and 23 per cent respectively. This represented a significant improvement over the situation at the turn of the century. At the workplace some employers took steps to promote vocational training for inexperienced workers. A modest premium in the remuneration of literate workers may have provided an incentive to acquire rudimentary skills.[31]

How did these changes translate into labour productivity? How far did they induce extra effort from workers? Adjusted for hours worked, output per person rose quite markedly during 1915 but fell back in 1916, at which point it was no higher than in the last year of peace. Thereafter productivity declined rapidly. Table 5.1 illustrates these trends.

The aggregate data conceal wide variations between branches of industry as well as between individual enterprises. Daily output per worker in machine-building increased by 32 per cent in the period 1913–1916, and in chemicals by 27 per cent. Other sectors, such as metal-working and clothing, also recorded an increase. These improvements were closely connected with the pressure created by the rising volume of military demand, which prompted firms to reorganise the labour process and install new

TABLE 5.1   *Labour productivity in large-scale industry, 1913–1918, USSR pre-1939 territory*

Year	Gross output, million rubles, 1913 prices	Employ-ment, millions	Hours worked, per day	Labour input adjusted for hours worked, millions	Output per person. Col.1/col.4, in 1913 rubles	Col.5 as per cent of 1913
1913	6,391	2.44	10.0	2.44	2,619	100
1914	6,429	2.48	9.7	2.40	2,679	102
1915	7,056	2.58	9.7	2.50	2,822	108
1916	7,420	2.87	9.9	2.84	2,613	100
1917	4,780	2.89	8.9	2.57	1,860	71
1918	2,160	2.25	8.5	1.91	1,131	43

Sources: Gross output of census industry, as reported by Gukhman, 1929, p. 173; employment data from Mints, 1975, p. 39; hours worked, including overtime, from Strumilin, 1964a, p. 365.

TABLE 5.2   *Mean output per day worked, by branch of industry, 1913–1918 (1913 = 100)*

Sector	1913	1914	1915	1916	1917	1918, 1st half
Stone & clay products	100	95.3	91.3	87.2	71.6	56.4
Mining	100	110.5	132.7	92.0	52.4	40.7
Metal-working	100	89.3	113.0	107.9	70.8	40.7
Machine-building	100	98.3	131.6	132.1	89.4	54.2
Wood products	100	95.8	80.1	69.0	49.4	44.2
Chemicals	100	88.8	110.2	127.2	91.7	44.4
Food, drink & drugs	100	121.2	106.9	87.7	62.7	31.4
Animal products	100	106.1	106.3	99.9	79.3	86.9
Leather	100	96.7	88.3	84.1	70.7	62.1
Cotton	100	98.8	95.1	85.1	62.2	50.8
Woollens	100	105.9	100.6	97.2	67.5	50.5
Silk	100	94.8	110.2	96.8	72.9	63.0
Flax	100	118.2	104.7	97.7	72.1	64.7
Hemp	100	95.9	103.3	105.3	80.4	58.5
Other fibres	100	93.6	100.0	129.6	86.2	56.6
Clothing	100	106.9	127.6	130.3	127.4	91.0
Paper	100	96.6	92.9	86.4	71.6	42.6
Printing	100	89.9	80.4	85.7	85.0	92.4
Art & craft products	100	77.1	94.3	66.0	56.3	83.5
Utilities	100	111.5	111.1	117.8	97.9	64.8
All sectors	100	100.9	108.3	104.1	76.0	49.7

Source: Sbornik statisticheskikh svedenii, 1924, pp. 170–71.

plant. Trends in output per day worked in different branches of industry are shown in Table 5.2.

Some employers complained of difficulties in ensuring that workers stuck to the task in hand. Workers at Kolomna took time off to look after their allotments. The same happened in the Donbass, where low morale – the product of dreadful conditions and treatment – and physical exhaustion also took their toll. Here a miner produced on average 12.5 tons of coal per month before the war. By 1916 this figure had fallen to 10.2 tons. In June 1917 output per person reached just 7.7 tons.[32]

5.3   Capital investment and the re-equipment of industry

Industrial investment during the war years presents a confused picture, complicated by the fact that we know virtually nothing about small-scale industry. Contemporary sources testified to an impressive increase in gross investment in large-scale industry. Domestic output of equipment in 1916 was already some 24 per cent higher than in 1913. In addition, supplies of equipment were boosted by imports from Russia's allies. Total gross investment in industrial equipment and structures amounted to around 1,050 million rubles between January 1914 and January 1918. Table 5.3 presents the annual changes to the capital stock in industry.

During the first year and a half of the war the 39 largest engineering firms spent 130 million rubles on new equipment. Smaller enterprises accounted for a further 50 million rubles and the public organisations had purchased 15 million rubles' worth of plant to equip their own enterprises, some of it acquired from firms that had been evacuated in 1915. Other new spending (including the re-equipment of evacuated factories) represented

TABLE 5.3   *Capital stock in large-scale industry, 1914–1918, million pre-war rubles*

	Value of capital stock	Annual investment	Depreciation	Net change
1 January				
1914	3,538	327	125	202
1915	3,740	291	132	159
1916	3,899	275	138	137
1917	4,036	153	143	11
1918	4,047	43	177	−134

Source: Davies et al. 1993, (Gatrell) Cambridge University Press, p. 320.

an additional 100 million rubles' investment. These outlays were equivalent to one-third of the total stock of equipment in engineering at the
outbreak of war – a significant replenishment.[33]

One bottleneck was the supply of machine tools and precision instruments. Before the war a small number of specialist suppliers had
manufactured tools 'according to their own plans and without any overall
direction'. In the early part of the war this scattergun approach continued,
as factories searched desperately for tools from any source.[34] By spring
1916 the Special Council decided to give domestic suppliers of machine
tools the same status as armaments producers, enabling them to secure
generous advances and privileged access to inputs. This was an important
acknowledgement of their role in the war economy.[35] Firms manufactured
drilling and cutting tools for the first time, usually for their own needs,
while the manufacture of complex precision tools was confined to a small
number of specialist suppliers.[36] Total production rose increased from
0.71 million rubles in 1913 to 7.13 million rubles in 1916, falling to 3.14
million rubles in 1917.[37] Imports made a big difference, Russian firms
placing more than half their orders with overseas suppliers in 1915.[38]
Russkii Renault imported tools from its parent company in France, and
other companies did the same. Inevitably there were complaints about
delays and about contracts not being honoured. Even so imports increased
sevenfold between 1914 and 1916.[39]

How was this investment financed? The government stepped in, on the
grounds that 'all Russian industry has been created on credit. We are
giving credit in order that industry will develop without falling into the
hands of the banks'.[40] At the height of the war effort, the government
advanced more than 1,000 million rubles to its contractors. The War
Ministry advanced up to 65 per cent of the value of the contract. (The war
industry committees obtained only 30 per cent.) Large engineering firms
sought assistance from the commercial banks to underwrite their activities
by providing letters of guarantee, but the relationship was sometimes
strained. Sormovo Engineering complained that 'not only are the limits
placed by the banks on these operations very quickly reached, but the commission charged by the banks on this assistance constitutes a fresh burden
on the costs of production'. In response, the government allowed firms to
lodge other forms of security with the procurement agencies, thereby
reducing the influence of the banks.[41]

Corporate profits represented another source of finance. A survey in
1917 indicated that, after tax, profits increased from 11 per cent of share
capital in 1913 to 19 per cent in 1915 and 31 per cent in 1916.[42]

Employers denounced the excess profits tax imposed in 1916, pointing out that 'the defence departments will hardly find new entrepreneurs willing to invest capital in defence production'. They campaigned in support of increased depreciation allowances to set against tax liabilities. The government conceded a 25 per cent depreciation allowance on equipment and 10 per cent on structures, subject to their being used for defence contracts and allowable only on assets that had been acquired or installed during the war. Industrialists had campaigned for 100 per cent, on the grounds that much of the investment would be redundant in peacetime.[43]

Other sources of finance played a less significant role. Except in isolated instances, foreign investment, which had financed as much as half of new corporate investment on the eve of the war, now ceased.

5.4 'All the instruments for causing pain': manufacturing munitions[44]

During the war defence requirements accounted for one-quarter of total production of large-scale industry and about 12 per cent of the output of small-scale industry. By 1916 two-thirds of output in the engineering industry was devoted to military production, compared with around one-quarter in the last full year of peace. This redirection of output came about because of the incessant claims made by the military.[45]

Against this background the productive effort in munitions shows a mixed picture. By 1916 the output of rifles increased nearly fourfold compared with 1914. The manufacture of machine guns was 13 times higher. Output of three-inch artillery had increased by a factor of ten, while the corresponding production of shell had multiplied by 30. In 1914 monthly deliveries of 3" shell from domestic sources averaged 150,000 rounds, but by 1915 this figure rose to 950,000 and in 1916 to 1.9 million. Figures for munitions output are given in Table 5.4.

Russian industry produced no heavy artillery and no military aircraft in peacetime but made modest strides in that direction during the war. Other areas of weakness included the manufacture of armoured vehicles and radios.[46]

The state sector occupied pole position in the armaments industry before the war, being responsible for the manufacture of small arms, heavy artillery and most naval vessels and explosives. Broadly speaking it maintained this position during the war. State arsenals had a torrid time during the early phase of the war when the Main Artillery Administration (GAU)

TABLE 5.4   *Trends in munitions production, 1914–1917, physical units*

Item	1914	1915	1916	1917	Total
Rifles, millions*	0.278	0.860	1.321	1.120	3.579
Index 1914=100	100	309	475	403	
Machine guns, units	833	4,251	11,072	11,320	27,476
Index 1914=100	100	510	1329	1359	
Cartridges, billions	0.345	1.022	1.482	1.209	4.058
Index 1914=100	100	296	430	350	
Artillery, 3", units	385	1,673	4,087**	3,538	12,834
Index 1914=100	100	435	1062	919	
Artillery, 4.8", units	78	361	637	391	1,467
Artillery, 12" fortress, units	n.a.	4	3	11	18
Shell, 3", million	0.616	10.062	19.420	11.739	41.837
Index 1914=100	100	1633	3153	1906	
Shell, 4.8", million	0.024	0.371	2.213	3.238	5.846
Shell, 12", units	n.a.	1,600	3,331	7,372	12,303
Fuses, time, millions	1.686	8.875	21.230	19.477	51.268
Fuses, HE shell, millions	0.380	1.455	10.852	14.418	27.105
Powder, metric tons	4,406	8,405	12,102	9,348	34,260

Sources and note: Manikovskii, 1930, volume 1, pp. 84–5, 127–30, 152–3, 165, 185–90, 285–90, 304–7, 341–3, 370, 374, 377; volume 2, pp. 267–8; Golovin, 2001, pp. 190, 195, 200, 211, 220. 1914 figures are for July to December. * Includes repairs; ** Not including 3,151 repairs

suddenly inundated them with new orders. In February 1915 the Sestroretsk arsenal was asked to produce up to 18,000 rifles each month, from scratch. Output per person increased 15-fold between 1914 and 1916. The Tula ordnance factory increased its production of machine guns from 60 per month before the war to 1,200 by October 1916.[47] Success hinged on the sector's vertical integration (for example, state steel works supplied ordnance factories with steel shapes) and its ability to retain skilled labour. Qualified workers were indispensable to the manufacture of small arms, involving a series of highly complex operations. By the end of 1916, around 310,000 workers were employed in state arsenals, explosives factories and dockyards, contributing around 15 per cent of defence production. This gave the state sector considerable leverage.[48]

The privileged position of government arsenals attracted negative comment (not for the first time) from entrepreneurs who viewed them as 'dead capital'. Businessmen complained that they lost skilled workers to the state arsenals,[49] but this argument did not get them very far in the frantic atmosphere of wartime. In May 1915 the government approved the construction of state facilities to produce nitric acid. Proponents of state enterprise became even more assertive. In October 1916 Manikovskii brought forward ambitious proposals for the construction of 38 state-owned factories to reduce Russia's reliance on foreign sources of supply. Other motives came into play, including the subjection of a greater number of workers to military discipline. Finally the GAU hoped to force private firms to bring down their prices. On these grounds Manikovskii's proposals encountered strong opposition from business leaders who put the total cost of the programme at a staggering 800 million rubles, nearly twice the price tag that the GAU attached to it. Nevertheless government ministers approved the scheme and construction work continued throughout 1917 and 1918.[50]

A small number of large firms dominated the commercial sector for armaments. The giants such as Putilov, Kolomna Engineering, Sormovo, Briansk and the Tula Cartridge Company maintained close connections with foreign specialists including Vickers and Schneider-Creusot.[51] Powerful private conglomerates emerged with the backing of the big commercial banks. These associations continued during the war, enabling private factories to invest in new plant. Putilov rivalled the state sector in the manufacture of heavy artillery. Other large enterprises sub-contracted work to smaller associates.[52]

Firms that had hitherto concentrated on civilian work now joined the headlong rush to manufacture shell and other items. By July 1915 more than 240 civilian machine-building firms, with a combined output of 140 million rubles (equivalent to 30 per cent of total machine-building production in 1913), contributed to munitions production. In Petrograd alone metal-working and machine-building firms employed 154,000 workers by November 1915 and were in receipt of orders worth 1,500 million rubles.[53] This commitment of resources did not go unchallenged. In July 1915 a group of technical specialists and lawyers criticised the slow pace of work among manufacturers in the Central Industrial Region and recommended concentrating equipment in a few factories: 'this is no time for standing on ceremony'.[54]

In the light of such recommendations the GAU sponsored an attempt to reorganise production in the armaments industry as a whole. One important initiative brought together dozens of firms in the private sector, whose responsibilities were carefully defined. This was the Vankov organisation, the brainchild of a technical specialist who had risen through the ranks of the GAU. Vankov distributed regular orders for large quantities of high explosive shell, enabling factories to concentrate on the mass manufacture of shell cases and fuses. The emphasis was on repeat manufacture and the inter-changeability of parts, as well as on pooling resources and technical know-how, including advice from French engineers. The significance of this doctrine was not lost on technical specialists who had long complained of the lack of standardisation in the engineering industry, which they attributed to irregular and haphazard market demand.[55] Manufacturers complained that their clients, including in defence procurement, regularly changed product specifications without any thought for the disruption this entailed. The Vankov organisation promised long production runs instead. By March 1916 it accounted for one-third of all shell production; towards the end of 1917 its share rose to nearly one-half. His genius for organisation and publicity won Vankov many admirers in the GAU, but this was no mere window dressing; Vankov delivered shell on time and at a competitive price. His organisation made great strides in terms of careful supervision of the manufacturing process, monitoring costs and profit margins, pooling equipment, and providing access to advanced foreign technology. Not surprisingly Vankov later became a role model for Soviet engineers.[56]

Basic steps were taken to secure increased output of munitions from available inputs. At the level of the firm, better arrangement of lathes and faster running times allowed factories to double their output per shift. Factories set aside dedicated space for tools, to enable them to be located and assembled as quickly as possible. Blueprints were carefully stored, again for ease of access.[57] Machinery was put to continuous use and workers were required to work extra shifts in order to ensure that factories operated round the clock. (The strain to which equipment was subject led to more breakdowns.) Firms simplified the production process. Mass manufacturing techniques and the use of interchangeable parts became more widespread. In the light of these measures one engineer grandly pronounced that 'on the day of victory, when the enemy sues for peace, industry will be prepared to fight on for at least another year'.[58]

Issues of product innovation, technical change, labour productivity and industrial organisation were at the forefront of debates during the war. New branches of industry emerged, such as the manufacture of military vehicles, although much remained to be done to standardise output and to improve the supply of quality forged steel.[59] The aviation industry was also largely a creature of the war.[60]

In chemicals, the war exposed a shortage of capacity to make explosives and pharmaceuticals. The sector as a whole relied heavily on imports of raw materials; Norway and Portugal supplied three-quarters of Russia's pyrites requirements needed to make sulphuric acid, a basic element in the manufacture of explosives, dyes and artificial fertiliser, as well as in oil refining. Before the war the manufacture of dyestuffs had been heavily concentrated in the Baltic provinces and Poland. Supplies of Russian pyrites were concentrated in the Urals, far from manufacturing centres. Investment in new plant led to a rapid increase in the output of pyrites and to an improved rate of deriving benzol and toluene from coal-tar, in which a consortium of private entrepreneurs played the leading role.[61] Strenuous efforts were also made to recruit labour to this dangerous work (an explosion killed 200 workers at the Okhtensk powder works in 1915). Employment in chemicals grew from 83,000 to 181,000 between 1913 and 1917, with women workers contributing close on half this increase. As a result of the commitment of labour and capital (and the corresponding diversion of resources from other branches of chemicals), the output of explosives increased tenfold, while the manufacture of dyestuffs and pharmaceuticals doubled. The GAU again played a key role in supporting research and development in the major state works at Okhtensk and Samara. Russian scientists set to work developing poison gas, gas masks and incendiary bombs.[62]

Manikovskii's scheme for the future organisation of the arms industry envisaged reserving small arms, grenades, time fuses, explosives and most types of shell for the state sector. Only those items 'that do not pose special difficulties for private industry', such as field artillery, gun carriages and gas masks, should be entrusted to the private sector. Industrialists fought back. Meshcherskii claimed that 'the mobilisation needs of the state may be realised most quickly and satisfactorily by an organisation that unites industry in its entirety. Such an organisation can allocate different parts of complex military orders to factories in accordance with their capacity and equipment'. He envisaged something akin to Manikovskii's ideas for the rapid conversion of civilian engineering firms to defence production, but under the control of private trusts.[63] Developments in 1916–1917 demonstrated that these ideas were taken seriously. In 1916 private businessmen founded 'Pulemet' ('Machine gun'). The following year leading firms established a 'Shell Union' which, like the Vankov organisation, organised firms according to their product specialisation. The central office re-negotiated contracts to help improve the financial condition of the member firms.[64]

Whatever the future form of ownership it was important to ensure that the additional capacity created during the war was maintained rather than dissipated. Officials in the Ministry of Trade and Industry argued that the government would need to reallocate industrial equipment in the interests of maximising productive potential.[65] This became a recurrent theme: left to their own devices, private firms concentrated on profitable and relatively straightforward items such as shell, when expertise, labour and equipment needed to be directed towards more complex items. Other critics drew attention to a relative lack of commitment to the manufacture of rolling stock and agricultural equipment, reinforcing the growing technocratic belief that corporate interest should be restrained to the advantage of national defence.[66]

5.5   Poor relations: other branches of manufacturing

The consequences of the changes described above were reflected in the pattern of total industrial output. In 1915, the real value of manufactured output destined for household consumption was sustained, thanks largely to the use of spare capacity. However, in the following year the first cracks began to appear in the edifice, as military demand rose in unstoppable fashion. By 1917, amidst a substantial decline in total output, the value of goods destined for household consumption dropped to two-thirds of the pre-war average.

Individual sectors tell the same tale. Firms producing agricultural machinery struggled to survive before the war, being caught between suppliers of iron and steel who kept input prices high and the zemstvos that colluded over purchases of agricultural equipment. The war impoverished the sector still further, because the zemstvos lacked the means to purchase equipment, while inputs dwindled to barely 10 per cent of the pre-war level. The output of agricultural machinery fell by 50 per cent between 1913 and 1916. Firms lost workers to the military draft and were saddled with unsold inventories and debts. Nor did the government encourage firms to manufacture more complex items of equipment, such as mobile steam engines, that had been imported before the war. Only firms that switched to munitions production managed to survive.[67]

Domestic suppliers of rolling stock increased their output from 763 units in 1914 to 917 in 1915; even the 600 locomotives produced in 1916 constituted a 30 per cent increase on the pre-war average. Many suppliers, however, found it more profitable and convenient to switch to shell or other munitions, securing generous advances on the contract price as well as supplies of metal and fuel.[68] Although locomotive producers were accused of working to just 50 per cent of capacity by 1915–1916, this reflected conversion to military production, rather than a collapse in overall levels of output. No significant reduction in the output of rolling stock took place before 1917.[69]

The withdrawal of labour contributed to a sharp decline in the output of wood and paper products, glass and pottery, cotton goods and processed foodstuffs. The labour force in cotton textiles and woollens fell by 14 per cent and 44 per cent respectively between 1913 and 1916. Around one in four firms producing cotton goods and mixed fabrics closed down in 1914. Nor did this eliminate only the weaker firms; each one was exposed to the shortage of imported cotton and the surviving firms went on to a three-day week. Only the bumper cotton harvest of 1915 helped to avert a disaster. The following year was less successful, because of the revolt in Central Asia.[70]

Most branches of consumer goods suffered a decline in labour productivity. Meanwhile labour productivity in consumer goods branches declined throughout 1916, reaching 85 per cent of its pre-war level in cotton textiles and paper products, 82 per cent in food and drink and just 70 per cent in wood products. Interruptions in supplies of fuel and raw materials, the mobilisation of skilled workers and the high turnover of workers who sought more remunerative employment in the defence sector all wreaked havoc with attempts to maintain productivity. So too did the deterioration in the quality of equipment. The clothing industry, uniquely, managed to sustain labour productivity, partly thanks to the efforts of the Zemgor which reorganised production and supplied knitting frames to producer co-operatives.[71]

Consumer goods were treated as a residual. To take one example, two-fifths of all cotton was directed to the army by the middle of 1915. A year later this figure soared to three-fifths. The military also had priority in the supply of hides and tanning extracts, leaving civilians to go to the back of the queue.[72] Deprived of labour, raw materials and fuel, the manufacture of furniture, matches, ceramics and musical instruments shrank. Theatres suffered shortages of nails, timber, paint and canvas. The fledgling motion picture industry found it difficult to obtain film.[73]

The consequences were registered in the behaviour of prices. Government demand pushed up the price of iron and steel, coal, copper, leather, cotton and other items. In July 1916 the government eventually instituted fixed prices for all transactions in cotton yarn and fabrics, but this decision merely encouraged suppliers to hold out for higher prices where they could. Other forms of intervention had a more overt impact. Firms supplying the domestic market could not import raw materials without official permission.[74]

Conclusions

The war posed vital issues about the need to secure additional output from existing resources and to develop industrial capacity. Certainly Russian industry had important achievements to its credit, in terms of developing new products and new branches of manufacturing and delivering munitions in sufficient quantities to banish some of the nightmares of 1915. New investment resulted in improvements to the capital stock, delivering output that was 'good, cheap and simple'. The technical specialist A.V. Pankin praised the introduction of continuous flow methods which 'will have favourable consequences on a wider scale. Russian industry will be mobilised for the future struggle for the domestic market and for standing on its own feet'.[75]

In making these advances the Russian government played a relatively passive role, although it belatedly recognised the importance of the machine tools industry by placing it on the same footing as armaments. Military and technical specialists were more active in supporting innovation; the semi-official Vankov organisation played an important role here. Spurred by the profit motive and by expectations of improved market share after the war, private firms also embarked on new ventures. The war created a climate in which chemistry attained a higher status and the industry received hitherto undreamed of resources. Government intervened in order to allocate fuel and other inputs to defence contractors. Its planning instruments, devised by committees for the allocation of ferrous and non-ferrous metals, were subsequently appropriated by the Bolshevik regime.

Yet in other respects a darker mood prevailed. There were bottlenecks in key sectors, brought about by the decline in imports and shortages of fuel that reached a critical level in the winter of 1916. In addition, and notwithstanding Pankin's optimistic remarks, new capital equipment was difficult to put to effective use in peacetime, because of its specialist character. The quality of industrial labour also left much to be desired. Difficulties in recruiting and retaining skilled labour had been well publicised. It was widely and correctly believed that Russia would have to develop improved vocational education and training after the war.

Industrialists organised to defend themselves from charges of sloth or greed. In February 1916, more than 100 representatives from 44 leading engineering firms assembled in Petrograd and established a permanent body to represent their interests before 'government departments and civic organisations'. The employers stressed that their contribution to the war effort had been made possible by massive new investment, but that it could only be justified if the procurement policy of the government became more secure and less haphazard.[76] Yet the entire edifice of capitalist ownership remained shaky. A strong current persisted of official distaste for the joint-stock company. Corporate opposition to the wartime profits tax won Russia's entrepreneurs few friends and labour relations reached a new nadir. Employers counted upon the threat of conscription to maintain the semblance of order in the workplace. The factory inspector who investigated the strike at the Nikolaev shipyards in 1916 concluded ominously that 'therapeutic measures are no use, what is needed is hospital, although the operation is dangerous and the patient may die.' This diagnosis overlooked the fact that the tsarist regime, rather than private enterprise, was terminally ill and liable to expire first. It was left to the Bolsheviks to pronounce the death of capitalism.[77]

Note on further reading

There is no up-to-date study of Russian industry or labour during the First World War in English or in Russian. This leaves the reader with the old and somewhat patchy work by Zagorsky, 1928. Overall dynamics are best approached by means of the 1918 Industrial Census. The economic role of the war industry committees has been much debated, notably by Sidorov, 1973, on the basis of research conducted during the 1930s and 1940s. The standard source on the armaments industry remains Manikovskii, 1930. On the labour force I have relied heavily upon the 1918 Census and on Strumilin, 1964a.

References

1 *Izvestiia TsVPK*, 1916, 117 (Goikhbarg); editorial, *B. ved.*, 15400, 23 February 1916; Sidorov, 1973, pp. 548–9.

2 Kafengauz, 1994, pp. 176–7, 356–7, 363. These figures refer to USSR pre-1939 territory and exclude the Dombrowa coal basin, which fell into German hands in 1914.

3 Zagorsky, 1928, p. 41.

4 Sheliakin, 1930, p. 65.

5 Coal imports fell from 7.7 million tons in 1913 to 0.95 million tons in 1916. *V.fin.*, 1917, 15 (Lomakin); *P&T*, 1917, 1 (Mertsalov); Sidorov, 1973, p. 522. Before the war the Donbass accounted for just one per cent of Petrograd's coal. By 1916 its share jumped to 25 per cent.

6 *Materialy k uchetu*, volume 2, 1917, pp. 36–8; Sidorov, 1973, pp. 524–44.

7 *P&T*, 1917, 1 (Mertsalov); Zagorsky, 1928, pp. 120–21.

8 *Vestnik inzhenerov*, 1916, 4, pp. 145–9 (K.V. Kirsh); *Proizvoditel'nye sily Rossii*, 1917, 6–7, pp. 18–20 (Artleben); Coopersmith, 1992, pp. 110, 118; Maevskii, 1957, pp. 227–8.

9 Tarnovskii, 1958, pp. 29–40, 203, 216, 229–30. Steelworks expected 1.98 million tons of coal and 0.42 million tons of iron ore in November 1916, but received only half these amounts.

10 Tarnovskii, 1958, pp. 57–72, 87–91, 95, 99.

11 Zagorsky, 1928, pp. 112–13; Tarnovskii, 1958, pp. 60, 67, 213. These figures are for iron and steel, expressed in terms of pig iron equivalent.

12 Tarnovskii, 1958, pp. 102, 131–3. The government increased the fixed prices in February 1917.

13 General Myshlaevskii, quoted in Tarnovskii, 1958, p. 123; *P&T*, 1917, 7, pp. 155–9 (anonymous).

14 *Doklad Soveta s"ezdov*, 1915, p. 136; *V.fin.* 1917, 15 (Lomakin); Breiterman, 1930, volume 3, p. 255; Tarnovskii, 1958, pp. 140, 158, 188–90, 194.

15 General Mikhel'son, quoted in Manikovskii, 1930, volume 2, p. 306; Rashin, 1958, pp. 92–3, citing a complaint by Moscow employers.

16 Quoted in Gaponenko, 1970, p. 76.

17 Bukshpan, 1929, p. 241; Pogrebinskii, 1941, p. 174; Golovin, 2001, p. 227, referring to a report by General Beliaev dated 22 February 1915. The Putilov Company secured the return of 3,500 workers, out of a total of 5,000 who had been called up. Pogrebinskii, 1941, p. 173.

18 *RVMV*, 1925, pp. 19, 84, 88; RGVIA f.369, op.1, d.39, ll.178–80 for comments by Polivanov and Guchkov; Kir"ianov, 1971, pp. 223–7.

19 RGIA f.1276, op.11, d.814, ll.1–16; Bukshpan, 1929, pp. 241–2.

20 Sidorov, 1973, pp. 166–7.

21 *ZhOSO*, 4 July 1915; 29 August 1915, referring to the Putilov investigation.

22 *ZhOSO*, 14 May 1916; Bukshpan, 1929, pp. 241–3; Grave, 1958, pp. 421–3; Sidorov, 1973, pp. 166–72.

23 Zagorsky, 1928, p. 56.

24 *Izvestiia TsVPK*, July, 114 (Sharyi).

25 *Promyshlennaia perepis'*, 1926, volume 1, p. 50; *Izvestiia MVPK*, 31–32, 1916 (Pal'chinskii); Gaponenko, 1970, p. 78.

26 Vorob'ev, 1923, p. 141. See also Rashin, 1958, pp. 92–3, and Mints, 1975, p. 53.

27 *RVMV*, 1925, p. 84; Kir"ianov, 1971, p. 31; Sidorov, 1973, p. 418.

28 *B. ved.*, 15091, 16 August 1915; *ZhOSO*, 15 July 1915; Sidorov, 1973, pp. 55–94.

29 Kir"ianov, 1971, p. 41; Gatrell, 1999, p. 135; Maevskii, 1957, p. 322.

30 Taniaev, 1927, pp. 135–6 quoting an engineer's report from the Urals. For a more critical view see Zagorsky, 1928, pp. 55–6; *Materialy k uchetu*, 1916, volume 1, pp. 40, 45.

31 *Promyshlennaia perepis'*, 1926, volume 2, pp. 20–40; *Izvestiia MVPK*, June 1916, 23–24 (Charnovskii); Rashin, 1958, pp. 593–609.

32 Gaponenko, 1970, p. 85; Sheliakin, 1930, pp. 29–33, 38, 41–5, 51, 82–6; Zagorsky, 1928, p. 39; Sidorov, 1973, pp. 513–21.

33 *Trudy Pervogo s"ezda*, 1916, pp. 54, 71; *Trudy Vtorogo s"ezda*, 1916, volume 2, pp. 435–6; Sidorov, 1973, p. 219.

34 Vankov, 1921, p. 16; Mikhailov, 1927, p. 499.

35 RGVIA f.369, op.3, d.93, ll.1–11.

36 RGVIA f.369, op. 1, d.98, ll.339–42, 30 July 1915 (Krestovnikov); op. 3, d.78, ll.170–2 (Litvinov-Falinskii); RGIA f.23, op.15, d.341, ll.3–17; Sidorov, 1973, pp. 454–8.

37 *Promyshlennaia perepis'*, 1926, volume 1, p. 184, in 1913 prices.

38 Charnovskii, 1921, pp. 48–9.

39 RGVIA f.369, op.1, d.96, ll.162, 245–7; op. 3, d.78, ll.170–72; *Trudy pervogo s"ezda*, 1916, p. 65.

40 Quoted in Sidorov, 1973, p. 242.

41 RGVIA f.369, op. 1, d.28, l.30; GIASPb f.1446, op. 1, d.20, ll.1–1ob., 29 July 1916; *ZhOSO*, 6 June 1915. See also Bukshpan, 1929, p. 335; Beliaev, 2002, pp. 274–87.

42 *Promyshlennaia perepis' 1918 goda*, volume 26, p. 59.

43 GIASPb f.1446, op. 1, d.19, ll.2-10.

44 This phrase belongs to W.H. Auden.

45 Manikovskii, 1930, volume 2, pp. 342–3. In November 1915 the army demanded 1.6 million 3″ shrapnel, but revised this upwards by 25 per cent in May 1916. Similar increases were demanded in the supply of high-explosive shell.

46 Golovin, 2001, pp. 188–227.

47 Sidorov, 1973, p. 433.

48 Manikovskii, 1930, volume 1, p. 78; Mikhailov, 1927, p. 504; Strumilin, 1964b, pp. 102–6.

49 Manikovskii, 1930, volume 1, pp. 129–31.

50 GIASPb f.2145, op.1, d.361, ll.191-194ob.; Sidorov, 1973, pp. 424–49; Gindin, 1959; Polikarpov, 1983. Manikovskii retained his post at the GAU after the Bolshevik revolution, until his premature death in 1920.

51 Bovykin, 1959; Gatrell, 1994, pp. 216–34.

52 Tarnovskii, 1958, pp. 242–3, 248–51.

53 RGVIA f.369, op.1, d.96, ll.38–41ob.

54 Bekin, 1915, pp. 8, 21–2. They also recommended 'laying a firm hand on Prodameta'.

55 Manikovskii, 1930, volume 2, pp. 298–301 (Mikhel'son).

56 RGVIA f.369, op.1, d.31, ll.229–31; d.96, ll.215–6; d.98, l.72; *Istoriia organizatsii Vankova*; *Nauchno-tekhnicheskii vestnik*, 1921, nos 4-6 (Vankov); Izmailovskaia, 1920, p. 103.

57 *Vestnik inzhenerov*, 1916, 17 (Kannegiser).

58 *P&T*, 1915, no. 13–14, 5–8 (N.N. Savvin); Pankin, 1915.

59 *Izvestiia TsVPK*, 1916, 97, (Piolunkovskii); Voronkova, 1965.

60 Duz', 1986; Odinetz and Novgorotsev, 1929, pp. 181–2.

61 Maevskii, 1957, pp. 125–39; Uribes, 1961; Beskrovnyi, 1986, p. 109. Sulphuric acid and nitric acid act upon toluene to produce TNT.

62 *Nar.khoz v 1915g.*, 1918, volume 3 (Pantiukov); Ipatieff, 1946, pp. 190–235; Mints, 1975, p. 87.

63 Manikovskii, 1930, volume 2, pp. 61–9; *Trudy pervogo s"ezda*, 1916, pp. 28–9.

64 *EPR*, 1957, volume 1, pp. 72–5.

65 Manikovskii, 1930, volume 2, pp. 293–7.

66 RGVIA f.369, op.3, d.78, ll.170–2. For a defence of the contribution of private enterprise to state defence see *Proizvoditel'nye sily Rossii*, 1917, 4 (Bernatskii).

67 Izmailovskaia, 1920, pp. 16–17, 58, 92–110; *Khoziaistvennaia zhizn'*, 1916, p. 60; *Promyshlennaia perepis'*, 1926, volume 1, p. 42.

68 Il'inskii and Ivanitskii, 1929, p. 106.

69 *Promyshlennaia perepis'*, 1926, volume 1, p. 42. On the haphazard procurement policy of officials who allocated orders for small quantities to a

range of suppliers, altered specifications at short notice, and discouraged standardisation, see Charnovskii, 1921, pp. 43–77; Rozenfel'd and Klimenko, 1961, p. 141; Vankov, 1921.

70 *Nar.khoz. v 1916g.*, 1922, volume 7, pp. 178–9; volume 1, p. 34; Vorob'ev, 1923, pp. 150–53; Sidorov, 1973, p. 383.

71 Tarnovskii, 1995.

72 Zagorsky, 1928, pp. 46, 129. Compare Laverychev, 1963, pp. 253–55, 318–20.

73 Jahn, 1995, pp. 135, 152.

74 Maevskii, 1957, p. 197; Sidorov, 1973, pp. 385–98; Zagorsky, 1928, pp. 134, 140.

75 Pankin, 1915; Manikovskii, 1930, volume 2, p. 306.

76 RGIA f.1276, op.11, d.248, ll.14-17; *Trudy Pervogo s"ezda*, 1916, pp. 58, 66.

77 N.I. Florinskii, report dated 28 February 1916, in Koshik, 1965, p. 143.

CHAPTER 6

Paying for the war, Russian style

After the war the system of government credit will sink ever firmer roots in the soil of the people.
>   *[Aleksei Shingarev, quoted in Strakhov, 2003, p. 39]*

In the apt words of a leading authority on English banking, 'financial policy is never a strong candidate for the attention of the man in the street, and in time of war it has spectacular rivals for the scanty newspaper space'.[1] Certainly the reading public in tsarist Russia was fed a diet of military and political propaganda, while financial matters – with the important exception of publicity given to war loans – were largely confined to the trade press. Behind the scenes, however, vital issues of national security, political power and social welfare were being played out against the backdrop of state finance. Russia's participation in an international coalition ensured that the chief players in this drama included British and French (and, later on, American) officials, advisers and financial magnates. This chapter seeks to integrate technical yet vital details of war finance with the broader political and social dynamics.

The budget deficit – the gap between government revenue and expenditure – could be financed either by incurring domestic debt (long-term and short-term) or by recourse to overseas borrowing, and by an expansion of the money supply. The tsarist government resorted to extensive borrowing during the war. Borrowing had an important political dimension, because creditors needed to be convinced that their investment was safe. A government perceived to be weak or to be devoting little attention to post-war financial viability would suffer in the unforgiving marketplace for loans. Tsarist Russia confronted precisely that difficulty during the war against

Japan and the revolution of 1905. At the outbreak of war, key questions arose in respect of domestic borrowing. By what means could the Russian population be persuaded of the need to save? How much emphasis could be placed upon an appeal to patriotism? To what extent would Russia be able to call upon financial assistance from the Allies?

The financial services sector underpinned economic activity and played its part in the modernisation of Russia before the war. Commercial banks fulfilled a vital role in supplying credit to industry. Russia's banks continued to juggle the various demands made by the state with the needs of their clients in the private sector.[2] Co-operative credit institutions also began to make a bigger contribution to the economy. On the eve of the war total membership stood at around 8.2 million. Loans enabled peasant farmers to acquire livestock and equipment or to tide them over short-term difficulties.[3]

6.1   War budgets, 1915–1917: fiscal convention and innovation

Government revenue and expenditure grew considerably before the war and budget revenue doubled between 1900 and 1913. As Minister of Finances, Vladimir Kokovtsov took much of the credit for balancing the budget after the turbulence of 1904–1906. Much of the growth in revenue was generated by long established items, such as excise duties and receipts from the spirits monopoly and from state-owned property. Attempts at fiscal innovation – substituting indirect taxes as well as a more discriminating portfolio of direct taxes – had relatively little impact. The Russian tax burden stood at a relatively modest 13 per cent on the eve of war.[4] In 1913 27 per cent of government spending went towards state enterprises including railways, 27 per cent to defence, 17 per cent to productive purposes, such as education and agriculture, 16 per cent to general administration and 13 per cent to debt payments.[5] On the eve of war the Treasury boasted a reserve (the so-called 'free balance', the accumulated unspent surpluses of ordinary revenue over ordinary expenditure). This amounted to more than 2,600 million rubles, equivalent to more than three-quarters of total government revenue in 1913, and constituted a kind of financial safety net.

One consideration that dominated official deliberations on financial preparedness was Russia's ability to borrow from domestic and overseas sources. Total government indebtedness increased from 7,858 million rubles in 1900 to 12,745 million rubles in 1914, 58 per cent of it held domestically. Russia accumulated multiple commitments to foreign creditors before 1914. However, the country's standing in the international financial community hardly improved since the Russo-Japanese War. (A foreign loan concluded in 1909 yielded 85 per cent of the nominal issue, only slightly better than in 1906 when tsarism's fortunes had reached their nadir.) Russia's total foreign debt stood at 5,404 million rubles in January 1914.[6] The annual interest charges and dividend payments that these holdings implied were met by generating revenue on the merchandise account (meaning that Russia committed its surplus of export earnings over payments for imports) and by recourse to additional borrowing. Most of the new commitments that Russia entered into on the eve of the war were closely related to defence preparations; chief among these was the foreign loan concluded in 1914 for 500 million rubles, to support the construction of strategic railway lines. Russian officials denied that war would seriously disturb this web of obligations, particularly since Russia maintained healthy reserves of gold and foreign currency. To be sure the former Minister of Finances, Sergei Witte, complained privately that 'from a financial point of view we are considerably less well prepared for war than we were ten years earlier', arguing that the accumulation of gold reserves had not kept pace with the rate of increase of paper rubles. But his crabby assessment is characteristic of many former statesmen who find themselves excluded from the political process.[7]

Table 6.1 provides a summary of the trends in government revenue and expenditure, with the last full year of peace as a means of comparison. In 1913 the Russian government reported a budget surplus, albeit a modest one when expressed in terms of total spending. Thereafter the gap between total expenditure and revenue mushroomed. By 1915 and 1916 the deficit was equivalent to nearly four-fifths of government expenditure. We shall see later how the government financed this deficit.

TABLE 6.1   *Russian government revenue and expenditure, 1913–1918 (million rubles)*

	1913	1914	1915	1916	1917	1918
Total expenditure	3,383	4,858	11,703	18,101	30,607	46,706
Revenue	3,417	2,898	2,828	3,975	5,700	15,580
Surplus/Deficit	+ 34	−1,960	−8,875	−14,126	−24,907	−31,126
Per cent financed by deficit	(1.0)	40.3	75.8	78.3	81.4	66.6

Sources: Michelson et al., 1928, pp. 70, 118–19, 129, 144; Malle, 1985, pp. 169–71.

Government spending consisted of expenditure on civil items and on war-related items, including service charges incurred on short-term debts. Russian officials referred to these twin items as ordinary and extraordinary expenditure respectively. In practice some war-related spending was attributed to the ordinary account, and vice-versa. By including some civil expenditure in the extraordinary budget, the tsarist regime evaded parliamentary scrutiny. For example, allocations in 1915 and 1916 for improvements to the rail network were charged to the 'war fund' (*voennyi fond*), the consolidated fund from which all spending on war was supposed to be drawn. On the other hand, some war-related expenditures, such as transfer payments to soldiers' families and to refugees, were periodically charged to the 'civil' account. Such manipulation went on all the time, usually in order to convey the public impression that the 'ordinary' budget was under tight control.[8]

Ordinary expenditure meant allocating resources to recurrent needs. After the outbreak of war, the war fund became the main means of identifying war-related items, although the 'ordinary' defence budget continued to appear as a separate item in the published accounts. Non-war expenditures stood at 2,927 (3,204) million rubles in 1914, fell to 2,643 (2,837) million in 1915, recovered to 2,922 (3,152) million in 1916, but increased to 4,800 (5,380) million rubles in 1917 ('extraordinary' spending, unrelated to the war, is included in parentheses).[9]

No dramatic change took place in the profile of the government's civil expenditure during the first two and a half years of war. The most noticeable change was the increased cost of procuring goods and services. Local government felt the pinch much more acutely. For example, stringent cuts were imposed on education spending by the zemstvos in 1915 and 1916.[10]

What of war-related spending? The first claim on belligerent government budgets was the cost of mobilisation. In Russia this alone amounted to approximately 540 million rubles, or one-third of the entire direct costs of fighting the Russo-Japanese War.[11] These outlays were followed by the immense cost of sustaining the war effort by purchasing munitions and all the other varied paraphernalia of war, such as uniforms, footwear, transport equipment and so forth. In addition, the war entailed the payment of benefits to the families of those who served in the armed forces. The average daily outlays on the war were as shown in Table 6.2.

The overall distribution of the funds approved by the government for expenditure on the war is summarised in Table 6.3.

Not surprisingly the largest item was for the maintenance and supply of the armed forces, reflecting the increase in the size of the Russian army and

TABLE 6.2   *Average daily outlay on the war effort in Russia, 1914–1917*

	Daily outlay, million rubles	Per soldier per diem, rubles
July–December 1914	10.0	1.8
January–June 1915	17.4	2.9
July–December 1915	27.9	4.1
January–June 1916	33.3	3.8
July–December 1916	46.3	4.2
January–June 1917	55.2	4.9
July–September 1917	82.3	7.5
Total	40.8	4.7

Sources: Prokopovich, 1918, p. 82; *RVMV*, 1925, p. 5.

TABLE 6.3   *Total Russian military appropriations by category of expenditure, 1914–1917*

Category	Million rubles	Per cent
Army	30,945	74.7
Navy	2,058	5.0
Transfer payments:		
Soldiers	3,264	7.9
Refugees	570	1.4
Post & telegraph	122	0.3
Railways:		
New lines	369	0.9
Extension to lines	1,173	2.8
Rolling stock	618	1.5
Port facilities	115	0.3
Waterways & roads	80	0.2
Other	2,080	5.0
Total	41,394	100

Sources and note: *RVMV*, 1925, p. 98; Prokopovich, 1918, p. 81; Michelson et al., 1928, p. 218. Figures refer to appropriations approved up to 1 September 1917; actual expenditure was 38,650 million rubles.

the rising daily costs of feeding and equipping the army over a prolonged period. Daily outlays per soldier increased from a mean of 1.8 rubles in the second half of 1914 to 4.1 rubles in the second half of 1915. The figure stabilised in 1916. However, the rising costs of food procurement in 1917 pushed the daily cost per soldier up to 7.5 rubles.[12] More generous terms were agreed for the upkeep of soldiers' families, equivalent to an extra 210 million rubles per month.[13]

The war led to a reduction in indirect sources of revenue, such as import duties and export levies. During the first year of the war the Treasury's receipts fell as a result of the general decline in the level of normal economic activity and especially the decision to abolish the monopoly on the sale of vodka. The decline in commercial freight traffic led to a reduction in revenue, and increases in the rate of tax on property and excise duties did not compensate for these losses. The situation improved in 1916, because the Treasury derived increased receipts from the transport of freight and passengers (including soldiers), as well as from duties imposed on imports of munitions and other finished goods. Inflation led to a nominal increase in the ruble value of receipts. However, the receipts that accrued to the Treasury became at the same time a charge on the expenditure account (i.e. the war fund), so the improvement was purely notional.[14]

It might be thought that there remained plenty of room for innovative fiscal thinking. However, experimentation was more significant in principle than in practice. Various proposals in 1915 to introduce a state monopoly on the sale of tobacco, matches, oil and insurance came to naught, apparently because of optimism about a speedy resolution of conflict on the battlefield.[15] Later on, arguments were put forward for the creation of state monopolies for the sale of bread, salt, tea, woollens, flax and other items, but the proposals were defeated. The Ministry of Finances believed that it would be difficult to set the retail price; besides, 'the introduction of a state monopoly implies a considerable immediate expenditure on the buying out of existing enterprises and on the construction of new plant.'[16] The government introduced a tax on the sale of wine, consumption of which had increased since the prohibition on the sale of spirits, but this had little impact.

The most important innovations took place during 1916. A novel step was the decision in May to levy a tax on corporate excess profits, at a basic rate of 20 per cent (kicking in at 'excess' profits of 8 per cent of nominal share capital) rising to a top rate of 40 per cent. As with the existing corporate taxes, firms were allowed various deductions (such as generous depreciation charges) to offset their tax liability. The rates doubled in 1917. The benchmark year for 'normal' profits was taken to be 1913–1914. However, the tax was not expected to raise more than 55 million rubles in its first year of operation.[17] This did not prevent industrialists from complaining that the new tax would harm their attempts to replenish Russia's capital stock after the war.[18]

The other innovation was the introduction of an income tax, preparations for which had already been made a decade earlier. In introducing the proposal the Ministry of Finances argued that:

If this tax is based on the total revenue of the taxpayer and is imposed on a progressive scale, and if it provides for a comparatively high limit of exemption, it should prove ... an efficacious remedy for the inequalities of the existing system.[19]

Personal income was taxed at a starting rate of 0.6 per cent (on incomes of 850–950 rubles per annum) rising to a top marginal rate of 12.5 per cent (levied on incomes of more than 400,000 rubles). Estimates of likely revenue from the income tax were, as in the case of the excess profits tax, quite modest: it was thought likely that around 130 million rubles would flow into the Treasury from this source. The wartime increase in wages and salaries led to an extension in the incidence of the income tax. By 1917 it was expected that members of more than one-half of all households would be liable to pay.[20] Set alongside a projection of 3,998.6 million rubles of ordinary revenue in 1917, the two new taxes would contribute less than five per cent of the total. Increases in the rate of duty levied on tobacco and sugar would bring in much the same, albeit with much less fanfare. The government was actually more successful in generating substantially greater sums from the higher volume of railway freight and passenger traffic. It relied heavily upon indirect sources of revenue.[21]

All the same, this new measure did represent a significant change in financial policy, indeed in political life more generally, since the income tax was levied on an individual's personal income. Traditional distinctions, notably those that derived from legal status (*sosloviia*), had no relevance to an income tax: no-one could claim exemption by virtue of belonging to a privileged estate category. The individual taxpayer came instead face to face with the tax inspector (backed by new district assessment boards), and disclosed personal financial details as part of a contract with the state. As one leading economist put it, 'the population ... should show greater willingness to reveal the true state of their incomes'. This amounted to an unprecedented emphasis upon civic duty.[22] The principle was somewhat weakened by the realisation that around half the population would not be liable. (The Duma having insisted on a relatively high threshold for liability, namely an annual income of 1000 rubles, the State Council fixed the limit at 850 rubles.) Even so, many manual workers were expected to be caught in the net.[23]

Setting these important considerations aside, however, three conclusions are inescapable. First, increases in ordinary revenue fell far short of what was needed to finance the war effort. Second, the old regime was not responsible for a fiscal revolution, even though it inaugurated a modern income tax. Third, new ideas of public duty were nevertheless beginning to emerge in the form of an obligation to declare one's personal income (irrespective of social rank) and to subscribe to war loans.

6.2   Government domestic borrowing

The increasing gap between government spending and revenue, a product of the rising costs of war, obliged the tsarist government to adopt various strategies to finance the budget deficit (see Table 6.4). In the first instance, the tsarist government had recourse to long-term and short-term borrowing on the domestic market. During the war the Russian government raised a total of 11,400 million rubles from domestic sources (long-term borrowing), equivalent to around 30 per cent of total war expenditure. The first war loan, for 500 million rubles, was floated in early October 1914. Further long-term loans followed in February, April and October 1915 and in February and October 1916, the latter for 2,000 and 3,000 million rubles respectively. Finally the Provisional Government floated the 'Liberty Loan', for an unrestricted amount, soon after taking power in February 1917.[24]

Between July 1914 and September 1917 Russia also contracted short-term liabilities in the form of 5 per cent Treasury bills that were discounted by the State Bank, on the basis that the bills would be renewed within 12 months, or else redeemed, either by revenue receipts or by long-term loans. The main purpose of these arrangements was to facilitate the issue of additional paper currency without which the war economy would have ground to a halt. By 1 January 1915 short-term floating debt amounted to 800 million rubles (twice the amount issued during the crisis of 1905), but this figure grew fivefold over the next twelve months. On 1 January it stood at 9,775 million rubles. By the beginning of October 1917 Treasury bills were outstanding to the tune of 18,747 million rubles. The State Bank's assets consisted largely of its operations in discounting these short-term Treasury bills.[25]

TABLE 6.4   *Financing the Russian budget deficit, 1914–1917 (million rubles)*

	1914	*1915*	*1916*	*1917*
Total expenditure	4,859	11,562	18,101	30,607
War-related	1,655	8,724	14,049	26,161
Ordinary revenue	2,961	3,008	4,345	5,039
Deficit	1,898	8,554	13,756	25,568
Long-term domestic debt	709	2,879	4,174	3,729
Overseas borrowing	82	2,140	3,665	2,554
Short-term debt	805	3,176	5,611	10,844

Sources: Michelson et al., 1928, pp. 214, 325; Davies, 1958, p. 8.

Private individuals and commercial organisations took up only modest amounts of these bills. Russia's joint-stock banks purchased Treasury bills and the government compelled its suppliers to accept such bills as part payment for goods and services. This produced a slight shift from the State Bank to the private sector: on 1 December 1915 private banks and individuals accounted for 17 per cent of all short-term paper, whereas 12 months later the proportion had risen to 27 per cent. However, by the summer of 1917 the private sector accounted for only 23 per cent.[26] In essence these arrangements resembled the system of war finance in Germany, which likewise depended on the issue of floating debt.[27] Russian practice was not idiosyncratic or irrational, but it testified to the relative unwillingness of the private sector to invest in government debt and to the government's dependence upon the State Bank.

Without entering into unnecessary detail on the terms of long-term loans, we can detect some general principles at work and offer some broad conclusions. The government attempted in late 1915 to extend the market for loans by inviting subscriptions in lower denominations than were normal. Other inducements included tax exemptions and generous advances on the security of government bonds. Strenuous propaganda efforts were made to encourage public subscriptions, for example by opening hundreds of new venues at railway stations, rural telegraph posts and even at paymasters' offices at the front. The government also printed thousands of posters and postcards with colourful images of high-explosive shell and dedicated soldiers. Propaganda films reinforced the message. Brusilov and Alekseev urged their men to subscribe. Appeals were made in 'native' languages. Muslim and Buddhist clerics were enlisted to preach the virtues of government stock.[28] The October 1915 loan was the first to be advertised as a 'war bond', deserving the attention of the 'small investor' who wished to demonstrate his patriotic duty and who (as Finance Minister P.L. Bark said) had money to spare. However, Bark's vision of recruiting peasants to his credit operations – 'democratising' the system, in his words – did not materialise. Most villagers preferred to hoard cash, rather than invest it. Workers, too, expressed little enthusiasm for war bonds and resented attempts to dock their pay in order to force them to subscribe. By late 1916 desperate officials urged the population not to resist war loans, even if they disagreed with government policy.[29] This government borrowing did not 'crowd out' the commercial sector, which continued to place stocks and shares with private subscribers, at least until the spring of 1917. Investment in private enterprise continued to flourish, as stock market activity during the war indicated.[30]

6.3   The import bill, Allied credits and Russia's balance of payments

Russia's reliance upon external borrowing, so crucial to its conduct of the war, must be set in the broad context of its overseas transactions as a whole. At the outbreak of war the web of international economic relations appeared to confer significant advantages on Russia. First, the country was a major exporter of grain and other primary products, the receipts from which were expected to enable Russia to pay for the imports needed to sustain the war effort. Second, Russia had substantial reserves of gold that could if needed be sold in return for foreign goods and services. Third, Russia entered the war as part of an international alliance. This meant, at least in principle, that Russia could call upon its traditional creditors, France and Britain, to extend new government loans. The entry of the USA into the war in April 1917 added a third powerful co-belligerent to the alliance against Germany and Austria–Hungary.[31]

Yet these advantages might prove illusory or at least problematic. Domestic claims on the grain surplus, particularly if it diminished, made it difficult for Russia to generate export earnings or at least required difficult decisions to be made about those imports that Russia could afford. Besides, in the short term there was a question mark over the practicalities of sending Russian grain abroad. In addition, Russia would be bound to enter into serious negotiations for fresh credit in a position of relative weakness, having been such a regular suitor on the international money market, and because doubts would certainly be raised about its long-term stability. This did little to inspire confidence abroad, and it placed Russian negotiators in a very difficult position, much as they had been during the Russo-Japanese War.[32]

Imports of finished goods, such as munitions and transport equipment, could be paid for either by current exports, by the sale of assets (such as securities), or by accumulating new obligations to foreign creditors. Each option entailed costs. By definition the export of goods and services deprived the domestic economy of those items. The value of those exports and thus decisions about the economic merit of exports was also related to the exchange rate. The second strategy, the sale of securities and other assets, was relatively straightforward, but a careful calculation had to be made about the terms and timing of any transaction. In practice, Russia was unable to make much use of this option. The third option, new borrowing from abroad, entailed a commitment on the part of the government to meet its obligations to lenders in the years to come. We shall look at the first and third options in turn.

The demands of war led to a sharp increase in imports. The value of imports remained stable during 1915, but by 1916 they showed an increase of 133 per cent, with Russia's purchases of goods from overseas amounting in total to 7,694 million rubles.[33] Government controls over foreign purchases were relatively weak throughout the war, and virtually non-existent in its first phase, something that aggravated relations between Russia and Britain. As an illustration of the implications for resource allocation one can cite Russia's decision to order wagons and locomotives from overseas. This represented an odd use of scarce foreign exchange, when the government could have used its powers to compel leading engineering firms to produce rolling stock. More serious bottlenecks could have been alleviated by importing machine tools for domestic industry or motorised vehicles for the front line.[34] Yet the Ministry of Transport insisted on importing railway equipment. Nor were decisive measures taken until after the February revolution to curtail the import of luxury items, such as caviar, and these, too, had to be paid for.[35]

Exports were hampered by the closure of established trade routes and the failure to develop alternative routes to any extent. The German frontier, across which a large proportion of goods had been transferred, was obviously closed to traffic. With the entry of Turkey into the war, the Black Sea was also no longer available. Goods could only be exported via ports on the Arctic and Pacific. Given the distances involved both options created enormous problems. The value of Russia's exports between 1913 and 1917 is illustrated in Table 6.5.

By 1915 the value of Russian exports had fallen by 75 per cent compared to their pre-war level and the pre-war surplus on the merchandise trade account had turned into a large deficit. There were no invisible earnings of any significance. As a consequence, the value of the ruble on the foreign exchanges plummeted. Nor were matters helped by the decline in foreign confidence that was brought about by the military reverses in the

TABLE 6.5   *Russia's merchandise trade, 1913–1917 (million rubles)*

	Exports	Imports	Balance
1913	1,520.1	1,374.0	+ 146.1
1914	956.1	1,098.0	− 141.9
1915	401.8	1,138.6	− 736.8
1916	577.3	2,451.2	− 1,873.9
1917	464.0	2,316.7	− 1,852.7

Source: Khromov, 1950, p. 455.

summer of 1915.[36] Financing this deficit required assistance from allied
creditors, in which the British government played the key role. Under the
terms of the huge loan agreed with the Allies in October 1915, Russia
received 500 million rubles from France and 3,000 million rubles from
Britain.[37] Further lines of credit were opened in 1916. By the end of the
war Russia had received nearly half of all credits agreed by the Allies,
enabling it to purchase goods in London and in the USA.[38] Figures for
Russia's balance of payments are given in Table 6.6.

Underlying some of the difficulties in inter-Allied financial relations
was a disagreement over the status and use of Russia's gold reserves.
Successive tsarist ministers of finance had built up substantial gold reserves
before the war, and these served to underpin the Russian currency. During
the war these reserves were swelled by current production. Wartime exigencies made it much more difficult to defend the view that the gold
reserves were sacrosanct. Gold now entered the equation of war finance as
a means of collateral for credit. British Treasury officials were sceptical of
Russia's ability to make full use of the resources put at its disposal. Keynes
maintained that Russia should ship its gold overseas rather than hoard it.
Russian resistance produced a compromise position, namely that Russia
would in effect lend its gold to the Bank of England.[39]

In the event, Britain extended credit far in excess of the gold that it
received from Russia, and the Russian government in turn cited its gold
held abroad, in order to justify further extensions of the note issue.
Russian shipments of gold, totalling 464 million rubles, took place on four
occasions, in October 1914, May 1916, November 1916 and July 1917.
Shipments were made in conditions of great secrecy: 'the English cruiser

TABLE 6.6   *Russia's balance of payments, 1913 and 1915–1916: a provisional
calculation (million rubles)*

	1913	1915	1916
Imports	− 1,374	− 1,138	− 2,451
Exports	+ 1,520	+ 402	+ 577
Deficit/surplus	+ 146	− 736	− 1874
Interest on public debt	− 221	− 307	− 490
Interest on private debt	− 150	− 136	
Repatriated profits	− 30	− 20	
Net tourist expenditures	− 292	− 29	
Other	− 13	− 192	
Total	− 578	− 1420	

Source: Harrison et al. forthcoming (Gatrell), Cambridge University Press.

Drake ... on arriving at Archangel, cast anchor on the high seas at a distance of thirty miles from the coast and the gold was carried out to them by night on lighters. Despite these precautions the Germans were apprised of this shipment'. Subsequently Russian gold was shipped via Vladivostok, thence to Vancouver and thence to Ottawa where the British had established a special depository.[40] In January 1916 the State Bank reported Russian gold reserves, held domestically and overseas, of 2,260 million rubles (646 million held abroad). A year later they stood at 3,617 million rubles (2,141 million held abroad). Most of these foreign reserves represented Russia's foreign borrowing.[41]

The transactions mentioned above, expressed in terms of Russia's total war debt held in foreign countries, beggared belief. External debt stood at 3,971 million rubles on 1 January 1914. By 1 March 1917 this had grown to 9,160 million rubles. On 25 October 1917 it reached 11,194 million rubles. However, even these enormous sums paled into insignificance when set alongside the newly acquired domestic debt. At the outbreak of war Russia's external debt represented 45 per cent of total debt. By October 1917 it had fallen to around 23 per cent.[42]

6.4   The behaviour of prices

Constraints on the government's capacity to raise revenue led inexorably to an increase in the rate of emission of paper money. Between July 1914 and March 1917 the amount of currency in circulation increased from 1,630 million to 9,950 million rubles (Table 6.7). By October 1917 the volume of notes in circulation had virtually doubled, reaching 17,290 million rubles, the Provisional Government having extended the right of issue on a further five occasions. At the outbreak of war, notes in circulation were entirely covered by gold, but by the February Revolution only 15 per cent of the currency was covered by gold. In the autumn of this year the figure had dropped to a mere 6 per cent. By October 1917 the government was issuing notes each day with a face value of 127 million rubles, three times the rate of issue a mere two months earlier.[43]

Generally speaking grain prices did not accelerate dramatically in the first 18 months of the war, because exporters now unloaded their goods on to the domestic market. The price of other commodities, however, rose at a faster rate. In 1914 prices as a whole rose by around 27 per cent and in 1915 by a further 20 per cent. During this phase the chief stimulus was military purchases.[44] Prices rose by 94 per cent in 1916, and in the first half of 1917 they increased by a further 125 per cent.

TABLE 6.7   *Monetary expansion in Russia, 1914–1917*

	Notes in circulation, million rubles	Index (July 1914 = 100)
1 July 1914	1,630	100
1 January 1915	2,947	181
1 July 1915	3,756	230
1 January 1916	5,617	345
1 July 1916	6,628	407
1 January 1917	9,097	558
1 March 1917	9,950	610
1 July 1917	13,055	801
1 October 1917	17,290	1061

Source: Katzenellenbaum, 1925, pp. 56–7.

Trends in wholesale and retail prices are given in Table 6.8. Underlying the rapid onset of inflation after 1916 was the creation of money and the growing intensity of competition between state and private sectors for limited available resources. To some extent the impact of price inflation was moderated by increases in taxation, which served to withdraw purchasing power from the economy. Yet the rise in note circulation pointed to difficulties being stored up for the future. As Prokopovich put it, 'it is possible not to subscribe to government loans, it is possible not to buy government paper, it is possible to refuse to pay one's taxes, but one cannot refuse payment in notes for one's goods and services'. He might have added that the alternative was to substitute barter for a money economy, a development that started to take root following the Bolshevik seizure of power.[45]

The behaviour of prices had serious economic, social and political consequences, some of which have already been mentioned in earlier chapters. Inflation disrupted established economic ties and stoked public resentment towards the tsarist regime. It divided the dispossessed, allowing urban workers to feel that peasants benefited at their expense. It convinced plebeian Russians that speculators had driven up the price of basic goods, in order to extract greater economic advantage. Radical politicians believed that industrial profiteers had made a killing at the expense of workers. Entrepreneurs rushed to renegotiate contracts with clients, in order to secure more favourable terms. Finally, inflation undermined the standard of living of hitherto relatively comfortable social groups. Those on fixed incomes, such as rentiers, or whose salaries were difficult to negotiate upwards, such as local government employees, became disillusioned by the conduct of a regime that displayed so little concern for their income and

TABLE 6.8　*Indexes of Russian wholesale and retail prices, 1913–1918*

Year	Col. 1 Wholesale prices	Col. 2 Wholesale prices		Col. 3 Wholesale prices, foodstuffs	Col. 4 Retail prices, USSR territory	Col. 5 Retail prices, Moscow
1913		100	100	100	100	100
1st half 1914	100	106	110		101	101
2nd half 1914	101			106	102	
1st half 1915	115	117	153	138	120	130
2nd half 1915	141			145	140	
1st half 1916	238	208	219	178	166	206
2nd half 1916	398			–	240	
1st half 1917	702	327	434	–	365	775
2nd half 1917	1171			–	982	
1st half 1918	–	639	953	–	–	5680

Source and notes: Harrison et al. forthcoming (Gatrell), Cambridge University Press. Column 1 is an unknown commodity sample, quoted in Sidorov, 1960, p. 147. Column 2 is taken from *Trudy TsSU*, 1926, volume 3, pp. 6–49; the left hand column refers to raw material inputs to wood, foodstuffs, mineral, leather and textiles, the right hand column to inputs to other branches of industry. Column 3 gives the wholesale prices of 13 food items according to Gosplan, quoted in Kokhn, 1926, p. 20. Column 4, Kokhn, 1926, pp. 160–61, is the price of a basket of 16 food items, 9 items of clothing and footwear, and 4 miscellaneous items, including soap, fuel and housing costs, weighted according to working class household budgets in 1918. Column 5 is a Gosplan index for Moscow city shop prices, from *Trudy TsSU*, 1926, volume 1, p. 11.

social status. Those who did relatively well out of the war – one thinks in particular of skilled workers in the defence industries – had no affection for the old regime in the first place.[46]

6.5　The Russian banking system

We have already alluded to aspects of the role played by the Russian banking system during the war, in financing defence industry. To what extent did the war bring about structural changes to the system, and how significant were those changes?

The banking system before the war comprised the State Bank, joint-stock (commercial) banks and secondary financial institutions such as state-owned savings banks, the Peasants' and Nobles' Land banks, mutual credit associations and municipal banks. As the bank of issue, the State Bank was ultimately responsible for the integrity of Russia's currency. In addition to this key role, the Bank supported the private sector by advancing funds to the commercial banks that were secured by various kinds of collateral. Finally, the State Bank also had a tradition of providing financial assistance – usually unpublicised – to industrial and other enter-prises.[47]

Russia's joint-stock banks, like the State Bank, held deposits on behalf of customers and in turn supplied credit to their clients. Russia's commercial banks demonstrated some heterogeneity in their business practices. The St Petersburg banks prided themselves on their international orientation and links to the financial centres of London, Berlin and Paris. The leading bankers enjoyed close ties to government officials (many of them having spent time in government service). Moscow banks tended to focus much more closely on the development of the Russian textile trade, which gave them a particular interest in the development of commercial links throughout the Russian empire as a whole. Moscow bankers criticised their counterparts in the capital for being dependent upon the government bureaucracy, whereas they portrayed themselves as guardians of a more authentically 'Russian spirit'. As we saw earlier, this stance led Moscow merchants to take the lead in forging new voluntary organisations that challenged the primacy of government and big business.[48]

The war inevitably affected the nature of banking. Discounting bills of exchange dwindled in importance as firms did more of their business in cash. Instead, the banks were mobilised. The money market responded to the issue of floating debt (in the form of short-term Treasury bills) as well as consolidated government debt, largely thanks to the support provided by the State Bank. Commercial banks and state savings banks supported the credit operations of the state, by mobilising private deposits belonging to their customers and by investing their own funds. A syndicate of leading commercial banks in Petrograd handled the loans. When the banks announced disappointing results in placing government debt on the market (even with an extension of the subscription period), they extracted favourable terms from the Treasury as a condition of absorbing the debt themselves. The arrangements demonstrated the close relationship between government and financial institutions, which depended in the last resort upon credits extended by the State Bank.[49] The State Bank also extended credit to its commercial clients to enable them to purchase other kinds of securities. By 1917 the commercial banks, having achieved a degree of independence from the State Bank, were once more seeking its help as business uncertainty intensified.[50]

By February 1917 the joint-stock banks held securities to the tune of 3,500 million rubles, the bulk of their portfolio comprising correspondents' accounts and other loans ('on call' loans), with share certificates acting as collateral.[51] The major players increased their grip on key sectors, acquiring stocks of sugar and cotton. The powerful Russo-Asiatic Bank controlled a network of companies, giving it influence over the trade in oil, grain, iron and steel, coal, timber and other products, and it also traded shares in railway companies.[52] However, this did not prevent commercial banks from expressing concern, in particular about the loss of business when private investors purchased stocks and shares with their surplus cash rather than placing it on deposit. Some industrialists, too, sought independence from the big banks by forming their own financial institutions, specialising in a particular branch of industry. When Russian bankers established an Association of Commercial Banks in 1916, this may have been an indication that they wished to retain their influence and sought to counter this growing tendency. They were worried about upstarts such as Vtorov and Iaroshinskii who were challenging the existing commercial banks, and they had rivals in the mobilisation of finance in the shape of rural savings banks, the Nobles' Land bank, insurance companies and mortgage banks. They were anxious about the growth of cash transactions, which undermined their role as financial intermediaries. Finally they were concerned to fend off the growing demand from 'educated society' for closer government supervision of their activities.[53]

Peasants, merchants and even workers whose money incomes grew as a result of transfer payments, sales of foodstuffs and increased wages deposited cash in interest-earning accounts, at least during the first 18 months of the war. No less significant for the bulk of the population were the loan and savings associations and credit associations that emerged before the war. The growth of their business continued during the war. Membership of these organisations increased from 8.2 to 10.5 million persons between 1914 and 1917 and, taking account of household size, this probably represented a total participation of around 60 million. However, these institutions made fewer loans to their members during the war. Available funds were instead invested in government stock as part of the ongoing process of financial mobilisation.[54]

Conclusions

Russia's First World War was an expensive business, reflecting its duration and the size and requirements of the armed forces. Total war-related spending amounted to 38,650 million rubles, compared with 2,295 million rubles spent on the Russo-Japanese War. Put another way, outlays on the war were equivalent to 12.4 years of total government expenditure during the last full year of peace. Of this amount, some 62 per cent was covered by domestic loans (long-term and short-term, including discounting Treasury bills) and foreign borrowing (foreign loans represented 20 per cent of the total means of covering war expenditure). The remainder was financed by spending the 'free balance', accounting for around 7 per cent, and by taxation.[55]

The tsarist regime thus financed its contribution to the European war effort by relying heavily upon loans and an expansion of the note issue. Domestic lenders can be credited with a substantial contribution – war loans raised more than 11,000 million rubles – but this was a modest sum when set against total war expenditure. The contribution of the banking sector and the investing public was greater during the first year of the war, whereas the proportion contributed by external loans rose slightly over time.[56] This does not, however, exhaust the significance of borrowing. Raising money was a matter of financial mobilisation. Subscription and conscription, financial contributions and citizenship were closely related and this explains why strenuous efforts were made to popularise war loans, by means of a concerted publicity drive and the involvement of lesser credit institutions alongside the big joint-stock banks.

The Russian state found itself encumbered by debt. By the time of its withdrawal from the war, total government debt stood at between 49,000 and 53,000 million rubles, of which 35 per cent comprised credits from the State Bank, 33 per cent various long-term loans and 12 per cent short-term Treasury bills. Externally held debt represented between 20 and 23 per cent of the total. The interest payable on this debt absorbed around 11 per cent of total spending during the war.[57] The Bolsheviks subsequently made much of the financial thrall in which Russia found itself in relation to the imperialist allies, seeing in this subordination yet another reason for leaving the war and cancelling Russia's debts.

Other things being equal, debt had important implications in terms of prospective interest payments. One leading Russian economist anticipated a long-term budget deficit once these payments were taken into account, alongside the obligation to reconstruct the shattered economy (including taking care of national security) and to make social welfare payments, not to mention the gaping hole left in the budget by prohibition. Fridman's solution was to increase income tax and property taxes (including death duties), to raise revenue from state monopolies on the sale of tea, sugar, oil and tobacco and to improve receipts from state forests. Sobolev, another critic of the government's financial policy, argued that the 'income tax ought to be made the foundation of the fiscal system and not be regarded, as it is at present by the Ministry of Finances, as subsidiary taxation'.[58]

The economic consequences of a large and sustained increase in the budget deficit took the form of sustained growth in the monetary base. In other words, Russia financed a significant part of the deficit by printing money. The money thus created flowed into the hands of those who, directly or indirectly, as entrepreneurs, intermediaries or workers, contributed to the war effort. It added to total demand and enabled household consumers to vie with central government for available goods and services. As a consequence, the government was confronted with an inflationary spiral that persisted beyond the collapse of the old regime. Paper money helped sustain the Russian war effort until February 1917. Thereafter, in the words of one authority, it financed both 'war and revolutionary ambition'.[59]

Only a modest proportion of total expenditure – around 24 per cent – was met out of taxation. (Russia was not alone in pursuing this course. In Britain this proportion was around 26 per cent, and in Germany it reached 17 per cent, with corresponding inflationary consequences.)[60] Government financial policy was unable to stem the rising tide of inflation. In vain did ministers pin their hopes upon voluntary savings as a means of absorbing the increased purchasing power in the hands of the population. The government mobilised money by encouraging the banks to invest private deposits in government war loans. Some of those who had cash in hand were tempted to place it with the banks. Before 1917 many peasants hoarded cash as the opportunities to exchange their cash for goods fast evaporated, and this contributed to the economic and financial crisis that sharpened following the February Revolution. By then – recalling Sayers's remarks at the beginning of this chapter – Russia's newspapers were full of little else.

Note on further reading

The standard account of Russian war finance in English is the collaborative volume by Michelson et al., 1928, which may be supplemented by other informative contemporary accounts, such as Eliacheff, 1919. There is no up-to-date treatment of the subject in English. Major works in Russian include Sidorov, 1960 (on financial policy), and Shepelev, 1973 (on joint-stock companies). See also the recent monograph by Beliaev, 2002, the relevant chapters of Prokopovich, 1918, and Volobuev, 1962. Foreign aid is best approached via Neilson, 1984. For a convenient summary of war finance in all belligerent countries see the relevant chapters of Ferguson, 1999, and Strachan, 2001.

References

1 Sayers, 1956, p. 2.

2 Crisp, 1976, Chapter 5.

3 Kayden and Antsiferov, 1929, pp. 260, 285.

4 Michelson et al., 1928, p. 246.

5 Raffalovich, ed., 1918, p. 331 (Bogolepov).

6 Shebaldin, 1959, pp. 178–9, 190; Gindin, 1957.

7 Sidorov, 1960, p. 102; Gatrell, 1994, pp. 311–12.

8 Prokopovich, 1918, p. 90; Michelson, et al., 1928, pp. 65, 77, 216. The tsarist government disguised some of the costs of regular business (such as the maintenance of railway lines, as well as sanitation, geodesic and irrigation work) by transferring them to the extraordinary budget.

9 Michelson, et al., 1928, pp. 65, 215, 244.

10 Odinetz and Novgorotsev, 1929, pp. 67–8, 90; Michelson, et al., 1928, pp. 191–4.

11 Prokopovich, 1918, pp. 75, 78–9. Bark had earlier put the cost at 458 million rubles.

12 Prokopovich, 1918, p. 82 for full breakdown of expenditure, daily expenditure, size of armed forces, and expenditure per soldier per day.

13 Michelson et al., 1928, pp. 193–4.

14 Michelson et al., 1928, p. 141. Death duties were also increased.

15 Michelson et al., 1928, p. 131.

16 Michelson et al., 1928, p. 53 for this quotation.

17 Kulisher, 1917; Tomsen, 1916. The windfall profits that many companies earned in 1914–1915 were not liable to tax. Furthermore, companies that did not exist in 1913 escaped the excess profits tax altogether. France and Britain introduced an excess profits tax in 1916, Germany did so only in 1918.

18 P&T, 1915, 33, pp. 669–72 (anonymous). The industrial lobby persuaded the Ministry of Finances to water down its initial scheme.

19 Quoted in Michelson et al., 1928, p. 148.

20 Sorin, 1916. The tax came into force on 1 January 1917; returns could be submitted up to and including 30 April. For the position in Germany (where income tax played a modest role in war finance) and Britain (where it played a more 'vigorous' part), see Balderston, 1989.

21 *Proekt*, p. 25. But see Prokopovich, 1918, pp. 92–5, for a critique of the tax on railway freight introduced in 1914, on the grounds that it discriminated in favour of luxury items.

22 Michelson et al., 1928, pp. 147, 161 (quoting Sobolev), 169–78. See also Kotsonis, 2004. Note the extension of surveillance implied in the rule that employers and financial institutions were obliged to report payments made to each individual. Meanwhile tax inspectors assumed the task of enforcing the citizen's duty to the state.

23 Michelson et al., 1928, pp. 172, 196. Michelson notes that in 1917 the depreciation of the currency made so many people liable 'that it became technically impossible to collect the tax'.

24 These figures take no account of short-term issues with a maturity of less than 10 years. Michelson et al., 1928, p. 249. For the Liberty Loan see Chapter 9.

25 Fisk, 1924, pp. 108–9; Michelson et al., 1928, pp. 220, 282.

26 The state's share included state savings banks. Michelson et al., 1928, p. 285.

27 Around three quarters of all Treasury bills in the Reich (prior to 1917) were held primarily by the Reichsbank, much the same proportion of bills as was held by the Russian State Bank. In Britain, by contrast, the London money market absorbed government Treasury bills with much greater alacrity. Balderston, 1989, p. 238.

28 Michelson et al., 1928, p. 269; Strakhov, 2003, p. 34.

29 Tugan-Baranovskii, ed., 1917; *EPR*, 1957, volume 2, p. 30; Strakhov, 2003, pp. 33, 35–7. This is not to say that the government's operations failed completely; the rate of interest on government loans and the issue price suggest that the government did succeed in driving a favourable bargain. In other words the terms did not deteriorate, such was the abundance of funds available for investment.

30 Shepelev, 1969; Shepelev, 1973, pp. 294–314.

31 Fisk, 1924, pp. 4–8, 31–33.

32 Beliaev, 2002, p. 368; Crisp, 1976, pp. 206, 214.

33 Babichev, 1956.

34 An argument made by Litvinov-Falinskii in November 1915. His memo is reprinted in Manikovskii, 1930, volume 2, pp. 293–7.

35 Michelson et al., 1928, p. 397.

36 See the table of the monthly ruble exchange rate in London between August 1914 and November 1917, in Michelson et al., 1928, pp. 398–9.

37 A further 2,000 million rubles were loaned in order to support an extension of the right of the Treasury to issue paper currency.

38 Michelson et al., 1928, p. 312; Hardach, 1977, p. 146.

39 Details in Beliaev, 2002, pp. 365–466; Neilson, 1984, pp. 65, 67.

40 Fisk, 1924, p. 135.

41 Barnett, 2001; Neilson, 1984, p. 67; Katzenellenbaum, 1925, p. 53; Beliaev, 2002, p. 574.

42 Volobuev, 1962, p. 379.

43 This figure includes the so-called 'Kerenskii' tokens. Different figures were reported by the State Bank. Beliaev, 2002, p. 574.

44 Michelson et al., 1928, p. 392.

45 Prokopovich, 1918, p. 111; Michelson et al., 1928, p. 259.

46 Compare Ferguson, 1999, pp. 425–6.

47 Crisp, 1976, pp. 106–7, 135–9.

48 Michelson et al., 1928, pp. 356–7, for the relative importance of these institutions in terms of deposits held. See also Crisp, 1976, pp. 144–5, 151–2; Gatrell, 1986, pp. 211–13; Rieber, 1982, pp. 366–70.

49 Michelson et al., 1928, pp. 249–59; Strakhov, 2003.

50 Shepelev, 1963, p. 163; Michelson et al., 1928, p. 262; Katzenellenbaum, 1925, p. 66.

51 Gindin, 1997, p. 110; Michelson et al., 1928, p. 264.

52 Kitanina, 1969.

53 RGIA, f. 1276, op.12, d. 344, ll. 9-10; *Novyi ekonomist*, 13 June 1915 (Migulin) and 5 November 1916 (Iazylich); Gindin, 1997, pp. 112–13; Shepelev, 1963, pp. 167–8.

54 Kayden and Antsiferov, 1929, pp. 260, 272. These figures exclude enemy-occupied territory.

55 Most of the free balances went to cover the costs of mobilisation. Michelson et al., 1928, pp. 235, 370; Fisk, 1924, p. 56.

56 Prokopovich, 1918, p. 122.

57 Volobuev, 1962, p. 379. Compare Hardach, 1977, p. 168, and Fisk, 1924, p. 31, and the caveat entered by Michelson et al., 1928, p. 241. The calculations in Gindin, 1957, exclude the short-term obligations of the Treasury held by the State Bank.

58 Michelson et al., 1928, pp. 157–61.

59 Katzenellenbaum, 1925, p. 51.

60 Balderston, 1989, p. 228.

CHAPTER 7

Feeding Russia: Food supply as Achilles' heel

The collapse of food supply, the frenzied speculation, the possible famine – these are the result of ignorant and incompetent policy. (Rodzianko to Nicholas II, February 1917)
I simply don't understand these questions ... (Nicholas II, September 1916)

[quotations in Kitanina, 1985, pp. 280, 301.]

None of the belligerent countries found it straightforward to secure a sufficiency of food for combatants and for civilian consumers during the war. Food supply entailed grappling with inputs and production, as well as with complex problems of storage, transport and finance. Decisions had to be taken about the mechanisms for extracting food from producers, including the extent to which market mechanisms should give way to administrative intervention. Food supply also involved issues of nutritional culture, as consumers wrestled with difficult choices about what to eat and what items to forego.

In Russia the production and distribution of food had been a matter of intense public debate for more than a generation. Concerns were expressed about the viability of privately owned farms and about the extent to which peasant farming could be relied upon to satisfy the needs of the Russian market. On the eve of the war the landed gentry accounted for only 12 per cent of total grain production but around 22 per cent of the marketable surplus. In normal circumstances peasants entered the market to buy and sell food, in order to obtain the cash needed to pay taxes and to buy consumer goods, but these arrangements were quite delicate and liable to be disrupted by changes in the terms of trade between town and country. Peasant family farms probably retained around two-thirds of their output, but peasant producers still accounted for some 78 per cent of available surpluses.[1]

The chief crops produced on peasant farms were rye, buckwheat, potatoes and flax, although peasants had begun to cultivate more wheat and barley, particularly in the southern provinces.[2] In the last year of peace, field crops accounted for around two-thirds of total agricultural production.[3] The rural economy was diversifying as peasants exploited the opportunities available by supplying new urban centres with fresh meat, fruit, vegetables and dairy products. Peasants who migrated to western Siberia found prosperity in livestock farming and in co-operative marketing of dairy products.[4]

The growth of agricultural output as a whole relied heavily on the cultivation of additional land rather than upon significant gains in yields or labour productivity, but no-one expected that Russia would go hungry as a result of a prolonged war. Large estates in the rich farmlands to the south and south-east ensured a substantial grain surplus which found its way on to European markets before 1914. In moments of extreme necessity this surplus could be diverted to domestic consumption and both the government and the private sector had invested in grain storage facilities and grain elevators. Russia's military planners had evolved a reasonably efficient system for procuring food. Unless the harvest failed badly, war seemed unlikely to create an intolerable strain.[5]

The crisis in Russia's food supply during the winter of 1916 helped topple the old regime and threatened to create sufficient upheaval in towns, garrisons and trenches to jeopardise the war effort itself. Why did shortages arise? Did they occur because of a failure in production, brought about by the notoriously erratic grain harvest, by a wartime shortage of labour, draught animals and equipment, or by some combination of these factors? Alternatively, did shortages occur because of a breakdown in the arrangements for obtaining grain from food producers and, if so, what role was played by policy errors?

7.1   Agriculture: the main inputs

The hired labour force in agriculture fell by around two-thirds between 1913 and 1916. Mobilisation immediately deprived large landowners of around 800,000 labourers, equivalent to two-fifths of the total agricultural labour force before the war. Overall this sector had a significant productivity advantage, with output per hectare being as much as 50 per cent greater than on the average peasant farm. However, reductions in the supply of agricultural equipment made it difficult to substitute capital for labour and, as a result, landowners harvested less grain, which was left to rot on the stalk.[6] In subsequent years sowings also declined. A decline in the sown area on larger farms was bound to have an adverse effect on grain marketings.

The consequences of mobilisation were not confined to the large estates. In some provinces individual peasant households were completely deprived of able-bodied men, an outcome that the system of conscription was supposed to avoid. The mobilisation of draught animals also placed Russian farmers in great difficulty. Middling peasant households reportedly sold animals in 1914, having no use for them once able-bodied men had been called up. Wealthier farmers tried to conceal their horses, moving them between districts in order to evade the draft.[7]

Traditionally Russian agriculture relied heavily on animate rather than inanimate forms of energy for the basic tasks of sowing, harvesting and threshing. In large-scale farming, steps had been taken since the turn of the century to mechanise farming operations, but landlords relied heavily on the labour of local peasants or on migrant labour from the Central Agricultural Region, 'Little Russia' and the south-west. Thus, for the most part, agricultural production meant back-breaking toil by human labour.[8]

On most farms a horse or team of oxen commonly pulled the traditional light wooden plough (*sokha*). By the beginning of 1917 the army had appropriated around 2.10 million horses, equivalent to ten per cent of the horse population.[9] Villagers were left with the oldest or youngest animals, oxen included, which were least suited for strenuous field work, and it was increasingly expensive to buy replacement animals. The large estates in the southern and Baltic provinces also suffered. Overall, however, Russian agriculture had a surfeit of horses, to the extent that one-third of available horse power may have been unutilised: 'peasants had horses enough and to spare during the war'.[10]

The burden of cultivating the fields and harvesting grain fell increasingly upon peasant women and elderly men. By 1916 able-bodied women outnumbered men by a factor of two to one. Refugee labour also helped to offset the drain of manpower to the army.[11] Up to 800,000 refugees were believed capable of making themselves available for work, although only 354,000 were actually employed in Russian agriculture by October 1916. Their numbers dropped to 250,000 by 1917, still an impressive total amounting to around eight per cent of the total labour force on private land.[12]

The war brought the manufacture of agricultural equipment and machinery to a virtual halt. By December 1914 domestic production had fallen by one-third. The Ministry of Agriculture at first took a sanguine view of the supply of farm implements and machinery, arguing that there were sufficient reserves to see farmers through the war.[13] Factory output declined by around 50 per cent between 1913 and 1916, and small-scale production could not possibly offset this. Imports, which had accounted for around 45 per cent of the market in 1913, fell sharply. As a result, total purchases of agricultural machinery by 1916 stood at little more than one-tenth of the pre-war level. Once again, large estates were hit badly. Peasant farmers, with their modest stock of capital equipment, made whatever running repairs were necessary. Those who had recently invested in more sophisticated machinery doubtless reverted ruefully to old habits, although co-operatives helped by supplying farm tools or arranging for the collective cultivation of land.[14]

7.2   The productive effort

No analysis of Russian food production can be undertaken without understanding the methods by which data were obtained. Prior to the war, the Central Statistical Committee (TsSK), a department of the Ministry of the Interior, obtained details of the area under crops and sample estimates of the grain yield. Multiplying the sown area by yield gave a total figure for the harvest, but the results were sensitive to the quality of the raw data on sown area and grain yields. One authority believed that the TsSK underestimated peasant grain sowings but heavily exaggerated the area sown on private estates. The official figures were also thought to have underestimated grain yields.[15] The TsSK continued to collect data in 1914 and 1915, but in 1916 statisticians employed by the zemstvos and the municipalities took part in an all-Russian agricultural census in an attempt to seize control of the collection and processing of economic data. The exercise was repeated the following year in preparation for a projected reform of land tenure. Consequently the published data for 1916 cannot be compared directly with the TsSK data for 1915 and earlier years. The results diverged quite sharply from those of the TsSK. Zemstvo statisticians claimed that their results gave a more accurate indication of the sown area and concluded that the TsSK data had under-stated sowings by around nine per cent. The 1916 and 1917 figures were themselves distorted by the reluctance of peasant informants to give accurate responses, lest they encourage official intervention to take grain.[16]

The two components of grain production were the area under crops and crop yields. Notwithstanding the difficulties mentioned earlier, the war did not result in a dramatic curtailment in the sown area on the territory that remained in Russian hands. During 1914 and 1915 the area sown to food and fodder grains, as well as potatoes, remained slightly above the pre-war level, although the area sown to minor crops fell quite sharply. In 1916 total sowings probably contracted by just over five per cent compared with the 1909–1913 average, most of this being accounted for by a reduction in the area sown to cereals. The most serious contraction took place on privately owned estates, where sowings fell by half between 1913 and 1915. An additional factor may have been the measures taken against German colonists.[17] Peasant farmers increased their sowings in 1915 by more than 20 per cent, and even more in the black-earth provinces and in Siberia. During 1917 peasants in some regions actually had more land under plough than during the previous year.[18]

A rough approximation of the size of the cereal harvest on the territory continuously in Russian hands reveals sharp differences in the behaviour of individual crops.[19] In 1914 the total harvest fell by more than one-fifth over the record set the previous year and was more than three per cent lower than the pre-war average. Since the sown area remained more or less stable, the contraction reflected a poor grain yield. Rye was much less badly affected than the other crops. Strong regional differences were also evident: an extremely good performance in central Asia, the Caucasus and parts of Siberia was offset by a poor harvest in Vitebsk, Vologda, Tula, Penza and Kazan, where production fell by more than 40 per cent compared with the average for 1909–1913.[20] Figures for the Russian cereal harvest are presented in Table 7.1.

In 1915 rye and wheat made a strong showing – yields of these crops were well above the pre-war average – but the modest recovery in oats and barley still left output of these crops below the pre-war level. Overall the harvest in 1915 exceeded the pre-war average by 10 per cent whereas the 1916 harvest was 10 per cent *lower* than in 1909–1913. Grain yields fell by around four per cent compared with the pre-war average. However, as Demosthenov stated, 'there is nothing very alarming revealed by these figures', particularly in view of the widespread conviction that the recorded figures for 1916 were too low.[21]

The war dislocated the food processing industries, which were deprived of skilled labour.[22] Flour milling suffered from a shortage of rolling stock and fuel and by spring 1916 the mills working for the civilian market had reduced their output by one-third. (Some millers exaggerated the extent of the crisis in order to obtain additional supplies of labour and fuel.) Shortages also reflected millers' attempts to evade price controls by with-

TABLE 7.1   *An index of the Russian cereal harvest (1909–1913 average = 100)*

Year	Total harvest	Rye	Wheat	Oats	Barley
1909–1913	100 (100)	100	100	100	100
1913	120.4 (117.8)	110.9	136.3	116.3	1204
1914	96.5 (99.7)	100.1	105.7	89.5	88.8
1915	110.2 (109.6)	123.2	112.7	98.1	97.2
1916	91.3 (90.3)	102.7	79.6	94.7	84.7
1917	87.6 (87.0)	83.1	93.8	87.6	84.7

Sources and notes: Struve et al., 1930, p. 308. Column 1 includes the 57 provinces of European Russia and Siberia (excluding Poland, the Caucasus and Kuban, Turkestan, Kovno, Courland, Vilna, Grodno, Volynia, Podolia, Iakutsk and the Far Eastern territories). Figures in brackets are from Wheatcroft, 1980, pp. 216–17. The total includes the four principal grains plus buckwheat and millet.

holding supplies of flour. According to Demosthenov, 'the root of the trouble was not in a smaller production of flour, but in the inability of the mills to work to their full capacity, so as to satisfy the heavier demand for flour'.[23]

The area sown to sugar beet remained constant until 1917. Several provinces increased sowings of beet, helping offset the loss of production in the vicinity of the front. Big refineries cultivated their own sugar beet. The output of refined sugar actually increased to record levels in 1915 and, despite a decline in the following year, output remained at around the 1914 level. Much more critical was the decline in the production of sugar beet during 1917, by as much as one-fifth on peasant allotments. Part of the crop was lost because of delays in gathering the harvest. Labour unrest contributed to a significant reduction in the production of refined sugar, which fell by around 21 per cent in 1917. Meanwhile, the cultivation of higher value crops such as sunflower, tobacco and flax expanded at the expense of hemp and potatoes, suggesting that the war did not interrupt qualitative improvements in arable farming.[24]

The production of meat and dairy products likewise gave no cause for immediate concern. Siberian butter – something of a success story before 1914 – was increasingly snapped up by the army and became a government monopoly in 1915. Although the figures should be treated with caution, peasants appear to have increased the stock of younger animals between 1914 and 1916, particularly pigs and sheep. Slaughtered livestock enabled farmers to sell meat and animal hides to the army, but there are also suggestions that peasants themselves consumed greater quantities of pork and lamb.[25]

7.3   Food supply: prescriptions and policies

Before the war, Russia had a fairly sophisticated system of grain distribution, as befitted a country that stood high in the world league of food exporters. The efforts of food dealers, co-operatives, warehouse owners and railway administrators were devoted primarily to the movement of grain from the main producing regions in the Central Agricultural Region and the south-west to the main centres of consumption and to Russia's ports. Around one-third of all cereal production reached the market, with roughly equal proportions being destined for the home and foreign markets. The main exporting provinces in Ukraine and the north Caucasus despatched wheat and barley to the Black Sea ports. Other provinces with surplus grain such as Samara, Bessarabia, Tambov, Saratov and Orenburg sent grain over long distances to the expanding home markets of the Central Industrial Region and the north-west. Storage facilities included around 50 large grain elevators, as well as several hundred warehouses and other granaries, including those at the chief seaports. The State Bank financed an expansion in the network of grain elevators. Commercial banks extended credit to producers using grain as collateral. The supply of meat and butter over long distances also began to improve as a result of the introduction of refrigerated freight cars. Thus the trade in foodstuffs was better organised when war broke out.[26]

Regional aspects of food production and consumption also need to be kept in mind. In 1914–1915, largely as a result of the increase in troop concentrations, the Northern Consumer Region (NCR) required additional grain, less than two-thirds of which could be supplied from within the regional economy. Both the Southern Producer Region (SPR) and the Eastern Producer Region (EPR) had significant surpluses available, the first because of the cessation of exports, the second because of a sizeable increase in the grain harvest. In the Central Producer Region (CPR) the harvest was poor but the situation was not critical, because grain could be imported from areas of surplus and peasants drew upon stocks accumulated from the 1913 harvest. Overall, there was a modest surplus of grain and no major disruption took place to the pre-war pattern of regional transfers of grain.[27]

Apart from feeding the army, government ministers regarded as their chief priority the control of food prices. To this end, the government imposed an embargo on the export of food from provinces close to the front and entrusted the procurement of grain to special commissioners who were empowered to buy grain at controlled prices and, if need be, to requisition stocks. The aim was to circumvent the middlemen or encourage them to sell before the officials had recourse to their new powers.[28] Subsequently these powers were extended throughout much of the Russian interior. Provincial governors in the producing provinces increasingly availed themselves of their new powers to prevent grain from leaving their territory, much to the alarm of their counterparts in the central industrial region and the north-west.

In a departure from pre-war practice, the main responsibility for buying grain was entrusted to the Ministry of Agriculture (headed since 1908 by A.V. Krivoshein) and at local level to zemstvo chairmen, who now became grain commissioners. This decision was intended to reduce the role of merchants and to deal directly with agricultural producers instead. Although they struggled heroically in troubling circumstances, made worse by administrative rivalry between the ministries of Agriculture and the Interior, the newly appointed commissioners were in no position to dispense with the services of grain merchants, who alone had facilities to store food. Furthermore, although the commissioners had the power to prevent shipments of grain outside their own province and to compel landowners and peasants to sell grain at a fixed price, they did not deliver improvements to local consumers.[29]

Aggressive intervention by the Russian military and by government officials had an immediate effect on the price of foodstuffs, in particular rye, oats and meat. For instance, 12 months after the outbreak of war, deliveries of oats to major urban centres had been drastically curtailed and the price doubled.[30] It was not the absolute quantity of purchases that influenced price movements so much as the fact that the army bought grain in provinces that traditionally disposed of relatively small surpluses per head of population. Other factors were also at work. In some provinces peasants began to consume more grain in order to convert it into higher value meat and dairy products. Prices also rose as a result of hoarding by consumers as well as by dealers who stockpiled grain for speculative purposes.[31]

Some provincial commissioners tried as we have seen to stabilise prices by experimenting with embargoes on the 'export' of grain. As prices rose, voices were raised in support of more aggressive intervention. Within the Union of Towns, for instance, the progressively minded economist Vladimir Groman argued in favour of closer controls over the grain trade, much to the indignation of grain merchants. Speculation became the peg on which to hang a broader campaign against private trade, which became more vitriolic the longer the war dragged on.[32]

By the summer of 1915 the central government began to panic that food supply was out of control. The army had intervened in a manner that disrupted established commercial networks. Rivalries between the ministries of agriculture and the interior hindered attempts to co-ordinate food supply. Zemstvos acted as intermediaries between the army's procurement authorities and local co-operatives, but their actions were sometimes hampered by inadequate storage facilities and relations were soured by delays in making payments to suppliers. Some regions had grain but no fuel for the flour mills; others had fuel but no grain.[33] Municipal authorities reported shortages, pinning the blame on grain merchants and 'speculators' who hoarded grain in expectation of rising prices. Responding to these various concerns, the government decided that greater powers to control the supply of food should be vested in the new Special Council for Food Supply.

The Special Council curbed the activity of private grain merchants. Municipal authorities were urged to accumulate stocks of grain and to offload them when prices began to rise. (In practice, the loans granted to town councils were spent at once, driving food prices upwards.) During the winter of 1915–1916 officials devised fixed prices for government purchases of the major foodstuffs, arguing that this was the best means of 'protecting the consumer from extortionate prices'. Other transactions took place at unregulated prices, although the situation was complicated still further by the decisions of local municipal authorities to regulate prices.[34] However, fixed prices were altered sufficiently often for producers to hold out in expectation of an upward revision. For their part, peasant producers pointed out their readiness to adhere to fixed prices, provided they applied to textiles and other consumer goods.[35]

These decisions took place against the background of a protracted debate about the role of government in wartime. If the state decided to fix food prices and seek to eliminate market transactions, what should be the appropriate level? Why should the state embark on systematic price control, instead of bringing order to the rapidly deteriorating transport system? Would not the control of prices simply encourage the black market in food?

The leading proponent of price regulation was the aforementioned Groman, whose proposals were advanced in a series of reports. Groman insisted that prices should be kept low. In his case, the battle to control prices formed part of a broader vision of economic 'planning'. He supported rationing, in order to ensure that consumers were treated fairly. The practical involvement of producers and consumers would, he maintained, ensure that the Russian public gained confidence in the extension of economic regulation. Groman proposed that the state should arrange in turn for peasants to receive manufactured goods in exchange for their food surpluses, anticipating the Bolsheviks' experiment with 'collective commodity exchange'.[36] His colleague on the special council, Petr Struve, representing the Union of Zemstvos, also supported fixed prices for all transactions, but parted company with Groman by arguing in favour of setting prices at a higher level, in order to provide greater incentives to Russian farmers. Groman took the view that peasants would respond to higher prices by reducing the sale of their produce. In the end, government procrastination caused a lengthy interruption to the sale of grain. Producers waited to see what prices were to be fixed, while dealers who had already bought grain were loath to part with their stocks until they too saw what prices would be posted in the autumn.[37]

These schemes entailed an unprecedented degree of state intervention, leavened – as Groman hoped they would be – by citizens' participation in the formulation of economic policy. But Groman was given short shrift; few government officials supported an extension of civilian involvement in matters of food supply. Members of the Union of Zemstvos joined forces with the Special Council for Food Supply to press for local participation in new purchasing agencies, but the new Minister of the Interior A.D. Protopopov complained that this would give a green light to all manner of people, including zemstvo professionals, co-operatives and others. The dreaded 'third element' would, he argued, 'obviously not work for the common good so much as for their particular needs'.[38]

Parallel moves were being made by government officials for a very different scheme. Lars Lih dubs this the 'gubernatorial solution', because it implied the extension of authority by central government, acting in conjunction with the provincial governors appointed by the Ministry of the Interior. According to this strategy the state would determine the total amount of grain needed for the war effort and impose an obligatory levy on individual producers. Any surplus could be disposed of as the producer saw fit.[39] In late November 1916 the new Minister of Agriculture A.A. Rittikh instituted a grain levy (*razverstka*), against the background of insistent demands for grain from the Russian high command and the dwindling quantities of grain that now reached the market. Rittikh opposed the use of force (believing it likely to be counterproductive) and believed that each district and village would accept its share of the levy as part of its contribution to state defence. If they refused, the state could threaten to use force. The scheme relied upon the co-operation of provincial zemstvo boards to assign quotas to districts. Four zemstvos refused and Rittikh was accused of imposing the levy in a high-handed manner. In practice, he permitted local agencies to temporise, particularly when they complained about the burden of assessment and the timetable they were expected to meet.[40] The success of the levy is difficult to gauge, because the projected deliveries of grain were not due to be completed until the summer of 1917, by which time it had been overtaken by the Provisional Government's grain monopoly. Rittikh's policy 'resulted in no real improvement' to food supply.[41]

7.4   Securing food: front line, town, and country

Competition between civil and military authorities, and between 'state' and 'society', contributed to a sense of administrative confusion in food supply. But how did the war alter established patterns of food production and consumption? How, in practice, did Russian consumers gain access to food, and were the mechanisms and strategies identical for urban and rural consumers, and for men in uniform?

Contemporaries were perfectly well aware of the impact that wartime population movements had on the market for food. One crucial factor here was the draft, as an elaborate system of military procurement came into being. Nearly one-fifth of the army's supply of grain and hay came from the co-operative organisations, the remainder from private transactions. By the end of 1914 the Russian army purchased substantial quantities of cereals, including buckwheat and millet that was turned into coarse grain meal. The army also bought vast amounts of meat, fish, sugar, butter, cheese, rice, vegetables and vegetable oil. Co-operative organisations also made a major contribution to supplying the army.[42]

Peasant conscripts consumed these items in far greater amounts after donning a uniform. In 1913 peasants ate an average of 5 kg of meat (urban workers consumed 70 kg on average), whereas the army expected to give its troops around 147 kg of meat per annum. Horses too were better fed than in peacetime.[43] This insatiable demand is reflected as shown in Table 7.2.

However, the trend did not continue beyond the second year of war. In the winter of 1916 soldiers wrote home about the deteriorating quality and

TABLE 7.2   *Procurement of foodstuffs and fodder by the Russian military, 1914–1917*

Year	Flour and grits, million tons	Fodder (oats and hay), million tons	Meat, million tons	Butter and fats, million tons	Total spending, million rubles, 1913 prices
1914	0.44	2.90	0.22	0.03	240.5
1915	2.18	5.97	0.83	0.11	410.9
1916	4.03	10.32	1.34	0.19	939.5
1917	4.16	11.00	1.27	0.18	882.8

Sources: Derived from *RVMV*, 1925, p. 60; Dikhtiar, 1960, pp. 215–16.

quantity of food, with cuts in the bread ration and watery soup heading the list of complaints. The War Minister told Stavka that he proposed to cut the food norms.[44]

Prevailing peacetime patterns of consumption also altered as a result of the growth of the urban population. Many towns in the Central Agricultural Region and Ukraine experienced a large influx of workers to the iron ore mines of Krivoi Rog and the coal mines and steelworks of the Donbass. Urban expansion in the north-west and Central Industrial Region created a huge problem, as Moscow and Petrograd competed for food with provincial towns such as Ekaterinoslav and Saratov, swollen in size by a large refugee population. Meanwhile peasants were able maintain their food intake by growing food for their own consumption and by purchasing foodstuffs hitherto beyond their means. Many of them consumed higher quality foodstuffs such as wheat flour, meat, tea and sugar that were not traditionally a regular part of the peasant diet.[45] Regional variations should also be kept in mind. Chaianov demonstrated that the average annual consumption of bread in rural Russia was 253 kg per person. However, in Viatka province it was 292 kg and in Kherson province closer to 450 kg, while in Kostroma and Tula it hovered around the 215 kg mark. Penza enjoyed a relatively high meat consumption, whereas Kostroma and Viatka were well below average. Other items similarly displayed a wide variation.[46]

In 1915–1916 the demands made upon food supplies by the main consuming region in the north (NCR) increased as a result of the growth in the transient population. However, the grain harvest here increased by 20 per cent over the previous year's figure and the region's dependence upon imports of grain from the major producing regions did not become any more critical in the first half of 1916. In the south (SPR) the decline in production in 1915 had few serious consequences. The bumper harvest in 1915–1916 in the CPR allowed the region to build up stocks and satisfy the demands placed upon it by the NCR. In these circumstances, the decline in the harvest from the EPR was by no means alarming. Wheatcroft has shown that the notional surplus (estimated production less estimated utilisation) in 1915-1916 may have trebled in comparison with the preceding year. Figures are given in Table 7.3.

The main problem in 1916–1917 was that the demands from the NCR continued to grow, whilst the SPR had no surplus at its disposal to release to the towns and garrisons in the north. The sharp fall in the grain harvest in the CPR implied a pronounced reduction in the availability of grain for consumption, which could only be offset by the import of grain from other regions. Unfortunately, such was the decline in production elsewhere that neither the SPR nor the EPR could satisfy the claims of the NCR and the CPR. The aggregate shortfall in grain available for consumption in 1916–1917 amounted to 10 million tons. In the following year the situation deteriorated further. This probably reflected the continued decline in grain production in the NCR, rather than an increase in the region's grain requirement. In the SPR, production failed to recover in 1917 and this region persisted in its inability to generate a potential surplus. More serious still was the behaviour of the CPR where the harvest fell yet again, creating a deficit that amounted to nearly one-third of estimated regional consumption. The modest increase in output in the EPR simply could not compensate for the shortages experienced in the NCR and the CPR. In that year the notional grain deficit for the country as a whole amounted to more than 13 million tons.

TABLE 7.3   *Estimated inter-regional grain balances, 1909/13–1917/18, million tons*

Year	NCR	SPR	CPR	EPR	All regions
1909/13–1913/14	−3.5	+10.0	+1.6	+0.8	+8.9
1913/14	−2.9	+11.0	+1.5	+1.0	+10.6
1914/15	−5.3	+3.5	−1.6	+4.1	+0.7
1915/16	−4.6	+3.6	+2.1	+1.0	+2.1
1916/17	−7.4	−0.8	−1.1	−0.7	−10.0
1917/18	−8.5	−0.6	−5.7	+1.5	−13.3

Source and note: Wheatcroft, unpublished paper, p. 17, summarising estimates of regional production and utilisation. The abbreviations refer to the Northern Consumer Region (NCR), Southern Producer Region (SPR), Central Producer Region (CPR) and Eastern Producer Region (EPR).

Thus the delicate inter-regional balance of grain production and utilisation came under intense pressure before 1916 and collapsed completely in 1917. This is evident in the failure of the traditional grain-producing regions, the Volga provinces and Ukraine, to meet the demands of local consumption, let alone the needs of the northern consuming areas. Difficulties in grain supply reflected the breakdown in inter-regional shipments, caused by the impact of the war on regional production and consumption patterns and exacerbated by the disruption in inter-regional transportation.[47]

In the municipal economy the shortages of food contributed to growing distress and anger. The urban population had been swollen by an influx of workers and refugees. In Petrograd the population stood at 2.32 million, according to the 1915 municipal census, an increase of 413,000 since 1910, largely as a result of immigration. Many of the new arrivals wanted wheat and meat, not the standard diet of rye flour, and they were often disappointed.[48] Against this background, some local authorities intervened more actively. Municipal officials stockpiled refrigerated meat, sugar, salt and other foodstuffs, which they either distributed through co-operative stores or sold direct to consumers at wholesale prices. The zemstvos performed a similar service for poorer households in the Russian village.[49]

Consumer co-operatives grew in number, in average size of membership and in social and economic significance. By 1915 Russia had as many consumer societies as Britain, France, Germany, Italy, Switzerland and Denmark combined. Their number trebled in the Volga region, in the Central Industrial Region and the central black-earth provinces. Co-operatives used their funds to buy sugar, flour, kerosene, matches, boots and shoes and other items on behalf of their members, to whom they extended credit. They also sold these items on to the general public. Total reported trade turnover in the consumer co-operatives increased from around 290 million rubles (1 January 1915) to 1,040 million rubles in January 1917, in pre-war prices. They accounted for 14 per cent of total retail trade in 1915, but this had risen to a staggering 46 per cent just two years later. The war witnessed the emergence of large co-operative societies, with optimistic sounding names such as 'Forward', 'Life' and 'Power', which operated warehouses and chain stores in provincial towns. By early 1917 there were more than a hundred such societies with a reported membership of 350,000. The most famous was the Moscow society, 'Co-operation'. In accordance with co-operative convention, its members subscribed a modest amount to purchase shares in the society. In all likelihood the thousands of additional consumers who joined had a much more positive view of co-operative organisations than they did of merchants or officialdom.[50]

Government officials certainly had the power to ration supplies, had they chosen to do so. However, the Special Council for Food Supply hoped to avoid a nation-wide scheme, lest it arouse expectations from consumers that could not be fulfilled. It was also deterred by the administrative complexities of issuing ration cards. Officials believed temporary difficulties could best be overcome by solving the transport question and concluded in October 1915 that stocks of food were 'plentiful'.[51] A further consideration was that local authorities ought to be free to arrange matters themselves, which many of them did. The tsarist government played no direct part, except in restricting meat consumption by prohibiting the sale of meat products on certain days of the week, the main effect of which was to encourage consumers to buy extra quantities on other days.[52] Gradually the state accepted the necessity of rationing supplies of sugar, without committing itself to the regular delivery of a specific amount to consumers. Rationing meant an entitlement, not a promise, and it applied only to urban consumers.[53] After the fall of tsarism the Provisional Government embarked on a more systematic approach, but ministers acknowledged that their attempts to prescribe 'norms' of consumption bore little resemblance to reality, 'nor do they impose an obligation on procurement organisations to deliver these quantities to consumers'. The government reaffirmed its stance when it introduced a bread ration.[54]

Supplementary rations could only be obtained via the black market, which was very active in meat products. Occasionally firms stepped in to make food available to their workforce, and some workers grew their own food on urban allotments. Displaced persons and prisoners of war struggled to maintain an adequate diet. Some refugees were fed by charitable agencies, but obtaining a decent meal was more a matter of individual and collective self-help. Those who worked on peasant farms may have shared in the broad improvement in rural consumption during the war. Prisoners who were deployed on back-breaking tasks in the mines, on construction projects or in arduous field work ate just enough to ensure their bare survival; the lucky ones received occasional food parcels via the Red Cross. The most adventurous managed to pilfer from those who guarded them. Prisoners who ended up in hospital fared badly: 'an attendant would go round throwing a piece of meat on to each bed'. Prison camp officials were expected to supply bread and meat, irrespective of cost, and to spend a fixed amount per head on daily supplies of potatoes, flour, onions, lard and salt. However, the falling purchasing power of the ruble took its toll on provisions.[55]

The consumption of food entails broader questions of community and culture that are less susceptible to measurement but are fundamental to any consideration of the relationship between war and nutrition.[56] Russian peasants knew better than anyone else how exposed domestic household production and consumption were to the erratic nature of the cereal harvest. In times of extreme dearth, where the peasant village proved unable to distribute stocks of grain among its most needy members, peasants had often been able to count on assistance or intervention by central and local government. Financial assistance also came from central government funds, which could be spent on foodstuffs.[57] In 1915 and 1916 the harvest was more than adequate and peasants enjoyed a moment of relative abundance, but the war did not convince peasant farmers that a permanent improvement in nutrition was just around the corner. The traditional vulnerability of peasant farming was further exposed by the loss of able-bodied labour. Where a father or brother had been maimed or killed in battle the household would need to be supported by the village. Members of the community had plenty of experience of dealing with the consequences of injury and disability on the farm, and in this respect the war reinforced traditional norms of solidarity.

In urban communities workers and middle-class consumers alike began to join new organisations, which entitled their members to basic goods. Workers side-stepped management run stores, which they regarded as a means of distributing scarce goods in order to exert control over the labour force. Stores now flourished exclusively for working-class families. In Kiev the labour society *Zhizn'* ('Life'), formed in October 1915 with 1,000 members, saw its enrolment rise tenfold in the first year of operation. Similar initiatives took place in Khar'kov, Irkutsk, Tomsk, Samara, Moscow and Petrograd. By August 1917 around 350,000 workers had enlisted in these organisations. Nor did they confine themselves to the distribution of food. They had a cultural purpose, too, maintaining reading rooms, playgrounds, entertainment, and social welfare. In this way food supply was joined to educational and political nourishment. The sense of affinity and obligation to organisations outside the state was not lost on their members.[58]

Conclusions

How did a deficit of food contribute to the collapse of tsarism? There is no simple answer to this question. There had been worse shortages within living memory, such as during the famine of 1891 and in 1902. On these occasions the tsarist regime managed to survive, and the newspapers and priests who delivered sermons from the pulpit could advise their audiences that the problems were God-given rather than man-made. However, short-ages in the winter of 1916 could not be blamed on an extreme failure of the grain harvest – human agency was invoked instead. One scapegoat emerged in the shape of middlemen who speculated in stocks of food. Petty traders were the targets of consumer wrath. So too were merchants who dealt in grain and the bankers who controlled the trade through issuing credits to the dealers. Traditional forms of expression were also deployed; clowns used the circus tent as a venue to tap into popular anger at price inflation, speculation and *nouveaux riches*.[59]

Tsarist officials shouldered part of the blame. Provincial governors failed to feed the civilian population, bureaucrats failed to devise a coherent strategy before eventually coming up with a futile scheme to req-uisition grain, and those responsible for transport had failed to organise the distribution of stocks. The irony is that the government early on ruled out a nation-wide system of food rationing, fearing that shortcomings in these arrangements would lead to a breakdown of public sympathy and support.

Tsarist food supply policies were inept and contributed to a growing perception of official incompetence. They were the product of competing visions of a war economy. Within the ministries of war and agriculture the view prevailed that government had a primary responsibility towards the armed forces, hence their acquiescence in embargoes early on in the war. The Ministry of the Interior developed a more cynical programme that encouraged urban consumers to pin the blame on shopkeepers and mid-dlemen. Meanwhile the new generation of specialists and the public organisations formulated an ambitious vision that required public partici-pation in the task of economic regulation. Their derivation of grain balances demonstrates a broader point about the politicisation of food in wartime Russia and the growing contribution of agricultural specialists in political and economic life. Both the zemstvos and central government sought to establish the quantities of food available for consumption. Among the statisticians and agricultural economists, scarcity was no longer used to justify the redistribution of land but became instead a means of thinking about administrative intervention in food supply. For many of these specialists, wealth and income distribution were less relevant than technical matters of food supply. Statistics, not social justice, held the key to the satisfaction of basic needs.[60]

Against the background of institutional conflict, the supply of food reached critical proportions. By December 1916 grain reserves stood at one-fifth of their level 12 months earlier.[61] At the outset, the government engaged in unprecedented purchases of food on behalf of the army, leaving civilian consumers to stand on the sidelines and watch retail prices climb steadily. No subsidies were introduced in order to protect consumers from the effects of inflation of food prices on the unregulated market. The attempt to impose a grain levy coincided with inflation in the price of man-ufactured goods, and the experiment was abandoned. There was even talk of famine.[62]

How then should the entire blame be apportioned? One problem was exogenous to agriculture. Mobilisation and military transport imposed intolerable pressures on the railway system, which buckled and then broke under the strain of having to cope with conflicting demands on rolling stock and railway lines. Secondly, the entire agricultural sector was poorly developed, making it difficult to promote changes in the production and consumption of food. Those responsible for food supply were confronted by a dense network of autonomous peasant households whose market pos-ition was strengthened by the decline in the capacity of large-scale producers to maintain, let alone increase, their share of agricultural pro-duction. Many Russian peasants improved their hitherto modest standard of nutrition not by engaging in commercial transactions but by diversifying production on the family farm and retreating into self-sufficiency. Others circumvented the levy and withheld grain, hoping to sell on the open market or to secure an increase in fixed prices. A declining percentage of crops reached the market. As one observer concluded, 'although the peas-ants had no grounds for deliberately producing less, they had no special inducement to produce more than they had done before the war'. Whereas in 1909–1913 around 12.4 per cent of all grain and fodder crops reached the market, by 1915 this had fallen to 7.4 per cent.[63]

Russia's urban consumers nevertheless expected the government to demonstrate greater success in food procurement. These expectations were frustrated. Neither the tsarist regime nor its short-lived successor devised a policy that could satisfy the wishes of producers and the needs of con-sumers. Russian consumers did not starve, but their access to food depended increasingly on their own efforts to obtain food by whatever means, including semi-legal initiatives and the outright seizure and redis-tribution of stocks during food riots. They could not count upon the state to guarantee adequate supplies. Co-operative organisations helped to some extent: 'when the average Russian suffered from the lack or shortage of goods ... he remembered gratefully that if it was at all possible to secure the things he sorely needed, anywhere, at a reasonable price, the place was the co-operative store'.[64] This activity underscored the extent to which civilians felt betrayed by officialdom as well as by shopkeepers. However, no-one expected middlemen to act in the public interest; that, surely, was the job of government. Thus, in the last analysis, Russian consumers pinned the blame on government incompetence, not on middlemen, misfortune or backwardness.

Note on further reading

The essential sources on Russian agriculture during the war are the contemporary studies by Kondrat'ev, 1922, reprinted 1991 (in Russian only), Struve et al., 1930, and Antsiferov et al., 1930. Food supply is the subject of valuable books by Lih, 1990, and Kitanina, 1985. Other historians, including Wheatcroft, 1980, Stanziani, 1995, and Matsuzato, 1998, have also made important contributions. The standard account of agricultural Russia during the war is by Anfimov, 1962. Kayden and Antsiferov, 1929, is a valuable source on co-operative marketing and credit.

References

1 Kondrat'ev, 1991, pp. 99, 315–35. The statistics of grain production and marketings before and after the 1917 revolution are examined by Wheatcroft, 1980.

2 The distribution of crops on the peasant allotment and on large farms in 1916 is shown in Pavlovsky, 1930, p. 215. On peasant farms 30 per cent of the area under crops was given over to rye (compared with 19 per cent on private farms), 21 per cent to wheat (26 per cent), 17 per cent to oats (20 per cent) and 11 per cent to barley (10 per cent). These figures are for European Russia, excluding Stavropol'. Rye dominated peasant farming in the central industrial, central agricultural, mid-Volga and western provinces. New crop rotations made slow headway on peasant farms.

3 Falkus, 1968, p. 59, referring to USSR inter-war territory. Income from hay and straw, and from animal products, made up the bulk of the remainder. Forestry and fishing products are excluded.

4 Gatrell, 1986, pp. 119–39.

5 Kitanina, 1978, pp. 201–21.

6 Prokopovich, 1917, pp. 135–9.

7 Anfimov, 1962, pp. 196–205.

8 Pavlovsky, 1930, pp. 203–8; Izmailovskaia, 1920, p. 34. 'Little Russia' comprised the Ukrainian provinces of Chernigov, Poltava and Khar'kov.

9 Antsiferov et al., 1930, pp. 117–8, 230.

10 Antsiferov et al., 1930, p. 125. Each horse required between 5 and 6 hectares of arable for it to be fully utilised. According to the 1916 and 1917 census returns, Russia made available only 3.5 hectares.

11 Struve et al., 1930, pp. 297–303; EPR, 1967, volume 3, pp. 33–71.

12 Peasant farms engaged only 20,000 POWs, far fewer than the numbers on private farms. Izvestiia VZS, 51, 1 December 1916, pp. 55–57; EPR, 1967, volume 3, p. 443.

13 Izmailovskaia, 1920, p. 52.

14 In vain did the war industry committees point out in February 1916 that the supply of agricultural equipment was a 'matter of state defence'. Trudy Vtorogo s"ezda, volume 1, 1916, p. 271.

15 Ivantsov, 1915, pp. 125–30. Ivantsov added that the zemstvo estimates might themselves err on the side of caution, given what he took to be a tendency of scribes to underestimate cereal yields.

16 The 1914 harvest was thought to have been underestimated by 6 per cent for rye, 1 per cent for winter wheat, 5 per cent for spring wheat and 13 per cent for barley. Ivantsov, 1915, pp. 124–5; Pallot, ed., 1998, p. 177 (Stanziani).

17 Kondrat'ev, 1991, pp. 121, 424–5; Wheatcroft, 1980, pp. 38–63.

18 Prokopovich, 1917, pp. 122–3; Antsiferov et al., 1930, pp. 122–3, 150–1. The sown area in 1915 on private land was only 47 per cent of its prewar level. In the Caucasus the corresponding figure was 74 per cent. In Siberia the sown area actually increased by 37 per cent, confirming the vitality of ('private') peasant farming. See also Antsiferov et al., 1930, pp. 144–5.

19 The figures exclude Asiatic Russia, where the sown area remained broadly stable. See Antsiferov et al., 1930, pp. 143, 146.

20 Ivantsov, 1915, pp. 144–5, 154; Groman, 1915, pp. 313–80.

21 Struve et al., 1930, p. 309; Kondrat'ev, 1991, pp. 124–5.

22 Details in Struve et al., 1930, p. 302.

23 There is some uncertainty about the scale of the problem. Struve et al., 1930, pp. 312–14 (quotation on p. 314).

24 Antsiferov et al., 1930, pp. 155–63.

25 Antsiferov et al., 1930, pp. 168–80, 298–300.

26 Antsiferov et al., 1930, pp. 62, 99.

27 Groman, 1915, pp. 330–31, 352.

28 Krivoshein appointed more than three thousand such agents by 1915. The relevant decree allowing tsarist officials to buy at fixed prices and to requisition stocks was issued on 17 February 1915. Barykov, 1915, p. 410.

29 Yaney, 1982, pp. 404–5.

30 'Luxury' items such as eggs and butter became cheaper as Russia lost its access to lucrative export markets. Maslov, 1915; Lipkin, 1915. Siberian farmers killed up to 10 million cattle, or one-fifth of the total herd, in order to reduce milk and butter production and to take advantage of the increased price of meat products. Dikhtiar, 1960, pp. 186–7, 203.

31 Groman, 1915, p. 353. The situation was exacerbated by the disruption to railway transport, which led to the accumulation of stocks in silos and warehouses.

32 Rieber, 1982, p. 402; Lih, 1990, p. 12.

33 Polner, 1930, p. 179.

34 Yaney, 1982, p. 411. In June 1916 the government embarked on a further extension of its powers by seeking to ensure that all flour mills received grain at a fixed price.

35 Anfimov, 1962, p. 310.

36 Malle, 1985, pp. 338–50.

37 Groman, 1916; Lih, 1990, pp. 25–8, 39–40; Kitanina, 1985, pp. 170–71; Pallot, ed., 1998, p. 178 (Stanziani).

38 Quoted in Lih, 1990, p. 47.

39 Lih, 1990, pp. 33, 42. There is an obvious parallel with the introduction of the New Economic Policy in 1921.

40 As Chaianov put it, 'the government feared hunger but it feared the public organisations even more'. Details of the Rittikh levy are in Lih, 1990, pp. 50–56 (Chaianov quotation on p. 53). See also Polner, 1930, pp. 184–5; Yaney, 1982, pp. 431–3 and Diakin, 1967, p. 313.

41 Kayden and Antsiferov, 1929, p. 101.

42 Kayden and Antsiferov, 1929, pp. 20, 291.

43 Fedorov, 1916, p. 22; Struve et al., 1930, pp. 330–1.

44 Gavrilov, 1986, p. 54; Diakin, 1967, p. 312.

45 Prokopovich, 1917, pp. 140–41, for peasant purchases in 1915 of *krupchatka*, a high-quality wheat flour.

46 Chaianov, 1915.

47 I draw here on an unpublished paper by S.G. Wheatcroft.

48 Fedorov, 1916.

49 *Izvestiia VSG*, 1915, 16, pp. 104–6.

50 Kayden and Antsiferov, 1929, pp. 18–19, 67–107, 292.

51 Bukshpan, 1929, pp. 162–3.

52 Struve et al., 1930, pp. 164–8; Bukshpan, 1929, p. 164.

53 Struve et al., 1930, p. 164; Bukshpan, 1929, p. 163; Diakin, 1967, p. 313.

54 Volobuev, 1962, pp. 457, 461, statement dated 29 April 1917.

55 Brändström, 1929, pp. 71–3.

56 Offer, 1991.

57 Porshneva, 2000, p. 119.

58 Kayden and Antsiferov, 1929, pp. 75–83.

59 Jahn, 1995, pp. 91–92, 152. The war hit the circus, because German owners were forced to close down their operations; others lost performers and horses to the army.

60 Stanziani, 1995.

61 Kondrat'ev, 1991, p. 150.

62 Yaney, 1982, p. 433.

63 Bubnoff, 1917, pp. 43–4.

64 Kayden and Antsiferov, 1929, p. 106.

CHAPTER 8

Economic nationalism and the mobilisation of ethnicity in 'the great patriotic war'

The era of dynastic war is at an end, and the era of popular participation has arrived
            [M.A. Tokarskii, Izvestiia MVPK, no. 1, September 1915, p. 2]

Domestic campaigns for the hearts and minds of the population took place in all belligerent states during the First World War. An important element of this process was the dissemination of images of friend and foe, and Russia shared in this common practice. To be sure, not all enemies were immediately demonised, but the strains of war increasingly produced an insidious current of hatred. Hundreds of thousands of enemy soldiers became prisoners of war. This captive population had the potential to become an instrument of national politics, particularly because of the 'national question' in Russia's arch-rival Austria-Hungary.[1]

Long before the war Russia's multinational empire had raised issues about the place of non-Russian minorities within the polity and about the extent to which greater freedom of self-expression could be permitted. The variety of ethnic groups reflected the history of imperial expansion and conquest. Although the most numerous group, with a population of 56 million, ethnic Russians fell some way short of half the total population. They were followed by other 'Great Russians' (22 million Ukrainians and six million Belorussians). Eight million Poles, five million Jews, four million Kirgiz, four million Tatars, and a multitude of other national groups made up the remaining population.[2]

The framework of nationality marked certain categories of population as trustworthy and others as inherently untrustworthy. The most obvious example was Russian Jews, all but one-tenth of whom were confined to the Pale of Settlement. Their homes and businesses in towns such as Odessa and Kishinev were regularly attacked, looted and destroyed. Russian generals expressed misgivings about the potential loyalty of the Tsar's Jewish subjects and accordingly prevented them from residing close to the state frontier. Jews were not allowed to become officers in the tsarist army. The war intensified the army's distrust of Jews, who were demonised as fifth columnists and deported.[3]

Military planners believed that war would be a test of imperial integrity and a 'test of loyalty' for non-Russians. Deeply ingrained in military consciousness was the memory that Poles had rebelled against tsarist authority in 1831 and 1863, and that revolution in 1905–1906 had again galvanised sections of Polish society into action against Russian overlordship. The state responded by embarking on a programme of Russification. Greater political freedom after 1906 permitted racist and nationalist groups to express themselves more openly. Thus the 'Society for the Russian Borders', established in 1908, expressed antipathy for Poles and Jews, and questioned their political loyalty. On the other hand, Russia's more astute leaders knew that to promote Russian nationalism might unleash the forces of non-Russian nationalism.[4]

The more the state succeeded in convincing the Russian population of the need for a sustained war of attrition, the more it encouraged feverish campaigns against ethnic groups that were perceived as inherently untrustworthy and even disloyal. A key moment here was the appointment of A.N. Khvostov as Minister of the Interior in September 1915. Khvostov targeted German settlers and businessmen. Thus, accompanying the formal patriotic fervour was a more insidious undercurrent of jealousy and persecution that extended to ethnic and religious minorities. Material considerations helped to turn sentiment into violent action. Economic nationalism became a means of settling old scores and transferring economic assets to 'loyal' populations.

The tsarist state also acknowledged the 'nationality factor' by permitting the establishment of national units in the imperial army as well as refugee committees defined in terms of nationality. This helped foster a sense of difference, and encouraged feelings of jealousy among refugee populations (particularly Russians) who were not so favoured. Furthermore, the existence of more than two million prisoners of war, many of them Slavs under the jurisdiction of the Habsburg empire, led some tsarist officials to entertain hopes of destabilising the enemy by encouraging disaffection. However, this was a dangerous card to play in Russia's own multinational empire.

The war effort had a direct impact on the fortunes of the tsarist state by demonstrating the weakness of imperial control on the periphery. Here, pre-war developments combined with wartime mobilisation to produce an explosive mix. Colonisation by Russian settlers had disadvantaged all but a small indigenous elite. A revolt in Andizhan in 1898, and further unrest during 1905–1906, provided a foretaste of what was to come. The war exacerbated social and economic tensions, because scarce resources now had to be shared with a growing population of prisoners and refugees. Finally, the tsarist authorities took the fateful decision to conscript Muslim men for construction work at the front. What followed was the most serious challenge to tsarist rule since 1905 – tsarist Russia's version of the Sepoy Mutiny of 1857. Tsarist repression was no less savage, and it left an equally bitter legacy.

Russia's wartime mobilisation encouraged the growth of a new popular politics. Stories of espionage occupied the pages of the popular press and played upon societal fears. Ironically, this groundswell of ethnic antagonism had troubling implications for the imperial Court, since it helped to foster a belief that the Romanov royal family deliberately adopted a pro-German attitude. If 'ordinary' Germans deserved only contempt, why should the Tsar be shown any mercy? Thus the frenzied wartime xenophobia helped to carry the royal family to its doom.[5]

8.1   The 'enemy within': targeting Germans, Jews and others

The incestuous milieu of the Moscow merchantry had long been home to the belief that Russia was in thrall to foreign economic interests, including German capital. The war offered an opportunity for Russian merchants to proclaim their patriotism and simultaneously rid the country of German 'domination'. Calls for a boycott of German enterprises soon turned into more aggressive action and German proprietors of shops and businesses were favourite targets for rioters. Before long civil servants and government lawyers drew up plans to seize and redistribute the property of German farmers and businessmen.[6]

At the outbreak of war German subjects proclaimed their loyalty to the Tsar. Many of them – unless, like Seventh-Day Adventists, they had religious objections – served in the Russian army.[7] Their reward was to be treated as the enemy. Although the government promised to respect the person and property of enemy subjects, public action and private behaviour were less benign. The Tsar banned the use of the German language, forbade public gatherings of those of German extraction and closed down their newspapers. A Russian actor, appearing on the streets of Petrograd in German uniform, caused a minor panic in August 1914.[8] Members of the Baltic German nobility were summarily dismissed from public office. Government officials and clergymen harassed religious communities, such as Baptists, Adventists and Pentecostalists, hoping thereby, as one police chief said, to 'use the passing moment to call down repression in relation to the sectarians, counting on this to paralyse their religious influence on the population'.[9]

More ominous still, the Russian high command and the Ministry of the Interior drew up plans as early as August 1914 for the deportation of German settlers from several districts in the western borderlands. One leading government official expressed a widely held view: 'the colonists ... live so detached an existence from the native Russian population that, all in all, they constitute a ready base for a German attack through our southern provinces'.[10] After a vitriolic press campaign, steps were taken to drive them all out of Russian Poland.[11] Around 200,000 individuals were affected, their journeys to Siberia supervised by armed military or police detachments. There was no respite in 1915. German settlers were driven from their farms in Volynia, Kiev and Podolia to designated destinations, despite the reservations expressed in some quarters. Nor did the deportations cease in the following year. Brusilov forced settlers out of Volynia during his offensive in June 1916 and despatched them to Penza, Riazan' and Tambov. Many Germans who had settled in Riga were also deported. Protestations of collective loyalty were to no avail, being countered by the claim that they were being deported for their own protection.[12]

More complex were the issues raised by measures taken against the property of the settlers. The government embarked on a series of legislative devices in February 1915 to expropriate German colonists (as well as Austrian and Hungarian farmers) who lived in the frontier zone. Exceptions were made in respect of those of Orthodox faith or Slavic nationality, as well as those who could demonstrate that current family members or ancestors had volunteered to fight in the Russian army.[13] Delays in implementing the new law prompted the military to take more direct action. In excess of 200,000 German settlers in the province of Volynia were forced to leave their homes during 1915, making way for 40,000 refugee settlers, who received land on the understanding that they would hand over part of the harvest to the state. Further measures followed in December 1915, which extended the coverage of the February law to 29 provinces of European Russia, as well as to Finland, the Caucasus and the Amur region. Whereas the earlier law exempted lands that had been granted to colonists at the time of their initial settlement, the December law subjected these lands also to expropriation. Families of German descent that had lived for generations in Volynia, Kiev and Podolia, as well as in the Volga region, were unceremoniously shipped to Siberia or Central Asia.[14]

The combined landholdings of German farmers probably exceeded three million hectares. In terms of the total area sown to crops, their farms accounted for a tiny fraction, but their output of cereals contributed around 3.3 million tons. This was equivalent to half the recorded decline in grain output during 1915, the result of land that had gone unplanted as a consequence of the measures taken against the German settlers.[15] The liberal parliamentarian Paul Miliukov criticised the legislation on political as well as economic grounds, arguing that it set a poor example to Russian peasants, among whom expectations had now been aroused of more radical measures to expropriate property owners.[16]

The Russian government did not hesitate to exploit popular hostility to what was conceived as German economic domination, which served as justification for attacks on factories, utilities, estates, shops, banks and film companies. In his annual report for 1914, the governor of Tula province described how 'the people have formed the view that Germans, even those who are Russian subjects, are enemies of the fatherland, that there is no place for them on Russian soil and that the land that belongs to them here should be given to Russian peasants'.[17] Workers at the Russian Locomotive Works in Khar'kov went on strike in August 1914 to demand the dismissal of German and Austrian supervisors; they quickly secured a victory.[18] In Moscow the sizeable German community (Moscow was home to around 22,000 Germans, second only to Petrograd, with 50,000) found itself harassed, demonised and eventually expropriated. German shops and warehouses were subject to frenzied looting and arson over several days at the end of May 1915, total losses being put at over 70 million rubles. Several individuals were murdered. These attacks, condemned by some officials as a 'pogrom' that revealed the base instincts of the 'mob', took place against a background of municipal inaction.[19]

Attempting to capitalise upon this popular hostility, the government took a more aggressive stance towards enemy aliens. The Duma too captured the public mood, agreeing on 3 August 1915 to establish a commission to 'fight the German yoke'. The new Minister of the Interior, A.N. Khvostov, leant vigorous support to this campaign.[20] Businessmen of

German origin suffered harassment. Orbanovskii, a director of the Putilov firm in Petrograd, was accused of undermining the Russian war effort. Firms such as Siemens and Kolomna, with close ties to German banks, were the subject of investigation. German-owned film studios and cinemas were shut down. Following an energetic campaign by the mayor of Moscow, M.V. Chelnokov, the Electric Company of 1886 was taken into state ownership, even though only one-fifth of its shares were actually held by German subjects. Finally, under a decree issued on 8 February 1917, the government liquidated shares held by enemy subjects, a measure that resulted in the transfer of around four per cent of all foreign stock in industry and utilities.[21]

The situation with regard to Jews was more complicated. The war provided an opportunity for their economic competitors to settle old scores. The relationship between refugees and economic activity became clear from the discussions that took place about the relaxation of residence restrictions on Russian Jews. The Minister of Trade and Industry urged that Jews be allowed to settle not only in towns, but also in rural areas, in order to permit them to re-establish businesses that were disrupted by the retreat from the western provinces in the summer of 1915. Colleagues accused him of under-estimating the degree of animosity that would arise between Jewish merchants and Russian peasants, and of over-estimating the capacity of police to maintain public order.[22]

Once it was recognised that the movement of Jews could no longer be controlled by government agencies, the Pale of Settlement dissolved itself. The first phase of this process came during the dramatic retreat from Poland and Galicia in 1915. The government reluctantly conceded that 'Jewish war sufferers' should be allowed to settle outside the Pale, but not to enter Petrograd and Moscow, nor to settle in the Caucasus or on Cossack land. Furthermore, and consistent with traditional official beliefs that Jews and peasants should be kept apart, Jewish refugees were forbidden to settle in villages. Jews were also forbidden to buy land or other real estate in the towns.[23]

Notwithstanding the perpetuation of civil disabilities, some members of the government sought to promote a more liberal regime. The Russian industrialist Protopopov, appointed Minister of the Interior on 16 September 1916 and noted for his moderately progressive views, hoped to integrate Jews more fully into Russia's economic life.[24] Some members of the tsarist elite kept up a rearguard action: a meeting of provincial governors in May 1916 expressed the hope that the Pale could be re-established after the war. However, they were fighting a losing battle, not so much against a tide of liberal opinion within Russia or of international disquiet as against the impact of population displacement. For a vocal lobby inside and outside the Duma, only full civic equality would render Russia 'indestructible'. Most officials were swayed less by such appeals than by difficult and unpleasant wartime realities that challenged old modes of thought and action. As Krivoshein put it, 'one cannot fight a war against Germany and against the Jews'.[25]

What of the initiatives taken by Jews themselves? In the first phase of the war a group of wealthy activists – mostly bankers and lawyers in Petrograd – established a central 'Jewish Committee for the Relief of Victims of War' (EKOPO). Given the internal rivalries within the Jewish elite, this was an indication that political differences had been set aside. EKOPO sponsored around 200 new schools, serving 30,000 Jewish children; many were secular Yiddish or Russian language schools. Funds were found for the traditional Jewish religious school (heder), which provided religious instruction and a place where children could be kept clean and warm. Some liberal Jewish commentators argued that refugeedom actually yielded cultural benefits, by 'mixing' Jews together and demonstrating the need for them to find a common language of communication: 'The wave of refugees has united all shades of Judaism and all languages. Jews who hitherto did not know or understand one another have been brought together. Mutual antagonisms have disappeared, to be replaced by excellent fraternal relations'.[26]

Popular prejudice and official hostility continued to provide the framework within which Russia's Jewish refugees struggled to survive. The use of Yiddish in public places led some Russians to think that German was being spoken, and this compounded the fear of Jewish otherness. Some municipal authorities made it clear that Jews should not venture out of doors. The governor of Tambov obstructed the distribution of allowances to Jewish refugees, giving as his reason the support they received from Petrograd's Jewish committee. Typical of bureaucratic unwillingness to renounce old attitudes was the decision by the Minister of the Interior in April 1916 to erect obstacles in the way of Jewish refugees who wished to return to their former homes. 'The issue of permits to Jews (wrote Stürmer) is unacceptable because Jews are not suited to agricultural work and because the army needs to be protected from espionage'.[27]

Germans and Jews bore the brunt of state violence towards the empire's ethnic minorities, but other minorities were not immune. Muslims were deported from Kars and Batum provinces to Khar'kov, Kursk, Orel, Tula and elsewhere. The aim was to expel them from the empire for good once the war ended, their farms being earmarked for Armenian refugees. Crimean Tatars were also targeted, on the grounds that they held Ottoman passports (in fact, these were papers entitling them to temporary work in Turkey). They had to wait for the Provisional Government to call a halt to their deportation. The new government removed the disabilities on the Jews, but did nothing to alleviate the problems faced by the German colonists.[28]

8.2   Combat units and prisoners of war: the new politics of ethnicity

Arguments in favour of creating ethnically defined military units made little headway in tsarist Russia before the war, but the war did encourage a more positive attitude on the part of the authorities. One factor was the need to find fresh sources of military manpower by tapping into 'national' sentiment. Poles and Armenians were encouraged to set aside misgivings about Russian imperial rule and to think of Germany and Turkey respectively as the greatest threat to their prosperity and 'national' survival. Polish loyalists early on advocated the creation of 'flying squads' that would fight behind enemy lines. Nothing came of this proposal, which in any case spoke to the conventional belief that separate units might be justified only where specific needs arose. A small company of Czech volunteers also formed in 1914, in the hope of freeing compatriots in the Habsburg empire from Austrian domination.[29] In a far greater departure from convention, in March 1915 the Tsar gave his permission for a new 'Polish legion' (there was even talk of Poles returning from America to enlist in it), no doubt swayed by the promise of an extra half million conscripts. Certainly Nicholas II scored a propaganda coup in German-occupied Poland and in Galicia, where Polish patriots urged their compatriots to refuse to take up arms against tsarist Russia. By the end of 1916 Brusilov trumpeted the success of this policy, albeit in a sentimental and patronising manner that dwelled upon the 'strong hand of friendship' that was extended to Russia's 'younger sister'.[30]

As its critics feared, and as its proponents hoped, this change of policy led to the formation of other such units, including a Latvian brigade (precursor of the famous Latvian Riflemen), as well as Armenian, Georgian and other units in the Transcaucasus. In part these concessions were a means of meeting the concerns of Russian subjects, who complained that they were being asked to shoulder a disproportionate burden. Not all minorities received this favourable treatment; Finns, for example, were refused permission to form ethnic units. Some minorities were believed to make poor soldiers; military planners deemed the Kirgiz to be 'useless military material'.[31]

The February revolution inspired more purposeful efforts to establish national units, partly because its leaders were committed to the principle of 'separate but equal' national relations, and partly because their tenuous grip over the empire might be reasserted by offering concessions to the emerging patriotic intelligentsia. As a result, new national formations came into being, including Finnish and Ukrainian regiments, the latter active on the South-Western and Romanian fronts. Josh Sanborn suggests that the experience was not a happy one, because it entailed the disruption of established military formations. As a result, many of the new units contained badly demoralised soldiers. Be that as it may, the formation of national units fostered a sense of national unity and pride, particularly where (as in the case of the famous and bloody 'Christmas battles' in Latvia) losses were severe and war could be expressed as a national sacrifice.[32]

The Russian army captured more than two million Austro-Hungarian and German prisoners of war. Most belonged to the Austrian army, having been captured in Galicia in 1914, or during the battles for Przemysl' and the Carpathians during 1915 and 1916 respectively. Half of them ended up in military districts far from the front line, including Moscow, Kazan, Omsk and Turkestan. Others were kept back for military work closer to the front, for example in Kiev and Odessa. Only relatively small numbers of ordinary soldiers were sent to purpose-built concentration camps (officers were more likely to be confined to camps), the rest being housed – like refugees – in makeshift accommodation such as theatres, circus venues, abandoned factories and farm outhouses.[33] They were subsequently transferred to designated prison camps, the largest of which in Siberia housed up to 30,000 POWs at a given time. Overcrowding became a major problem, and prisoners were vulnerable to outbreaks of typhus, as at Krasnoiarsk and Novo-Nikolaevsk in the winter of 1914 and Totskoe (Orenburg) in 1915, where conditions were scandalous.[34] The unlucky ones were sent to build the new Murmansk railway in 1915–1916, where some 25,000 died during the project.[35]

The regime everywhere was harsh. Mortality rates in the camp at Sretensk housing German POWs rose sharply during the harsh winter of 1914, and at Totskoe a terrible epidemic of typhus brought about widespread deaths in late 1915 and early 1916. Unlike rank and file soldiers, officers – making up less than three per cent of the total POW population – enjoyed relatively favourable conditions in 'prison universities', where they used their monthly salaries to sustain a decent standard of living.[36] Prisoners devised their own forms of recreation, including sports, theatre and music; and the camps provided an opportunity to develop literacy programmes. However, material conditions were poor, owing to inescapable difficulties in supplying food, fuel, clothing and medicines to the prison camps. Reports reached neutral authorities that prison guards embezzled the funds meant to alleviate the plight of the POWs, but Russian officials evinced little sympathy for the plight of prisoners of war, whose numbers increased following the Brusilov offensive of 1916, precisely at the time when Russia's food supplies began to deteriorate. Ordinary soldiers experienced an improvement in their conditions in 1917, thanks to the organisation of relief efforts by the Austrian and German authorities, as well as the reduced rate of influx of new prisoners.

The ethnic composition of the POWs was diverse – Austrian, Hungarian, Czech, Slovak, Ukrainian, Serb, Croat, Jewish and others. Some tsarist officials planned to give prisoners of war of Slav origin relatively favourable treatment, in the hope that they could be turned against their Austrian overlords. However, it proved difficult to implement this policy, largely because it was impossible to cushion prisoners from the privations that ordinary Russian citizens suffered by 1916–1917. To be sure, the tsarist government created 'propaganda camps' for anti-Habsburg volunteers, but conditions were no better than in other camps. Recent work suggests that rank rather than nationality was the key determinant of tsarist policy towards POWs. An Austro-Hungarian official, writing in August 1916, concluded that 'the great majority of prisoners of the Czech nationality groan under oppressive and inhumane treatment, just like their companions in distress from other nationalities of the monarchy'.[37]

Following the February Revolution, more concerted attempts were made to disseminate revolutionary propaganda in German, Hungarian, Czech and Polish newspapers. Miliukov, the new Minister of Foreign Affairs, publicly called for 'liberation of the oppressed peoples of Austria-Hungary'. He gave permission for the leading Czech nationalist politician Tomas Masaryk to enter Russia, in order that he might conduct a recruiting campaign among prisoners of war. In June 1917 Kerenskii, the Minister of War, was so impressed by the performance of Czech troops that he undertook to sponsor a Czech national army.[38] These attempts met with relatively little success, because most POWs tended to be more concerned with basic survival than political agitation. Around 40,000 Czech and Slovak POWs did volunteer to fight against the Habsburg empire, most of them in 1917–1918. In practice, however, the Russian authorities were more interested in POWs as a source of labour than as instruments of imperial subversion.[39]

8.3   Refugees and 'national' identity

A British military observer described the movement of refugees as a 'national migration'.[40] Around 5 per cent of all refugees were Jewish; some two-thirds were officially classed as Russians, but this made no distinction between Russian, Ukrainian and Belorussian refugees; a further 11 per cent were Polish and 5 per cent Latvian; Armenians, Lithuanians, Estonians and others made up the remainder.[41] In Petrograd the proportions were quite different: only one-fifth of refugees were Russian compared with 23 per cent Polish and 23 per cent Latvian. Much further south, in Kursk province more than one-third of refugees were Ukrainian, 25 per cent Polish, 12 per cent Belorussian and only 17 per cent Russian.[42]

Crucially, because resources were thinly stretched, the tsarist state devolved some of the responsibility for refugee relief on to newly formed 'national committees' (Latvian, Armenian, Polish, Jewish and Lithuanian – although not Russian, Ukrainian, Belorussian, still less German). These committees mobilised 'national' opinion at home and abroad. Refugeedom (*bezhenstvo*) inspired among an emerging patriotic elite a sense of national calamity that in turn gave rise to a vision of national solidarity. Deliberate action was needed, in the words of the Latvian activist Janis Goldmanis, to ensure that Latvians avoid 'the lot of the Jews, to be scattered across the entire globe'. Polish activists spoke of 'preserving the refugee on behalf of the motherland'. Goldmanis was not alone in articulating a vision of a reclaimed homeland, whose farms should in due course be re-populated by 'people who think and act in a Latvian manner'. The leader of the Lithuanian Welfare Committee, Martynas Yčas, a lawyer and former Duma deputy, boasted in his memoirs that his organisation had 'prepared the people for future action and created the foundations for a future cultural and political edifice. It unearthed the buried name of Lithuania and forced even non-Lithuanians to recognise that we ourselves were masters of our country'.[43]

Members of the Committee proclaimed the need to ensure that Lithuanian refugees retained a sense of what it meant to be 'Lithuanian', meaning that they needed to stay together. Refugeedom gave these elites direct access to a nascent national community. Refugee relief instructed the displaced farmer or labourer what it meant to be Armenian, Polish, Jewish or Latvian. Even where (as in the case of Ukrainian and Belorussian refugees) the tsarist state frustrated attempts by a patriotic elite to create dedicated national organisations, the very act of denial fostered a sense of disappointment and a readiness to confront official discrimination. Thus Belorussian refugees were invited to reflect on the iniquity of their having been amalgamated with Poles for the purposes of refugee relief.[44]

More direct encounters between refugees and the host population reinforced the sense of national difference. Press reports drew attention to the fact that ordinary Russian people considered the Latvians to be 'nemtsy', or Germans, because the decisive factor in determining a person's identity was their religion, and most Latvians were Lutheran. Portrayed as Germans, Latvian refugees were often denied work, while in the larger cities they were the victims of street fights and organised attacks. As a result of these attitudes, in August 1915 the Latvian press began publishing the slogan, 'Refugees, get yourselves proof of your nationality!'[45]

Refugees were given a green book registering their name, place of origin and ethnic affiliation, with the aim of deterring fraudulent claims for assistance from more than one national committee. National committees transacted their business with refugees in their native language, but also devoted much of their time to arrangements for tuition in the mother tongue. Schools taught in the native language. The Latvian organisation *Dzimtene* created a network of schools for refugee children where the curriculum was designed to assist children to cope with the new circumstances by including instruction in Latvian and Russian, as well as religious study, maths, nature study, singing and gymnastics. The main difficulty they faced was a dearth of good staff. National committees struggled to overcome such limitations; like other activists, they were keen that schooling should stem the rising tide of juvenile crime and immorality. National organisations also arranged cultural events, such as choral competitions, music festivals and art exhibitions.[46]

The national dimension of refugeedom provoked some unease in official circles, yet little could be done to prevent the efflorescence of relief organisations catering for specific nationalities, whose efforts were grudgingly accepted by government as a means of lightening the burden on hard-pressed officials and on the public purse. Local authorities welcomed the intervention of national committees as a means of relieving the strain on municipal budgets and concentrating on provision for the indigenous population. Contrasts were sometimes drawn between the speed and efficiency of the national committees and the hesitant manner in which

Russian authorities handled refugee relief. The national committees also offered the advantage, so far as the government was concerned, of being an alternative to the politically troublesome voluntary organisations.[47]

From the refugees' point of view the experience of war appears to have contributed to the growth of national consciousness, buttressed by their sense of betrayal and oppression at the hands of Russian officials. Collective action helped to bridge the gap between the educated national elite, refugee members of the national intelligentsia and the 'common' refugee. It was no longer possible to retain the conventional sharp distinction between members of the educated intelligentsia and the 'dark' narod, because they had suffered a common exposure to the dehumanising and debilitating consequences of refugeedom. Non-refugee members of national minorities bound themselves together by taxes levied on the entire community. Refugeedom conferred respectability upon the rhetoric of national consciousness and imparted vitality to actions that were couched in a national idiom. Refugees were mobilised for a crusade in support of national regeneration. This was one of the most remarkable and unexpected consequences of the war.[48]

8.4   Crisis in the periphery: the revolt in Central Asia, 1916

One of the notable aspects of Russia's First World War was the way in which it entailed mobilisation at the level of empire. The demand for new sources of manpower brought the Russian army face to face with colonial subjects. The most serious repercussion was the revolt in Central Asia in 1916.

The revolt cannot fully be explained without considering the prolonged process of Russian colonisation before the war. Russian peasants had settled in Turkestan in large numbers during the 1880s and 1890s, and again during the era of the Stolypin reforms. They received land that the imperial government had seized from indigenous nomadic pastoral farmers. The government controlled access to scarce water resources, favouring Russian settlers at the expense of Kazakh natives. In the southern steppe provinces of Syr Daria and Semirech'e, the land settlement and expropriation policies of the regime deprived indigenous nomads of access to winter pasture. As a consequence, herds of cattle were being depleted.

Not surprisingly, relations between the indigenous population of Turkestan and Russian officials had for many years been characterised by mutual suspicion and antagonism, culminating in sporadic outbreaks of violence. However, none of the outbreaks of unrest in Central Asia before the war reached the pitch of the 1916 revolt, when resistance took the form of a full-blown attack on imperial power.

The outbreak of the revolt can be attributed directly to the war, chiefly in four respects.[49] First, the war led to severe shortages of manufactured consumer goods as well as foodstuffs. The blame for the increased price of basic necessities was laid at the door of local merchants. Local cotton producers complained of the low prices that the government offered them for their crops. Some farmers were forced into bankruptcy. Second, these difficulties were compounded by the disruption to the regional balance of food supply brought about by the government's decision to send tens of thousands of prisoners of war and refugees to Turkestan, something that local residents and displaced persons alike resented bitterly. Third, the army obliged local Kazakh farmers to supply horses, either well below market prices or even without compensation. But the most serious consequence of all was that the state finally overcame its objections to drafting the empire's 'foreigners' (inorodtsy) in an already volatile region.[50]

The over-stretched Russian army needed to find new sources of manpower for construction work. On 25 June 1916 the government decreed that indigenous males aged 18 to 43, who had hitherto been exempt from the draft, should register immediately for military service. Officials expected to conscript 390,000 men in accordance with a regional quota system, including 87,000 from Semirech'e, 60,000 from Syr-Daria and 60,000 from Turgai; the remainder would be supplied from Akmolinsk, Ural'sk and Semipalatinsk. These demands coincided with the cotton harvest, a highly labour intensive activity. Cultural considerations were also at stake. Wealthy locals resented the imposition of physical labour, feeling demeaned by the expectation of having to mix with men of a lower social status; ironically, military service would have given them an opportunity to use their prized skills of horsemanship. Although the Ministry of War tried to sugar the pill, stating that 'we do not call these persons as soldiers into the army, but for work necessary for the army in return for pay and provisions', the damage was already done.[51]

Some local Kazakh leaders tried to find a negotiated solution to the crisis, even sending representatives to Petrograd to meet with the Minister of War. They offered to supply cash in lieu of manpower. Muslim representatives in the State Duma published an appeal to Prime Minister Stürmer, urging him to improve relations between the local native administration and the military. The government suspended conscription in

Fergana, in order to enable farmers to gather the cotton harvest, so vital to the needs of manufacturing industry in the Central Industrial Region. Many prisoners and refugees were shunted out of Central Asia, to alleviate pressures on food supplies. However, all these efforts at compromise came to naught. Moderate spokesmen yielded to Kazakh radicals who declared that they would not serve the Russian Tsar and would kill anyone who did. In August they attacked Russian shopkeepers and local officials. Record offices containing the lists of names of those liable for service were a favourite target. (These 'family lists' were widely believed to contain incorrect information and to provide easy opportunities for officials to exempt relatives and friends.) By and large – with the exception of the area around Lake Issyk-Kul – Russian settlers were left alone. Local police, administrators and native scribes, as well as Russian soldiers, were not so lucky. Tens of thousands were killed.[52]

The revolt spread to engulf Semirech'e and Syr-Daria. The Kazakh, Kirgiz and Uzbek rebels were well organised and levied dues on the local population in order to finance their campaign. Potential conscripts went into hiding, rebels blockaded the town of Turgai and demanded the release of prisoners and rail links between major centres of population were severed. More significant still was the emergence of a new regional Kazakh politics. Kazakh leaders overcame local rivalries and met in regional assemblies to debate the course of action.

Labour conscription, the original cause of the rebellion, turned out to be something of a shambles. The authorities in Turgai succeeded in conscripting only 10,000 workers, less than one-fifth of the original quota, although higher rates of conscription were reported in Akmolinsk and Semipalatinsk. Livestock numbers were decimated, partly because rebels killed their animals to avoid seizure by tsarist officers and partly because fodder stocks had declined drastically.

Repression was merciless. The regime deployed Cossack punishment squads as well as regular army troops who found themselves fighting the rebels rather than Germans or Austrians, a state of affairs that they resented. When the siege of Turgai was lifted, in November 1916, the Kazakh inhabitants were brutally deported, in atrocious weather and without adequate clothing. Those who evaded capture crossed over the border into China, preferring exile to the risk of execution. Estimates range from one quarter of a million to half a million. Many died en route. By the end of 1916 the revolt had subsided, although pockets of resistance continued well into 1917.[53]

Following the revolt, the tsarist government launched an official inquiry headed by General A.N. Kuropatkin, the recently appointed governor general of Turkestan. Kuropatkin concluded that the revolt in Semirechie was a consequence of government resettlement and dispossession of the indigenous population, but the commission also had harsh words to say about Russian colonists, whom he described as 'rubbish' and as 'criminals'. There were reports of native villagers having been robbed by unscrupulous and racist Russian settlers.[54] Other factors were also at work. In the northern part of Turkestan, many Kazakhs adhered to shamanist beliefs. Further south, in areas of sedentary agriculture, the deeply religious Uzbek farmers espoused Islam. Local Muslim clerics instructed them about the implication of the mobilisation decree. Some clergy declared *jihad* (holy war) against the Russians, encouraging the rebels to think of themselves as martyrs to the Muslim faith. Another dimension was introduced by those who found evidence of German, Jewish and Turkish influence. One local governor arrested flour millers whom he accused of speculation. They were convenient scapegoats.

The situation in the region changed in important respects following the February Revolution. At the end of March 1917 the Provisional Government introduced a new administration. It proclaimed an amnesty for those who had taken part in the revolt and land that had been seized was returned to its original owners. Nonetheless, martial law continued in many districts and the government procrastinated over the issue of land that had been granted to Russian settlers prior to the war.[55]

After the October Revolution, leaders of the revolt – some of whom joined the Bolshevik Party – fell out among themselves. Divisions opened up between a liberal elite and conservative forces, over such issues as the position of women in Kazakh society, the role of Islam in an autonomous polity and the respective status of Kazakh natives and Russian settlers. However, the memory of revolt against Russian rule helped to fuel further resistance, and a catastrophic famine in the winter of 1917–1918 hardened local sentiment. Throughout the civil war period and beyond, the Basmachi ('bandits') in the Fergana valley maintained a kind of guerrilla warfare against Soviet rule, protesting the requisitioning of food and – in an eerie echo of 1916 – the forced conscription of Muslim troops into the Red Army.[56]

What were the lessons of the revolt in Central Asia? The conclusion is inescapable: first, that the revolt was brought about by the strains of war, in so far as pressures in the labour market dictated a search for additional sources of manpower. Wartime exigencies thus spread from the centre to the periphery of the Russian empire. Second, the revolt constituted another element in the 'nationalisation' of political life. The government itself attributed partial responsibility for the revolt to Germans, Turks and Jews, and concluded that Kazakhs could not, by virtue of their ethnicity, be trusted to be loyal members of the imperial polity. Kuropatkin told a Kazakh audience that 'the Russian empire is great and powerful, but the main role in its formation, strengthening, and expansion is played by the Russians ... The many peoples inhabiting Russia are all children of one father, the Great Sovereign Emperor'. But they owed a duty to the 'father'; the alternative was permanent exclusion from the body politic.[57] Third, the tsarist government targeted Kazakhs. In the pre-war period displacement had been given an economic rationale, in terms of the need to find land for Russian settlers who could devote themselves to the permanent cultivation of farmland. During the war the rationale shifted to a 'population politics', in which the inherent disloyalty of the Kazakhs justified their deportation and resettlement. This only reinforced their sense that it was someone else's war.[58]

Conclusions

Patriotism during Russia's First World War gave vent to troubling expressions of sentiment and belief. The most overt expression was the doctrine and practice of economic nationalism, whose consequences included attacks on the persons and property of entire ethnic groups. The war unleashed a campaign against ethnic Germans, German residents and German culture. Latvian refugees were mistaken for Germans. The campaign against the 'German yoke' was targeted at German ownership of land, industrial and financial assets. Russia's High Command deported German farmers from the land on which many of them had settled for generations, and German residents in towns and cities faced opprobrium and even violence from their neighbours. This hostility was subsequently translated into legalised expropriation. Expropriation and deportation anticipated the practices adopted by the Bolsheviks after 1917.

The state pursued a policy of economic nationalism, targeting German businesses and settlers, exploiting the xenophobia of Moscow merchants while playing to the popular gallery. The resulting frenzy caught other subjects of the Tsar in the net. The borderlands were 'cleansed' of elements deemed 'subversive' by virtue of their ethnic identity. However, their relocation created the paradox whereby (as one military official put it) 'purely Russian provinces are being completely defiled by elements hostile to us'.[59]

Another product of forced migration was the emphasis upon a new national politics. Targeted groups learned the hard way that their ethnicity marked them as different and vulnerable. The imperial state no longer offered ethnic minorities the prospect of assimilation. However, ethnic solidarity in turn held the key to the salvation of minority groups; thus would refugee relief entail the provision of welfare by new national organisations. While Russian refugees were excluded from that process, non-Russian refugees relied upon omnipresent national organisations, whose leaders gained valuable lessons in the conduct of government.

Prisoners of war also began to be described and organised in national terms. By 1918 this had profound implications for Czech POWs who took up arms against Austria–Hungary. A final acknowledgement of the power of national sentiment was the decision of the tsarist state, albeit reluctantly, to approve the formation of national units in the imperial army. In these various ways, the war contributed to the 'nationalisation' of politics.

The revolt of Kazakhs in Central Asia during 1916 brought home to Russia's rulers the high costs of imperial administration. Wartime economic imperatives clashed with indigenous culture. Resistance to imperial rule demonstrated the complex interaction of economic, social, ethnic, religious and political considerations. At one level the issue was about access to land and water, but questions of political order were also at stake, including the responsibility for controlling Turkestan's natural resources and on whose behalf. Perhaps, too, the revolt demonstrated the powerful grip that the doctrine of war as an instrument of politics now held on ordinary people. If government leaders in Petrograd were prepared to go to war to defend their interests, and to demand sacrifices from Kazakhs, why should the indigenous population of Turkestan not shed blood in order to protect their lands and their way of life?

Much of the material presented here is consistent with a less benign reading of wartime government than is usually depicted. The focus has not been on ineffectual attempts by the Tsar to organise his troops or to bring recalcitrant ministers to heel. Instead we have witnessed the use of harsh measures to deprive ordinary civilians of their livelihood and to discipline those who sought liberation from tyranny. The chosen instruments of repression – forced migration and expropriation – are more often associated with the excesses of Stalinism than with Romanov Russia. Stalin needed no lessons from Nicholas II, but he was not the first to embark on systematic brutality towards Russia's civilian population, as a means of purging society of dangerous 'elements'.[60]

Note on further reading

Economic nationalism can be traced in the work of Nolde, 1928. A more up-to-date account, drawing upon an extensive range of sources, is Lohr, 2003. On prisoners of war see Rachamimov, 2002, and (in German) the comprehensive study by Nachtigal, 2003. For refugees and national politics see Gatrell, 1999. A full discussion of the tsarist army and nationality politics remains to be written; a start has been made by Sanborn, 2003. The 1916 revolt is the subject of a monograph by Sokol, 1954, now very difficult to obtain. More up-to-date but brief treatments in English include the relevant sections of Pierce, 1960, Olcott, 1995, and Brower, 2002.

References

1 Horne, ed., 1997, pp. 173–91 (Cornwall); Ferro, 1973, pp. 15–18, 98–100.

2 Kappeler, 2001; Service, ed., 1992, pp. 35–63 (Jones).

3 Rogger, 1986, pp. 56–112; Löwe, 1992.

4 Fuller, 1985, p. 206.

5 Grave et al., 1927, p. 137, quoting a police report dated 30 October 1916.

6 For details see Lohr, 2003, pp. 27–30, 66–8, 100–101.

7 Klibanov, 1982, p. 145. 'How is one to manage with Baptists among whom German influence and sympathies are clearly visible?' asked N.B. Shcherbatov, Minister of the Interior, in August 1915. Quoted in Cherniavsky, ed., 1967, p. 193.

8 Jahn, 1995, p. 152; Lohr, 2003, pp. 13, 61.

9 Klibanov, 1982, p. 335.

10 RGVIA f.2005, op.1, d.28, ll.5–7ob., chief of Odessa military district to Ianushkevich, 25 October 1914.

11 *Novoe vremia* excelled itself on 30 December 1914 with the comment: 'Let us hope that we shall soon get rid of these poisonous spiders that suck the best juices from our land and systematically undermine the Russian state idea'.

12 RGVIA f.2032, op.1, d.281, ll.75–84, 308–22; f.2005, op.1, d.28, ll.238–9; Lohr, 2003, p. 137.

13 The frontier was defined as up to 150 km from the western borders (from Finland to the Black Sea), and included the whole of Poland. Nolde, 1928, pp. 103–15.

14 Nolde, 1928; Lohr, 2003, pp. 100–109.

15 Kondrat'ev, 1991, p. 124; Lohr, 2003, p. 113.

16 *Gosudarstvennaia Duma: stenograficheskii otchet*, fourth session, fifth sitting, 3 August 1915, cols 497–508; Rempel, 1932.

17 RGIA f.1284, op.194, d.22–1915, l.3.

18 Porshneva, 2000, p. 169.

19 Lohr, 2003, pp. 31–50; Mal'kov, ed., 1998, pp. 434–5 (Kir''ianov). The riots followed the sinking of the passenger ship *Lusitania* and the fall of Przemysl' fortress. They claimed the Minister of the Interior, N.A. Maklakov, as a victim.

20 *Birzhevye vedomosti*, 15007, 5 August 1915; Sidorov, ed., 1968, pp. 227–38 (Diakin).

21 Maevskii, 1957, pp. 267–71; Jahn, 1995, p. 152; Lohr, 2003, pp. 71–6.

22 Cherniavsky, ed., 1967, pp. 59, 61, 65–66. Krivoshein argued that, although competition in the towns would be healthy for the national economy, 'the village was another matter entirely. Not only must one not allow Jews there, one must also fight illegal penetration in every way'.

23 Rogger, 1986, p. 169; Löwe, 1992, pp. 325–31.

24 Löwe, 1992, p. 377; Rogger, 1986, p. 105.

25 Cherniavsky, ed., 1967, pp. 61, 70, 85.

26 Gatrell, 1999, p. 148.

27 Gatrell, 1999, p. 149.

28 Lohr, 2003, pp. 150–52, 160.

29 Rachamimov, 2002, p. 116.

30 Sanborn, 2003, pp. 74–82; Wildman, 1980, pp. 103–4; Sidorov ed., 1968, pp. 158–69 (Beliakevich), quotation on p. 167.

31 Sanborn, 2003, pp. 75–8; Frenkin, 1978, pp. 211–40.

32 Sanborn, 2003, pp. 81–2.

33 For a reference to 'concentration camps' see *Materialy k uchetu*, volume 2, 1917, p. 66.

34 In Brändström's words, ' "healthy" are those with inflammation of the kidneys, tuberculosis, diarrhoea, dysentery, boils and gangrene, in short, every disease but typhus and smallpox'. Brändström, 1929, pp. 101–5.

35 Kohn and Meyendorff, 1932, pp. 37–41; Brändström, 1929. For the treatment of civilian prisoners see Davis, 1983, pp. 164–5. On the Murmansk railway see Nachtigal, 2001, pp. 124–6; Rachamimov, 2002, pp. 112–13.

36 Volkov, 1930, p. 77; Rachamimov, 2002, pp. 9, 89–107.

37 Davis, 1983, pp. 168–9, 172; Nachtigal, 2003; Rachamimov, 2002, pp. 96, 118 (quotation on p. 96).

38 Rachamimov, 2002, pp. 118–19.

39 Volgyes, 1973.

40 Knox, 1921, volume 1, p. 322.

41 *Izvestiia VSG*, 1916, 34, p. 223. Different figures were reported by the Tatiana Committee. See Kohn and Meyendorff, 1932, p. 34.

42 Gatrell, 1999, pp. 211–15.

43 Gatrell, 1999, pp. 159, 283.

44 Gatrell, 1999, pp. 165–8.

45 *Līdums*, 170, 1915, p. 3; ibid., 175, 1915, p. 2; ibid., 202, 1915, p. 3.

46 *Izvestiia VZS*, 34, 1 March 1916, pp. 98–101.

47 *B. ved.*, 15001 and 15004, 3 and 6 August 1915.

48 Gatrell, 1999, pp. 168–70.

49 Daniel Brower argues instead that the war was of secondary importance and that the revolt was 'a judgement on the empire's half-century of colonial rule'. Brower, 2002, p. 152.

50 Pierce, 1960, p. 267; Pallot, ed., 1998, pp. 194–209 (Buttino).

51 Kastel'skaia, 1972, p. 86; Sokol, 1954, p. 111. No major uprising took place in the Caucasus.

52 Details in Piaskovskii, ed., 1960. According to Sokol, 1954, pp. 158–60, 3,600 Russian settlers were killed, a number greatly exceeded by deaths of the indigenous inhabitants.

53 Olcott, 1995, pp. 121–25.

54 Kuropatkin, 1929, diary entries for August 1916 through February 1917. Kuropatkin's appointment was announced on 21 July; he arrived in Tashkent on 8 August.

55 Olcott, 1995, pp. 129–37.

56 Buttino, 1993, pp. 257–77.

57 My interpretation differs from that of Pierce, 1960, pp. 284–5, who stresses Kuropatkin's conciliatory stance.

58 Olcott, 1995, p. 125, puts the numbers of resettled Kazakhs at 200,000.

59 M.D. Bonch-Bruevich, writing in June 1915, quoted in Lohr, 2003, p. 155.

60 Holquist, 2002; Sanborn, 2003; Lohr, 2003, pp. 82–3, 111, 163.

CHAPTER 9

Hierarchy subverted: the February Revolution and the Provisional Government

The authorities must be certain of victory over the internal enemy which has long been more dangerous and fierce and brazen than the external enemy.

Essentially you are declaring all of Russia the internal enemy.

> *[From an exchange between N.A. Maklakov and the chairman of the Extraordinary Commission of Investigation in 1917. Quoted in Miliukov, 1967, p. 316]*

Beset by popular protest over shortages of food and fuel, confronted by opposition within and outside parliament, and unable to count upon the support of the military leadership, the old regime exhausted its capacity to survive. The Tsar abdicated, yielding to a Provisional Government in which some of his fiercest detractors now 'shared' power with the new Petrograd Soviet.[1] The plethora of alternative agencies – voluntary organisations, professional associations, national committees, co-operatives and the like – came into their own. Patriotism was now associated with loyalty to the revolution rather than to the discredited tsarist regime.

Revolution afforded an opportunity to re-define attitudes towards the war. Existing institutions were 'democratised' which meant a recasting of existing social relations. A government commission under a leading Moscow lawyer began to investigate the 'dark forces' of the old regime.[2] In many towns and cities new 'committees of public organisations' came to the fore, to foster co-operation between educated and plebeian Russia. However, they quickly became a site of conflict between the liberal version of reform, which sought to protect the interests of property within a newly democratised polity, and a popular class-based assault on capital.[3]

The Provisional Government re-dedicated the country to the cause of war and lost no time in reasserting Russia's commitment to the Allied war effort, by explicitly ruling out a separate peace with Germany. Most soldiers and workers endorsed this message, their leaders emphasising that it was time to 'redouble efforts' having 'drunk at the well of freedom'.[4] Some government ministers went a great deal further, arguing that Russia had a right to dominate Constantinople and the Dardanelles, a stance that claimed the scalp of Paul Miliukov, the Provisional Government's first foreign minister, in April 1917.[5] Miliukov's resignation opened the way for Soviet leaders to join a coalition government.[6] In May the USA entered the war, promising a fresh infusion of credit for the Russian war effort and an improved supply of munitions. In June 1917 the newly installed Minister of War, Aleksandr Kerenskii, embarked on a fresh military offensive, with disastrous political consequences.

The war effort – and its corollaries, discipline and duty – supported a powerful rhetoric about the need to quell radical enthusiasms. Yet the more vociferously Russia's leaders used the language of wartime obligation and enjoined people to behave 'responsibly', the more they established the connection in the popular mind that genuine freedom could be secured only by bringing about a rapid end to the war. On the political left, the Mensheviks demanded greater state control over the economy, in order to stem its disintegration. At a grass roots level, radical political forces moved into the open. The Socialist Revolutionary (SR) Party campaigned for immediate land reform, by which they meant the dispossession of the landed gentry. The Bolsheviks, tiny in number in February, gained new numbers rapidly during the summer of 1917 and unleashed an outspoken campaign for peace, bread, land and workers' control.[7]

Social and economic relations were closely intertwined with political practice, and the war inflicted insidious damage on the conduct of both. The relationship between economics and politics was reflected in debates about control. Control meant many things, not all of them mutually compatible. First, it meant control by 'responsible' politicians over the revolutionary forces unleashed by the events of February, lest the actions taken by workers, peasants, soldiers and sailors provoke a counter-revolutionary backlash. This doctrine found its expression in frequent utterances by the Provisional Government and the Petrograd Soviet.

Second, it suggested the application of mechanisms of economic control by 'disinterested' agents of the state who were motivated by a desire to steer the economy to safety, whether by improving the supply of raw materials, securing additional supplies of food or increasing the productivity of labour. Third, control meant the exercise of supervision over one's social superiors and holding them to account. At its extreme it entailed the application of the elective principle to ensure that foremen, managers and even officers were answerable to a newly enfranchised 'electorate'. Finally, control implied self-control. Its antonym was a personal loss of responsibility and the abandonment to fantasy, resulting in increased rates of criminal behaviour, in drunkenness, in prostitution and other social 'maladies'. These afflictions might be an unfortunate by-product of wartime, but they threatened the foundations of civic responsibility upon which the Provisional Government staked its claim to legitimacy.[8]

9.1   Regime change: the Provisional Government and the war effort

During the winter of 1916 Nicholas II received reports of impending economic disaster. In February the chairman of the Duma, Mikhail Rodzianko advocated a 'national economic plan', which would include public management of the railway network and greater rights for organised labour. Once public confidence had been restored, the government could encourage Russia's citizens to invest in government stock.[9] The Tsar treated Rodzianko's assessment with contempt, but it coincided with more dire news. Colonel A.P. Martynov, head of the Moscow political police, lamented that 'it is difficult to say what measures could be taken to rekindle the patriotism of the people'.[10] Daily reports drew attention to the rising price of food and fuel. The mayor of Moscow, Mikhail Chelnokov, wrote to Rittikh complaining that 'we have grain at the flour mill which has no fuel, flour where there are no wagons to transport it, and wagons where there is no freight'. In February the army received barely half its anticipated shipments of grain, but Russia's cities received only 25 per cent of its expected supply. Moscow had sufficient flour for one and a half days.[11]

Popular despondency turned into concerted action ('The revolution is there in the nerves before it comes out on the street', in Trotsky's memorable words[12]). In Petrograd, workers took to the streets to commemorate the twelfth anniversary of Bloody Sunday. Close on 100,000 men and women came out on strike one month later, demanding bread and an end to the war. On International Women's Day (23 February), women textile workers downed tools. Troops belonging to the Petrograd garrison – ironically, many of them sent there as punishment for earlier militancy – sided with the protestors. Having done his best to hold on to power, Nicholas had insufficient forces at his disposal. His generals, led by Alekseev, urged him to abdicate in favour of his brother, a decision he took on 2 March 1917.[13] There was widespread relief and rejoicing. Peasants submitted petitions greeting the Tsar's overthrow, but pledging support for the war effort.[14]

The new government sought to recast the relationship between state and society, in order to sustain the war effort. They called upon 'the citizens of great and free Russia' to back the new government by deed, word and money. Only constant vigilance and dedication to the war effort would force the enemy to retreat, and only then would the risk of a return to the 'old, dead and discredited regime' be averted.[15] The language of patriotism, linked to a commitment to equality and justice, ran through the proclamations of the first revolutionary cabinet. The Orthodox Church quickly switched its allegiance, reminding soldiers of the need to fight until Russia's enemies conceded defeat.[16]

At the same time, the old divisions between erstwhile opposition elements proved difficult to overcome. In the first place, the Provisional Government brought together liberals of a quite different hue. The Prime Minister, Prince Georgii L'vov, believed that narod should rally behind its patriotic 'duty', setting aside self-interest in pursuit of the common good. The new Minister of War, Guchkov, was also wholly committed to the war effort. Miliukov emphasised the need for Russia to maintain its treaty obligations and military commitments. Other ministers, such as the new Minister of Trade and Industry, A.I. Konovalov, and Kerenskii, Minister of Justice, had fewer qualms about rocking the boat. Konovalov believed in making major concessions to workers and peasants, as a condition of securing their active commitment to the war effort. Liberal opponents of the Tsar had not hitherto mentioned Kerenskii's name as a potential cabinet minister, and by taking office he had to overcome profound misgivings in the revived Petrograd Soviet about the desirability of collaborating with the new regime. The Soviet adhered to the doctrine of 'dual power', according to which it would hold the government to account, which it could only do by maintaining its distance. However, Kerenskii was an immensely popular choice on the streets of Petrograd, where he was seen as the people's champion and an important element in the new cabinet.[17]

The first measures taken by the new government demonstrated its intention to harness administrative reform to the patriotic impulse. Provincial governors were dismissed, their place being taken by the chairmen of zemstvo boards, symbolising the government's determination to recognise the achievements and ambitions of reformist local authorities. The Provisional Government embarked on other reforms. It lifted restrictions on the formation of co-operatives, paving the way for a national congress. At the lower tier of local government zemstvo members were appointed by the new provincial and district 'commissars' and charged with the task of improving supplies to the armed forces, 'eliminating shortages and high prices of food and articles of prime necessity', and of maintaining public order. However, these measures did nothing to reduce either peasant scepticism or the suspicions of the 'third element' about the new personnel.[18]

Cabinet ministers depicted the prospects of the country in glowing terms, since they were deemed to rest upon a new political legitimacy and greater commercial liberty. But the long-awaited 'social reconstruction', combined with the ever-present demands of war, imposed ever more heavy claims on the state budget. Civil servants, including employees of the state-owned railways and those employed in post and telegraph services, secured a substantial pay rise. In addition, the number of employees grew as a result of the extension of economic regulation. Revisions to government contracts also inflated the cost to the state of acquiring goods and services.[19]

Popular pressure mounted on the Provisional Government to enact further fiscal reform, in the interests of fairness. The All-Russian Congress of Soviets in late June argued that the new income tax and excess profits tax should be 'only the first steps in the general reform of the entire system of taxation'. The congress advocated a 'high single tax' as preferable to the current mix of direct taxes, and also advocated a radical revision of death duties and other unearned income.[20] The government responded by preparing an 'extraordinary levy on incomes'. Since the basis for the levy was the income earned during 1916, since high-income earners had suffered financial loss during 1917, and since new death duties were about to come into force, the financial health of the rich appeared precarious. Shingarev, who occupied the post of Minister of Finances between May and July 1917, proclaimed that new taxes should be 'introduced decisively and even severely'. The Petrograd Society of Factory Owners and Manufacturers denounced the 'inopportune and risky tax experiment'.[21]

By far the most dramatic attempt to raise funds from the Russian population was the 'Liberty Loan' of 1917. The new Minister of Finances, M.I.

Tereshchenko, explicitly regarded this as a touchstone of public support for the new regime, whose legitimacy would also help restore foreign confidence. Originally conceived as a 'Victory Loan', socialist members of the new cabinet felt that this was too bellicose a term. The launch of the 'Liberty Loan' on 6 April was accompanied by a fanfare of publicity.[22] As Tereshchenko predicted, subscriptions to the new loan proved to be a good barometer of public opinion, albeit not in the way that he had originally hoped. Early enthusiasm gave way to disillusionment, particularly on the part of workers who were expected to demonstrate a commitment to the fledgling democracy by making a contribution. In June 1917, the Petrograd Soviet attempted to assert its authority by calling upon all soviets to compel workers and peasants to subscribe to the loan (critics pointed out that the element of 'liberty' had given way to a 'forced loan'). Middle-class subscribers were deterred by a lack of confidence in the Treasury and by the evidence of growing economic and social turmoil; they also complained that the Provisional Government's tax increases had left them short of funds.[23]

Ministers now argued that external financial support 'alone offered the prospect of our salvation'. Tereshchenko maintained that Russia's credit-rating had improved dramatically and he proposed seeking assistance from the American and Japanese money markets. (Striking a bargain with the USA offered the hope of reducing Russia's dependence upon the British government.) His hopes were soon dashed. Russia's new rulers mistook the expressions of support in the corridors of power in Paris and London for a collective vote of confidence on the part of international bankers, but they were much more sceptical about Russia's prospects. Given this hard line, Russia was placed in an impossible predicament.[24]

Against this background, the Provisional Government embarked on a fateful attempt to break the military deadlock by pouring heavy artillery and troops into a campaign in Galicia in mid-June. Other objectives played a part. Moderate opinion in Russia (this included the Soviet leadership) espoused the offensive as a means of restoring order in the armed forces. Medium-term considerations included forestalling the danger of counter-revolution and exerting Russian influence over a future peace settlement.[25] Unfortunately, new lines of British credit dwindled; nor did France come up with fresh funds. Russia kept going by drawing upon unexpended credits from agreements reached at the Allied conference at Chantilly in November 1916. Worse still, the planned offensive inflamed political passions. Moderate socialist leaders who earlier adopted a 'revolutionary defencist' stance on the war came face to face with a hostile public.[26]

Kerenskii pinned great hopes on the campaign, which he regarded as a test of his personal authority as Minister of War, but the military objectives would only be realised if there were adequate supplies of hardware and ammunition. Here the picture was mixed. Russia expected deliveries of small arms and heavy artillery from abroad, but domestic production of medium calibre ordnance remained weak. In the short term, the Russian army was comparatively well equipped with heavy artillery,[27] but other preparations were more uncertain and controversial. The British refused to commit additional tonnage.[28] Military leaders expressed their anxiety about the shortage of trained manpower and about the commitment of men in uniform who fraternised with the enemy and – disillusioned by the stance of the Soviet – had begun to disobey orders and to desert.[29] Kerenskii could do little about the first point, but in addressing the second ('disgraceful behaviour') he committed himself to the re-introduction of the death penalty, a measure that outraged soldiers who felt that he had abandoned one of the most important gains of the revolution.[30] Nor did it prevent a further breakdown in discipline, wrecking any short-term advantage that Brusilov and his commanders managed to gain from the bombardment of German and Austrian positions.[31]

The Provisional Government also believed that the war effort was jeopardised by national 'particularism', most evident in the claims made by Ukrainian nationalists for greater autonomy. The proper relationship between the government and the 'imperial borderlands' divided government ministers and led to the withdrawal of the Kadets from the cabinet in early July, following a decision to make concessions to the Ukrainians.[32] The 'national question' disclosed the awkward mix of problems facing the government in the midst of war, and the readiness of the centre-right to denounce claims for autonomy as tantamount to treason. On the whole, however, national aspirations did not have a significant impact on the war economy. When Ukrainian miners went on strike it was in support of the emancipation of labour. They did not withdraw their labour in order to secure autonomy for Ukraine.[33]

9.2   Hierarchy and democracy: wars in the workplace, trench and village

Industrial harmony appeared a realistic possibility in the immediate aftermath of the February Revolution. The prevailing discourse, embraced by the Petrograd Soviet, was imbued with ideas of patriotism, duty and sacrifice: 'Workers, remember that soldiers in the trenches work without respite'.[34] However, the government and the Soviet acknowledged the sacrifices that workers had made and the need for concessions. Konovalov persuaded employers to agree to the establishment of conciliation chambers, an initiative that had long been dear to his heart and that held out the prospect of forestalling militant action by workers.[35] He introduced labour reforms, including the abolition of child labour in factories and the restriction on hours worked by juveniles aged between 15 and 17 years. Employers did not reject out of hand demands for substantial improvements in pay and hours of work. In Petrograd factory owners granted workers the eight-hour day and the right to form factory committees, but employers elsewhere took a less conciliatory line.[36]

Particularly significant for future relations between workers and employers were the new workers' militias and factory committees, which united workers across the plant irrespective of differences in trade or skill. Moderate socialists had in mind a different kind of organisation, looking to trade unions and the new soviets as the cornerstone of a disciplined labour movement. However, unions took time and money to establish, whereas a mass meeting was all it took to create a factory committee or militia. Workers regarded factory committees as inclusive institutions that defended jobs by taking practical steps to secure fuel, food and raw materials. By seeking to maintain internal factory discipline they also demonstrated working-class capacity to govern their own affairs. For their part, employers dug in their heels when workers demanded access to company accounts or sought the dismissal of managers. The successful prosecution of the war effort required order and obedience, not accountability or syndicalism.[37]

Rank and file soldiers wrote home to express a multitude of grievances. First and foremost, they complained of undignified treatment, including arbitrary punishments that seemed wholly at odds with the responsibilities expected of them and the risks to which they were exposed. The Kronstadt naval base was notoriously brutal.[38] The second area of disquiet related to the poor quality and irregular supply of food, clothing and medicines. Army rations had been reduced. Quartermasters dispensed second-hand uniforms and boots, leaving men with the uncomfortable feeling that they were literally stepping into dead men's shoes. There were complaints that food parcels never arrived. 'At least the dead no longer have to worry about the hunger or cold', wrote one soldier bitterly.[39] A related set of complaints identified the disadvantage they faced vis-à-vis their better equipped German and Austrian counterparts. Fourth, soldiers complained that exemption certificates had become a pretext for cushioning privileged groups in society from the realities of warfare. Fifth, they demanded an increase in dependants' allowances whose value had been eroded by inflation. This litany of complaint was reinforced by a sense that Russia's leaders were corrupt and incompetent, and too ready to turn soldiers into 'cannon fodder' whose lives were being sacrificed on the altar of a 'senseless war'.[40]

Soldiers and sailors believed that they had a licence to improve their status in society. Men in uniform held their superiors to account, not only for the treatment shown to their subordinates but also for their political stance, as revealed by a tendency to conceal from soldiers at the front the significance of the revolution. Following Order Number One and Kerenskii's subsequent 'Declaration of Soldiers' Rights' (11 May 1917), committees sprang up in defence of the popular understanding of 'democracy' and 'revolution'. Many of these committee men espoused the Soviet's defencist stance, something that alienated common soldiers.[41] In May 1917 naval ratings at Kronstadt went a step further, declaring their adherence to 'soviet power' rather than to the Provisional Government.[42]

Popular culture reflected this new dispensation. Traditional folk verses gave way to more belligerent soldiers' songs that welcomed the long-awaited dawn of freedom.[43] Against this background, the government and the Supreme Military Command struggled to make their voice heard. Guchkov and Alekseev attempted to rally the troops in March with a 'Manifesto to Soldiers and Citizens'. It sang the praises of the revolution but insisted that soldiers obey orders and defend the motherland: 'at the dawn of freedom we are under the threat of being turned into German hirelings'. The manifesto restated Russia's commitment to 'war to a victorious end'.[44] Far from restoring calm, however, the message encouraged further dissent and protest, reinforcing the belief in government circles that the war effort was being undermined.

The problems were no less acute in rural Russia. Peasant misgivings were magnified by the government's land and food supply policies. Land had long been at the core of the peasantry's political disaffiliation. Now they had a chance to rectify the wrongs done in earlier times.[45] The government disowned the village committees that were established in spring 1917 and recognised only its own approved organisations. Peasant militants protested that this was a top-down approach. A peasant assembly in Samara in late May, dominated by local SRs, heard speeches from leaders who supported the government, but the local delegates spoke in favour of direct action: 'we are always being told 'later, later, not until the

Constituent Assembly'. . . But the land question must be solved now and we should not put our trust blindly in the political parties'. The assembled delegates rejected the authority of the Ministry of the Interior and the police.[46]

In the short term, peasant activism meant refusing to pay rent and trespassing on private estates. The Kadet newspaper *Russkie vedomosti* maintained that 'various anarchistic forces have emerged and are threatening to lead the country to new losses of sown area and to new national disasters'.[47] This view was supported by private landowners, by wealthy peasants as well as the nobility. A leading voice at the congress of the Union of Landowners in late 1917 adopted the military tone that was becoming commonplace in political debate: 'we must go all out, even if it means risking our lives, but at all costs we must be victorious'.[48]

Elsewhere a climate of greater openness – accompanied by the abolition of censorship – allowed greater scope for public criticism. Schools and universities became a hotbed of political debate, albeit less so than in 1905. Students who had been expelled by the old regime were allowed to resume their studies, and professors who had been dismissed were allowed back. Lectures were cancelled or hurriedly rewritten to allow university staff to comment on the events taking place. More immediately troubling were the shortages of food and fuel that led to staff absenteeism and the closure of schools and laboratories. By June there were reports that 'academic life was completely dislocated' by a growing rift between staff and students. However, more serious was the division that pitted right against left – those who thought that the revolution had been completed against those for whom it had only just begun.[49]

Underlying the authorities' attitude towards the various claims advanced by 'society' was the belief that individuals and social groups had to be self-disciplined, and not to press their claims for special treatment or prior satisfaction of their wishes, which would disrupt the war effort. The imperatives of war and the assertion of selfish desire were incompatible. By committing themselves to war and curbing their instincts the people would demonstrate their entitlement to citizenship within 'free Russia'. This message was for the Allies as well as for domestic consumption.

9.3   Government regulation and the economic crisis

Russia's war economy suffered mixed fortunes during 1917. The output of military goods reached a peak in the winter of 1916. Thereafter it was jeopardised by emerging shortages of raw materials and fuel that were intensified by the disruption unleashed by revolution. Employers and government ministers bemoaned the decline in labour productivity, which averaged 70 per cent of the pre-war level; by mid-1917 it fell to below 40 per cent in the Donbass mines. In May 1917 Konovalov spoke of the failure of the revolution to deliver improved prospects for the development of Russia's productive forces. Instead, Russia was beset by 'destruction, anarchy and the annihilation of public and national life'.[50] Table 9.1 gives output and procurement figures for selected items in 1917.

In truth, revolutionary activism was not the sole factor contributing to economic instability. The Russian transport system had come under enormous strain long before labour militancy erupted. The government failed to deliver on its promise to supply villagers with cloth, fuel and other necessities, instead continuing to pump additional purchasing power into the economy, fuelling inflation. The large network of co-operatives was powerless to assist. As the terms of trade worsened for food producers, peasants lost interest in bringing their produce to market. In an ominous move, local soviets of workers demanded that 'firm measures' be taken

TABLE 9.1   *Output and procurement of selected products, January to December 1917*

Month	Coal Output 000 tons	Oil Extracted 000 tons	Cotton Yarn 000 tons	Grain Procured 000 tons	Per cent of stipulated amount
1916 monthly average	2390.1	n.a.	24.8	665	
1917					
January	2,555.3	406.2	26.8	934	77%
February	2,349.0	366.9	23.5	672	62%
March	2,529.1	378.4	22.7	1,130	98%
April	1,965.7	380.0	13.9	491	38%
May	2,185.2	394.8	21.1	1,261	88%
June	2,152.4	373.5	19.6	1,106	112%
July	1,967.3	381.7	14.2	459	57%
August	1,887.0	370.2	15.9	324	17%
September	1,801.8	288.3	16.7	765	31%
October	1,883.7	309.6	15.8	449	19%
November	1,867.0	334.2	14.3	640	38%
December	1,280.9	327.6	14.4	136	7%

Sources and note: Industrial products from Kafengauz, 1994, pp. 213, 466. Grain procurements from Kondrat'ev, 1991, p. 231. Oil output refers to the four largest fields in Baku.

against those who engaged in 'sabotage', while in Tomsk peasants angrily refused to sell grain: 'we'll give to the army, but the towns can get their own food'. Relations between town and country reached new depths.[51]

The urban revolution gave rise to grave economic uncertainty at the level of the individual enterprise. Jobs were on the line. Factories closed down at an alarming rate; during the spring and summer months the largest plants were the most vulnerable. The economic and social repercussions made themselves strongly felt in Petrograd. Famous victims of the economic collapse included the Franco-Russian Works, Nevskii Shipyards and Engineering, the Baranovskii Pipe and Fuse Works and Atlas Engineering. As a result the production of artillery and small arms began to collapse. The manufacture of consumer goods also ground to a halt as supplies of sugar, flour, cotton and paper dwindled.[52]

Leading government officials argued that the difficulties in keeping Petrograd supplied with fuel and raw materials made it imperative to shift defence production elsewhere. Now it was the turn of proletarian leaders to express outrage at this attempt to subvert working-class solidarity. Factory committees attempted to secure jobs by intervening at the level of the enterprise to challenge industrialists' claims about their insolvency. Here, too, the language of 'sabotage' was widely disseminated – and believed. Employers reacted negatively to this rhetoric: 'the demands of the workers are not based on law and if met would lead to the complete destruction of factory life'.[53]

Microeconomic problems fuelled entrepreneurial misery and helped to intensify a sense of impending doom. Engineering enterprises had laboured under grave financial difficulties since the second half of 1916. Partly these were a reflection of increased costs of labour, fuel and raw materials, particularly iron and steel. Suppliers reneged on old contracts and paid the financial penalty before renegotiating terms with their clients. Costs also rose because many of the leading firms offered workers subsidised housing, food and medical care, in order to retain skilled labour. The February Revolution raised the stakes by bringing about a sharp increase in wages. In the south Russian iron and steel industry, for example, the average wage in June 1917 was twice what it was a year earlier. Meanwhile output per person had fallen by nearly a half.[54] In Moscow, Bromley Engineering reported an increase in its operating expenditure, because of a need to pay higher wages, to maintain the new canteen, bakery and factory shop and to subsidise workers' purchases of galoshes and calico.[55] Against this background, employers argued that further wage claims would simply lead to financial insolvency. This argument cut little ice with workers, whose real wages continued to fall. By August 1917 an unskilled worker earned in real terms only half as much as in January 1917.[56]

According to government supporters, the modest initial success of the Liberty Loan was undermined by the 'intolerable' demands made by organised labour. Desperate officials contemplated various measures to compel middle-class taxpayers to make a minimum contribution to projected loans.[57] Bolder spirits such as Tugan-Baranovskii suggested that the government impose a levy on current accounts held by the commercial banks, a proposal backed by the SR Party,[58] but these radical schemes found no favour with ministers who declared them a last resort. Even so, he was unable to stop a flight of capital to safer havens abroad, such as Finland and the Far East. Not surprisingly, the most strident voice was that of the Bolshevik Party. Lenin called upon the government to annul all public debts and thus rid itself of the burden of paying interest, part of his 'revolt against capitalism'.[59]

What did economic mobilisation now mean? The war industry committees, having failed to turn themselves into a new ministry of supply, largely faded from public view. They set their sights a good deal lower, taking charge of arrangements for the supply of specific commodities such as cotton yarn. No new business came their way.[60] The Special Councils continued in existence, with more 'democratic' participation. But a sense of paralysis pervaded the government. Typical of government indecision was the debate over the regulation of the labour market. In the summer of 1917 proposals emerged for a 'Central Committee for the Allocation of Manpower', which would be responsible for allocating labour to all sectors of the economy, bearing in mind also the needs of the armed forces. Its purpose was to ensure that 'all those capable of work take part in productive labour'. Nothing came of this proposal.[61]

The Provisional Government moved quickly to 'democratise' the Special Council for Food Supply (now renamed the 'State Food Committee') and to declare its readiness to harness the network of co-operatives to assist in the task of grain procurement. Other measures were more assertive, notably the declaration on 25 March of a state grain monopoly. The brainchild of Vladimir Groman, and backed by the Petrograd Soviet, the monopoly was to be administered by food supply committees. Food producers protested that it would be impractical to implement and advocated instead free trade in grain. Other critics feared that it was the thin end of the wedge – indeed Groman had already floated the idea of controlling the prices of basic consumer goods.[62] The government sugared the pill by agreeing subsequently to an increase in maximum grain prices, despite having promised earlier that it would do no such thing. Meanwhile the peasantry, complaining that the 'bourgeoisie' dominated the new committees, spent the spring and summer months 'democratising' their membership.[63]

Other kinds of intervention followed. In a sop to peasant militants, the government declared that a farmer who refused to sow grain should have his land assigned to someone who would. Aimed primarily at landowners who claimed that a shortage of labour prevented them from sowing arable land, this populist measure showed how the patriotic card might be played to good effect.[64] The government also embarked on a more systematic approach by arranging for the distribution of inputs such as fertiliser and farm tools to farmers. The State Food Committee took charge of these arrangements, which anticipated the Bolshevik programme of 'organised commodity exchange' in 1918. These steps simply encouraged the peasantry in their belief that the state procrastinated over the one issue that really mattered, namely the redistribution of privately owned land.[65]

The procurement of grain through official channels continued to be beset by grave difficulties. In August, according to official figures, grain procurement plummeted to just 17 per cent of the expected amount.[66] Several local food supply committees refused to implement the new fixed prices that were imposed in August. A modest improvement in grain deliveries in September (the harvest was just in) proved short-lived, and the crisis in rail transport exacerbated official anxieties. Farmers with any surplus held out in expectation of a further increase in prices or converted their grain into spirits. Notwithstanding the monopoly, grain was traded on the open market. 'Bagmen' (and women) began to scour the countryside for grain to take back to the towns; although demonised as 'speculators', they performed a vital service in preventing urban consumers from starving. Hungry peasants ransacked storage depots.[67]

Under the old regime, individual local authorities had been allowed to ration available supplies of food, but in June 1917 the Provisional Government introduced a nation-wide scheme of bread rationing for all towns. Later on the scheme was extended to grits, fat and (in August) to meat and eggs. However, expectations were dashed when falling deliveries forced a cut in the prescribed rations.[68] Relatively privileged urban consumers hurriedly joined credit co-operatives in the hope of securing access to basic necessities. Quickly dubbed 'March' or 'kerosene' members, they were condemned as polluting the ideals of traditional Russian co-operation.[69] For their part, workers complained during the later summer that they had to queue for four or five hours after work in order to stand any chance of buying bread.[70]

Meanwhile government ministers increasingly deployed militarised rhetoric, rather than the language of class collaboration. To be sure, Shingarev pinned his hopes on the co-operative movement, but in doing so he called for 'the great army of industrial ants to take upon their broad and powerful shoulders the heavy burden' of organising food supply.[71] Aleksei Peshekhonov, the last 'bourgeois' Minister of Food Supply before the October Revolution, urged his food procurement agents to think of themselves as 'armed detachments' (*voinskie druzhiny*) whose task was to secure grain at all costs, even if this meant using force. Thus the desperate efforts to improve food supply were associated with a more violent rhetoric.[72]

Broadly speaking the revolution encouraged economists to develop wide-ranging ideas for the regulation of the entire economy. One embodiment of these ideas was a 'Chief Economic Committee', established in July, in order 'to work out a general plan for the organisation of national economic life and labour'. It enjoyed an uneasy co-existence alongside other bodies. Lenin – with some justification – derided the multiplication of organs of regulation, 'complicated, cumbersome and bureaucratically lifeless'.[73] The key questions were how and by whom regulation would be implemented. Liberal ministers had already nailed their colours to the mast by dismissing political experiments that incorporated 'persons who are inexperienced in economics into the majority of enterprises'.[74] By extension they bemoaned attempts to democratise the apparatus of centralised economic control or to involve factory committees in the business of economic regulation.[75]

9.4   Radical solutions and outcomes

The June offensive exposed a conflict between competing visions of military organisation. Russian generals asserted the need for clear hierarchy and unquestioning obedience to authority, whereas the rank and file challenged the lack of accountability inherent in the established army and sought to question the legitimacy of authority. Furthermore, the offensive opened up a clear rift between the Soviet leadership and the rank and file troops whose numbers were being replenished by radical replacements from the rear. The mood of Russian front-line troops improved as the offensive faltered and the German army advanced. The army – some 7.2 million strong in June 1917 – remained intact, but it had not been cowed into submission. Soldiers re-elected the delegates to the trench committees, replacing Mensheviks and SRs with Bolshevik representatives. The response of Russian generals, predictably, was to blame the committees for undermining the army's fighting effectiveness.[76]

Employers' attitudes towards working-class organisations also hardened. Riabushinskii argued in mid-August that only complete economic collapse and 'the bony hand of hunger' would bring workers to their senses. Von Ditmar, a leading figure in the Association of Industry and Trade, called for an end to talk of class war and greater emphasis upon the rights of property. However, their statements suggested that there was some truth to the radical view that employers sabotaged industry in order to defeat the organised working class. As Trotsky wrote, their stance 'cost the capitalists dear'.[77] Workers lost faith with the government in August 1917, following the decision by the Menshevik Minister of Labour, Matvei Skobelev, to issue two notorious circulars, restricting the rights of factory committees and appearing to side with the employers.[78] Skobelev had come round to the view that the salvation of Russian industry required the imposition of order in place of 'anarchy' – a term in widespread use.[79] However, he misread the situation; in fact many committees did their utmost to maintain production even where this caused workers material hardship.[80]

Strikes continued throughout the summer months. The figures are presented in Table 9.2. In August and September workers' demands stood much less chance of being accepted by employers, and this contributed to an increase in the average length of stoppages.[81] A rapid jump in prices during October prompted more workers to advance claims for an increase in wages. However, the authors of a specialised study of labour protest point out that militancy was just as much associated with a loss of confidence in the government.[82]

Relations between workers and government and employers reached rock bottom. Outbreaks of physical violence and the destruction of property in September, particularly in the mining and metallurgical industry in the south and the Urals, fostered a sense of industrial 'anarchy' among the propertied elite. It was not just violence that antagonised the employers. Increasingly workers intervened in the day-to-day operations of the enterprise, in the hope that their 'control' would form the prelude to more systematic state intervention and regulation. This translated into growing support for the Bolsheviks who appeared to offer the best chance of safeguarding the workers' revolution. Workers recognised in Bolshevism an ideology of class struggle consistent with their own daily experience of being belittled by management.[83]

TABLE 9.2   *Strikes and 'economic demands' made by workers during 1917*

	Minimum estimated number of strikers	Per cent making 'economic demands'	Percentage change in price index
March	41,640	38	6
April	17,700	92	13
May	91,140	96	18
June	114,270	91	28
July	384,560	26	16
August	379,480	57	2
September	965,000	83	9
October	441,450	97	38

Source: Koenker and Rosenberg, 1989, © 1989 Princeton University Press, pp. 167, 272.

In Petrograd a group of conservative bankers and industrialists led by Putilov and Vyshnegradskii activated the 'Society for the Economic Regeneration of Russia' in order to back Lavr Kornilov, the new commander-in-chief of the armed forces. (He replaced Brusilov on 18 July.) Painting a picture of the imminent fall of towns and cities in the northwest, including a threat to the Russian capital itself, Kornilov proposed to impose martial law in the defence factories and on the railways, to ban meetings in factory premises and to threaten strikers with capital punishment. Guchkov lent him total support and remnants of the war industry committees called for 'iron discipline at the front and in the rear'.[84] Although Kornilov's attempted coup ended in fiasco, workers concluded that some industrialists and cabinet members would stop at nothing to crush the revolution.[85]

The government faced mounting evidence of desertion and labour militancy, which came to a head with a walkout on the railways and a strike of textile workers in the Central Industrial Region. Bereft of popular support and unable to secure the instruments of repression, Kerenskii fled Petrograd on 25 October. Early the next morning the Bolshevik Military Revolutionary Committee placed the remaining members of the Provisional Government under arrest. Lenin came to the Second Congress of Soviets and placed before it decrees on peace and land.[86] His utterances captured perfectly the popular mood of disillusionment with the Provisional Government and the Menshevik leadership in the Petrograd Soviet:

Six months of revolution have elapsed. The catastrophe is even closer. Unemployment has assumed a mass scale. . . . What better evidence is needed to show that after six months of revolution (which some call a great revolution, but which so far it would perhaps be fairer to call a rotten revolution), in a democratic republic, with an abundance of unions, organs and institutions which proudly call themselves 'revolutionary democratic', absolutely nothing of any importance has actually been done to avert catastrophe, to avert famine? We are nearing ruin with increasing speed. The war will not wait and is causing increasing dislocation in every sphere of national life.[87]

Lenin's devastating remarks confirmed the politicisation of economic collapse and social upheaval.

Conclusions

During 1917 vital issues of democracy, organisation and control were debated in the glare of publicity. These revolutionary keywords meant different things to different groups. Government ministers such as Guchkov and Konovalov berated the 'dark instincts of the mob' that had been unleashed by the transition to democracy. Liberals complained that workers pursued their own interests and overlooked the needs of 'national economic life'. Many workers saw no incompatibility between initiatives taken to organise production at the level of the enterprise to secure fuel or raw materials and measures devised by state authorities to regulate economic activity.[88] Soldiers, sailors and workers practised democracy by electing delegates to representative institutions such as soviets and grass roots committees, and by appropriating and transforming the symbols of tsarist authority.

By the autumn, having been exposed to workers' attempts to replace managers and foremen with elected representatives, leading industrialists pinned their hopes on a dictatorship. Among the beleaguered industrial elite, Riabushinskii's choice of words – the 'bony hand of hunger' – showed how the rhetoric had shifted from apoplexy to apocalypse. Analogously, within the armed forces, military commanders asserted their right to 'manage' soldiers and sailors. In the countryside, too, officials stood firm against the 'anarchy' represented by seizures of food, fodder, timber and land that threatened starvation and collapse.

The formation of the Provisional Government brought to prominence a group of progressive economists such as Vladimir Groman, for whom the challenge was to regulate the entire 'national economy' by harnessing the forces of 'new Russia'. Specifically this meant organising at a central level the distribution of consumer goods and foodstuffs. If planning proved impossible to implement – and the decline in output imposed severe constraints – then government had no alternative but to contemplate the use of force. The alternative was a complete free-for-all and the unravelling of the economic nation.

The language of war and revolution intersected in interesting and complex ways. To speak of 'sacrifice' was to invoke the unequal contribution made by plebeian Russia. To speak of 'duty' was to raise the question: duty to what? The language of war shifted from defending Russia from the Teutonic foe to declaring war on one's class enemies, settling scores with those much closer to home. To utter the word 'sabotage', as did Lenin and many activists in the factory committees, was to portray bosses as opponents to whom no quarter should be given. To target 'idlers and parasites' was to demonise non-proletarians, whether merchants, officials or refugees. Russian workers also singled out immigrants who swelled the population of Russia's towns and cities as a direct result of the war. By these various means, the war sharpened existing antagonisms and cultivated fresh fields of social conflict. In the autumn of 1917, plebeian society – the elements that Maklakov in February termed the 'internal enemy' – declared open war on the propertied elite and the state.

Note on further reading

There is no full-length study of the Provisional Government. Its activities are best followed in the collection of documents edited by Browder and Kerensky, eds, 1961. Economic policy is treated in the classic book by Volobuev, 1962. The best guide to industrial politics in 1917 is Galili, 1989. Important studies of working-class activism in English include Smith, 1983, and Koenker, 1981. Peasant radicalism awaits a comprehensive modern treatment. The best study of the Russian army during 1917 is the two-volume work by Wildman, 1980–1987.

References

1 Browder and Kerensky, eds, 1961, volume 1, p. 135. The Prime Minister (G.E. L'vov), the Foreign Minister (Miliukov), the Minister of War and Navy (Guchkov), as well as the ministers of Finances (Tereshchenko), Trade and Industry (Konovalov) and Agriculture (Shingarev) all played a prominent part in the voluntary organisations. The new government was 'provisional', because Russia's post-tsarist form of government would be decided at a later stage by a Constituent Assembly.

2 The Extraordinary Commission of Investigation was headed by N.K. Murav'ev. Most of the leading members of Nicholas's various wartime cabinets were imprisoned by the Provisional Government. Stürmer died in 1917, A.N. Khvostov and Protopopov were executed by the Bolsheviks. Bark and Rittikh emigrated.

3 Orlovsky, 1989, pp. 103–5.

4 Sobolev, 1973, pp. 174–5.

5 Wade, 1969, pp. 26–50. The Foreign Minister earned the soubriquet 'Miliukov of the Dardanelles', according to Mazon, 1920, p. 51. He was replaced by Tereshchenko.

6 The key figures were Kerenskii (replacing Guchkov as Minister of War), Viktor Chernov (SR), Matvei Skobelev and Irakli Tsereteli (both Menshevik).

7 See the surveys by Wade, 2000, and Steinberg, 2001.

8 The speeches given to the State Conference in August 1917 bear this out. *Gosudarstvennoe soveshchanie*, 1930; Browder and Kerensky, eds, 1961, volume 2, pp. 1479–80.

9 *EPR*, 1957, volume 2, pp. 18–32.

10 Quoted in Coetzee and Shevin-Coetzee, eds, 1995, p. 47 (Zuckerman).

11 Diakin, 1967, p. 314; Kayden and Antsiferov, 1929, p. 101.

12 Trotsky, 1934, p. 65.

13 Mikhail Aleksandrovich immediately renounced the throne. The Russian royal family were held prisoner, first by the Provisional Government and then by the Bolsheviks, before being executed in Ekaterinburg in July 1918. Diakin, 1967, p. 315.

14 Maliavskii, 1981, p. 10.

15 *ZhZVP*, 26 March 1917.

16 Senin, 1993, p. 49.

17 Lincoln, 1986, p. 351.

18 Emmons and Vucinich, eds, 1982, pp. 383–421 (Rosenberg); Kayden and Antsiferov, 1929, pp. 24–6.

19 Volobuev, 1962, p. 414, referring to the costs of the grain monopoly.

20 Michelson et al., 1928, pp. 197–8, 205–7; Volobuev, 1962, p. 324. The Provisional Government continued to debate the introduction of state monopolies on tea, tobacco, coffee and matches.

21 Michelson et al., 1928, pp. 200–201; Volobuev, 1962, pp. 319, 329.

22 *ZhZVP*, 26 March 1917; *EPR*, 1957, volume 2, pp. 373–5, 395–9; Volobuev, 1962, pp. 339–41; Strakhov, 2003, p. 36.

23 Daily subscriptions ran at an average of 33 million rubles in early April, but fell to 16 million by early May. A month later they climbed back to 28 million rubles and still ran at 20 million at the beginning of July. Thereafter the slide was impossible to stop. Michelson et al., 1928, p. 275; Volobuev, 1962, pp. 327, 342–7.

24 Bernatskii, 24 July 1917, quoted in Volobuev, 1962, p. 365; *ZhZVP*, 4 March 1917.

25 Browder and Kerensky, eds, 1961, volume 2, pp. 921–76; Wade, 1969, pp. 88–91. The Allies agreed at the Chantilly conference that an offensive should take place on Russia's south-western front in May 1917. Neilson, 1984, p. 162.

26 Browder and Kerensky, 1961, volume 3, pp. 1386–7; Sobolev, 1973, pp. 282–322.

27 *EPR*, 1957, volume 2, pp. 169–94.

28 Neilson, 1984, pp. 266–8.

29 Gavrilov, 1986, pp. 55–6 for expressions of concern in the autumn of 1916; Wildman, 1987, p. 18; Mal'kov, ed., 1998, pp. 593–7 (Zhilin).

30 Reed, 1970, p. 45; Browder and Kerensky, eds, 1961, volume 2, pp. 982–4, 985–6; Wildman, 1987, pp. 127–33. Kerenskii did not see this as inconsistent with his earlier repudiation of the use of force. Kolonitskii, 2001, p. 6.

31 Brusilov replaced Alekseev as commander-in-chief in May. The offensive is described in Wildman, 1987, pp. 89–111.

32 The left-wing newspaper Den' reported that 'the Government has lost a more or less important group of militant Kadets but has won the sympathies of many millions of Ukrainians'. Quoted in Browder and Kerensky, eds, 1961, volume 3, p. 1384.

33 Consistent with its view on the other 'questions', the government enjoined citizens to wait for the convocation of the Constituent Assembly.

34 An appeal to steelworkers, dated 20 March 1917. *EPR*, 1957, volume 1, pp. 513–144.

35 Smith, 1983, pp. 172–3; Hogan, 1982; Galili, 1989, pp. 93–6.

36 *EPR*, 1957, volume 1, pp. 511–13; Koenker and Rosenberg, 1989, pp. 131–2.

37 Smith, 1983, pp. 80–102; Freidlin, 1967, pp. 126–62; Browder and Kerensky, eds, 1961, volume 2, pp. 718–27.

38 Porshneva, 2000, pp. 238–41; Mawdsley, 1978, p. 14.

39 Gavrilov, 1986, p. 54, quoting a letter intercepted in January or February 1917. For military food rations see Volobuev, 1962, p. 461.

40 Porshneva, 2000, pp. 241–2, 247.

41 Wildman, 1980, pp. 220–23; Browder and Kerensky, eds, 1961, volume 2, pp. 848–9, 880–83.

42 Getzler, 1983, p. 69; Buldakov, 1997, p. 57. Buldakov attaches more significance than seems warranted to what he terms 'archaic and non-political mob violence' (*buntarstvo*). Getzler, 1983, and Wildman, 1980, 1987, offer a more nuanced treatment.

43 Rayfield, 1988. Sailors retained the traditional 'Andreev' flag, but it flew alongside the Red flag. Kolonitskii, 2001, pp. 113–21.

44 Browder and Kerensky, eds, 1961, volume 2, pp. 854–6.

45 Browder and Kerensky, eds, 1961, volume 1, pp. 244–6, 282–94.

46 Figes, 1989, pp. 42–3.

47 Kingston-Mann, 1983, p. 130.

48 N.N. L'vov, quoted in Osipova, 1976, p. 123. See also Volobuev, 1962, pp. 392, 409; Browder and Kerensky, eds, 1961, volume 2, pp. 582–95.

49 Odinetz and Novgorotsev, 1929, pp. 124–8, 223–5; Gleason et al., eds, 1985, pp. 39–56 (Orlovsky).

50 Browder and Kerensky, eds, 1961, volume 2, pp. 668–9. Konovalov delivered his speech to a congress of the war industry committees on 16 May. He resigned a week later.

51 Volobuev, 1962, pp. 409, 411, 418, 420, 466–8; Lih, 1990, p. 98; Kayden and Antsiferov, 1929, p. 102.

52 Vorob'ev, 1923, p. 118; Kovalenko, 1970, p. 47; *EPR*, 1957, volume 2, pp. 180–84, GAU memo dated 29 June 1917.

53 Smith, 1983, pp. 158, 167, 171–4.

54 *EPR*, 1957, volume 2, pp. 141–2.

55 Venediktov, 1917, p. 6; Gatrell, 1995.

56 Strumilin, 1964a, p. 334; Smith, 1983, pp. 70–73.

57 Michelson et al., 1928, pp. 266–7; Prokopovich, 1918, pp. 113–14.

58 Michelson et al., 1928, pp. 277–80; Volobuev, 1962, p. 349.

59 Lenin expressed this view in a speech on the war, delivered at the First All-Russian Congress of Soviets on 9 June 1917; see also Lenin, 1977. By October, in a discussion of the Party's programme, he appeared to be more cautious, referring to the need to accommodate the 'small bondholder'.

60 Zagorsky, 1928, p. 229; Siegelbaum, 1983, pp. 202–4.

61 Bukshpan, 1929, p. 246; Zagorsky, 1928, pp. 181–2.

62 *Pervyi Vserossiiskii torgovo-promyshlennyi s"ezd*, 1917, pp. 85–7; Lih, 1990, p. 84.

63 Bukshpan, 1929, pp. 389–93, 507–16; *EPR*, 1957, volume 2, pp. 343–4; Volobuev, 1962, pp. 389–404, 413. The fixed prices in March were 65 per cent higher than in the autumn of 1916.

64 Lih, 1990, pp. 91–4; Maliavskii, 1981, pp. 73–87.

65 Yaney, 1982, p. 441.

66 *EPR*, 1957, volume 2, pp. 353–69; Kondrat'ev, 1991, p. 231, drawing on Narkomprod data.

67 Volobuev, 1962, pp. 431, 435–8, 442; Lih, 1990, p. 107.

68 Strumilin, 1964a, p. 350; Volobuev, 1962, p. 461.

69 Kayden and Antsiferov, 1929, pp. 74, 293.

70 Volobuev, 1962, p. 463.

71 Cited by Kayden and Antsiferov, 1929, p. 102.

72 Yaney, 1982, p. 442.

73 Lenin, 1977, p. 329; *ZhZVP*, 21 June 1917; Bukshpan, 1929, pp. 516–28; Volobuev, 1962, p. 141.

74 Browder and Kerensky, eds, 1961, volume 2, p. 670 (Konovalov).

75 Smith, 1983, pp. 151–60.

76 Wildman, 1987, pp. 37–8, 141–7, 230; Gavrilov, 1986, p. 58.

77 *Gosudarstvennoe soveshchanie*, 1930, p. 255; McDaniel, 1988, pp. 458–9; Trotsky, 1934, p. 639.

78 *EPR*, 1957, volume 1, pp. 555, 558; Browder and Kerensky, eds, 1961, volume 2, pp. 721–2; Koenker and Rosenberg, 1989, pp. 278–9.

79 Bailes, 1978, pp. 20–21. Compare Wildman, 1987, pp. 148–83, on the generals' views of soldiers' committees.

80 Izmailovskaia, 1920, pp. 134–6; Smith, 1983, pp. 180–81.

81 Galili, 1989, pp. 374–5; Gaponenko, 1970, p. 386.

82 Koenker and Rosenberg, 1989, p. 273.

83 *EPR*, 1957, volume 1, pp. 533–4, 539; Galili, 1989, p. 375; Koenker and Rosenberg, 1989, pp. 281–8.

84 Cited in Siegelbaum, 1983, p. 207.

85 Smith, 1983, pp. 171–2. Kornilov's abortive intervention in Russian politics is discussed in Lincoln, 1986, pp. 412–25, White, 1994, p. 141, and Swain, 1996, pp. 20–38.

86 White, 1994, pp. 165–7.

87 Lenin, 1977, pp. 327–8.

88 Browder and Kerensky, eds, 1961, volume 2, p. 669.

CHAPTER 10

Economic meltdown and revolutionary objectives: between European war and Civil War, 1917–1918

The war taught us much, not only that people suffered, but that those who have the best technology, discipline, and machinery come out on top; it is this that the war taught us, and it is a good thing it taught us.

[Lenin, cited in Bailes, 1978, p. 49]

The Bolsheviks came to power on a tide of popular support for 'peace, bread and land', powerful slogans that captured the spirit of exhaustion after nearly three and a half years of war. The old regime bequeathed to the new not only a backward economy but also a society ravaged by war. Russia's victorious revolutionaries inherited a country on the verge of complete collapse. The output of basic manufactured goods had plummeted, a fuel crisis threatened the lives of vulnerable people, severe shortages of food made mass starvation a strong possibility, particularly in Russia's swollen towns and cities, and inflation undermined economic transactions.

If the strains of war set the seal on the Bolshevik Party's triumph in October 1917, then the revolution was validated by popular expectations of peace. The revolutionaries hoped to reach a settlement with Russia's enemies, in the expectation that it would provoke a crisis in Europe and deliver a world revolution. Lenin's government (Sovnarkom, the Council of People's Commissars) declared a ceasefire in the middle of November, followed shortly by an armistice. The Allies promptly cut the supply of munitions to the Russian army. In March 1918 Russia and Germany signed a peace treaty at Brest-Litovsk. Lenin termed this a 'breathing space', but his authority was severely tested by those within his own party who questioned the wisdom of ceding valuable territory and resources to German imperialists. Soviet plans for demobilisation were put on hold. By the summer of 1918 the Bolsheviks needed a military force in order to confront the emerging armed opposition in the Urals and the Don region.[1]

The Bolsheviks took power with a strong commitment to political, social and economic transformation. Their programme envisaged no compromise with the private landowners and capitalists who stood in their way. Whereas many decision makers in western Europe hoped to restore pre-war economic arrangements and structures, the Bolsheviks deliberately sought to rupture them or (as with the apparatus of wartime regulation) to appropriate and bend them to their wishes. This radical ideological stance inevitably invited confrontation and conflict.

Lenin devoted a great deal of time to justifying the Bolshevik revolution and outlining his intentions before the Russian public. He related the revolution to the structural transformation of the economy during the war. Lenin exposed the opposition between the public purpose of production and private ownership of the means of production. Ownership had become yet more divorced from society and socialism alone could resolve the resulting contradictions.[2] But ownership was a contested term. Did it mean direct ownership by workers themselves, making use of the powerful factory committees they established in 1917? Or did it mean nationalisation, taking assets into the hands of a state that acted in the name of the proletariat? As with the Bolsheviks' agenda as a whole, it was not clear how far these questions could be resolved without unleashing more violence.

The revolution provoked other kinds of disturbance. The collapse of the Russian empire and the Civil War profoundly affected the displacement of population. As a result of the world war, the number of displaced persons (defined as men in uniform, foreign prisoners of war and refugees) exceeded 17.5 million, equivalent to more than 12 per cent of the total Russian population. The revolution generated fresh internal population displacement, adding to Russia's woes. In towns and cities, the severe economic collapse in 1917–1918 compelled Russian workers to leave for the village in search of the means of subsistence, thereby reversing a generation of sustained urbanisation.[3]

10.1   Class war and economic collapse

Most historians now accept that civil war began at the moment the Bolsheviks seized power in October 1917. By rejecting a coalition with others on the left, Lenin gave an explicit foretaste of what was to come. The long awaited Constituent Assembly (for which the Bolsheviks received one-quarter of the popular vote) was dispersed after just one session in January 1918. Opposition parties including the Socialist Revolutionaries (SRs) were given short shrift. When elections to local soviets failed to go in their favour in the spring of 1918 the Bolsheviks resorted to terror and class war.[4]

The Bolsheviks' enemies among the propertied classes were left in no doubt of the seriousness of Soviet purpose. In the countryside the peasantry took their inspiration from the Decree on Land, which abolished private property in land and placed this land fund at the disposal of volost land committees and village soviets, pending the convocation of the Constituent Assembly. In Lenin's words, 'the root of the matter is that the peasantry should be given the assurance that there will be no more landed proprietors in the village'. Where the land fund was insufficient for local needs, the 'surplus' population was liable to 'voluntary resettlement'. This was bound to affect the claims of refugees in the first instance, although the decree spoke of 'the depraved (*porochnye*) members of the commune, deserters etc.'. But the most dramatic impact of the decree was the removal of around 100,000 landed gentry and their families.[5]

The Decree on Land was part of an impressive paper chase of revolutionary edicts. Taking their cue from the Decree on Workers' Control (14 November 1917) workers began to settle accounts by confiscating the enterprise. There may have been an element of xenophobia in some of the attacks on factory managers; had not Lenin spoken of the 'tribute' paid to foreign bondholders by workers and peasants?[6] Bolshevik leaders were concerned lest this 'spontaneous' behaviour get out of hand and further disrupt the already fragile basis for maintaining industrial production. However, the genie of protest had already been let out of the bottle and it would be difficult to put it back in. 'Conscious' workers were praised for having established control commissions to assess available supplies of fuel and raw materials and the financial health of the enterprise, but their action alarmed factory owners who simply closed up shop, demonstrating that they too were capable of 'spontaneous' action.[7]

The Bolsheviks favoured a centralised system of economic administration, akin to the old special council apparatus, in order to 'regulate' production, supply and prices. Accordingly a Supreme Council for the National Economy (Vesenkha) took over the offices of the old agencies for metal and coal supply. Vesenkha appropriated the war industry committees, recasting them as 'people's industrial committees' and giving workers' groups an equal role in decision making. Eventually, the committees were liquidated along with the biggest industrial syndicates. However, the process of appropriation and central administration did not satisfy radical proponents of workers' control.[8] Soviet officials deployed a remarkable rhetoric in their enthusiasm for adapting the system of economic administration. Larin, one of the main figures in Vesenkha, announced that he 'took the German *Kriegsgesellschaften*, translated them into Russian, poured into them some real working-class spirit and got them going under the name of *glavki*'.[9] In practice these 'central administrations' for the supply of raw materials were sovietised versions of the committees that had been created in 1915 and 1916. Like their predecessors, the *glavki* played an important role in the allocation of inputs. Vesenkha, its name (and the aspirations of some of its personnel) notwithstanding, concerned itself largely with issues of industrial organisation and production. In effect, it became the 'commissariat for industry'.[10]

Even more divisive than economic centralisation was the issue of 'one-man management' that Lenin advocated in March 1918. His preference for 'unqualified submission to a single will' first appeared in Lenin's analysis of the chaotic situation in Russian railway transport, whose mobilisation required that one person take executive responsibility. Lenin spoke in mechanistic terms of the need for the economic system to function 'like clockwork'. On other occasions he likened one-man management to 'the mild leadership of a conductor of an orchestra'. His proposed abandonment of collegial decision making angered the 'Opposition' Workers' the implementation of one-man management was shelved for the time being. The debate – and Lenin's advocacy of an unpopular doctrine – demonstrated how contentious the discourse of mobilisation had become. It would continue to be a source of discord within the Bolshevik Party throughout the Civil War, just as it divided the old regime.[11]

Even progressive commentators expressed concern that popular enthusiasm for revolutionary action stifled economic recovery. The Social Democrat Petr Maslov likened the bitter conflict between capital and labour to the squabbles between passengers for a place at the captain's table whilst the ship was sinking. He called for decisive action to rescue the process of economic decline; 'the fact that Trotsky is driving around rather than Rasputin, and that Lenin has replaced Plehve in the palace has not produced any change'. Maslov argued that it was imperative to cut down on 'unproductive consumption' by the state and to direct resources to productive investment instead.[12]

Maslov's vision went unrealised. Orders dried up, although the Special Council for State Defence did its best to subsidise the leading industrial enterprises during the winter months. Investment declined. The intensity with which equipment was used and the failure subsequently to maintain and repair the capital stock in large-scale industry resulted in negative net investment during 1917–1918. Fuel supplies dwindled. The output of coal and anthracite fell to 1.3 million tons in December 1917, less than half of the equivalent figure a year earlier.[13] Workers who held on to their jobs became increasingly exhausted and demoralised, with damaging consequences for productivity per shift.[14] But at least they still had a job. At the Putilov works, the management urged workers to support themselves beyond the factory gates, either by using family connections or drawing upon any funds they might have accumulated. The message was directed in particular at 'comrades' who retained a link with the village or joined the factory during the war.[15]

This desperate appeal raised interesting questions about the relationship of workers to the land. The 1918 Industrial Census revealed that one-third of Russian factory workers either had a plot of land or were employed as agricultural labourers in the summer months. The figure may under-estimate the strength of the connection, because of the exodus of workers that had already taken place.[16] One way – the Bolshevik way – of thinking about the departure of workers to the villages was that it strengthened the proletarian core. A Petrograd worker told Lenin (who repeated the claim in May 1918) that 'there were forty thousand of us [sic] at Putilov but most of them were "short-termers", not proletarians, not to be trusted, a flabby lot. But now there are just 15,000 of us – proletarians, experienced and hardened in battle'. His view was shared by the new People's Commissariat for Labour, which lauded the winnowing of 'petty bourgeois elements' from the factories.[17] The surviving proletarian cadres would be able to establish food detachments to search for 'hidden' reserves of grain. By these means the economic crisis could be given a positive gloss.

The assault on capital did not prevent the Soviet leadership from entering into discussions in early 1918 with leading industrialists and financiers, such as Meshcherskii, chairman of the International Bank and the key figure in the Kolomna-Sormovo engineering conglomerate. Lenin needed to lay the basis for industrial recovery, now that Brest-Litovsk had given Russia a breathing space.[18] In June the government finally committed itself to nationalisation. Even so, it was justified as much by circumstance as by ideology: the decree was a pre-emptive measure designed to forestall German claims for compensation following Brest-Litovsk, which restored land and capital assets to enemy nationals, unless they had been taken into state ownership before 1 July.[19]

Food procurement became even more problematic as officials tried and failed to meet supply norms. In the shops and street markets of Petrograd such food as was available stretched workers' budgets to the limit. Workers dipped into their savings or sold their belongings to feed themselves and their families, or turned to charities to help them out. They also ventured into the countryside to look for food.[20] Grain supplies for the period 1917–1918 are illustrated in Table 10.1.

Optimists continued to believe that the Russian countryside had substantial surpluses of grain, but the great challenge was to find some means of extracting it. The armistice and the promise of land led to an influx of young adult males into the villages. They could now feed themselves. The seizure and redistribution of privately owned land led to the creation of new peasant households of smaller size that were less likely to have surplus grain.[21] Lenin espoused the cause of 'compulsory commodity exchange', which he entrusted to the People's Commissariat for Food Supply (Narkomprod), but distribution was immensely difficult to arrange. Trade became the preserve of 'bagmen' who scoured the countryside. Some peasants willingly sold grain if they were offered a realistic price.[22] As they had

TABLE 10.1   *The supply of grain, 1917–1918*

Month	Grain procured, million tons	Comparison with equivalent month in the preceding year
October 1917	448	56%
November	641	100%
December	136	13%
January 1918	46	5%
February	41	6%
March	46	4%
April	38	8%
May	4	0.3%
June	2	0.2%
July	7	2%
August	26	8%
September	126	16%
October	381	85%

Source: Derived from Kondrat'ev, 1991, p. 231.

done before 1917, urban consumers berated speculators. Popular protest manifested itself in attacks first on traders and other 'non-proletarians', then on 'rich peasants' who were 'well fed and secure, having amassed enormous sums of money during the war'.[23]

In this atmosphere the government embarked on an attack on the 'rural bourgeoisie'. A decree of 13 May 1918 required peasants to hand over surplus grain if ordered to do so by the government. The aim was to destroy the bagmen and the rich peasantry (kulaks): 'the reply to the violence of holders of grain upon the rural poor must be to inflict violence upon the bourgeoisie'. Peasants who refused to comply (including those who converted grain into homebrew) were brought before revolutionary courts, jailed for a minimum of ten years and expelled from the peasant land commune. Their belongings were confiscated. This was followed by the decree (11 June) establishing committees of poor peasants (*kombedy*) under the control of the People's Commissariat of Supply. Members of the *kombedy* were entitled to a share in the grain they seized from kulaks. Lenin justified the measures as a temporary solution to the problem of grain supply but also as a political tactic designed to move from a 'bourgeois' to a socialist revolution in the countryside.[24]

Private trade establishments found it difficult to sustain their position. Co-operative organisations proved much more dynamic, more than doubling in average size between 1917 and 1918, and boasting a total membership of 12 million in January 1918, compared with around 6.8 million a year earlier and 1.7 million in 1915. The real value of trade turnover in the co-operatives increased from 1.04 million to 1.30 million rubles between January 1917 and January 1918. In percentage terms co-operatives accounted for two-fifths of all retail trade by 1918. The famous Moscow chain-store, 'Co-operator', not only dealt in food and other commodities but also established libraries, kindergartens and playgrounds, and arranged concerts, film shows and lectures. In April 1918 the Bolsheviks reached an understanding with the leaders of the co-operative movement according to which any citizen could join a co-operative, irrespective of his or her social status. In return the co-operatives had to accept closer regulation by the state.[25]

Economic restructuring also manifested itself in the turbulent world of banking and finance. Lenin and Bukharin followed the German economist Hilferding in drawing out the implications of the wartime concentration of financial resources in the hands of a small number of banks as a crucial factor in enabling a socialist government to impose control over the national economy. With this in mind the Bolsheviks made provision for the nationalisation of private banks, a policy implemented in December 1917 after the levelling of charges of 'sabotage' and counter-revolution against Russia's bankers. (The immediate pretext was the refusal of some banks to finance enterprises that had been occupied by factory committees.) The State Bank (renamed the 'National Bank') was 'mobilised' to help finance the needs of government.[26] The chaos in finances was signalled by the spiralling budget deficit, associated in part with the increased expenditure on economic administration and other branches of government, as well as with the costs of food procurement. Revenue covered only 5 per cent of estimated expenditure in the first half of 1918. Some taxpayers refused to pay, claiming exemptions or an inability to meet their obligations. Arrangements for the collection of taxes ground to a halt. The rate of increase of currency in circulation was checked during the winter months but then revived. Even so, in March 1918 Lenin complained of a 'money famine' that hampered the payment of wages. The Soviet government attempted to bring inflation under control by instituting a compulsory 'Red' loan to absorb excess purchasing power, but they had no greater success than the Provisional Government.[27]

Throughout the industrial sector, established economic ties began to be wrenched apart. Writing from Khar'kov, in the midst of a bitter conflict between Whites and Reds for the control of the resources of Ukraine, Grinevetskii spoke of 'industrial separatism'. Enterprises used a variety of informal methods in order to secure dwindling supplies of fuel and raw materials, including bartering finished goods in exchange for supplies of coal and steel.[28] Transactions between employers and their workforce also took a money-less form, as firms paid workers in kind and workers exchanged manufactured goods for food. In the Central Industrial Region factory workers removed farm equipment to use on their household plots, a further sign of economic disarray.[29]

10.2   Population displacement and territorial fragmentation

The picture of social and economic upheaval must also take account of continued population displacement that complicated the search for the means of social reconstruction. Population displacement meant the exchange of prisoners, as well as the return migration of hundreds of thousands of those who had been displaced in 1915–1917.[30]

The October Revolution had profound consequences for the external relations of Russia and for the internal configuration of territory. It brought about the fragmentation of the old imperial polity, as Lenin's doctrine of self-determination implied. In January 1918 Germany recognised Ukrainian independence (the Germans had already invited a Ukrainian delegation to the negotiations at Brest-Litovsk). Within two months Lithuania and Latvia received similar recognition, although (as in Poland) this remained something of a fiction, given the continued presence of German occupation forces. Belorussian nationalists also declared independence, although Lithuania disputed their claim to statehood. Russia's new rulers accepted the independence of Finland in December 1917, but they drew a distinction between their recognition of Finnish independence and the independence granted to 'puppet' states by imperialist powers.[31]

Far from bringing peace and stability, Lenin's stance exposed Russia's borderlands to continued German and Turkish encroachment, partly because German patience with Trotsky's negotiating stance ('neither war nor peace') ran out, and partly because the collapse of the Russian army meant that no military force stood in their way. German troops entered Ukrainian territory, while consolidating their position in Belorussia and the Baltic region. Turkish troops advanced into Armenia, leading to the recapture of Erzindzan and Erzerum in February 1918; the fortress of Kars fell two months later. Turkey added to the humiliation by demanding that Russia cede the border provinces of Kars, Ardahan and Batum that had been in Russian hands since 1878. When they finally signed the treaty of Brest-Litovsk, the Bolsheviks renounced all the tsarist empire's western regions, not only Poland but also the Ukrainian, Belorussian and Baltic borderlands, 1.3 million square miles of territory with a population of 62 million.[32]

This process of 'partial amputation' (the term used by the German ambassador in Moscow) had immediate implications for population displacement. Many refugees made plans to return home, in the hope of contributing to a radical reconstruction of their homeland. These plans were difficult to implement because of fresh military conflict, the devastation of the means of communication and the loss of personal documents. All the same, between May and November 1918, around 400,000 refugees of various nationalities left Soviet territory for lands that were now under German occupation. More cautious elements adopted a wait-and-see policy. Other refugees threw in their lot with the Bolsheviks for the time being, from their temporary base in cities such as Viatka, Perm, Rostov and Kiev.[33]

Exchanges of POWs took place before 1917 under the auspices of neutral countries, but Russia's withdrawal from the war held out the prospect of repatriating prisoners in much larger numbers. Many German and Austrian POWs anticipated a formal agreement by making their own way home via German-occupied Ukraine, in extremely difficult conditions. Negotiations between Germany and Russia were complicated by the uneven number of POWs on either side; Russia held around 167,000 German prisoners whereas Germany retained 1.4 million Russians. The dispute was not resolved until June 1918. The Civil War turned organised repatriation into something of a nightmare and the prolonged process only came to an end in 1922. Complaints on both sides about the 'spontaneous' drift of POWs homewards eerily echoed the language employed to describe the movement of refugees during 1915–1917. Returning prisoners, many of them sick, encountered mistrust and hostility whatever their final destination.[34]

The struggle for supremacy in Russia after October 1917 took the form of prolonged and bloody encounters between the new Red Army and the Bolsheviks' White opponents. Since the Whites were committed to maintaining the integrity of the old empire, it was clear that the outcome of the Civil War would ultimately decide the fate of self-determination. In Siberia the struggle for supremacy took a vicious turn. The first phase of the struggle was marked by the uprising of Czech POWs in 1918, who hoped to take part in the war against Germany and achieve Czech independence. Taking up arms against the Soviet regime, whose troops stood in the way of their departure from Siberia, they joined forces with the Bolsheviks' SR opponents. By the end of the year, Admiral Kolchak had imposed his own authoritarian but short-lived rule on these anti-Bolshevik forces in Siberia. Prosperous citizens sought to escape from Bolshevik supremacy in central European Russia by taking refuge in the major towns controlled by the Whites, notably Cheliabinsk and Omsk. Many refugees, having sold their valuables, found themselves in desperate straits and eventually fled east to Vladivostok, in the company of Kolchak's bedraggled army. One eyewitness depicted them as 'men moving like living dead through the taiga'. Others likened them to locusts. Their fate is beyond the scope of this book.[35]

Elsewhere, too, military confrontation gave rise to continuous movements of population. Following Brest-Litovsk, German generals were anxious to secure control of Ukrainian territory, either directly or through puppet governments. At the end of March 1918 Kiev came under the control of the fiercely anti-Bolshevik Hetman Skoropadskii. White Russian refugees from Soviet-controlled territory quickly entered the city in order to take shelter from Bolshevik terror, many of them finding work in Ukrainian government agencies. However, this proved a short-lived refuge. Skoropadskii was driven out, along with his German masters, at the end of the year. Bewildering changes of regime subsequently gave rise to further demographic turbulence in Ukraine. The continued encroachment of German troops had similar consequences in the Crimea.[36]

Population displacement was closely connected with the availability of food. When living conditions in the countryside deteriorated, relations between refugees and host communities turned sour. Refugees normally found themselves excluded from the redistribution of land; in any case, few of them had the equipment or draught animals to work the land on their own account. Their only hope was to make the journey back to their former homes in the west, a hope that the chaotic condition of Russian transport and the military uncertainty often rendered futile.[37]

Nor did the October revolution bring to an end the shocking phenomenon of abandoned or 'unaccompanied' children (*besprizorniki*). These children had lost contact with their parents or had become orphaned between 1914 and 1917. Some were cared for by the Church or by the Tatiana Committee, others scavenged for food and swelled the ranks of Russia's petty criminals. After 1917 many of these facilities closed down. Those who could not be cared for in new state orphanages or in private homes roamed the streets of Russia's towns and cities. The *besprizorniki* represented another instance of wartime upheaval that reverberated far beyond 1917.[38]

10.3   Demobilisation and re-mobilisation

The Bolsheviks envisaged that the old army would be replaced by a citizens' militia, drawn from the ranks of the proletariat and the poor peasantry. Officially the Red Army came into being on 15 January 1918,[39] but widespread war weariness meant that few men came forward to enlist: three months later only 154,000 volunteers had enrolled, a large number of them workers from Petrograd whose job prospects were bleak. The situation was transformed by the renewed German offensive following the breakdown of the negotiations at Brest-Litovsk. When peace was finally signed the Soviet leadership established a Supreme Military Council, which prepared the ground in earnest for the Red Army. Conscription began in May and June 1918, following the Czech revolt, but it proved chaotic. Attempts to operate a systematic levy of soldiers on a regional basis foundered on a lack of organisation and administrative personnel. Only by conscripting workers and (especially) peasants at gunpoint did recruitment begin. Mass evasion contributed to the difficulties encountered by the Soviet authorities, who finally hit on the idea (as Trotsky put it) of an 'intelligent combination of repression and agitation'. Villages and railway stations were combed for deserters. These measures were accompanied by a renewed commitment by the state to provide benefits to soldiers' families.[40]

The economic underpinning of the infant defence effort was the Central Administration of Supply, accompanied by various military procurement agencies including the organs of food supply. The Main Artillery Administration (GAU) was subsumed into the People's Commissariat for War. By August 1918 this apparatus gave way to an Extraordinary Commission for Supplying the Red Army, with similar powers to the old Special Council for State Defence. One scholar describes this as the persistence of a 'military enclave' that by-passed civilian authorities altogether. Soviet policy obliged all able-bodied citizens either to work or to serve in the armed forces. The management of defence plants secured exemptions for skilled workers.[41]

During 1918 (and beyond) the Red Army depended not on fresh output from dedicated defence establishments but upon stocks of military items that had been accumulated during the war as a result of the productive effort in 1915–1917 (see Table 10.2).

'Bourgeois specialists' carefully audited stocks of weaponry. This was an immensely difficult task, given that so much material lay scattered in numerous enterprises, military depots and railway yards, all under different and frequently competing authorities. Specialist arsenals concentrated on repairing small arms and ordnance that had been recov-

TABLE 10.2   *Munitions production and supply, 1914–1917*

	Light ordnance	Medium calibre	Heavy guns	Machine guns	Rifles, millions
Stocks, July 1914	7200	1031	nil	4157	4.124
Production	7800	2466*	87	30354**	5.088**
(Repairs)	(3410)	(496)	n.a.	n.a.	n.a.
Stocks, June 1917	9800	2874	62	18269	4.664
Wartime losses	5000 approx.	1369	25	16172	5.087

Source and notes: EPR, 1957, volume 2, pp. 173–5. Stocks include front line and reserve – * includes 500 units of old (1877) model; ** includes imports.

ered. Small workshops contributed uniforms, footwear and other items. Military production, in other words, was something of a hit and miss affair.[42]

All this activity put paid to the formal efforts that had been made to prepare for demobilisation. Attempts by the tsarist government and the Provisional Government to manage the process of economic demobilisation had achieved very little, but not for want of trying. Already in early 1915 the Association of Representatives of Industry and Trade called for the establishment of a body dedicated to post-war planning. The industrialists hoped to use this as a vehicle to propound their view that nothing good could come of continued state intervention in Russia's economic life. The proposal was revived by the State Council later that year, in the hope of forging a better working relationship between the bureaucracy and the educated public. Prime Minister Boris Stürmer pre-empted further discussion by creating a 'Financial-Economic Commission' under the State Auditor, N.N. Pokrovskii, in March 1916, ostensibly to prepare for the Paris economic conference scheduled for May. However, the commission was a purely consultative body and it failed to conduct any significant business, apart from drawing up a schedule of questions that required 'consideration' at some stage, of which the need for a Ministry of Labour was perhaps the most controversial. According to one anonymous source, it dealt in 'vermicelli'.[43] The Provisional Government established a Chief Economic Committee in June 1917, but its deliberations on the post-war world amounted to little.[44]

The Soviet government turned its attention to industrial demobilisation at the end of November 1917 and issued a decree on 9 December that called for the conversion of enterprises to peacetime production.[45] Demobilisation compelled factory committees reluctantly to lay off workers. Large defence plants in Petrograd felt the chill more severely than most. Total registered unemployment stood at around 325,000, including 50,000 in the Petrograd region and 32,000 in Moscow. No sector or region was immune.[46]

Economic re-mobilisation attracted a lot of interest. Typically the technical specialists advocated the creation of several tiers of enterprise, with a core or 'cadre' of factories that would handle technically demanding and specialised contracts, for rifles, machine guns, revolvers, fuses, explosives and cartridges. Their task would be to keep abreast of technical changes and to incorporate improvements to design and performance, as well as to meet the recurrent demands of the military in peacetime, such that stocks of weaponry were maintained at an adequate level. They would ensure that civilian enterprises were ready to convert to defence production at a moment's notice. Other defence producers would constitute a kind of reserve capacity. The final tier would normally supply civilian needs in peacetime and then convert to the manufacture of technically more straightforward items such as shell, tanks, motorised vehicles and other equipment. This proposed reorganisation was driven by technical rationality rather than by private profit or by administrative convenience and bureaucratic rivalry. However, there are few signs that ambitious ideas about convertibility bore much fruit.[47]

10.4   Reconstruction and the war on backwardness

Social and economic reconstruction hinged on available resources of capital, labour and professional expertise. The capital stock was badly depleted. Capital investment meant serving the needs of industry and transport, two sectors that had been badly damaged during the revolution by physical destruction and increased wear and tear. It meant finding resources to realise radical visions, such as regional power stations capable of serving a broader population.[48] It meant an extension of health care and educational provision, both of which had been strained by wartime exigency. However, there was no blueprint for social welfare, and no quick decision could be reached about the form that a Soviet health service – centralised or de-centralised? – should take, and how demobilisation would affect the hospitals and clinics in the short term.[49]

Economic and social reconstruction was not confined to the Russian heartland. The collapse of commercial links became apparent in the rupture of economic ties between the regions of the former Russian empire, which the German intervention in the first half of 1918 helped to exacerbate. Decades of carefully cultivated economic relationships were being torn asunder. War in the Caucasus caused enormous damage. Armenia's agricultural economy lay in ruins, with fewer than 6000 goats and cows left out of a pre-war herd of one million. Most dwellings had been damaged beyond repair. In Kars oblast and Erevan province alone 30 million rubles were needed in order to rebuild shattered farms. As a result, 'we who live in the twentieth century have had to turn to forgotten forms of barter exchange and a natural economy'.[50] This reinforced the point that the war on backwardness could only begin once the devastation wrought by the 'imperialist' war had been overcome.

Three months after Brest-Litovsk the Soviet authorities approved an ambitious attempt to assess the impact of war, revolution and demobilisation on the industrial economy. The All-Russian Congress of Statisticians drew up plans for a census of factory ('large-scale') industry, which the government approved in June 1918. It was conducted towards the end of 1918, in immensely difficult circumstances, including rebellions against Soviet rule and the scourge of influenza. Around 3,800 enumerators took part. The geographic coverage was largely confined to the Central Industrial Region, the north-west, part of the Urals, the Central Black-Earth Region and the Mid-Volga. No account could be taken of the Southern Industrial Region, the Caucasus or Central Asia. The census provided details on the labour force, on the behaviour of industrial production, on the capital stock in industry, and on the condition of industry as of 31 August 1918. The enumerators obtained data on 9,750 enterprises, although only 6,066 actually continued to operate. Many of these worked only partially, because of the shortages of fuel and raw materials or a lack of orders.[51]

No-one under-estimated the scale of the task revealed by the Industrial Census. Economic reconstruction needed to begin with massive investment, particularly in extractive industries, in transport, and in electrification. Grinevetskii called upon Russia to attract fresh foreign investment on a massive scale – 15 or 20 billion rubles over the next decade. In May 1918 Lenin advocated an economic rapprochement with Germany, which would have meant a huge loan to the Soviet government in return for German access to Russian raw materials, coupled with concessions to German companies.[52] Other private investors came forward, many of them entertaining grandiose ambitions that fed Russian fantasies as well. Even the old Central War Industry Committee, now on its last legs, negotiated with American banks for a massive loan to rebuild the railway network between Moscow and the Donbass. Grinevetskii, loyal to the old vision espoused by Sergei Witte in the 1890s, attached particular importance to improvements in labour productivity that he anticipated from a combination of foreign investment and 'scientific organisation'.[53]

The lessons to be drawn from wartime agriculture were less clear-cut. The agricultural sector badly needed resources to cope with under-investment during the war. Certainly the war did little to dissuade the Bolsheviks of the virtue of large-scale farming. The forests and other lands belonging to the royal family and the Church were soon expropriated. During 1918 the Bolsheviks began to address the bigger issues of arable and pastoral farming by formulating plans for the creation of new state farms.

However, the main form of land tenure in the immediate post-revolutionary period was the peasant family farm, whose small scale and commitment to subsistence hardly encouraged technical progress. Some economists, including Chaianov, advocated greater investment in peasant farming, agricultural co-operatives and agronomic science in order to raise productivity. Groman and others countered that the priority was to invest in industry and in transport, anticipating the industrialisation debates that took place during the 1920s.[54]

In pursuit of a vision of a transformed Russia, the Bolsheviks embraced the cause of large-scale and planned scientific research. The Committee for the Development of Productive Forces (KEPS) reached an agreement with the Soviet state whereby it would conduct pure and applied research, working 'on topics originating from the needs of state-building, while acting as the organisational centre of the national research effort'. This initiative had its origins in wartime assessments of 'backwardness' and national endeavour.[55]

Economic recovery and expansion placed a premium upon technical expertise. Many professionals committed themselves to working for the Bolsheviks on the grounds that the new regime was committed to the restoration of order. Technical specialists who had worked for the Central War Industry Committee joined a 'council of experts' set up within Vesenkha and gained the respect they felt was their due. Lenin supported the 'bourgeois specialists' not merely as a pragmatic necessity, but as a matter of 'culture' and modernity. He favoured 'intellectuals who sought knowledge as a guide to action'. His stance caused enormous political controversy during the first half of 1918, putting him on a collision course with the Workers' Opposition and with rank and file workers.[56]

Some of the ideas of experts had already been anticipated during the war, including a commitment to the mass manufacture of standardised products, such as machine tools, boilers, refrigerators and agricultural equipment.[57] Vesenkha took up arguments about the need for better record keeping and accounting practices.[58] Other specialists pointed to the need to improve the location of industry, in order to bring manufacturing enterprises closer to the source of energy and raw materials.[59] Agricultural specialists in the new People's Commissariat of Agriculture who wished (in George Yaney's words) 'to immerse themselves in villages and blend their science with peasant practice could do so while singing hymns to social and economic advance. Those who wished to collect information and concoct programmes could predict results, estimate costs and rhapsodise about scientific advances'. Given a weak Bolshevik presence in the countryside, the agricultural specialists were left alone to carry on with land consolidation and other schemes.[60]

The war on backwardness opened on other fronts as well. As perceived embodiments of tradition, the church and the family attracted the attention of Russia's new rulers. A decree of January 1918 provided for the dis-establishment of the Orthodox Church, depriving it of the right to hold property in its own right and of the right to charge for religious services. The Church also lost its control over the private lives of Russia's citizens, who were free to divorce without restriction following the law of 19 December 1917. Other changes followed. The Code on Marriage, Family and Guardianship, adopted in October 1918, legalised civil marriage and abolished the concept of 'illegitimacy'. It also affirmed that marriage 'does not establish community of property'. This meant that peasant women could now hold allotment land and other property in their own right. But the new Code was at odds with customary law, which supported community of property; it was not clear, for example, what assets a woman could take with her if she divorced her husband. What should happen, asked one jurist, if her dowry had been used to build a shed – was she entitled to take it with her? In practice Soviet lawyers found it difficult to reconcile modern legal norms with peasant custom. The Bolsheviks also supported projects to socialise menial household chores and to provide socially regulated childcare, but these projects foundered on the rock of spending constraints. Thus the new regime ended up embracing the conventional household as the basis for social wellbeing, particularly in rural Russia.[61]

If social and economic reality undermined the radical or modernising agenda, Bolshevik political culture itself tended to reaffirm traditional gender roles. Here Bolshevik language was revealing. The dominant discourse depicted the epic revolutionary struggle against propertied elites in a way that reinforced gendered distinctions. Party leaders called for iron discipline (less 'squabbling'), strong organisation and the pitiless prosecution of their opponents. The tendency was to describe the revolution itself as a fundamentally masculine project. In this context it is important to remember how much significance the Bolsheviks attached to the preservation of a masculine 'core' within the working class. What many of its most fervent adherents feared was 'spontaneity' (*stikhiinost'*), the uncontrolled flow of elemental forces that undermined consciousness and compromised 'rational' action. Here, too, the language of control was deployed to counteract 'destabilising' forces in society.[62]

Conclusions

The October Revolution appeared to solve everything and yet it solved nothing. The Decree on Peace did not bring peace nor did it free Russia from the need to pick up the pieces after a devastating war. The Bolshevik Party's programme remained a set of proposals without clear details concerning the future of the economic or political system. The Party lacked a strong social base outside towns and garrisons. Workers became victims of the collapse in industrial production. This was immensely disconcerting to a regime founded on the principle of proletarian strength and solidarity. Proletarian support was problematic. Workers lent the Party their support, rather than commit themselves to Bolshevik government unconditionally. Many workers who backed the Party in the heady days of 1917 voted just a few months later for non-party candidates, in protest against early signs of dictatorship, 'bureaucratism' and the loss of jobs. Lenin's response was to buy time, making peace with Germany while extending the war within.

The decision to leave the European war meant a radical change in the relations between Russia and the Allies. Wartime agreements over external economic assistance quickly collapsed and, in the medium term, the complex web of external economic ties – trade, capital movements and labour migration – was ruptured. It would be hard to rebuild the trust that evaporated with the Bolshevik seizure of power and the consequent decision to sue for peace with Germany. Revolutionary diplomacy inevitably imposed costs in terms of securing the necessary resources for economic reconstruction.

It is a truism to say that the Bolsheviks came to power in the midst of a long, bloody war of destruction. Losses had to be made good and jobs would have to be found for demobilised soldiers. But the war had other dimensions. It promoted close economic regulation and thus an apparatus capable of being deployed for revolutionary ends. It also enabled the emerging technical intelligentsia to articulate a vision of expert knowledge, capable of serving the needs of social transformation and economic planning, in order to 'possess the future'.[63] At its most extreme, the war sustained a vision of government intervention in the sphere of property relations. The old regime engineered the seizure of privately owned assets, expropriating the businesses and farmsteads owned by the Tsar's German and Jewish subjects. Expropriation in 1917–1918 took place on a quite different scale, and the Bolsheviks justified it in terms of class rather than ethnicity. However, the principle had already been embodied in state practice.

Pronounced upheaval manifested itself in social conflict, redrawing social boundaries and population displacement. Social conflict meant continued confrontation between workers and employers, and between peasants and the landlords, in each instance being resolved in favour of the dispossessed. Existing social boundaries collapsed in the face of class war. These processes were not confined to Russia, but they took an extreme form there, where the revolution propelled large numbers of the propertied elite into permanent exile. Russia took on the form of a 'quicksand society'.[64]

Wartime shifts were represented in cultural terms. It is no accident that the Bolsheviks' appeal to class consciousness and revolutionary order was accompanied by a fresh emphasis upon military virtues and 'iron discipline'. The ground had already been prepared during the war. The First World War gave rise to militarised metaphors, above all the doctrine of 'mobilisation'. Other expressions also gained currency, such as an 'economic general staff', the 'battle' for metal and fuel, the 'campaign' for labour productivity and the need for 'struggle' to improve Russia's position in world markets. This terminology was related to ongoing concerns about economic backwardness. Of course the war was more than a metaphor for planning, productivity and improved economic prospects. Mobilisation embodied a complex set of meanings that were deployed in the interests of national security and 'forging a social movement'.[65]

Contemporary discourse betrayed a pronounced concern with 'control' and its antithesis, 'spontaneity' (stikhiinost'). Before the February Revolution liberal politicians sought to rein in government officials and neutralise the 'dark forces' that operated in Russia. After February, officials and politicians of all hues expressed anxiety about the loss of control within plebeian Russia, whether it took the form of wildcat strikes, looting food stores, peasant jacquerie or refugee 'criminality' and 'disease'. This discourse persisted beyond 1917. It was reflected in Lenin's controversial espousal of one-man management and Bukharin's rejection of the 'anarchy of production' under capitalism.[66] It emerged in an affirmation of the 'manly' virtue of discipline, which Lenin coupled with technology and machinery in an ideological triptych that described his understanding of the conditions for success in the modern world. In this respect, the Bolshevik revolution and the language of obedience reinforced the brutalising message of the world war.

Note on further reading

The best guide in English to the economic arrangements called 'war communism' is Malle, 1985, which readers of Russian can supplement by consulting the informative book by Drobizhev, 1967. Contemporary comment includes Grinevetskii, 1919. Two excellent surveys of the origins and politics of the Russian Civil War are Swain, 1996, and Mawdsley, 2000, which can be read in conjunction with Lewin, 1985, and Holquist, 2002. The link between population movement and state building is traced in Baron and Gatrell, eds, 2004.

References

1 Carr, 1972, volume 3, pp. 15–68; Neilson, 1984, p. 294.

2 Lenin, 1977.

3 Davies, et al., eds, 1994, pp. 60–62 (Wheatcroft and Davies).

4 Swain, 1996, pp. 50–51, 62–9, 146–62; McAuley, 1991, pp. 87–111.

5 Remizova, 1954, pp. 113–16. This and other relevant decrees are printed in Bunyan and Fisher, 1961, pp. 125–8, 129–32, 308–10.

6 Volobuev, 1962, p. 365. Compare Malle, 1985, p. 58.

7 Smith, 1983, pp. 231–3, 235. Compare Keep, 1976, pp. 263–75.

8 Drobizhev, 1967, pp. 46, 50, 62–79.

9 Drobizhev, 1967, p. 8. See also Carr, 1972, volume 2, pp. 78–80, 359. *Glavki* were the abbreviated form of the 'chief administrations' that organised production by branch of industry.

10 Drobizhev, 1967, p. 186.

11 Lenin, 1972a; Carr, 1972, volume 2, pp. 190–94; Malle, 1985, pp. 110–13. Compare Mints, 1982, pp. 199–235.

12 Maslov, 1918, p. 229. Plehve was Minister of Interior until his assassination in 1904.

13 Kafengauz, 1994, p. 213; Somov, 1972; Gatrell, 1994, pp. 222, 320.

14 Strumilin, 1964a, pp. 358–63 (first published in 1919); McAuley, 1991, p. 195.

15 Drobizhev et al., 1975, p. 36.

16 *Promyshlennaia perepis'*, 1926, volume 2, pp. 130–33; Rashin, 1958, pp. 572–6.

17 Lenin, 1972b, pp. 391–8; Drobizhev et al., 1975, pp. 37–8.

18 Drobizhev and Volobuev, 1957; Gatrell, 1995; Carr, 1972, volume 2, pp. 93–5. The negotiations were called off in April.

19 Malle, 1985, p. 60; Drobizhev, 1967, pp. 93–100.

20 Strumilin, 1964a, pp. 342, 359; McAuley, 1991, pp. 296–9.

21 Malle, 1985, pp. 327–8.

22 Malle, 1985, pp. 326, 338–49; Volobuev, 1962, pp. 438–9; Lih, 1990, pp. 128–37.

23 Carr, 1972, volume 2, p. 58; Koenker et al., eds, 1989, pp. 158–79 (McAuley); Lih, 1990, pp. 135, 138–66.

24 Carr, 1972, volume 2, pp. 58–61; Malle, 1985, pp. 359–61.

25 Kabanov, 1973, pp. 52, 91; Kayden and Antsiferov, 1929, pp. 71, 83, 94.

26 Bukharin, 1972; Lenin, 1972a; Carr, 1972, volume 2, pp. 136–43.

27 Volobuev, 1962, p. 337; Malle, 1985, pp. 161–8.

28 Grinevetskii, 1919, p. 199. Like K.V. Kirsh, another engineer who specialised in energy utilisation, Grinevetskii died from typhus in 1919.

29 Izmailovskaia, 1920, pp. 130–31.

30 Kulischer, 1948, pp. 36–78.

31 Roshwald, 2001, pp. 120–22, 146–52.

32 Debo, 1979, pp. 157–69; Swain, 1996, pp. 127–32.

33 Baron and Gatrell, eds, 2004, 10–34 (Gatrell).

34 Rachamimov, 2002, pp. 191–4.

35 Smele, 1996, p. 593. Kulischer, 1948, p. 41.

36 Reshetar, 1952, pp. 158–9; Debo, 1979, pp. 206–11.

37 Okninskii, 1998, pp. 140–41; Kulischer, 1948, p. 38.

38 Polner, 1930, pp. 141–5; Goldman, 1993, pp. 59–67.

39 Wildman, 1987, p. 379.

40 Sanborn, 2003, pp. 38–55 (quotation on p. 52); Drobizhev et al., 1975, p. 35; Mawdsley, 2000, pp. 59–63.

41 Malle, 1985, pp. 466–78; Kovalenko, 1970, p. 69.

42 Gorodetskii, 1958; Kovalenko, 1970, pp. 14, 116–39, 385; Malle, 1985, pp. 477–8.

43 Bukshpan, 1929, pp. 454–6; Florinskii, 1988, pp. 64–93.

44 ZhZVP, 21 June 1917; EPR, 1957, volume 1, pp. 273–4; Volobuev, 1962, pp. 135–46.

45 Drobizhev et al., 1975, pp. 35–6.

46 Smith, 1983, pp. 243–5; Freidlin, 1967, p. 255; Drobizhev et al., 1975, p. 38.

47 Mikhailov, 1927, summarises the contributions made between 1918 and 1924 to specialist journals. See also Vishnev and Mikhailov, 1928.

48 Coopersmith, 1992, pp. 111–14, 147–50.

49 Solomon and Hutchinson, eds, 1990, pp. 97–120 (Weissman).

50 Gatrell, 1999, p. 153.

51 *Promyshlennaia perepis'*, 1926, volume 1, pp. iii–iv, 16, 23; *Vestnik statistiki*, 1919, 1, pp. 140–46 (A.R. Briling). An enterprise qualified if it employed more than 16 workers, or if it employed fewer than 16 workers but used mechanised motive power.

52 Debo, 1979, pp. 318–20; Swain, 1996, pp. 53–62.

53 Grinevetskii, 1919, pp. 105, 184, 202–4; Bailes, 1978, p. 21; Coopersmith, 1992, pp. 139–50.

54 Malle, 1985, p. 411; Lewin, 1985, pp. 296–300; Izmailovskaia, 1920, pp. 63–70; Stanziani, 1995, p. 178.

55 Quoted in Kojevnikov, 2002, p. 256.

56 Bailes, 1978, pp. 23–5, 47–9, 52, 57; Balzer, ed., 1996, p. 53 (Bailes).

57 Izmailovskaia, 1920, pp. 69–70, attached greater significance to 'planning' than to ownership.

58 *Tekhnika*, 1918, 1 (Lavrov); Anon., *Dva goda diktatury proletariata*, 1919, p. 97.

59 Manikovskii, 1930, volume 2, pp. 298–301, quoting a memo from General Mikhel'son to the OSO, 16 December 1915; Fersman, 1917.

60 Yaney, 1982, p. 509.

61 Goldman, 1993, pp. 90–100, 155–60.

62 Clements, 1997, pp. 61–2; Gleason et al., eds, 1985, pp. 238–60 (Farnsworth).

63 Rudoi, 1925, p. 91.

64 Lewin, 1985, pp. 211–13, 265.

65 Holquist, 2002, pp. 45–6, 143–4.

66 Bukharin, 1978, p. 34.

CHAPTER 11

Russia's First World War: an overview

It was believed that the economic backwardness of Russia ... ought to render Russia less sensitive to the economic shocks of war. On the other hand there was a widespread notion that war was bound to aggravate the impoverishment of the people and to tend to sap the strength of the nation. Both these assumptions, however, although in different degrees and in different sense, were belied by the results.

[Struve et al., 1930, xiii.]

The First World War left millions of people dead, bereaved, wounded or captive. In Russia its demographic impact was registered in terms of direct population losses and a population deficit. In other words, what difference did the war make to the size of the Russian population? What about those who survived? Challenging questions were posed about the health status of military personnel and civilians alike. The Russo-Japanese War had yielded information about the impact of war on the physical and mental health of men in battle. However, no preparations were made for the scale of injury and infection brought about by the world war. Here, as in other spheres, government and military specialists came into conflict with 'educated society'.

Issues of loss and reparation also emerged in the sphere of material production. Russia's headlong rush to secure additional quantities of military goods took place at the expense of civilian needs. In the words of Alexander Meyendorff:

The mobilisation took from the factories those who were essentially needed for the conduct of the war. The only ports left ... were inadequately equipped for the indispensable imports. The railway system broke down by the end of the first year, and railway repair shops were

*converted into munitions factories. All output being diverted for the
needs of the army, the open market was short of everything.*[1]

According to this interpretation, economic mobilisation was shortsighted,
because policy makers simultaneously failed to deliver basic goods to
Russian households and to commit sufficient resources to the maintenance
of infrastructure. However, Russia was also constrained by economic
backwardness, which narrowed the options available to policy makers.

The war also recast international economic relations. Beyond issues of
alliance strategy, such as the commitment of military forces to different
theatres of war, Russia's place in the world economy also came under scrutiny. How would the war affect Russia's future economic ties, for example
with Germany, which had been a vital economic partner before the war?[2]
To what extent could Russia look further afield, to emerging partnerships
with the USA or Japan?

Assessments of the war's impact on economy and society raised
broader questions about how it should be remembered. Death and destruction occasioned an outpouring of grief as well as anger. However, we
know very little of the way in which news of death was received by peasant
or working-class households who suffered bereavement. Russian intellectuals such as Paul Miliukov spoke movingly of the loss of loved ones.[3]
Beyond the suffering of individual families it is possible to establish something of the steps taken by voluntary and semi-professional organisations
to accumulate an archive of their activities during the war. These initiatives
were quickly overtaken by the Bolshevik revolution with its emphasis on
class struggle rather than the 'great patriotic war'.

11.1   Casualties of war: population and public health

Russia's population on the eve of the war stood at around 168 million.[4]
The population grew by a further 2.6 million between July 1914 and
January 1917. However, this fell far short of the increase that would have
been realised in the absence of war; extrapolating from pre-war trends
would have delivered growth of around 7.5 million over the same period.
After 1917 the growth in numbers was reversed: between 1917 and 1923
the total population fell by at least 9 million and possibly as much as 14.5
million.[5] Population figures for the period are given in Table 11.1.

The aggregate birth rate fell sharply in the period 1915–1917.
Marriage rates fell because conscription removed men of marriageable age

TABLE 11.1   *Russian population, 1914–1917 (USSR pre-war territory), millions*

1 January	1914	1915	1916	1917	1918
Total	139.9	142.6	142.3	142.3	140.9
Armed forces	0.4	5.1	7.1	8.0	7.9
Active duty	–	4.2	5.2	5.2	
Non-active	0.4	0.9	1.9	2.8	7.9
Displaced population	–	1.1	4.2	7.8	9.7
Per cent of total population		0.8	3.0	5.5	6.9
including refugees	–	0.9	3.3	6.1	7.4
including POWs	–	0.2	0.9	1.7	2.3

Source and note: Volkov, 1930, pp. 86–7, 90, 270–71. Other estimates of population on 1 January 1914 are summarised by Vainshtein, 1960, p. 452.

from Russia's villages and because those who remained behind chose to postpone marriage.[6] In urban areas the exemption of young adult men contributed to a less marked decline than in the villages. In Moscow province the marriage coefficient (marriages per 1000 population) fell from 7.4 to 2.2 in just two years; in the city it fell from 5.9 to 4.1 between 1913 and 1915. Marriage rates recovered slightly in 1917 as soldiers began to return from the war and establish their own households. The war 'cost' Russia some 1.7 million marriages. Part of the loss was made good when the war came to an end, as reflected in the rising number of peasant households between 1917 and 1920.[7]

The falling birth rate was accompanied by a less rapid decline in the crude death rate. In 1917 the death rate exceeded the birth rate for the first time. Table 11.2 gives the indexes of urban and rural mortality between 1913 and 1916.

The fate of those conscripted into the Russian army cannot be established with certainty, and estimates are subject to a wide margin of error. One careful calculation summarises the losses as shown in Table 11.3.

TABLE 11.2   *Urban and rural mortality indexes, 1913–1916*

Year	Urban population	Rural population
1913	100	100
1914	100	95
1915	116	89
1916	119	82

Source: Kohn and Meyendorff, 1932, p. 117.

TABLE 11.3   *Russian military losses, 1914–1917 (thousands)*

Year	Killed in action	Woun- ded in action	Deaths from wounds	Contrac- ted disease	Deaths from disease	Taken prisoner	POW deaths
1914	90.9	368.4	134.8	83.1	16.4	371.7	13.3
1915	226.7	842.1	308.6	423.0	88.4	2,004.5	71.5
1916	269.6	987.1	361.9	629.5	28.9	1,799.9	64.2
1917	102.4	454.1	165.0	1,292.6	22.0	918.2	32.9
Total	689.6	2,651.7	970.3	2,428.2	155.7	5,094.3	181.9

Source: Volkov, 1930, pp. 54, 56, 59, 60, 68.

These estimates put war-related deaths at just under two million men. Some scholars believe the figure to be higher still. Nearly half of these fatalities resulted from wounds inflicted in the course of battle. Just over one-third of all casualties were killed in action. The remaining fatalities were the result of infectious disease or deaths in captivity. The death rate among Russian prisoners of war appears to have been relatively light.[8]

Military casualties represented something like five per cent of Russia's male population of working age (15 to 49 years). This was roughly equivalent to the losses sustained by the UK. France, Italy, Romania and (above all) Serbia suffered proportionately greater losses. So, too, did Russia's enemies. German losses, for example, amounted to around 13 per cent of the male population of working age.[9]

Our knowledge of civilian casualties directly attributable to enemy action is not very thorough. One estimate puts them at around 318,000 for the years 1914 and 1915. Most of these were refugees caught up in heavy fighting on Russia's western frontier.[10]

The health status of Russia's civilian population was closely related to population movements. In rural Russia the crude death rate declined on account of the improved living conditions of the peasantry. The urban experience was very different. Towns and cities became still more overcrowded, and the volume of displaced persons contributed to the spread of infectious disease.[11] A survey published in the journal of the Union of Towns found that the 'core' population of Briansk increased from 35,000 to 90,000, of whom 27,000 were refugees. In Samara the pre-war population increased by 50 per cent to a total of 300,000. One in ten was a refugee. The population of the Black Sea port of Nikolaev (whose inhabitants in 1913 numbered around 118,000) reached 150,000, of whom 40,000 were troops and 20,000 were workers at the expanded shipyards.

Having failed to invest in a proper water supply, most towns lacked any kind of adequate sanitation. They paid the price in terms of rising rates of typhus and dysentery.[12]

An American archaeologist, Thomas Whittemore, travelled throughout European Russia in the winter of 1915, reporting on the consequences of population displacement. In Tambov refugees were scattered throughout the town; their dispersion 'kept them out of reach of organised control and rendered any kind of general supervision impossible'. Further east, in Orenburg, Ufa and Tashkent, conditions were even worse: 'I do not (he concluded) wish to support the impractical and the impossible. But the problem is a desperate one and unless something is done there will be in the spring an epidemic of unparalleled violence'.[13]

How did these measures affect public health in general? In 1916 tsarist officials discussed plans for a ministry of public health. Public health in pre-revolutionary Russia meant the primacy of general hygiene, emphasising environmental factors. This doctrine was challenged by an emerging group of bacteriologists, as well as by the proponents of community medicine for whom social factors were critical, but by 1917 general hygiene retained its predominant position. The Soviet state planned to move towards a centralised system, with doctors as government employees. Doctors and fel'dshers who were part of the zemstvo tradition hoped to maintain a semblance of professional autonomy. Recurrent public health crises during the Civil War period and its immediate aftermath helped to boost their role, in a greatly altered institutional context.[14]

Before 1914 the zemstvos had made provision for mental illness, but the scale of wartime responsibilities greatly exceeded the capacity of existing facilities. Nurses were hurriedly trained to assist with the evacuation of mentally ill soldiers to asylums in Moscow and its environs. Some psychiatrists envisaged the extension of wartime measures into an era of post-war 'planning' for mental health, taking account of the complex range of mental and physical response to extreme trauma, whether bursting shells, population displacement, rape or mass murder. Again, however, there were questions about the available resources for this level of commitment.[15]

Gains were made as a result of prohibition. Zemstvo activists applauded the improvements in health that followed the closure of the vodka shops, but they believed the Russian public should take greater responsibility for their own health. Broader opportunities for wellbeing were also anticipated. Observers of the new spirit of sobriety coupled this with the 'moral' improvement of village youth, who had put aside their 'excesses' in favour of a search for knowledge. Would the war dissipate these gains? Here the zemstvos refused to let the government off the hook, complaining that officials had done nothing to establish reading rooms or to introduce more 'rational recreation'. Many young people still preferred to spend their time playing cards. Government had a duty to invest in leisure and recreation.[16]

11.2   Economic activity as a whole

How was the war reflected in overall trends in economic activity? The only estimate of national income in wartime was compiled in 1918 by the Russian economist S.N. Prokopovich.[17] His underlying observations are neither secure nor very extensive. Prokopovich computed his index for industry by tracing output per person in the Donbass coal industry and derived an index of 'agricultural productivity' from estimates of the sown area in 45 provinces of European Russia. He then assembled a composite index by applying the 1913 weights for agriculture and industry. There are obvious difficulties with this procedure, notably that the Donbass coal industry cannot be taken as representative of the performance of industry as a whole. Second, Prokopovich's data on agriculture overlook the improvement in output in 1915 and under-estimate the decline in output in 1917. Third, he made no allowance for other sectors of the economy. The cereal harvest represented only between 35 and 50 per cent of the total value of agricultural production in 1913, and cannot necessarily be taken as representative of the entire sector. Since cereals accounted for only around 28 per cent of national income, and large-scale industry for 16 per cent, it is clear that more than half of all economic activity, based upon 1913 sectoral shares, was missing from Prokopovich's estimates.

TABLE 11.4   *Russian national income, 1913–1917: a new estimate*

Year	Large-scale industry	Small-scale industry	Agriculture	Forestry	Trade	Transport	Construction	Total
1913	100	100	100	100	100	100	100	100
1914	101	98	100	79	84	73	96	94.5
1915	111	78	110	59	68	71	100	95.5
1916	104	88	90	31	50	43	81	79.8
1917	76	78	87	18	37	29	68	67.7

Source and note: Harrison et al. Forthcoming (Gatrell), Cambridge University Press. Agriculture excludes sugar beet and potatoes.

Table 11.4 improves on Prokopovich's estimates, by recalculating his index of agricultural and industrial production and by incorporating other elements of national income. It allows us to draw some broad conclusions about the stages of the war effort. First, Russian national income declined by around five per cent during the first phase. In 1915 the decline was reversed to a slight extent, contrary to Prokopovich's view. In the following year national income began to fall more steeply, and the drop would have been still greater but for the resilience of output in large-scale industry. By 1917 national income reached barely two-thirds of its pre-war level. The declining output of basic commodities confirms how serious the situation had become. In the absence of an increase in total output during the third year of the war, consumption plummeted. By 1916–1917 it was probably less than half its pre-war level.[18]

Further light is shed on wartime trends by the 1918 Industrial Census. The war brought about a growth in total output, accompanied by the re-direction in the pattern of industrial production. The gross value of output in large-scale industry grew by about 17 per cent between 1913 and 1916, before going into reverse in 1917. This is illustrated in Table 11.5.

The aggregate increase disguised the very different fortunes of capital goods and consumer goods industries. In 1916, output in the former was already 62 per cent above the 1913 level; by contrast, output of consumer goods was 15 per cent lower.

Defence needs accounted for 30 per cent of total production in 1916, up from 5 per cent before the war. The share of output represented by investment goods declined from 9 per cent in 1913 to 5 per cent in 1916, largely as a result of the collapse in the production of transport equipment. The proportion absorbed by households fell from over 80 per cent in 1913 to not much more than 60 per cent by 1916. In absolute terms the value of

TABLE 11.5   *Gross industrial production, 1913–1918, USSR pre-1939 territory, million rubles, 1913 prices*

	Large-scale industry	Group A enterprise	Group B enterprise	Small-scale industry	Total (col. 1 + col. 4)	Index
1913	6,391	2,582	3,809	2,040	8,431	100
1914	6,429	2,726	3,703	2,000	8,429	100
1915	7,056	3,359	3,697	1,600	8,656	103
1916	7,420	4,170	3,250	1,800	9,220	109
1917	4,780	2,667	2,113	1,600	6,380	76
1918	2,160	980	1,180	1,500	3,660	43

Source: Gukhman, 1929, pp. 173, 191.

production destined for household use remained stable through 1915, but declined by around 11 per cent in 1916. By 1917 consumers took delivery of finished goods equivalent to just two-thirds of the pre-war figure.[19] Table 11.6 illustrates these trends.

Small-scale industry behaved less erratically, although the figures are less secure. Production declined at the beginning of the war but recovered by 1916, before falling back in 1917 to stand at around three-quarters of the pre-war total. These trends are consistent with the story of industrial mobilisation. Smaller enterprises were hit by conscription and unable to compete for labour with larger firms. They were also hampered by shortages of fuel and raw materials. Without the support of the voluntary organisations they would have been in an even worse plight.[20]

Industrial investment increased during the war as a result of the incentives given to firms to acquire the capacity to manufacture military hardware and ammunition. However, this did not mean that newly acquired plant could be used in civilian manufacturing. Pokrovskii believed that 'during the war a large number of factories have purchased a huge quantity of machine tools and equipment that they will not need in peacetime or that will be surplus to requirements'. Allowing for an element of special pleading (factories wanted a tax break), some factories acquired specialised equipment that proved redundant after the war.[21]

The transport sector was universally regarded as having failed to deliver. It badly required investment. The increase in total traffic during the war imposed a severe strain on the rolling stock. Fewer ailing locomotives would help to maintain momentum on the railways; as it was, the relative shortage of functioning locomotives put additional pressure on the available stock, resulting in increased wear and tear and therefore high casualty rates. The quality of the Russian rolling stock attracted derisory

TABLE 11.6 *Manufacturing output to final demand, 1913–1918, per cent*

Year	Investment goods	Construction goods	Household consumption	Defence
1913	9.1	3.7	81.8	5.4
1914	9.7	3.6	79.0	7.7
1915	7.3	3.9	68.1	20.7
1916	5.4	3.9	61.9	28.8
1917	4.5	3.6	59.8	32.6
1918 (1st half)	5.7	1.9	85.6	6.7

Source and note: Derived from *Promyshlennaia perepis'*, 1926, vol. 1, p. 41. Investment goods include rolling stock, industrial machinery and agricultural equipment.

comments from experts who drew unfavourable comparisons with foreign stock. An American engineer described Russian trains as 'strings of match-boxes coupled by hairpins and drawn by samovars'. The war also exposed a problem that originated from the decision to purchase heavier foreign locomotives for Russia's railways: most rails were too brittle and light to accommodate them. Other elements of transport, such as the merchant fleet, presented an equally dismal picture.[22]

In his survey of the post-war prospects of Russian industry, Grinevetskii concluded that Russia needed to allocate around 7.5 billion gold rubles to the construction over ten years of 64,000 km of new lines. He maintained that the costs could be met by domestic and foreign borrowing, by underwriting private ventures and by granting concessions to private operators. The latter option seemed to him most likely to bear fruit, and indeed the idea attracted the interest of an American railway mission in 1917.[23] Besides, the creation of such a network would create jobs, stimulate industry and open up new regions for exploitation. Railways should be the 'axis' of government economic policy, but it soon became apparent that they were in competition with other sectors for scarce funds. The obvious example was electrification, which – by concentrating on the generation and transmission of energy over long distances – would challenge the position of the railways as carriers of coal.

Where would this investment come from? For private entrepreneurs, the answer lay in creating a favourable climate for enterprise to encourage foreign investment and to release domestic entrepreneurial energy. That vision was not universally shared. At the first All-Russian Congress of Trade and Industry the Moscow industrialist Mikhail Riabushinskii argued that 'our borders must not be wide open to foreign capital', lest it score a 'victory' over Russian industry. Stakheev shared his concern.[24] Nor did the Soviet state neglect the issue of capital investment, as negotiations during 1918 between leading businessmen and the Bolsheviks demonstrated. The collapse of these negotiations placed Soviet leaders in a quandary that would only slowly be resolved after 1921.

Did the war act as a midwife, helping to encourage investment and economic modernisation? In industry the war fostered concentration. In agriculture the reverse process took place. Industrial enterprises employed on average 130 workers in 1913; by 1916 this figure had increased to just under 170. In chemicals the average increased from 164 to 197, and in metal-working from 159 to 234. Newly opened firms in particular tended to have a larger than average workforce, while firms that closed before 1917 were smaller.[25] Technocratic opinion was markedly in favour of this tendency. General Mikhel'son reported that 'unification is power', arguing that this power needed to be directed towards the production of better and cheaper products.[26] Small-scale enterprise had a harder time. However, large firms were more vulnerable to the economic crisis that set in during 1917 and 1918. In agriculture privately owned estates found it difficult to secure labour and equipment, giving the small peasant family farm a more prominent role in agricultural production. Thus the revolution left much work to be done to revive larger units in industry and agriculture that could support an increase in labour productivity.

11.3   Russia in the Allied war effort

Russia did not fight alone in World War 1. What principles governed Russia's relations with its Allies? What difficulties arose? What difference did it make to Russia to belong to an international coalition? To state the obvious, Russia would have found it impossible to act alone in its campaigns on three fronts against Germany, Austria-Hungary and Turkey. The alliance enabled some of the pressure to be relieved, as when Winston Churchill countenanced the disastrous campaign in Gallipoli in 1915. Participation in the international coalition also gave Russia access to overseas money markets. Foreign loans enabled Russia to pay for imports of munitions and other items, to support the exchange rate and to help meet its obligations to foreign creditors. Yet government officials never tired of pointing out that Russian industry should in future produce armaments and other manufactured goods, thereby saving scarce foreign exchange.[27]

Relations between Russia and its partners were never easy. The obstacles to achieving an informal mutual understanding of the possibilities of an international alliance should not be under-estimated. A great deal was at stake in the Alliance, including issues of national pride, trust and equity. Throughout the war differences of opinion arose between Alliance members over military strategy, disagreements that were mirrored within each member state. Thus, throughout 1916, Russia's military leaders urged Britain and France to increase the level of their activity in the Balkans, in order to ease the pressure on Russia's south-western front. However, this option would have meant diverting British and French resources from France, where an offensive against Germany was believed to be badly needed.[28] The war demonstrated how difficult it was to achieve sustained and meaningful co-ordination over military strategy. For example, the Russian offensive at Lake Narotch in March 1916 caused a good deal of irritation among its Allies. Heavy Russian casualties only confirmed their misgivings.[29]

Communication was also difficult, less for linguistic reasons (most negotiations were conducted in French) than because of a cultural distance between the various ministers, generals, diplomats and their staff. The British tended to discount Russian proposals as being driven by 'mercenary' considerations. Rather than complaining explicitly of bribery and corruption, British officials used oblique language, referring to Russians as 'Orientals' who behaved as if in the 'bazaar'.[30] For their part, the Russians felt that Britain under-valued their contribution to the war effort – in particular the heavy loss of life on the eastern front – and failed to acknowledge the mistakes made by British firms that had promised to supply munitions, but had failed to deliver. France's participation in the alliance added to the potential for discord and incomprehension, and the issues were further complicated by the participation of the USA, first as creditor and then as co-belligerent.[31]

Disagreements over priorities as well as confusion over lines of responsibility inevitably characterised issues relating to imports of military hardware, ferrous metal or other scarce items. The Russian government appointed its own licensed representatives in London (the Russian Government Committee) and in the USA. Meanwhile various unofficial middlemen acted independently and lined their own pockets.[32] In order to eliminate inter-governmental competition in third markets, the French and British formed a *Commission Internationale de Ravitaillement* in August 1914, and invited the Russians to nominate members. However, this did not bring an end to the scramble for contracts. Russian procurement officials failed to keep even their own delegates on the commission informed, so all attempts at co-ordinating purchases came to naught. Faced with overwhelming evidence that too many agencies were involved in ordering munitions Lord Kitchener, the British Secretary of State for War, established a Russian Purchasing Committee in London. This did not deter Russian procurement agents, including members of the Russian Government Committee, from making their own arrangements, further contributing to an atmosphere of mutual mistrust between the British and Russians that persisted beyond the February Revolution.[33]

Lack of co-ordination meant that foreign suppliers soon had more orders than they could cope with. By late 1915 officials in London complained that their Russian counterparts failed to understand that the British firms had reached full capacity. Manpower was required to sustain domestic production, not only to satisfy British military demand but also to export goods to the USA and uphold the sterling exchange rate and thus to maintain Britain's own credit-worthiness on the other side of the Atlantic.[34]

Other contentious areas included technical yet vital issues of shipping and port facilities. The Russian merchant fleet was of modest size, so goods needed to be delivered by British or American vessels, adding to the strain on existing merchant shipping capacity. As a result of these various difficulties, many orders placed by the Russians during the war failed to reach Russian shores on time or even to arrive at all. For example, Russia ordered 31,000 wagons and 1,300 locomotives from overseas, of which only 13,000 and 400 respectively reached their destination.[35] Industrialists complained that they had placed orders with suppliers in the USA, Britain, Sweden and Denmark, having been promised delivery within five months, but that by early 1916 they were being told to wait for up to 12 months.[36] Some authorities concluded that, explosives apart, Russia could not rely upon foreign producers. General Alekseev argued in June 1916 that it was time to focus instead on boosting domestic manufacturing capacity.[37] Even when goods did reach Russian ports there were difficulties in transporting them to the interior. Stocks of scarce copper ore accumulated at Vladivostok and Archangel. One major but very costly initiative was the construction of the railway from Murmansk to Petrozavodsk, which enabled supplies to be sent on to Petrograd and thence to the front line.[38]

Tortuous financial negotiations took place with the British and French, and subsequently with the Americans as well. None of them were keen to write Russia a blank cheque. The State Auditor, P.A. Kharitonov, complained that the Allies 'held a knife to our throat'.[39] At a meeting of Allied ministers in Paris in early February 1915 Russia's Minister of Finances Peter Bark, conscious of the shortage of foreign currency brought about by the interruption to Russia's grain exports, secured permission to raise £100 million on the London and Paris money markets, in order to settle Russia's import bill and pay dividends to foreign bondholders. In the interim, France and Britain undertook to extend loans for half that amount, provided that Russia released part of its gold reserves.[40] The same considerations applied throughout 1915 and 1916. Russia needed foreign currency to settle its accounts with existing creditors and to make advance payments or settle invoices for goods ordered from overseas suppliers. Needless to say, its creditors expressed alarm about Russia's ability to meet its obligations after the war. Bark offered to convert Russia's short-term obligations into long-term debt, but his suggestion met with a frosty response in Paris.[41]

The burden of overseas debt that Russia had accumulated by 1917 would inevitably saddle any post-war regime with enormous balance of payments difficulties. Lenin, true to his word, immediately abrogated all

Russia's outstanding external liabilities to bondholders, British, American, Japanese and above all French. While the Bolsheviks could hardly be expected to weep for foreign bondholders, and while their ruthlessness contributed yet further to a souring of international relations, the abrupt decision only underscored the risks that the Allies took when extending credit to Russia. The alliance had been built on shifting sand, and Lenin merely dug the final scoop.[42]

When he took the fateful decision to cancel Russia's obligations Lenin may have done out of ideological considerations what others in the same circumstances might have done for pragmatic reasons. Russia could not have sustained its contribution to the war effort without foreign assistance. Ironically much of the Civil War was fought with little direct foreign assistance, unless one counts stocks of foreign-made weaponry that remained on Russian soil. When the war was over, Russia's new rulers promised to scrutinise the country's external economic relations carefully. In the heady days of revolution it seemed as if proletarian Russia would be at the centre of a new web of revolutionary allies. When that vision evaporated, Russia had to go it alone.

11.4   Remembering – and forgetting

In many societies the aftermath of war is inscribed in collective remembrance, embodied in public ceremonial and encoded in personal memory. These processes have often been contested – ceremonial can divide as much as it unites – but all belligerents except Russia invested heavily in commemorative work following the Great War. Apart from a handful of Soviet studies on specialist topics, little work of note saw the light of day in Russia, certainly not in comparison with the vast outpouring of revolutionary propaganda.[43] During the Civil War the Bolsheviks were too busy fighting their own enemies to dwell overmuch on the 'imperialist war' as a conflict in its own right. Their emphasis upon a revolutionary rupture in October 1917 was extremely effective in marginalising the history of the eastern front. By the same token their opponents defined themselves in opposition to Bolshevism and not primarily in relation to the experience of the 'great patriotic war'.[44]

To be sure, in the midst of the conflict important efforts were made to come to terms with the war. Beyond the narrow world of officialdom, teachers, psychologists and social workers recorded the war's unprecedented impact. A group of pedagogues attached to the Kiev Froebel Society collected some of the drawings done by children, one of whom produced a cartoon-like mini-history of the outbreak of the war. The collection, entitled 'Children and the War', included letters written by children to soldiers at the front, offering them encouragement about the conduct of the war and reassuring them about the care lavished on their families and wounded comrades.[45] This material was presumably assembled to enable child psychologists to engage with the mental world of the next generation of citizens. Serious efforts were also made to collect folksongs from Russian, Ukrainian, Lithuanian and Georgian soldiers serving at the front and in the rear. The most active collector was the peasant turned feld'sher V.I. Simakov (1879–1955) who traced the emergence of a diversified popular culture in which traditional soldiers' songs were mixed with urban ballads, outlaws' songs, *chastushki* and other genres.[46]

Contemporaries also sought to historicise the war, by deliberately generating material that would contribute to a future account of the war. The famous historian Sergei Platonov (1860–1933) was emphatic about the need for testimony to be sought from displaced persons, in order to supply raw material for the 'future historian.' He had in mind collections of letters, stories, poems, etc., extracts of which appeared in the periodical press and in specialist publications dedicated to the refugee 'problem'.[47] The need to remember was particularly acute for the non-Russian patriotic intelligentsia for whom death and displacement spelled national disaster – the erasure of the nation through occupation and enforced migration. The leading Jewish historian Simon Dubnow wrote in 1918 that:

The historic events of the last four years are so profound that many years will be needed for the preparatory work to be undertaken, in order to allow the future historian to make sense of them.[48]

Russia's educated elite acted upon these injunctions. In this regard, the Tatiana Committee played an important part, launching an ambitious programme to publicise the history of refugeedom with a special exhibition scheduled for 1917. Underlying this initiative was a belief that the Russian public needed to be better informed about the living conditions and activities of refugees, who were not all 'beggars, idlers and spongers.'[49] Four main themes were to be highlighted: conditions in Russia's borderlands before and during the war (including 'the destruction of settlements, property and artistic monuments'); the 'sorrowful journey' of refugees, including the background to their displacement, the course of their movement and the assistance given by government and public organisations; the living conditions in their new homes (including 'the work undertaken by refugees and their impact on the local population'); and lastly the restoration of normal life in the regions cleared of enemy occupation.[50] Although nothing came of these elaborate plans (the timing was judged inappropriate in April 1917), many items of refugee provenance were submitted from far afield.[51]

In a related initiative the Tatiana Committee sponsored a remarkable project designed to gather material from refugees at first hand about their experiences. Refugees were encouraged to describe their experiences in their own words. If they needed help in formulating a coherent narrative the Tatiana Committee obligingly published a schedule of 24 questions to put to them. The aim was to secure stories from 'simple people' and not just from the refugee intelligentsia. Other kinds of testimony were also sought: photographs, drawings, reports, memoirs, stories and belles lettres:

The material that is collected ... will be collated and organised systematically and will form part of a projected volume of 'Collected materials on the history of the refugee movement during the world war.[52]

The project yielded several published accounts of episodes in the lives of refugees and relief workers. One sympathetic relief worker recorded that the exhausted and frightened refugee had 'the eyes of a wounded animal.' Another wrote of his encounter with a distraught father who had just buried his young daughter, concluding that 'I comforted him.' One refugee spoke not only of the pain and torment of displacement, but also of the fact that his experience was 'interesting for an observant individual', who had access to 'unexpected and different places, peoples and customs.'[53] Another project was conducted by the Jewish ethnographer Solomon Rapoport (1863–1920), who carried out relief work among Jewish refugees in Russian Poland, Galicia and Bukovina during the war. In his diaries he made much of his wish to record as much as possible of the Jewish experience, whether recounted in stories, poems or song. He sought to convey how Jewish civilians made sense of their experiences by recourse to traditional systems of belief.[54]

As self-conscious revolutionaries the Bolsheviks sought a rupture with the past. They deliberately distanced themselves from the 'imperialist war'. Revolution became instead their point of reference. To be sure, the military lessons of the war were recorded in specialist journals. A 'Commission for researching and applying the experience of the world and civil wars' met between 1920 and 1922 under the chairmanship of the military theorist A.A. Svechin. One of its members, the economist Iakov Bukshpan, emphasised that personal experience imparted authority to his own published work on economic regulation. In 1920 the People's Commissariat for Health established a 'Commission for investigating the effects of the war on public health', which trawled through hundreds of thousands of card indexes in the army archives.[55]

Elsewhere in Europe the centrality of wartime experience was clearly inscribed in military memoirs and ceremonial. In Soviet Russia the Red Army deliberately refused to cultivate continuities with the old army. Military units were dismantled and reordered, so there was no regimental continuity and an absence of institutional devices for remembering one's fallen comrades. The kind of camaraderie evident in the veteran's organisations of the French, British and Germans lacked any equivalent in Russia's generation of 1914, except among small numbers of émigré officers. What mattered was a commitment to the cause of the revolution. This discontinuity completely eroded any sense that fighting before 1917 was historically significant. The Civil War became the 'formative experience' for the ordinary soldier, although it is worth noting that Soviet soldiers often went into battle in 1941 singing the same songs as their fathers did in 1914.[56]

The example of the Latvian Riflemen is instructive. Formed in 1915, and allowed to bear Latvian flags and insignia, they went into battle to defend Latvia against German invasion, in which cause they suffered grievous losses in the winter of 1916. Even as, famously, they fought in defence of Lenin's revolution, they symbolised the claims of Latvia for recognition. Nationalists subsequently claimed the Riflemen as martyrs of Latvia who deserved to find a place of honour in Riga's national cemetery, whereas in Soviet historiography they belonged to the pantheon of revolutionary heroes. Military comradeship, radical political zeal and invented national tradition thus coalesced.[57]

More generally the widespread preoccupation in 1917–1918 with the 'class enemy' dovetailed with Bolshevik doctrines of social conflict. Thus the Russian population found meaning in intense social antagonism rather than in the sacrifice of war as such. Whatever its mainsprings, Soviet forgetting found expression in the absence of public monuments akin to the Cenotaph and the Menin Gate. There were no gardens of remembrance or village war memorials. No graves marked the spot where soldiers fell in battle or civilians perished en route to a place of safety. No official provision was made for those who wished to transcend grief. Oblivion was officially sanctioned. The Moscow city cemetery where 'fallen soldiers' were buried in 1915–1917 (and which was earmarked for a proposed war museum) became instead the site of mass burial of the Cheka's victims, until it was bulldozed to make way for a cinema.[58]

Conclusions

The decline in total output by 1917 restricted the options available to the Russian government, but officials had already committed themselves to a narrowly conceived strategy. The enormous energies directed towards defence needs – by 1916 close on one-third of industrial production was devoted to the military – contributed to a neglect of other sectors. Russia's leaders failed to see that 'non-defence' activity underpinned the defence effort as a whole. In vain did some contemporaries point to the need for a broader conception of defence.[59] The economist Mikhail Bogolepov, an employee of the tsarist Ministry of Finances, spoke of the state as having a dual capacity, first as a midwife helping to deliver new sectors of economic activity, and second as an 'intelligent gardener' capable of cultivating and developing existing enterprise.[60] Even more broadly, the war lent itself to a conception of mobilising the 'national economy' as a whole, a programme that entailed devoting due attention to the needs of civilian sectors.[61]

Whether the focus is on economic performance or public health, the First World War was a breeding ground for internal division at a political level, between officialdom and 'educated society'. Thus one of the lessons of war was that it exposed rather than masked acute political faultlines. Zemstvo activists gave the government credit for its initiatives in weaning the population off vodka, but warned that more needed to be done to substitute books for the bottle. The health crisis provided the public organisations with an opportunity to berate the old regime for failing to stem the tide of refugees or to plan their resettlement. The language deployed by the educated public spoke of planning and of 'rational' recreation. It is hardly surprising that these doctrines should have been central to debates following the revolution. They were not instituted by the war, but the war brought them greater prominence and appeal.

The war exposed a tangled web of credit between Russia and the Allies. Most players in this complex game concentrated on their own national interests to the exclusion of broader Allied considerations. Russia pressed Britain and France to support its purchases overseas, sometimes overlooking the fact that its military partners themselves needed to maintain their credit standing with the USA. The Allies' unwillingness to throw caution to the winds created enormous resentment in Russia, best expressed by the government minister who believed that 'we have jumped from the frying pan into the fire, swapping the German economic yoke for the English. What is worse, only the future will tell'.[62]

Most Bolsheviks pinned their hopes on international revolutionary solidarity. Events conspired to defeat that vision. Russia was left in its own proletarian fortress to pick up the pieces of a prolonged war. From that vantage point they contemplated the difficulties that bourgeois nation-states encountered in settling the financial obligations that Russia had incurred. Far better, it seemed, to be free from the grip of international finance. Yet this only underscored the fact that the Bolsheviks would have to rely upon their own resources in order to deal with the destruction of capital that the war bequeathed.

In what terms were memories of war couched? The Bolsheviks owed their victory to the strains of war, but they neglected to acknowledge the fact, apart from acknowledging in specialist publications structural changes in economic organisation. They discouraged public reflection on the war as a compelling human struggle and did nothing to sustain its commemoration. Memories of wartime campaigns, comradeship in the trenches and wartime population displacement were largely obliterated. The Bolsheviks turned their attention instead to revolutionary state-building. In so doing they helped to unleash fresh turbulence and violence.

The Russian poet Anna Akhmatova once wrote of the twentieth century as having 'really' begun only in 1914. A peasant girl born in Russia in 1914 lived the first seven years of her life knowing nothing except uninterrupted bloodletting. Then, as she reached her teenage years, her life would change beyond all recognition, as a result of the Stalinist economic and social transformation. In her full adulthood she would become embroiled in yet another 'great patriotic war', inflicting huge losses on the Soviet population. If she survived that terrible conflict, she could look back on a life of unrelenting struggle.[63]

Note on further reading

For thinking about economic change I have relied upon the pioneering work of Prokopovich, 1918. On social and demographic change the starting point for an informed discussion in English is Kohn and Meyendorff, 1932. Even less well studied (either in English or in Russian) are issues of military medicine and public health in wartime. Neilson, 1984, is a very informative work on the politics and diplomacy of external economic assistance to Russia.

References

1 Kohn and Meyendorff, 1932, pp. 158–9.

2 Bonwetsch, 1973, p. 184.

3 Miliukov, 1967, pp. 310–11.

4 Vainshtein, 1960, pp. 452–3 discusses the rival estimates.

5 Davies, Harrison and Wheatcroft, eds, 1994, p. 64. Compare Mal'kov, ed., 1998, pp. 476–77 (Stepanov), who puts the population deficit at 10 million (July 1914 to November 1918).

6 See the summary in Kohn and Meyendorff, 1932, p. 65.

7 Il'ina, 1977, p. 51.

8 Mal'kov, ed., 1998, pp. 478–9 (Stepanov).

9 Ferguson, 1999, p. 299.

10 Poliakov, 2000, p. 79.

11 Kohn and Meyendorff, 1932, pp. 117–20.

12 Details in *Izvestiia VSG*, 1916, 34, pp. 179–222.

13 Report printed in *Izvestiia VSG*, 1916, 29–30, pp. 326–30.

14 Solomon and Hutchinson, eds, 1990, p. 176 (Solomon), and pp. 121–45 (Ramer).

15 Polner, 1930, p. 122.

16 *Izvestiia VZS*, 17, 15 June 1915, p. 77; 19, 15 July 1915, p. 46; 37–38, 15 April–1 May 1916, p. 285.

17 Prokopovich, 1918, p. 173.

18 Maslov, 1918, p. 223; Prokopovich, 1918, p. 134.

19 *Promyshlennaia perepis'*, 1926, volume 1, p. 41.

20 Gukhman, 1929, pp. 174–5; Adamov, ed., 1972, pp. 333–45 (Ol'khovaia).

21 *Proizvoditel'nye sily Rossii*, 1916, 1, p. 57 (Pokrovskii). Grinevetskii was more sanguine. *Trudy Pervogo Ekonomicheskogo s"ezda*, 1918, pp. 48–52, 96–100.

22 Davies, ed., 1990, p. 174, Westwood; Heywood, 2002; Bogolepov, 1921, p. 71.

23 Grinevetskii, 1919, pp. 128, 132–4. The Americans floated the idea of committing $50 billion over 100 years, in return for a concession on the line from Vladivostok to western Siberia. Ganelin, 1969, pp. 317–18; Saul, 2001, pp. 142–7.

24 *Pervyi Vserossiiskii torgovo-promyshlennyi s"ezd*, 1917, pp. 3–11; Kitanina, 1969, p. 115.

25 *Nar. khoz. v 1916*, 1922, volume 7, pp. 128–9; *Statisticheskii sbornik*, 1921, volume 1, table 2; *Promyshlennaia perepis'*, 1926, volume 1, pp. 35–6.

26 Manikovskii, 1930, volume 2, pp. 298–301.

27 Manikovskii, 1930, volume 2, pp. 293–7; *Snabzhenie Krasnoi Armii*, 1922 9, p. 4.

28 Similarly, Grand Duke Nikolai, Viceroy of the Caucasus, called for Allied action in Persia, in order to tie down Ottoman forces. Neilson, 1984, pp. 142, 144.

29 Stone, 1975, pp. 230–1.

30 Neilson, 1984, pp. 103, 184, 243. J.M. Keynes, already a leading official in the Treasury, used the word 'mercenary', as did Lieutenant-Colonel Alfred Knox, who was seconded to the Russian army during the war.

31 Neilson, 1984, p. 180; Ganelin, 1969.

32 RGIA f.1276, op.12, d.1083, ll.54–56ob.; Babichev, 1956; Neilson, 1984, p. 66.

33 Neilson, 1984, pp. 51–3, 91–2, 100–102, 127, 257.

34 Horn, 2002, pp. 93–116, 121–2; Neilson, 1984, p. 308.

35 Grinevetskii, 1919, p. 111.

36 *Trudy Pervogo s"ezda*, 1916, p. 65.

37 Mikhailov, 1927, p. 500; Manikovskii, 1930, volume 2, pp. 342–3.

38 Tarnovskii, 1958, p. 212; Nachtigal, 2001.

39 Quoted in Beliaev, 2002, p. 373. Kharitonov was speaking in August 1915.

40 Neilson, 1984, p. 65; Horn, 2002, p. 111; Beliaev, 2002, p. 371.

41 Beliaev, 2002, p. 377.

42 Fisk, 1924, pp. 133, 302–4.

43 Khmelevskii, 1973.

44 Cohen, 2003.

45 Afanas'ev and Levitskii, eds, *Deti i voina*, 1915.

46 Rayfield, 1988.

47 *Izvestiia Vserossiiskogo komiteta dlia okazaniia pomoshchi postradavshim ot voennykh bedstvii*, 15 May 1917, p. 8.

48 Dubnow, ed., 1918, p. 195.

49 RGIA f.1276, op.12, d.1382, ll.387–90.

RUSSIA'S FIRST WORLD WAR: AN OVERVIEW 263

50 *Izvestiia KTN*, 1 February 1917, p. 10; *Trudovaia pomoshch'*, 10, 1916, p. 512, where this initiative was seen as a contribution to 'the history of war in general.'

51 *Zinojums* 51 (22 December 1916); RGIA f.1322, op.1, d.13, l.142ob.

52 *Izvestiia KTN* , 1 October 1916, pp. 5–6; *Trudovaia pomoshch'* , 1916, 9, p. 394; *Izvestiia KTN*, 1 January 1917, pp. 10–11; Gatrell, 1999, Appendix 2.

53 E. Glukhovtsova, 'Skazka zhizni,' *Izvestiia KTN*, 15 February 1917, pp. 21–28; Iakov Vol'rat, 'Begstvo ot germantsev i skitaniia,' ibid., 19, 15 April 1917, pp. 17–22.

54 Roskies, 1984, p. 135.

55 Bukshpan, 1929, p. 7; Polner, 1930, p. 97. Economists such as Prokopovich and Jasny, who went into exile, left accounts of the war that drew upon their own participation. Military specialists, such as Manikovskii (who died in 1920) and Golovin (who died in exile in 1944), contributed to the historiography of mobilisation and munitions production. Several émigrés made valuable contributions to the historical record, notably as authors of monographs in the Russian series of the famous Carnegie Economic and Social History of the War, under the general editorship of the distinguished historian Paul Vinogradoff. Several projected volumes, including studies of transport, labour and key industrial sectors, never appeared.

56 Gleason et al., eds, 1985, pp. 57–76 (Fitzpatrick); Mal'kov, ed., 1998, p. 555 (Shatsillo); Cohen, 2003. Some personal testimony saw the light of day. See Pireiko, 1935 (first published 1926). Pireiko's book, which carried the subtitle 'Memoirs of a Bolshevik', portrayed the imperialist war as a stepping stone to proletarian revolution.

57 Bilmanis, 1951, p. 281.

58 Gronsky and Astrov, 1929, p. 258; Smirnov, ed., 1999, pp. 49–57 (Orlovsky).

59 *Trudy Vtorogo s"ezda*, 1916, volume 1, p. 271; Sviatlovskii, 1926, p. 385.

60 Bogolepov, 1916. See also *V.fin*, 1915, 47 (Gol'dberg) on the need for a 'general plan'.

61 Sviatlovskii, 1926, pp. 373–4, arguing that mobilisation meant preserving the 'vitality' of the national economy as well as its defensive capability.

62 Cabinet meeting, 25 March 1916, quoted in Gal'perina, ed., 1999, p. 325.

63 Merridale, 2000.

Conclusion: Russia's First World War in comparative perspective

A lone of the belligerent powers, Russia endured a political and social revolution in the midst of the Great War. The old imperial polity was swept away in February 1917. The new Provisional Government confronted profound challenges against the backdrop of continued warfare and of Russia's commitment to its allies. Its vision of universal citizenship based upon the integrity of private property proved short-lived. Russia's participation in the war came to an end when the Bolsheviks seized power. Depending upon one's point of view this amounted either to a catastrophic misfortune or a liberating revolution. For those who pinned their hopes on a revolutionary transformation, Russia blazed a path that others might follow. Radical opinion lamented the loss of life that Russia had borne during the world war and attributed it to the discredited, secretive and malign influence of imperialism on national and international politics. Liberals and conservatives meanwhile shared the general horror at the sacrifices made by so many of their fellow Russian countrymen, particularly when their suffering had done nothing to prevent the Bolshevik seizure of power.

So far, one might say, so distinctive. But how far should we press Russia's claim to uniqueness? One of the assumptions that govern the coupling of war and revolution is that Russia's experience in 1914–1918 had few parallels with experience elsewhere. Yet many supposedly unique elements dissolve on closer inspection. What appear from a Russian perspective to be extraordinary manifestations of political uncertainty, social upheaval and economic collapse often had their counterpart in other belligerent countries. This point tends to be overlooked, because the historiography of the war has been located largely within a national framework. The purpose of this conclusion is to establish points of convergence as well as divergence.

A mood of fatalism rather than mass enthusiasm characterised European society at the outbreak of war, although this was masked by the torrent of official propaganda. Historians who have examined the climate of opinion, whether in Berlin or Birmingham, Paris or Petrograd, have noted a resigned acceptance of the need to fight. Italian peasants, for example, regarded it as a misfortune over which – like drought or famine – they exercised no control. In the short term at least, European workers abandoned the strike weapon, partly persuaded by the widespread mood of patriotism, but also because conscription disrupted existing organisations in the workplace. Tsarist Russia conformed to the general pattern.[1]

In Russia the famous shortages of shell and the loss of manpower to conscription early in the war figure in accounts of its military weakness and industrial disruption. Yet the armies on the western front had also exhausted their supplies of shell by the middle of November 1914. Industrial production in Germany and Italy suffered badly from the sudden depletion of the labour force. In France the labour force haemorrhaged as a consequence of conscription. The proximity of mines and factories to the frontier exposed them to enemy invasion. The domestic political repercussions of these shocks were everywhere profound. Cabinet ministers lost their jobs and government departments were reorganised. Parliamentary politics became less meaningful.[2] To some extent Russia was not noticeably out of step with these developments. However, the critique of military procurement had lasting political and economic consequences, creating an opportunity for the new voluntary organisations and fashioning a fixation with defence production to the neglect of civilian needs.

The lack of any decisive military outcome meant stalemate on the battlefield. For most military planners and civil servants, the war would only end when the enemy had been crushed on the field of battle or forced to concede defeat as a result of economic exhaustion. This explains the commitment by all states to securing additional resources for war. Huge resources were poured into the manufacture of munitions as well as other supplies. In Russia the labour force grew rapidly, as employers drew upon reserves of unemployed, migrant and refugee labour, much of it female, to expand defence production. Russia's experience was mirrored elsewhere. The factories of Milan absorbed thousands of rural immigrants from other parts of Italy. As in Russia this blurred distinctions between 'worker' and 'peasant'. The intensity of mobilisation was registered in the absorption of labour into the armed forces. Threatening workers with conscription also served as a useful weapon in the hands of employers.[3]

Widespread military influence in the political sphere was one reflection of the new constellation of forces in wartime. In most belligerent states the army extended its administrative control over public affairs, including managing resources and interfering in the rewards to be given to capital and labour. Germany's military commanders laid claim to emergency powers over army corps areas, much as their Russian counterparts did across a broad swathe of the empire. Intervention by the Russian army disrupted established economic networks, but the German army too embarked on 'sporadic and haphazard mustering of resources' at the end of 1916. The Turkish and Austrian armies were no less interventionist.[4]

The politics of mobilisation was also marked by the growth of corporate influence. The administration of raw materials in Germany, Britain, France or Russia – with its characteristic mixture of state supervision and day-to-day control by semi-public agencies run by businessmen – did not differ in fundamental respects. No government had sufficient civil servants to cope with the minutiae of allocating stocks of fuel or metals, and so these tasks were devolved upon the private sector, under the watchful eye of the state. In the headlong rush to increase the supply of armaments each belligerent facilitated the expansion of capacity in the private sector. The German war ministry embraced the private sector rather than counting upon state arsenals to deliver the huge additional quantities of munitions that were required in wartime. Similar expectations were heaped upon Schneider-Creusot in France, Vickers in Britain and the Russian firm Putilov.

In one important respect Russia manifested a distinctive approach to managing the industrial war economy. In Britain the Trades Union Congress became directly involved in the war economy, in return for union leaders' acceptance of the dilution of labour and restrictions on labour mobility. In Germany, too, organised labour played a part in the arrangements for exempting workers from conscription. Shortages of shell and labour forced a radical rethink of the relationship between army, industry and labour, reaching its apogee in December 1916 with the Auxiliary Service Law that provided for formal arbitration and workers' councils in return for universal labour conscription and restrictions on mobility. In January 1917 the French Minister of Munitions, Albert Thomas, imposed compulsory arbitration on employers and workers; subsequently he introduced a minimum wage. The Italian government imposed compulsory arbitration and introduced a range of welfare measures that improved conditions in the workplace. Organised labour was either co-opted to help manage the war effort or mollified by concessions.[5]

These options never attracted serious attention in Russia. Trade unions played a marginal role before 1914 and government officials refused to change tack during the war. In vain did the public organisations call for the recognition of organised labour. After February 1917 the management of the war effort was entrusted to political leaders who were prepared to explore avenues for co-operation with organised labour, but this came too late to affect the course of industrial politics. There were no formal arrangements for institutionalised bargaining and no incorporation of labour in the Russian war economy. While Germany reached an accommodation between capital and labour, Russia ended up instead with factory committees and workers' control – in the one case collaboration, in the other communism.[6]

Attempts in Germany, France and Russia to accelerate defence production were initially frustrated by manufacturers' inexperience and by the dissipation of effort. They were resolved in each case by reorganising the production process, developing new capacity in the private sector (largely paid for by generous government advances) and creating public–private partnerships in the allocation of raw materials. At the level of individual sectors the talk was of mass manufacturing and standardisation as the wave of the future. Productivity improved more markedly in armaments and chemicals than in non-defence industry, but the investment that made this possible was normally written off. In Russia the decline in the manufacture of consumer goods disrupted the flow of goods from town to country, contributing to the food crisis in 1917. This failure was largely attributable to policy errors, namely the decision to favour the military and to neglect consumers. However, Russia's economic backwardness narrowed the options of the policy makers, by making it difficult to secure a sufficiently rapid increase in fuel and raw materials. Yet we should also not forget the severe strains to which the equivalent Hindenburg programme subjected the more advanced German economy.[7]

In most belligerent societies steps were taken to circumscribe private enterprise, either by regulating production and distribution or by expanding the range of state enterprise. In Russia the Main Artillery Administration invested heavily in government arsenals and explosives factories, as a means of curbing the ambition of the private sector. Its strategy seems to have been more deliberate than that pursued by procurement agencies in France and Britain, if not in Germany.[8] Russia's distinctiveness emerged more clearly in the decision by businessmen in medium and small enterprises to create new organisations designed to supply military items. The war industry committees regarded the manufacture of uniforms and footwear as a means to demonstrate the viability of a new kind of enterprise, owned neither by the state nor by the big banks.

The war was a technocrat's dream world, providing an opportunity to influence the organisation of production in pursuit of a vision that recognised disinterested expertise over private gain.[9] Experts constituted themselves as such by defining what 'problems' were in urgent need of attention. Much more was at stake than technical issues. In Russia discussions of economic policy and organisation posed fundamental questions about the nature of the state and the meaning of the narod. Discussion focused on the need to relocate manufacturing industry closer to the sources of raw materials and fuel. This formed part of the rhetoric of revolutionary rationality. In the words of one engineer, who advocated a 'rational beginning' for the national economy: 'Organisation and construction are the slogans of our time, and by them *we shall possess the future*'. Technical specialists believed that the state had a duty to override private interests in favour of what they defined as the common good.[10]

The war exposed antagonism of a more traditional kind, in which the people were victims of privilege and an 'amoral economy'. This antagonism was not exclusive to Russia. It reflected a feeling that 'polite society' managed to evade the draft. The longer the war dragged on the more these sentiments became generalised. Issues of fairness were at stake. Businessmen made unwarranted profits; shopkeepers were corrupt; the rich secured a comfortable billet – these observations became commonplace. They fed the idea that the war had become illegitimate and a means of exploitation. Popular sentiment demanded that those who had prospered should be called to account. Most states devised strategies to combat these sentiments, including redistributive policies, which went hand in hand with what one scholar has called 'pervasive mind control' and traditional forms of patrimony. However, there was little sign of redistribution in Russia, where neither property taxes nor a belated income tax moderated a sense that the burden of war fell upon the poorest sections of society.[11]

Russia had greater recourse than the other major powers to non-budgetary means of raising revenue. The Tsar's decision to abolish the spirits monopoly dislocated the budget, but other countries also struggled with the need to find fresh resources. Like Russia, France belatedly introduced taxes on personal incomes and on war profits. New sources of revenue still left a huge hole in the budget. The war was financed by issuing Treasury bills, enabling the government to print money. However, inflation was not confined to Russia. The impact of rising prices – yielding relative advantages to government contractors and skilled workers, disadvantaging those on fixed incomes – was everywhere the same. Other countries, however, had more success with subsidies and price controls.[12]

Exports having dwindled rapidly, Russia relied heavily on its Allies to help pay for imports of munitions, machine tools, rolling stock and raw materials. France, too, was heavily indebted to Britain and later the USA for imports of coal and pig iron, having seen three-quarters of its capacity seized by the enemy or cut off by military activity. It is hard to conceive of France's continued participation in the war effort without the contribution of its Allies, or of Britain's ability to fight without the contribution of the dominions. However, Russia's membership of an international coalition, important though it was in the supply of credit, did not translate into a sustained and reliable flow of munitions and scarce raw materials. In other words, imports did not relieve the pressure on the Russian economy by enabling more domestic resources to be devoted to household consumption and investment. It did not help matters that the USA entered the war just as the Russian war effort began to falter and then collapse.[13]

Accounts of the Russian war economy have properly drawn attention to the difficulties experienced by Russian farmers, such as shortages of manpower on large estates, inputs of equipment, feed and fertiliser. But these were no greater than the problems confronted by Germany. Indeed, policy measures and producers' responses followed a broadly similar pattern in the two countries. In Germany the balance of food production and consumption was altered by the mobilisation of 11 million men, who enjoyed a superior diet to the one they were fed before the war.[14] Restrictions on international trade convinced the Reich of an impending food crisis and thus of the need to impose strict controls on key products. However, price controls were haphazard and farmers switched to livestock farming because there were no controls on the price of meat and because they could use potatoes and grain as fodder, circumventing the controls that had been imposed. The government tried to get round the problem by ordering a widespread slaughter of pigs. When this measure failed, ministers opted for a policy of direct confrontation with farmers by creating requisition detachments to search farm buildings. Farmers turned against the government, which they blamed for strong-arm tactics, and against the urban consumers whose interests had taken precedence. The parallels with Russian food policy are striking. Rittikh, the last tsarist Minister of Agriculture, attempted to extract surplus grain by means of apportioning regional quotas at fixed prices. He could not prevent the use of force by local plenipotentiaries. Here, too, government regulation and intervention saddled the state with popular opprobrium when things went wrong.[15]

Shortages of food in Germany provoked urban food riots during the late autumn of 1915, reaching a peak in the summer of the following year. Eventually the Reich government imposed food controls, administered by the War Food Office. Unlike Russia, whose officials believed that rationing could actually be 'dangerous for the government', German authorities did ration foodstuffs. However, this procedure was not straightforward. The failure of the harvest led to a cut in the ration. The situation deteriorated during the first half of 1917 and shortages provoked a further crisis in the summer of 1918. Nutritional culture in Germany favoured the consumption of meat and fats, and the enforced restriction on their intake was perceived as 'deep deprivation'. Workers went on strike because they could no longer afford to pay black market prices for basic foodstuffs. In the autumn of 1918 German sailors mutinied in response to shortages at home.[16]

There was little to choose between the privations endured by Russian consumers in the winter of 1916 and German consumers a year later. During the 'turnip winter' Germans managed to secure a basic level of subsistence, partly as a result of rationing but also by having recourse to the black market, by which means they obtained up to one-third of foodstuffs. Those who were unable to afford black market prices deployed other methods, becoming 'potato pilgrims' or pilfering from village allotments, behaviour that shattered pre-war notions of 'respectable' behaviour. In Russia, when official mechanisms of supply proved inadequate, urban consumers packed themselves off to surrounding villages in order to bargain with peasants. There was less sense here of a collapse of pre-war norms – until, that is, the October Revolution turned the bourgeois world upside down and compelled remnants of the propertied strata to fend for themselves as best they could.[17]

Nor were Germany and Russia alone in experiencing serious shortages of food. Italian families suffered extreme privation. In the Near East, the civilian population of Ottoman-controlled Syria suffered widespread starvation in 1915. It is also sometimes forgotten that, following the German decision to launch unrestricted submarine warfare, by April 1917 Britain had sufficient grain for just six weeks. This level of stocks sufficed in peacetime, when Britain relied on imports from five or six different sources, but the uncertain circumstances of war caused officials to take a hard look at public consumption. However, Britain (and to some extent France) managed to overcome the potential crisis, partly because of American assistance and partly because of inducements to farmers to expand the sown area, whereas Germany, Italy and Russia experienced shortages, deprivation and despair.[18]

What of social stratification and inequality more broadly? Those who made relative gains during the war were closely connected with the productive effort, in particular skilled and unskilled workers in defence industry. Industrialists who held defence contracts enjoyed a sharp upturn in their fortunes. At the other extreme, workers in non-essential occupations struggled to make ends meet. Those on fixed incomes, such as rentiers, teachers and students, found themselves at a great disadvantage. So too did white-collar workers whether in industry or the tertiary sector. As for displaced persons, the war wreaked havoc on their opportunities for gainful work, whether they were Belgian, Serbian, Polish or Latvian refugees.[19]

After several months of excruciating torment, troops on both sides expressed a fervent wish that it should end as soon as possible so that they could go home. Soldiers vented anger on those who were thought to have profited from the war. The often-noticed willingness of Russian troops to translate these grievances into action against the propertied elite had their counterpart in France, Germany and Austria-Hungary, where they subsequently fuelled mutiny and revolution. However, Russia differed in a crucial respect. The old regime did not attempt to motivate the common soldier by linking personal sacrifice to notions of citizenship, and pinned its hopes instead on rhetoric and a modest allowance to soldiers' families. For the Provisional Government, too, the requirement to make a sacrifice came before the entitlement to citizenship. The Bolsheviks finally cemented this link when they created the Red Army.[20]

War also tested other kinds of authority. As a key institution in imperial Russia the Orthodox Church was weakened by its association with the regime and by its unreflective support for the war. At a lower level, it is true, soldiers may have taken comfort from the presence of army chaplains. Workers observed religious holidays, but as a relief from drudgery rather than a commitment to faith. Elsewhere the authority of the established church does not appear to have suffered anything like this loss of authority, and in France the Catholic Church actually saw a reverse of anti-clericalism. However all societies witnessed an increasing attachment to older forms of devotion and superstition.[21]

Rural households were transformed by conscription, with profound consequences for the family. Anna Bravo exploded the myth of female passivity among the Italian peasantry.[22] In Russia, too, peasant women assumed primary responsibility for the family farm when their husbands left for off-farm work. During the war these women acquired higher levels of literacy, helping them to deal with local officials and to run the household. The Russian peasant woman 'began to develop a new consciousness of the value of her own work, a sense of personal dignity, and a jealous regard for her rights'.[23] The other side of this coin was complaints that the collapse of patriarchal authority led to moral decline, crime and prostitution. Such fears were equally marked in Germany, Britain and other societies at war. These anxieties reflected the extent to which female participation in the labour market and in the public arena challenged existing gender boundaries.

Political and social upheaval in Russia's imperial borderlands also found echoes elsewhere. Generally speaking, the challenge posed by Russia's national minorities to imperial rule was a consequence and not a cause of the February revolution. These centrifugal tendencies had their counterpart in Austria-Hungary, where the army tried in vain to curb nationalist sentiment. Under tsarism the single most dramatic wartime social explosion occurred in Central Asia in 1916, but this revolt mirrored challenges to imperial rule elsewhere: against British administration in India, Egypt, Nyasaland and above all Ireland, against Ottoman rule in Syria, and against the German presence in Tanganyika. In each case, external sponsorship of rebellion (however vigorously asserted by those in power) played a much less important role than the potent combination of the rural dispossessed and local intellectual and religious elites.[24]

Arguably one area in which Russia's war was singular lay in the scale and implications of forced population displacement, and its consequences for public health. Refugees intruded suddenly on provincial society and challenged central and local government and voluntary organisations to meet their needs. Yet here too Russia was not unique. The Austrian invasion of Serbia in 1915 produced the catastrophic forced displacement of uniformed personnel and of the civilian population, amounting to one third of the pre-war total. Contemporary descriptions spoke of 'the Great Retreat . . . only the first stage of a Calvary which was to endure for several weeks', as soldiers and civilian refugees made their way across the mountains into Albania.[25] However, population displacement in Russia strongly reinforced a popular sense of bureaucratic inadequacy and mobilised the patriotic intelligentsia among the empire's ethnic minorities. It contributed also to the emergence of a profound health crisis.

To a greater or lesser extent all belligerents practised forms of discrimination and incarceration on 'elements' of the population that were deemed to be dangerous 'outsiders'. Internment, deportation and resettlement were features of British politics towards Germans, and economic rivalries were sometimes settled in a brutal fashion.[26] What determined the characteristics of discrimination in Russia? First, the impact of humiliating defeat encouraged the Russian High Command to search for scapegoats. Combined with long-established and officially sanctioned anti-semitism, the military had no compunction in promoting a brutal campaign against the Tsar's Jewish subjects. This does not, however, explain the actions taken against Germans, Latvians and others. Here, a groundswell of populist anti-capitalist sentiment came into play. Russian parliamentarians and the tsarist army went along with this, hoping thereby to deflect attention from their own shortcomings. To be sure, we should not exaggerate popular violence. Many thousands of non-Russian refugees entered 'Russian' space without encountering extreme hostility. None the less, severe impoverishment could help unleash bloody confrontation, as happened to ethnic Germans in 1915 and to Jews in 1918–1919.[27] In addition, the democratising impact of the war in Russia encouraged a willingness to think in national terms. However, the same was true of the Ottoman empire, where the Young Turks turned on the long-established Armenian community with terrifying consequences.

What of revolutionary aftermaths? Russia was not alone in falling victim to continued violence. The strains of war in all countries were immense. Demobilisation was a protracted business. Despair and anger helped contribute to a culture of hatred. One thinks of the terror inflicted by German Freikorps in the Baltic, the civil war in Ireland (typified by the paramilitary Black and Tans), and the cult of violence in Italy. In some instances – notably Hungary and Germany – state institutions were weakened and unable to withstand the challenge of revolutionary violence. Similarly, the culture of anti-capitalism was not confined to Russia, but elsewhere it took different forms and had different outcomes. In Germany, France and Italy, as Charles Maier has shown, corporate interest groups, representing capital and labour, were enlisted in the task of organising capitalism. This process helped to nip in the bud radical programmes for economic transformation, including rearranging ownership of the means of production. The emphasis shifted instead towards technical modernisation, consumption and stability.[28]

On the face of it, then, the same social and economic malaise afflicted all belligerent countries, which endured prolonged conflict and suffered grievous losses of able-bodied men. Shortages of basic goods became commonplace and, in Germany, calamitous. Labour protest was well nigh universal. Soldiers mutinied, on a spectacular scale in France during 1917. The European empires, Britain included, faced civil and sometimes military unrest. Why, then, did war produce such a marked transformation in

Russia? Part of the answer is that – to repeat – war *did* engender social and political upheaval across the entire continent. By the end of the war, the old imperial regimes disintegrated: no more Romanovs, but also no more Hohenzollerns, Hapsburgs or Ottoman dynasty. Yet Russia alone experienced something akin to a total transformation. To be sure, the basic institutions of peasant society, the peasant household and communal assembly, survived the upheaval remarkably well, but other institutions – political, social and economic – were changed beyond recognition.

Under tsarism, government intransigence sharpened existing antagonisms in the workplace and the village. The Provisional Government adopted a more reformist stance, but by that stage the strains of war – shortages, population losses, a sense of unequal sacrifice – had become deeply entrenched and politicised. Besides, the new government remained committed to an unpopular war. Elsewhere, European governments persisted with the war effort but married it to a vision of concession and social reform designed to secure a political accommodation between rulers and ruled. They were also adept at knowing when to use the instruments of repression. In the absence of concessions or guarantees, the social movement in Russia chimed perfectly with the uncompromising and clear message of Bolshevism. In Europe, citizens expected the state to intervene in order to maintain their welfare and security, whereas in Russia the post-February regime manifested itself as remote and blinkered, not the 'cold monster' of old but a feeble force.[29]

In Russia a combination of processes refashioned state and society. In the first place, a new political system was born, based not upon privilege or universal citizenship but upon class position, whether 'objective' or 'ascribed'.[30] The triumph of the Bolsheviks inscribed the victory of the proletariat and labouring peasantry over capitalists and landlords. Organised social forces took responsibility for the expropriation of property in pursuit of the goal of ending exploitation. Second, the empire founded upon rule by the Romanov dynasty yielded to a more complex polity, the structure of which took several long and violent years to resolve. However, the essential features were clear, and they included centralisation based upon the political domination of the Bolshevik Party, coupled with a new ethno-territorial structure that recognised and institutionalised the rights of the ethnic minorities that inhabited 'Russian' space. Third, the revolution renounced capitalism and recognised the power of the proletariat. This too was institutionalised in the form of 'soviet power' and the creation of new bodies that legitimised the seizure of key assets on behalf of the new class. Rival versions of a socialist order – such as a syndicalist organisation of industry and the extension of workers' control – proved short-lived, although dissident Bolsheviks and others on the left continued to make the case. Fourth, the imperial army was replaced by the Red Army. It emerged (after tense and angry debates about the advantages of a people's militia) as a conventional conscript army offering education and advancement.

Thus the revolutionaries drew a dividing line between the old order and the new. This had important consequences for the commemoration of the war and for the sense of obligation to its victims. With the virtual obliteration of much wartime experience by those who gave pre-eminence to revolution and civil war, the trauma suffered by veterans of the tsarist army received little attention. In Germany and elsewhere war widows lobbied for attention and resources, veterans' organisations flourished, commemoration activity began at once and the war produced an unstoppable torrent of literature. However, in Russia this activity was subsumed into an abiding avowal of the significance of the Bolshevik revolution, a process that afforded no scope for serious consideration of the impact of the imperialist war.[31]

When ordinary people in countries other than Russia protested, they usually had shortages in their sights that could be attributed to the war. Only rarely did they question the entire social and political edifice, and these voices were hurriedly suppressed or silenced by reformist measures. In 1917 Russian workers and peasants objected to the war, but in their minds it became a means of challenging privilege, property and state legitimacy. Elsewhere in Europe, peace became an opportunity to introduce reforms while affirming 'business as usual'. In Russia, the only business as usual was a return to the issues left unfinished in 1905, but on a far more ambitious and terrifying scale.

References

1 Becker, 1985; Ferguson, 1999, pp. 174–211; Procacci, 1989, pp. 36–7.

2 Maier, 1975; Hardach, 1977, pp. 87–8; Strachan, 2001, pp. 993–1005.

3 Procacci, 1989, p. 35.

4 Yaney, 1982, pp. 418–19; Feldman, 1966, pp. 253–6.

5 Feldman, 1966, p. 52; Kocka, 1984, p. 47; Procacci, 1989; Strachan, 2001, pp. 993–1005.

6 McDaniel, 1988, pp. 300–301.

7 Hardach, 1977, pp. 70–72.

8 Hardach, 1992.

9 Strachan, 2001, p. 1032 (but see p. 1039).

10 P. Gurevich, quoted in Coopersmith, 1992, p. 116, italics mine; Kayden and Antsiferov, 1929, p. 97.

11 Procacci, 1989, pp. 46–7; Ferguson, 1999, pp. 278–9; Geyer, 1989, p. 74.

12 Hardach, 1977, p. 90.

13 Geyer, 1989, pp. 82–3; compare Neilson, 1984, pp. 315–17.

14 Offer, 1991, p. 27.

15 Lih, 1990, pp. 48–56. The French government subsidised food prices in order to limit popular discontent.

16 Bukshpan, 1929, p. 163; Offer, 1991, pp. 64–5.

17 Kocka, 1984, pp. 24, 39, 50, 190; Offer, 1991, p. 53; Malle, 1985, p. 379; McAuley, 1991.

18 Offer, 1991, part one; Winter and Robert, eds, 1997, pp. 305–41 (Bonzon and Davis); Procacci, 1989, pp. 34, 40.

19 Winter and Robert, eds, 1997, pp. 229–54 (Lawrence); Gatrell, 1999, pp. 129–35.

20 Horne, ed., 1997, pp. 12–17 (Horne).

21 Audoin-Rouzeau and Becker, 2002, pp. 113–34; Lewin, 1985, on popular religion in Russia.

22 Bravo, 1982; Bessel, 1993, pp. 24–6.

23 Polner, 1930, pp. 157–8; Engel, 1994, p. 50.

24 Roshwald, 2001, pp. 111–13; Horne, ed., 1997, pp. 173–91 (Cornwall).

25 Mitrany, 1936, p. 245.

26 Panayi, ed., 1993, pp. 3–25 (Panayi).

27 Gatrell, 1999, pp. 179–81; Abramson, 1999, pp. 111–31; Lohr, 2003, pp. 31–54.

28 Maier, 1975; Procacci, 1989, pp. 40–41.

29 This phrase was originally coined by Friedrich Nietzsche.

30 Fitzpatrick, 1993.

31 Gleason et al., eds, 1985, pp. 57–76 (Fitzpatrick). Note the remarks of Audoin-Rouzeau and Becker, 2002, p. 233, on selective remembrance in France.

Bibliography

A: Abbreviations

B. ved.   *Birzhevye vedomosti.*

EPR   *Ekonomicheskoe polozhenie Rossii nakanune Velikoi Oktiabr'skoi sotsialisticheskoi revoliutsii: dokumenty i materialy*, Moscow–Leningrad: Izdatel'stvo Akademii nauk SSSR, 3 vols., 1957–1967.

GIASPb   Gosudarsvennyi Istoricheskii Arkhiv Sankt Peterburga (St Petersburg).

P&T   *Promyshlennost' i torgovlia.*

RGIA   Rossiiskii gosudarstvennyi istoricheskii arkhiv.

RGVIA   Rossiiskii gosudarstvennyi voenno-istoricheskii arkhiv (Moscow).

RVMV   *Rossiia v mirovoi voine 1914–1918 gg v tsifrakh*, Moscow: Tsentral'noe statisticheskoe upravlenie, 1925.

TKISD   *Trudy Komissii po izucheniiu sovremennoi dorogovizny*, Moscow: Gorodskaia tipografiia, 1915.

V.fin.   *Vestnik finansov.*

ZhOSO   *Zhurnaly Osobogo soveshchaniia po usileniiu snabzheniia deistvuiushchei armii glavneishimi vidami dovol'stviia*, general ed., L.G. Beskrovnyi, Moscow: AN SSSR, 1975–1982.

ZhZVP   *Zhurnaly zasedanii Vremennogo pravitel'stva*, 4 vols, general ed., V.F. Dodonov, Moscow: Rosspen, 2001–present.

B: Official and semi-official sources

Doklad Soveta s"ezdov o merakh k razvitiiu proizvoditel'nykh sil Rossii, Petrograd: Sovet s"ezdov predstavitelei promyshlennosti i torgovli.

Dva goda diktatury proletariata, Moscow: VSNKh.

Dvizhenie tsen za dva goda voiny, Petrograd: Glavnyi komitet VSG, 1916.

Gosudarstvennoe soveshchanie, 12–15 avgusta 1917 g., eds, M.N. Pokrovskii and Ia. A. Iakovlev, Moscow–Leningrad: Gosudarstvennoe izdatel'stvo, 1930.

Istoriia organizatsii upolnomochennogo Glavnym artilleriiskim upravleniem po zagotovleniiu snariadov po frantsuzskomu obraztsu general-maiora S.N.Vankova 1915–1918 gg., Moscow: n.p., 1918.

Khoziaistvennaia zhizn' i ekonomicheskoe polozhenie naseleniia Rossii za pervye deviat' mesiatsev voiny, Petrograd: Ministerstvo finansov, 1916.

Materialy k uchetu rabochego sostava i rabochego rynka, 2 vols, Petrograd: TsVPK, 1916–1917.

Narodnoe khoziaistvo v 1915 godu, Petrograd: Vestnik finansov, 1918.

Narodnoe khoziaistvo v 1916 godu, 7 vols, Petrograd: Narkomfin, 1921–1922.

Pervyi Vserossiiskii torgovo-promyshlennyi s"ezd v Moskve, 19–22 marta 1917 goda: stenograficheskii otchet i rezoliutsii, Moscow: Vserossiiskii soiuz torgovli i promyshlennosti, 1917.

Proekt gosudarstvennoi rospisi dokhodov i raskhodov na 1917 god, Petrograd: Kirshbaum, 1917.

Promyshlennaia i professional'naia perepis' 1918 g.: Fabrichno-zavodskaia promyshlennost' v period 1913–1918 gg., Trudy TsSU, volume 26, Moscow: Tsentral'noe statisticheskoe upravlenie, 1926.

Rossiia v mirovoi voine 1914–1918 gg. v tsifrakh, Moscow: Tsentral'noe statisticheskoe upravlenie, 1925.

Sbornik statisticheskikh svedenii po Soiuzu SSR, 1918–1923, Trudy TsSU, volume 18, Moscow: Tsentral'noe statisticheskoe upravlenie, 1924.

Statisticheskaia razrabotka dannykh o deiatel'nosti glavnogo po snabzheniiu armii komiteta Vserossiiskogo Zemskogo soiuza i

Vserossiiskogo Soiuza Gorodov i voenno-promyshlennykh komitetov po vypolneniiu planovykh zakazov voennogo vedomstva pervoi ocheredi, Moscow: Mamontov, 1917.

Statisticheskii sbornik za 1913–1917 gg., Trudy TsSU, volume 7, parts 1 & 2, Moscow: Tsentral'noe statisticheskoe upravlenie, 1921–1922.

Trudy komissii po obsledovaniiu sanitarnykh posledstvii voiny 1914–1920 gg., eds. M.M Gran, P.I.Kurkin, and P.A.Kuvshinnikov, Moscow: Narkomzdrav, 1923.

Trudy komissii po promyshlennosti v sviazi s voinoi, volume 3, Petrograd: Imperatorskoe Russkoe tekhnicheskoe obshchestvo, 1915.

Trudy Pervogo Ekonomicheskogo s"ezda Moskovskogo promyshlennogo raiona 18–20 dekabria 1917 goda, Moscow: n.p., 1918.

Trudy Pervogo s"ezda predstavitelei metalloobrabatyvaiushchei promyshlennosti, Petrograd: n.p. 1916.

Trudy s"ezda predstavitelei voenno-promyshlennykh komitetov 25–27 iiulia 1915 g., Petrograd: n.p., 1915.

Trudy Vtorogo s"ezda predstavitelei voenno-promyshlennykh komitetov 26–29 fevralia 1916 g., 2 vols, Petrograd: Gershunin, 1916.

Zhurnaly Osobogo soveshchaniia po usileniiu snabzheniia deistvuiushchei armii glavneishimi vidami dovol'stviia, general ed., L.G. Beskrovnyi, Moscow: AN SSSR, 1975–1982.

Zhurnaly zasedanii Vremennogo pravitel'stva, 4 vols, general ed., V.F. Dodonov, Moscow: Rosspen, 2001–present.

C: Secondary sources

Abramson, Henry (1999), *A Prayer for the Government: Ukrainians and Jews in Revolutionary Times, 1917–1920*, Cambridge, MA: Harvard University Press.

Acton, Edward, Vladimir Cherniaev and William G. Rosenberg, eds (1997), *Critical Companion to the Russian Revolution, 1914–1921*, London: Arnold.

Adamov, V.V., ed. (1972), *Voprosy istorii kapitalisticheskoi Rossii*, Sverdlovsk: Akademiia nauk.

Afanas'ev, G.E. and V.M. Levitskii, eds (1915), *Deti i voina: sbornik statei*, Kiev: izdanie Kievskogo Frebelskogo obshchestva.

Anfimov, A.N. (1962), *Rossiiskaia derevnia v gody pervoi mirovoi voiny, 1914–fevral' 1917 gg.*, Moscow: Izdatel'stvo sotsial'no-ekonomicheskoi literatury.

Anfimov, A.N., ed. (1965), *Krest"ianskoe dvizhenie v Rossii v 1914–1917 gg.*, Moscow: Nauka.

Anon., ed. (1929), 'Soveshchanie gubernatorov v 1916g.' *Krasnyi arkhiv* 33 pp. 145–69.

Antsiferov, A.N., A.D. Bilimovich, M.O. Batshev and D.N. Ivanstov (1930), *Russian Agriculture during the War*, New Haven: Yale University Press.

Ascher, Abraham (1988, 1991), *The Revolution of 1905*, 2 volumes, Stanford: Stanford University Press.

Audoin-Rouzeau, Stéphane and Annette Becker (2002), *1914–1918: Understanding the Great War*, London: Profile Books.

Babichev, D.S. (1956), 'Deiatel'nost' russkogo pravitel'stvennogo komiteta v Londone v gody pervoi mirovoi voiny, 1914–1917 gg.' *Istoricheskie zapiski* 57 pp. 276–92.

Babichev, D.S. (1969), 'Rossiia na parizhskoi soiuznicheskoi konferentsii 1916 g. po ekonomicheskim voprosam' *Istoricheskie zapiski* 83 pp. 38–57.

Baburina, N.I. (1992), *Russkii plakat pervoi mirovoi voiny*, Moscow: Iskusstvo i kul'tura.

Bailes, Kendall (1978), *Technology and Society under Lenin and Stalin*, Princeton: Princeton University Press.

Baker, Mark (2001), 'Rampaging *soldatki,* cowering police, bazaar riots and moral economy: the social impact of the Great War in Kharkiv province' *Canadian-American Slavic Studies* 35 pp. 137–55.

Bakhturina, A.I. (2000), *Politika Rossiiskoi imperii v Vostochnoi Galitsii v gody pervoi mirovoi voiny*, Moscow: AIRO–XX.

Bakhturina, A.I. (2004), *Okrainy rossiiskoi imperii: gosudarstvennoe upravlenie i natsional'naia politika v gody pervoi mirovoi voiny 1914–1917gg.*, Moscow: Rosspen.

Baklanova, I.A. (1966), 'K voprosu o militarizatsii truda v period imperialisticheskoi voiny', in L.M. Ivanov, ed., *Rabochii klass i rabochee dvizhenie v Rossii 1861–1917 g.*, Moscow: Nauka, pp. 304–13.

Balderston, T. (1989), 'War finance and inflation in Britain and Germany, 1914–1918' *Economic History Review* second series 42 pp. 222–44.

Balzer, Harley, ed. (1996), *Russia's Missing Middle Class: The Professions in Russian History*, Armonk, NJ: M.E. Sharpe.

Barnett, Vincent (2001), 'Calling up the reserves: Keynes, Tugan-Baranovsky and Russian war finance' *Europe-Asia Studies* 53 pp. 151–69.

Baron, Nick, and Peter Gatrell, eds (2004), *Homelands: War, Population Displacement and Statehood in Eastern Europe and Russia, 1918–1923*, London: Anthem Press.

Baron, Salo (1987), *The Russian Jew under Tsars and Soviets*, revised edition, New York: Schoken Books.

Barsukov, E.Z. (1948), *Artilleriia russkoi armii 1900–1917 gg. Tom 2: Artsnabzhenie*, Moscow: Voenizdat.

Barykov, S.I. (1915), 'Snabzhenie Moskvy khlebnymi produktami vo vremia voiny', *TKISD*, volume one, pp. 381–412.

Bashkirov, V.G. (1976), 'Mobilizatsiia promyshlennosti Sibiri v gody pervoi mirovoi voiny', in I.M. Razgon, ed., *Nekotorye voprosy rasstanovki klassovykh sil*, Tomsk: Izdatel'stvo Tomskogo universiteta, pp. 171–90.

Becker, Jean-Jacques (1985), *The Great War and the French People*, Oxford: Berg.

Bekin, A.G. (1915), *Spravka o rabote Moskovskogo promyshlennogo raiona nu nuzhdy oborony gosudarstva*, Moscow: n.p.

Belevsky, A.S. and B. Voronoff (1917), *Les organisations publiques russes et leur rôle pendant la guerre*, Paris: Librairie Hachette.

Beliaev, S.G. (2002), *P.L.Bark i finansovaia politika Rossii 1914–1917 gg.*, St Petersburg: Izdatel'stvo Sankt-Peterburgskogo universiteta.

Berezhnoi, A.F. (1975), *Russkaia legal'naia pechat' v gody pervoi mirovoi voiny*, Leningrad: Izdatel'stvo Leningradskogo universiteta.

Berkevich, A.B. (1947), 'Krest''ianstvo i vseobshchaia mobilizatsiia v iiule 1914 g.' *Istoricheskie zapiski* 23 pp. 3–43.

Beskrovnyi, L.G. (1986), *Armiia i flot Rossii v nachale XX veka: ocherki voenno-ekonomicheskogo potentsiala*, Moscow: Nauka.

Bessel, Richard (1993), *Germany after the First World War*, Oxford: Clarendon Press.

Bilmanis, Alfred (1951), *A History of Latvia*, Princeton: Princeton University Press.

Binshtok, V.I., and L.S. Kaminskii (1929), *Narodnoe pitanie i narodnoe zdravie*, Moscow–Leningrad: Osoaviakhim.

Bogolepov, M.I. (1916), *Puti budushchego: k voprosu ob ekonomicheskom plane*, Petrograd: Ministerstvo finansov.

Bogolepov, M.I. (1921), *Evropa posle voiny: ekonomicheskii ocherk*, Petrograd: Pravo.

Bokhanov, A.N. (1994), *Delovaia elita Rossii 1914 g.*, Moscow: RAN.

Bonwetsch, Bernd (1973), *Kriegsallianz und Wirtschaftsinteressen: Russland in der wirtschaftsplänen Englands und Frankreichs 1914–1917*, Düsseldorf: Bertelsmann.

Bovykin, V.I. (1959), 'Banki i voennaia promyshlennost' Rossii nakanune pervoi mirovoi voiny' *Istoricheskie zapiski* 64 pp. 82–135.

Bradley, Joseph (2002), 'Subjects into citizens: societies, civil society, and autocracy in tsarist Russia' *American Historical Review* 107 pp. 1094–123.

Brändström, Elsa (1929), *Among Prisoners of War in Russia and Siberia* (first published in Swedish, 1921), London: Hutchinson.

Bravo, Anna (1982), 'Italian peasant women and the First World War', in Paul Thompson, ed., *Our Common History*, London: Pluto Press, pp. 157–70.

Breiterman, A.D. (1930), *Mednaia promyshlennost' SSSR i mirovoi rynok*, 3 vols, Leningrad: Akademiia Nauk SSSR.

Broadberry, Stephen and Mark Harrison, eds (2005) *The Economics of World War 1*, Cambridge: Cambridge University Press.

Browder, Robert P. and A.F. Kerensky, eds (1961), *The Russian Provisional Government, 1917: Documents*, 3 vols, Stanford: Stanford University Press.

Brower, Daniel (1990), *The Russian City between Tradition and Modernity, 1850–1900*, Berkeley: University of California Press.

Brower, Daniel (2002), *Turkestan and the Fate of the Russian Empire*, London: Routledge Curzon.

Bubnoff, J.V. (1917), *The Co-operative Movement in Russia: Its History, Significance and Character*, Manchester: Co-operative Printing Society.

Buchanan, Sir George (1923), *My Mission to Russia and Other Diplomatic Memories*, 2 vols, London: Cassell.

Bukharin, N.I. (1972), *Imperialism and World Economy* (first published 1917), London: Merlin Press.

Bukharin, N.I. (1978), *Economics of the Transformation Period*, London: Pluto Press.

Bukin, B. (1926), 'Zheleznye dorogi v mirovuiu voinu' *Voina i revoliutsiia* 3 pp. 100–18; 4 pp. 87–100.

Bukshpan, Ia.M. (1929), *Voenno-khoziaistvennaia politika: formy i organy regulirovaniia narodnogo khoziaistva za vremia mirovoi voiny 1914–1918 gg.*, Moscow-Leningrad: Ranion, Institut ekonomiki, Gosizdat.

Buldakov, V.P. (1997), 'Ot voiny k revoliutsii: rozhdenie 'cheloveka s ruzh'em'', in P.V.Volobuev, ed., *Revoliutsiia i chelovek*, Moscow: Institut istorii RAN, pp. 55–75.

Bunyan, James and Fisher, H.H. eds (1961), *The Bolshevik Revolution 1917–1918*, Stanford: Stanford University Press.

Bushnell, John (1985), *Mutiny Amid Repression: Russian Soldiers in the Revolution of 1905–1906*, Bloomington: Indiana University Press.

Buttino, Marco (1993), 'Politics and social conflict during a famine', in M. Buttino, ed., *In a Collapsing Empire: Underdevelopment, Ethnic Conflicts, and Nationalisms in the Soviet Union*, Milan: Feltrinelli, pp. 257–77.

Carr, Edward Hallett (1972), *The Bolshevik Revolution 1917–1923*, 3 vols, London: Macmillan.

Chaadaeva, O.N., ed. (1927), *Soldatskie pis'ma 1917 goda*, Moscow–Leningrad: n.p.

Chaianov, A.V. (1915), *Normy potrebleniia sel'skogo naseleniia po dannym biudzhetnykh issledovanii*, Moscow: Ekonomicheskii otdel VSG.

Charnovskii, N. (1921), 'Mashinostroitel'naia promyshlennost'', *Narodnoe khoziaistvo v 1916 godu*, volume 4, Petrograd, pp. 43–77.

Chelintsev, A.N. (1918), *Sostoianie i razvitie russkogo sel'skogo khoziaistva po dannym perepisi 1916 g. i zhelezno-dorozhnykh perevozok*, Khar'kov: Agronomiia.

Cherniavsky, M., ed. (1967), *Prologue to Revolution: Notes of A.N. Iakhontov on the Secret Meetings of the Council of Ministers, 1915*, Englewood Cliffs, NJ: Prentice-Hall.

Claus, Rudolph (1922), *Die Kriegswirtschaft Russlands bis zur bolschewistischen Revolution*, Bonn/Leipzig: Schroeder.

Clements, Barbara (1997), *Bolshevik Women*, Cambridge: Cambridge University Press.

Clowes, Edith W., Samuel Kassow and James L.West, eds (1991), *Between Tsar and People: Educated Society and the Quest for Public Identity in Late Imperial Russia*, Princeton: Princeton University Press.

Coetzee, Frans and Marilyn Shevin-Coetzee, eds (1995), *Authority, Identity and the Social History of the Great War*, Providence: Berghahn.

Cohen, Aaron J. (2003), 'Oh, that! Myth, memory, and the First World War in the Russian emigration and the Soviet Union' *Slavic Review* 62 pp. 69–86.

Cohen, Theodore (1943), 'Wartime profits of Russian industry, 1914–1916' *Political Science Quarterly* 58 pp. 217–38.

Coopersmith, Jonathan (1992), *The Electrification of Russia, 1880–1926*, Ithaca: Cornell University Press.

Crisp, Olga (1976), *Studies in the Russian Economy to 1914*, London: Macmillan.

Curtiss, John S (1940), *Church and State in Russia: The Last Years of the Empire 1900–1917*, New York: Columbia University Press.

Danilov, N.A. (1922), *Vliianie velikoi mirovoi voiny na ekonomicheskoe polozhenie Rossii*, Petrograd: Gosudarstvennoe izdatel'stvo.

Davies, R.W. (1958), *The Formation of the Soviet Budgetary System*, Cambridge: Cambridge University Press.

Davies, R.W., ed. (1990), *From Tsarism to the New Economic Policy*, Houndmills: Macmillan.

Davies, R.W., Mark Harrison and S.G. Wheatcroft, eds (1994), *The Economic Transformation of the Soviet Union*, Cambridge: Cambridge University Press.

Davis, George H. (1983), 'The life of prisoners of war in Russia 1914–1921', in Samuel R.Williamson Jr and Peter Pastor, eds, *Essays on World War 1*, New York: Columbia University Press, pp. 163–96.

Debo, Richard K. (1979), *Revolution and Survival: The Foreign Policy of Soviet Russia, 1917–1918*, Toronto: University of Toronto Press.

Diakin, V.S. (1967), *Russkaia burzhuaziia i tsarizm v gody pervoi mirovoi voiny, 1914–1917 gg.*, Leningrad: Nauka.

Diakin, V.S. (1968), 'Pervaia mirovaia voina i meropriiatiia po likvidatsii tak nazyvaemogo nemetskogo zasil'ia', in A.L. Sidorov, ed., *Pervaia mirovaia voina*, Moscow: Nauka, pp. 227–38.

Dikhtiar, G.A. (1960), *Vnutrenniaia torgovlia v dorevolutsionnoi Rossii*, Moscow: Gosstatizdat.

Drobizhev, V.Z. (1967), *Glavnyi shtab sotsialisticheskoi promyshlennosti: ocherki istorii VSNKh, 1917–1932 gg.*, Moscow: Mysl'.

Drobizhev, V.Z. and P.V.Volobuev (1957), 'Iz istorii goskapitalizma v nachal'nyi period sotsialisticheskogo stroitel'stva v SSSR' *Voprosy istorii* 9, pp. 107–22.

Drobizhev, V.Z., A.K. Sokolov and V.A. Ustinov (1975), *Rabochii klass Sovetskoi Rossii v pervyi god proletarskoi diktatury*, Moscow: MGU Press.

Dubnow, S.M., ed. (1918), 'Iz 'chernoi knigi' rossiiskogo evreistva: materialy dlia istorii voiny 1914–1915 g.' *Evreiskaia starina* 9 pp. 195–296.

Dumova, N.G. (1988), *Kadetskaia partiia v period pervoi mirovoi voiny i fevral'skoi revoliutsii*, Moscow: Nauka.

Duz', P.G (1986), *Istoriia vozdukhoplavaniia i aviatsii v Rossii, iiul' 1914 – oktiabr' 1917 gg.*, 2nd edition, Moscow: Mashinostroenie.

Efremtsev, G.P. (1973), *Istoriia Kolomenskogo zavoda za 110 let*, Moscow: Mysl'.

Eklof, Ben and Stephen Frank, eds (1988), *The World of the Russian Peasant*, London: Unwin Hyman.

Eliacheff, Boris (1919), *Les finances de guerre de la Russie*, Paris: Giard et Brière.

Emets, V.A. (1965), 'O roli russkoi armii v period pervoi mirovoi voiny 1914–1918 gg.' *Istoricheskie zapiski* 77 pp. 57–84.

Emmons, Terence and Wayne Vucinich, eds (1982), *The Zemstvo in Russia: An Experiment in Local Self-Government*, Cambridge: Cambridge University Press.

Engel, Barbara A. (1994), *Between the Fields and the City: Women, Work, and Family in Russia, 1861–1914*, Cambridge: Cambridge University Press.

Engel, Barbara A. (1997), 'Not by bread alone: subsistence riots in Russia during World War One' *Journal of Modern History* 69 pp. 696–721.

Engelstein, Laura (1992), *The Keys to Happiness: Sex and the Search for Modernity in Fin-de-Siècle Russia*, Ithaca: Cornell University Press.

Falkus, M.E. (1968), 'Russia's national income, 1913: a revaluation' *Economica* 35 pp. 52–73.

Fallows, T.S. (1978), 'Politics and the war effort in Russia: the Union of Zemstvos and the reorganization of the food supply, 1914–1916' *Slavic Review* 37 pp. 70–90.

Fedorov, M.P. (1916), *Voina i dorogovizna zhizni 1916 g.*, Petrograd: Gorodskaia finansovaia komissiia.

Feldman, Gerald D. (1966), *Army, Industry, and Labor in Germany 1914–1918*, Princeton: Princeton University Press.

Ferguson, Niall (1999), *The Pity of War*, London: Penguin Books.

Ferro, Marc (1973), *The Great War 1914–1918*, London and New York: Routledge.

Fersman, A.E. (1917), *Otchet o deiatel'nosti Komissii po izucheniiu estestvennykh proizvoditel'nykh sil Rossii*, Petrograd: KEPS.

Figes, Orlando (1989), *Peasant Russia, Civil War: The Volga Countryside in Revolution, 1917–1921*, Clarendon Press: Oxford.

Figes, Orlando and Boris Kolonitskii (1999), *Interpreting the Russian Revolution: The Language and Symbols of 1917*, New Haven: Yale University Press.

Fisk, Harvey E. (1924), *The Inter-Ally Debts: An Analysis of War and Postwar Public Finance 1914–1923*, New York: Bankers Trust Company.

Fitzpatrick, Sheila (1993), 'Ascribing class: the construction of social identity in Soviet Russia' *Journal of Modern History* 65 pp. 745–70.

Fleer, Matvei G., ed. (1925), *Rabochee dvizhenie v gody voiny*, Moscow: Voprosy truda.

Florinskii, M.V. (1988), *Krizis gosudarstvennogo upravleniia v Rossii v gody pervoi mirovoi voiny: Sovet ministrov v 1914–1917 gg.*, Leningrad: Nauka.

Florinsky, Michael T. (1931), *The End of the Russian Empire*, New Haven: Yale University Press.

Freidlin, B.M. (1967), *Ocherki istorii rabochego dvizheniia v Rossii v 1917g.*, Moscow: Nauka.

Frenkin, Mikhail S. (1978), *Russkaia armiia i revoliutsiia 1917–1918*, Munich: Logos.

Fuller, William C. (1985), *Civil–Military Conflict in Imperial Russia 1881–1914*, Princeton: Princeton University Press.

Fuller, William C. (1992), *Strategy and Power in Russia, 1600–1914*, New York: The Free Press.

Galili, Ziva (1989), *The Menshevik Leaders in the Russian Revolution*, Princeton: Princeton University Press.

Gal'perina, B.D., ed. (1999), *Sovet ministrov Rossiiskoi imperii v gody pervoi mirovoi voiny*, St Petersburg: Bulanin.

Ganelin, R.Sh. (1969), *Rossiia i SShA 1914–1917 gg.*, Leningrad: Nauka.

Gaponenko, L.S. (1961), 'K voprosu o chislennosti promyshlennogo proletariata v Rossii nakanune Oktiabria' *Istoricheskii arkhiv* 5 pp. 158–65.

Gaponenko, L.S. (1970), *Rabochii klass Rossii v 1917 godu*, Moscow: Nauka.

Gatrell, Peter (1986), *The Tsarist Economy 1850–1917*, London: Batsford.

Gatrell, Peter (1994), *Government, Industry and Rearmament in Russia, 1900–1914: The Last Argument of Tsarism*, Cambridge: Cambridge University Press.

Gatrell, Peter (1995), 'Big business and the state in Russia, 1915–1918', in J.M. Cooper, Maureen Perrie and E.A. Rees, eds, *Soviet History, 1917–1953: Essays in Honour of R.W. Davies*, Macmillan: London, pp. 1–21.

Gatrell, Peter (1999), *A Whole Empire Walking: Refugees in Russia during World War One*, Bloomington: Indiana University Press.

Gatrell, Peter (forthcoming), 'Poor Russia, poor show: mobilising a backward economy for war, 1914–1917', in Stephen Broadberry and Mark Harrison, eds, *The Economics of World War One*, Cambridge: Cambridge University Press.

Gatrell, Peter and Mark Harrison (1993), 'The Russian and Soviet economies in two world wars' *Economic History Review*, second series **46** pp. 425–52.

Gavrilov, L.M. (1986), 'Russkaia armiia nakanune fevral'skoi revoliutsii' *Istoricheskie zapiski* **114** pp. 48–72.

Gerschenkron, Alexander (1962), *Economic Backwardness in Historical Perspective*, Cambridge, MA: Harvard University Press.

Getzler, Israel (1983), *Kronstadt, 1917–1921: The Fate of a Soviet Democracy*, Cambridge: Cambridge University Press.

Geyer, Dietrich (1987), *Russian Imperialism: The Interaction of Domestic and Foreign Policy, 1860–1914*, Leamington Spa: Berg.

Geyer, Michael (1989), 'The militarisation of Europe, 1914–1945', in John Gillis, ed., *The Militarisation of the Western World*, New Brunswick: Rutgers University Press, pp. 65–102.

Gindin, I.F (1957), 'O velichine i kharaktere gosudarstvennogo dolga Rossii v kontse 1917 goda' *Istoriia SSSR* 5 pp. 166–72.

Gindin, I.F. (1959), 'K istorii kontserna br. Riabushinskikh', in A.L. Sidorov, ed., *Materialy po istorii SSSR*, volume 6, part 4, Moscow: AN SSSR, pp. 603–40.

Gindin, I.F. (1997), *Banki i ekonomicheskaia politika v Rossii (XIX-nachalo XXv.)*, Moscow: Nauka.

Gleason, William (1982), 'The All-Russian Union of Zemstvos and World War 1', in Terence, Emmons and W. Vucinich, eds., *The Zemstvo in Russia: An Experiment in Local Self-Government*, Cambridge: Cambridge University Press, pp. 365–82.

Gleason, Abbott, Peter Kenez and Richard Stites, eds (1985), *Bolshevik Culture: Experiment and Order in the Russian Revolution*, Bloomington: Indiana University Press.

Golder, Frank (1927), *Documents on Russian History, 1914–1927*, New York: The Century Company.

Goldman, Wendy Z. (1993), *Women, the State and Revolution: Soviet Family Policy and Social Life, 1917–1936*, Cambridge: Cambridge University Press.

Golovin, N.N. (1931), *The Russian Army in the World War*, New Haven: Yale University Press.

Golovin, N.N. (2001), *Voennye usiliia Rossii v mirovoi voine* (first published Paris, 1939), Moscow: Kuchkovo pole.

Gorodetskii, E.N. (1958), 'Demobilizatsiia staroi armii' *Istoriia SSSR* 1 pp. 3–31.

Graf, D.W. (1974), 'Military rule behind the Russian front, 1914–1917: the political ramifications' *Jahrbücher für Geschichte Osteuropas* 22 pp. 390–411.

Grave B.B., ed. (1927), *Burzhuaziia nakanune fevral'skoi revoliutsii*, Moscow–Leningrad: Gosudarstvennoe izdatel'stvo.

Grave, B.B. (1958), 'Militarizatsiia promyshlennosti i rossiiskii proletariat v gody pervoi mirovoi voiny', in M.V. Nechkina, ed., *Iz istorii rabochego klassa i revoliutsionnogo dvizheniia*, Moscow: AN SSSR, pp. 416–30.

Gregory, Paul (1982), *Russian National Income 1885–1913*, Cambridge: Cambridge University Press.

Grinevetskii, V.I. (1919), *Poslevoennye perspektivy russkoi promyshlennosti*, Khar'kov: Vserossiiskii Tsentral'nyi soiuz potrebitel'nykh obshchestv.

Groman, V.G. (1915), 'Issledovanie tsenoobrazuiushchikh faktorov v gody voiny', *TKISD*, volume 1, Moscow: Gorodskaia tipografiia, pp. 313–80.

Groman, V.G. (1916), *Deiatel'nost' Osobogo Soveshchaniia po prodovol'stviiu i osnovnye zadachi ekonomicheskoi politiki*, Moscow: Vserossiiskii Soiuz Gorodov.

Gronsky, P.P. and N.J. Astrov (1929), *The War and the Russian Government*, New Haven: Yale University Press.

Gross, Helmut (1981), 'Selbstverwaltung und Staatskrise in Russland 1914–1917' *Forschungen zur osteuropäischen Geschichte* **28** pp. 205–378.

Gukhman, B.A. (1929), 'Na rubezhe' *Planovoe khoziaistvo* **5** pp. 164–93.

Gurko, Vladimir I. (1939), *Features and Figures of the Past: Government and Opinion in the Reign of Nicholas II*, Hoover Institution, Stanford: Stanford University Press.

Haimson, Leopold (2000), 'The problem of political and social stability in urban Russia on the eve of war revisited' *Slavic Review* **59** pp. 848–75.

Haimson, Leopold and G. Sapelli, eds (1992), *Strikes, Social Conflict and the First World War: An International Perspective*, Milan: Feltrinelli.

Hamm, M.F. (1974), 'Liberal politics in wartime Russia: an analysis of the Progressive Bloc' *Slavic Review* **33** pp. 453–68.

Hardach, Gerd (1977), *The First World War, 1914–1918*, London: Allen Lane.

Hardach, Gerd (1992), 'Industrial mobilisation in 1914–1918', in Patrick Fridenson, ed., *The French Home Front 1914–1918*, London: Berg, pp. 57–88.

Harrison, Mark, ed. (1998), *The Economics of World War II: Six Great Powers in International Comparison*, Cambridge: Cambridge University Press.

Haumann, Heiko (1980), *Kapitalismus im zaristischen Staat, 1906–1917*, Hain: Königstein.

Heywood, A.J. (1999), *Modernising Lenin's Russia: Economic Reconstruction, Foreign Trade, and the Railways, 1917–1923*, Cambridge: Cambridge University Press.

Heywood, A.J. (2002), 'Russia's foreign supply policy in World War I: imports of railway equipment' *Journal of European Economic History* **32** pp. 77–108.

Hickey, Michael (1996), 'Local government and state authority in the provinces: Smolensk, February–June 1917' *Slavic Review* **55** pp. 863–81.

Hoffmann, David L. and Yanni Kotsonis, eds (2000), *Russian Modernity: Politics, Knowledge, Practices*, Houndmills: Macmillan.

Hogan, Heather (1982), 'Conciliation boards in revolutionary Petrograd: aspects of the crisis of labor-management relations in 1917' *Russian History* 9 pp. 49–66.

Hogan, Heather (1993), *Forging Revolution: Metalworkers, Managers, and the State in St. Petersburg, 1890–1914*, Bloomington: Indiana University Press.

Holquist, Peter (2002) *Making War, Forging Revolution: Russia's Continuum of Crisis, 1914–1921*, Cambridge, MA: Harvard University Press.

Horn, Martin (2002), *Britain, France, and the Financing of the First World War*, Montreal: McGill-Queen's University Press.

Horne, John, ed. (1997), *State, Society and Mobilisation in Europe during the First World War*, Cambridge: Cambridge University Press.

Hovannisian, Richard G. (1967), *Armenia on the Road to Independence, 1918*, Berkeley: University of California Press.

Hutchinson, John F. (1990), *Politics and Public Health in Revolutionary Russia, 1890–1918*, Baltimore: Johns Hopkins University Press.

Il'ina, I.P. (1977), 'Vliianie voiny na brachnost' sovetskikh zhenshchin', in A.G.Vishnevskii, ed., *Brachnost', rozhdaemost', smertnost' v Rossii i SSSR*, Moscow: Statistika, pp. 50–61.

Il'inskii, D.P. and V.P. Ivanitskii (1929), *Ocherk istorii russkoi parovozostroitel'noi i vagonostroitel'noi promyshlennosti*, Moscow: Transpechat'.

Ipatieff, V.N. (1946), *The Life of a Chemist*, edited by Xenia Eudin, Helen D. Fisher and H.H. Fisher, Stanford: Stanford University Press.

Ivanov, P.G. (1920), *Ocherk istorii i statistiki russkogo parovozostroeniia*, Petrograd, n.p.

Ivantsov, D.N. (1915), 'Urozhai 1914 goda po dannym TsSK', *TKISD*, volume 1, Moscow: Gorodskaia tipografiia, pp. 123–201.

Izmailovskaia, E.I. (1920), *Russkoe sel'sko-khoziaistvennoe mashinostroenie*, Moscow: VSNKh.

Jahn, Hubertus (1995), *Patriotic Culture in Russia during World War 1*, Ithaca: Cornell University Press.

Jones, David R. (1976), 'The officers and the October revolution' *Soviet Studies* 28, pp. 207–23.

Jones, David R. (1988), 'Imperial Russia's forces at war', in Allan R. Millett and Williamson Murray, eds, *Military Effectiveness, Volume 1: The First World War*, Boston: Unwin Hyman, pp. 249–328.

Kabanov, V.V. (1973), *Oktiabr'skaia revoliutsiia i kooperatsiia, 1917–mart 1919g.* Moscow: Nauka.

Kafengauz, L.B. (1994), *Evoliutsiia promyshlennogo proizvodstva Rossii (posledniaia tret' XIXv. – 30e gody XXv.)*, Moscow: RAN.

Kandidov, B.P. (1929), *Tserkovnyi front vo vremia mirovoi voiny*, Moscow: Nauchnoe obshchestvo ateizma.

Kappeler, Andreas (2001), *The Russian Empire: A Multiethnic History*, Harlow: Longman.

Kastel'skaia, Z.D. (1972), *Osnovnye predposylki vosstaniia 1916 goda v Uzbekistane* (first published 1937), Moscow: Nauka.

Kats, A. (1925), 'Bor'ba s bezrabotitsei v gody voiny', *Materialy po istorii professional'nogo dvizheniia v Rossii*, volume 3, Moscow: Vserossiiskii tsentral'nyi sovet profsoiuzov, pp. 60–87.

Katsenelenbaum, Z.S. (1917), *Voina i finansovo-ekonomicheskoe polozhenie Rossii*, Moscow: Izdatel'stvo kul'turno-prosvetitel'nogo biuro studentov Moskovskogo Kommercheskogo Instituta.

Katzenellenbaum, S.S. (1925), *Russian Currency and Banking 1914–1924*, London: P.S. King.

Kayden, E.M. and A.N. Antsiferov (1929), *The Co-operative Movement in Russia during the War*, New Haven: Yale University Press.

Keep, John (1976), *The Russian Revolution: A Study in Mass Mobilisation*, London: Weidenfeld.

Kenez, Peter (1973), 'A profile of the pre-revolutionary Russian officer corps' *California Slavic Studies*, 7 pp. 121–38.

Khmelevskii, G. (1973), *Mirovaia imperialisticheskaia voina, 1914–1918: sistematicheskii ukazatel' literatury za 1914–1935 g.* (first published Moscow, 1935), Cambridge: Oriental Research Partners.

Khromov, P.A. (1950), *Ekonomicheskoe razvitie Rossii v XIX–XX vekakh*, Moscow: Gosudarstvennoe izdatel'stvo politicheskoi literatury.

Kingston-Mann, Esther (1983), *Lenin and the Problem of Marxist Peasant Revolution*, New York: Oxford University Press.

Kir"ianov, Iu.I. (1971), *Rabochie Iuga Rossii 1914–fevral' 1917g.*, Moscow: Nauka.

Kir"ianov, Iu.I. (1993), 'Massovye vystupleniia na pochve dorogovizny v Rossii (1914–fevral' 1917 g.)' *Otechestvennaia istoriia* 3 pp. 3–18.

Kir"ianov, Iu.I (1994), 'Byli li antivoennye stachki v Rossii v 1914 godu?' *Voprosy istorii* 2 pp. 43–52.

Kir"ianov, I.Iu., ed. (1999), *Politicheskie partii i obshchestvo v Rossii 1914–1917 gg.*, Moscow: RAN INION.

Kitanina, T.M. (1969), *Voenno-infliatsionnye kontserny v Rossii 1914–1917 gg.*, Leningrad: Nauka.

Kitanina, T.M. (1978), *Khlebnaia torgovlia Rossii v 1875–1914 gg.*, Leningrad: Nauka.

Kitanina, T.M. (1985), *Voina, khleb i revoliutsiia: prodovol'stvennyi vopros v Rossii, 1914 – oktiabr' 1917 g.*, Leningrad: Nauka.

Klibanov, A.I. (1982), *A History of Religious Sectarianism in Russia, 1860s to 1917*, Oxford: Pergamon Press.

Knox, Alfred (1921), *With the Russian Army, 1914–1921*, 2 vols, London: Hutchinson.

Kocka, Jürgen (1984), *Facing Total War: German Society 1914–1918*, Leamington Spa: Berghahn.

Koenker, Diane P. (1981), *Moscow Workers and the 1917 Revolution*, Princeton: Princeton University Press.

Koenker, Diane P. and William G. Rosenberg (1989), *Strikes and Revolution in Russia, 1917*, Princeton: Princeton University Press.

Koenker, Diane P., W.G. Rosenberg and R.G. Suny, eds (1989), *Party, State and Society in the Russian Civil War: Explorations in Social History*, Bloomington: Indiana University Press.

Kohn, S. and Meyendorff, A.F. (1932), *The Cost of the War to Russia*, New Haven: Yale University Press.

Kojevnikov, Alexei (2002), 'The great war, the Russian civil war, and the invention of big science' *Science in Context* 15 pp. 239–75.

Kokhn, M.P. (1926), *Russkie indeksy tsen*, Moscow: Ekonomicheskaia zhizn'.

Kolonitskii, B.I. (2001), *Simvoly vlasti i bor'ba za vlast': k izucheniiu politicheskoi kul'tury rossiiskoi revoliutsii 1917 goda*, St Petersburg: Bulanin.

Kol'tsov, A.V. (1999), *Sozdanie i deiatel'nost' Komissii po izuchaniiu estestvennykh proizvoditel'nykh sil Rossii, 1915–1930 gg.*, St Petersburg: Nauka.

Kondrat'ev, N.D. (1991), *Rynok khlebov i ego regulirovanie vo vremia voiny i revoliutsii* (first published 1922), Moscow: Nauka.

Kopylov, V.R. (1967), 'Kak voennoplennye prazdnovali 1 maia 1917 g.' *Istoriia SSSR* 3 pp. 32–7.

Korelin, A.P. (1964), 'Politika krupnogo kapitala v oblasti fabrichno-zavodskogo zakonodatel'stva v Rossii v gody pervoi mirovoi voiny' *Vestnik Moskovskogo universiteta: istoriia* 6 pp. 66–79.

Korelin, A.P. (1978), 'Krupnyi kapital i ekspluatatsiia rabochikh v gody pervoi mirovoi voiny', in S.V. Tiutiukin, ed., *Rabochii klass Rossii v period burzhuazno-demokraticheskikh revoliutsii*, Moscow: Akademiia nauk, pp. 65–93.

Korelin, A.P., ed. (1995), *Rossiia 1913 god: statistiko-dokumental'nyi spravochnik*, St Petersburg: Blits.

Koshik, A.K. (1965), *Rabochee dvizhenie na Ukraine v gody pervoi mirovoi voiny i fevral'skoi revoliutsii*, Izdatel'stvo Kievskogo universiteta, Kiev.

Kotsonis, Yanni (2004), '"Face-to-face": the state, the citizen, and the individual in Russian taxation, 1863–1917' *Slavic Review* 63 pp. 221–46.

Koval'chenko, I.S., N.B. Selunskaia and B.M. Litvakov (1982), *Sotsial'no-ekonomicheskii stroi pomeshchich'ego khoziaistva Evropeiskoi Rossii v epokhu kapitalizma*, Moscow: Nauka.

Kovalenko, D.A. (1970), *Oboronnaia promyshlennost' sovetskoi Rossii v 1918–1920 gg.*, Nauka, Moscow.

Krupina, T.D. (1969), 'Politicheskii krizis 1915 g. i sozdanie Osobogo soveshchaniia po oborone' *Istoricheskie zapiski* 83 pp. 58–75.

Krupina, T.D. (1970), 'Rossiia i Frantsiia i mezhsoiuznicheskie voenno-ekonomicheskie otnosheniia v gody pervoi mirovoi voiny', in F. Braudel, ed., *Franko-russkie ekonomicheskie sviazi*, Moscow: Nauka, pp. 397–430.

Kulischer, E.M. (1948), *Europe on the Move: War and Population Changes, 1917–1947*, New York: Columbia University Press.

Kulisher, I. (1917), 'Nalog na voennuiu pribyl'' *Vestnik finansov* **32** pp. 149–53; **33** pp. 184–90.

Kuropatkin, A.N. (1929), 'Vosstanie 1916 g. v Srednei Azii' *Krasnyi Arkhiv* **34** pp. 39–94.

Laverychev, V.Ia. (1961), 'Vserossiiskii soiuz torgovli i promyshlennosti' *Istoricheskie zapiski* **70** pp. 35–60.

Laverychev, V.Ia. (1963), *Monopolisticheskii kapital v tekstil'noi promyshlennosti Rossii, 1900-1917 gg.*, Moscow: Nauka.

Laverychev, V.Ia. (1967), *Po tu storonu barrikad: iz istorii bor'by moskovskoi burzhuazii s revoliutsiei*, Moscow: Mysl'.

Laverychev, V.Ia. (1988), *Voennyi gosudarstvenno-monopolisticheskii kapitalizm v Rossii*, Moscow: Nauka.

Leiberov, I.P. (1963), 'Stachechnaia bor'ba petrogradskogo proletariata v period pervoi mirovoi voiny', in V.A. Ovsiankin, ed., *Istoriia rabochego klassa Leningrada*, volume 1, Leningrad: Izdatel'stvo LGU, pp. 156–86.

Lenin, V.I. (1972a), 'The immediate tasks of the Soviet government' (April 1918), in Lenin, *Collected Works*, 4th English edition, volume 27, Moscow: Progress Publishers, pp. 235–77.

Lenin, V.I. (1972b), 'A letter to the workers of Petrograd' (22 May 1918), in Lenin, *Collected Works*, 4th English edition, volume 27, Moscow: Progress Publishers, pp. 391–8.

Lenin, V.I. (1977), 'The impending catastrophe and how to combat it' (September 1917), in Lenin, *Collected Works*, 4th English edition, volume 25, Moscow: Progress Publishers, pp. 323–69.

Lewin, Moshe (1985), *The Making of the Soviet System*, London: Allen & Unwin.

Lieven, D.C.B. (1983), *Russia and the Origins of the First World War*, London: Macmillan.

Lih, Lars T. (1990), *Bread and Authority in Russia, 1914–1920*, Berkeley: University of California Press.

Lincoln, W. Bruce (1986), *Passage Through Armageddon: The Russians in War and Revolution*, New York: Simon & Schuster.

Lindeman, Karl (1917), *Prekrashchenie zemlevladeniia i zemlepol'zovaniia poselian sobstvennikov*, Moscow: n.p.

Lindenmeyr, Adele (1996) *Poverty Is Not A Vice: Charity, Society and the State in Imperial Russia*, Princeton: Princeton University Press.

Lipkin, F.A. (1915), 'Obshchie usloviia obrazovaniia khlebnykh tsen' *TKISD*, volume 1, pp. 267–312.

Liudkovskii, Sh.S. (1955), 'Antivoennaia zabastovka 1916 goda v Nikolaeve: dokumenty' *Istoricheskii arkhiv* 5 pp. 97–109.

Liulevicius, Vejas G. (2000), *War Land on the Eastern Front: Culture, National Identity and German Occupation in World War One*, Cambridge: Cambridge University Press.

Lobanov-Rostovsky, Andrei (1935), *The Grinding Mill: Reminiscences of War and Revolution in Russia 1913–1920*, New York: Macmillan.

Lohr, Eric (2003), *Nationalizing the Russian Empire: The Campaign Against Enemy Aliens during World War 1*, Cambridge, MA: Harvard University Press.

Löwe, Heinz-Dietrich (1992), *The Tsar and the Jews: Reform, Reaction, and Anti-Semitism in Imperial Russia, 1772–1917*, Chur: Harwood Academic.

McAuley, Mary (1991), *Bread and Justice: State and Society in Petrograd, 1917–1922*, Oxford: Clarendon Press.

McDaniel, Tim (1988), *Autocracy, Capitalism and Revolution in Russia*, Berkeley: University of California Press.

McDonald, David (1992), *United Government and Foreign Policy in Russia, 1900–1914*, Cambridge, MA.: Harvard University Press.

McKay, John P. (1970), *Pioneers for Profit: Foreign Entrepreneurship and Russian Industrialization, 1885–1913*, Chicago: Chicago University Press.

McKean, Robert (1990), *St Petersburg Between the Revolutions: Workers and Revolutionaries, June 1907–February 1917*, New Haven: Yale University Press.

McReynolds, Louise (1993), 'Mobilising Petrograd's lower classes to fight the Great War' *Radical History Review* 57 pp. 160–80.

Maevskii, I.V. (1957), *Ekonomika russkoi promyshlennosti v gody pervoi mirovoi voiny*, Moscow: Gospolitizdat.

Maier, Charles S. (1975), *Recasting Bourgeois Europe: Stabilization in France, Germany, and Italy in the Decade after World War 1*, Princeton: Princeton University Press.

Maliavskii, A.D. (1981), *Krest"ianskoe dvizhenie v Rossii v 1917 g., mart-oktiabr'*, Moscow: Nauka.

Mal'kov, V.L., ed. (1998), *Pervaia mirovaia voina: prolog XX veka*, Moscow: Nauka.

Malle, Silvana (1985), *The Economic Organization of War Communism*, Cambridge: Cambridge University Press.

Manikovskii, A.A. (1930), *Boevoe snabzhenie russkoi armii v mirovuiu voinu 1914–1918 gg.*, 2 vols, second edition, Moscow: Gosudarstvennoe izdatel'stvo.

Markevich, A.M. (2001) 'Stimuly k trudu v metallurgicheskoi i metalloobrabatyvaiushchei promyshlennosti Rossii v gody pervoi mirovoi voiny' *Ekonomicheskaia istoriia: obozrenie*, 6 pp. 64–84.

Maslov, P (1915), 'Dvizhenie tovarnykh tsen i vliianie ikh na raspredelenie natsional'nogo dokhoda', *TKISD*, volume 1, pp. 29–115.

Maslov, P.P. (1918), *Itogi voiny i revoliutsii*, Moscow: n.p.

Matsuzato, Kimitaka (1996), 'The fate of agronomists in Russia: their quantitative dynamics from 1911 to 1916' *Russian Review* 55 pp. 172–200.

Matsuzato, Kimitaka (1998), 'Inter-regional conflicts and the decline of tsarism', in Mary S. Conroy, ed., *Emerging Democracy in Late Imperial Russia*, Niwot: University Press of Colorado, pp. 243–300.

Mawdsley, Evan (1978), *The Russian Revolution and the Baltic Fleet*, London: Macmillan.

Mawdsley, Evan (2000), *The Russian Civil War*, second edition, Edinburgh: Birlinn.

Mazon, André (1920), *Lexique de la guerre et de la révolution en Russie, 1914–1918*, Paris: Champion.

Merridale, Catherine (2000), *Night of Stone: Death and Memory in Russia*, London: Granta.

Meyer, Alfred G. (1991), 'The impact of World War 1 on Russian women's lives', in Barbara E. Clements, Barbara Engel and Christine Worobec, eds, *Russia's Women: Accommodation, Resistance,*

Transformation, Berkeley: University of California Press, pp. 208–24.

Michelson, A.M., P.N. Apostol and M.W. Bernatzky (1928), *Russian Public Finance during the War*, New Haven: Yale University Press.

Mikhailov, V.S. (1927), 'Promyshlennost' i oborona', in E.I. Kviring, ed., *Promyshlennost' i narodnoe khoziaistvo*, Moscow: Ekonomicheskaia zhizn', pp. 494–509.

Miliukov, Paul (1967), *Political Memoirs 1905–1917*, edited by Arthur P. Mendel, Ann Arbor: University of Michigan Press.

Mints, I.I. (1982), *God 1918*, Moscow: Nauka.

Mints, L.E. (1975), *Trudovye resursy SSSR*, Moscow: Nauka.

Mitrany, David (1936), *The Effect of the War in Southeastern Europe*, New Haven: Yale University Press.

Murzintseva, S.V. (1959), 'Iz istorii ekonomicheskogo polozheniia rabochikh na predpriiatiakh voennogo i morskogo vedomstv v 1907–1914 gg. v Peterburge' *Uchenye zapiski LGU* **270** pp. 217–41.

Nachtigal, Reinhard (2001), *Die Murmanbahn: Die Verkehrsanbindung eines kriegswichtigen Hafens und das Arbeitspotential der Kriegsgefangenen*, Grünbach: Verlag Greiner.

Nachtigal, Reinhard (2003), *Russland und seine österreichisch-ungarischen Kriegsgefangenen (1914–1918)*, Remshalden: Verlag Greiner.

Neilson, Keith (1984), *Strategy and Supply: The Anglo-Russian Alliance 1914–1917*, London: Allen and Unwin.

Netesin, Iu.N. (1974), *Promyshlennyi kapital Latvii, 1860–1917*, Riga: Zinatne.

Neuberger, Joan (1993), *Hooliganism: Crime, Culture and Power in St Petersburg, 1900–1914*, Berkeley: University of California Press.

Nol'de, A.A. (1918), *Russkaia l'nianaia promyshlennost' vo vremia voiny i revoliutsii*, Moscow: Somovoi.

Nol'de, B.E. (1916), *Organizatsiia narodnogo khoziaistva voiuiushchei Germanii*, Petrograd.

Nolde, Boris E. (1928), *Russia in the Economic War*, New Haven: Yale University Press.

Odinetz, Dimitry M. and Paul Novgorotsev (1929), *Russian Schools and Universities in the World War*, New Haven: Yale University Press.

Offer, Avner (1991), *The First World War: An Agrarian Interpretation*, Oxford: Clarendon Press.

Okninskii, A.L. (1998), *Dva goda sredi krest"ian* (first published 1936), Moscow: Russkii put'.

Olcott, Martha Brill (1995), *The Kazakhs*, Stanford: Hoover Institution Press.

Orlovsky, Daniel (1989), 'Reform during revolution: governing the provinces in 1917', in Robert Crummey, ed., *Reform in Russia and the USSR*, Urbana: University of Illinois Press, pp. 100–125. ⚡

Osipova, T.V. (1976), 'Vserossiiskii soiuz zemel'nykh sobstvennikov v 1917g.' *Istoriia SSSR* 3, pp. 115–29.

Paléologue, Maurice (1921), *La Russie des tsars pendant la grande guerre*, 3 vols, Paris: Librairie Plon.

Pallot, Judith, ed. (1998), *Transforming Peasants: Society, State and the Peasantry, 1861–1930*, London: Palgrave.

Panayi, Panikos, ed. (1993), *Minorities in Wartime*, Oxford: Berg.

Pankin, A.V. (1915), 'Organizatsiia massovogo proizvodstva predmetov artilleriiskogo dovol'stviia' *Artilleriiskii zhurnal*, 5–6 pp. 25–45.

Pavlovsky, G.A. (1930), *Agricultural Russia on the Eve of the Revolution*, London: Routledge.

Pearson, Raymond (1977), *The Russian Moderates and the Crisis of Tsarism, 1914–1917*, London: Macmillan.

Petrone, Karen (1998), 'Family, masculinity, and heroism in Russian war posters of the First World War', in Billie Melman, ed., *Borderlines: Genders and Identities in War and Peace, 1870–1930*, London: Routledge, pp. 95–119.

Piaskovskii, A.B., ed. (1960), *Vosstanie 1916 goda v Srednei Azii i Kazakhstane: sbornik dokumentov*, Moscow: Akademiia Nauk.

Pierce, Richard (1960), *Russian Central Asia, 1867–1917: A Study in Colonial Rule*, Berkeley: University of California Press.

Pireiko, A. (1935) *Na fronte imperialisticheskoi voiny: vospominaniia bol'shevika*, Moscow: Staryi bol'shevik.

Pogrebinskii, A.P. (1941), 'Voenno-promyshlennye komitety' *Istoricheskie zapiski* 11 pp. 160–200.

Pogrebinskii, A.P. (1948), 'Mobilizatsiia promyshlennosti tsarskoi Rossii v pervuiu mirovuiu voinu' *Voprosy istorii* **8** pp. 58–70.

Pokrovskii, M.N. (1925), 'Ekonomicheskoe polozhenie Rossii pered revoliutsiei' *Krasnyi arkhiv* **10** pp. 69–81.

Poliakov, Iu.A. (1986), *Sovetskaia strana posle okonchaniia grazhdanskoi voiny: territoriia i naselenie*, Moscow: Nauka.

Poliakov, Iu.A. (2000), *Naselenie Rossii v XX veke: istoricheskie ocherki*, volume 1, Moscow: Rosspen.

Polikarpov, V.V. (1983), 'O tak nazyvaemoi "programme Manikovskogo" 1916 goda' *Istoricheskie zapiski* **109** pp. 281–306.

Polner, T.J. (1930), *Russian Local Government during the War and the Union of Zemstvos*, New Haven: Yale University Press.

Porshneva, O.S. (2000), *Mentalitet i sotsial'noe povedenie rabochikh, krest"ian i soldat Rossii v period pervoi mirovoi voiny (1914–mart 1918 g.)*, Ekaterinburg: UrORAN.

Procacci, Giovanna (1989), 'Popular protest and labour conflict in Italy 1915–1918' *Social History* **14** pp. 31–58.

Prokopovich, S.N. (1918), *Voina i narodnoe khoziaistvo*, second edition (first edition, 1917), Moscow: Sovet Vserossiiskikh kooperativnikh s"ezdov.

Prusin, Alexander V. (2002), 'The Russian military and the Jews in Galicia, 1914–1915', in Eric Lohr and Marshall Poe, eds, *The Military and Society in Russia 1450–1917*, Leiden: Brill, pp. 525–44.

Rachamimov, Alon (2002), *POWs and the Great War: Captivity on the Eastern Front*, Oxford: Berg.

Raffalovich, Arthur, ed. (1918), *Russia: Its Trade and Commerce*, London: P.S. King.

Raleigh, Don (2002), *Experiencing Russia's Civil War: Politics, Society, and Revolutionary Culture in Saratov, 1917–22*, Princeton: Princeton University Press.

Rashin, A.G. (1958), *Formirovanie rabochego klassa Rossii: istoriko-statisticheskie ocherki*, Moscow: Sotsekgiz.

Rayfield, Donald (1988), 'The soldier's lament: World War One folk poetry in the Russian empire' *Slavonic & East European Review* **66** pp. 66–90.

Reed, John (1970), *Ten Days that Shook the World* (first published 1926), London: Penguin Books.

Remizova, T.A. (1954), *Agrarnaia politika Sovetskoi vlasti, 1917–1918 gg.: dokumenty i materialy*, Moscow: Nauka.

Rempel, David G. (1932), 'The expropriation of the German colonists in south Russia during the great war' *Journal of Modern History* 4 pp. 49–67.

Reshetar, John S. (1952), *The Ukrainian Revolution, 1917–1920: A Study in Nationalism*, Princeton: Princeton University Press.

Rich, David Alan (1998), *The Tsar's Colonels: Professionalism, Strategy, and Subversion in Late Imperial Russia*, Cambridge, MA.: Harvard University Press.

Rieber, A. J. (1982), *Merchants and Entrepreneurs in Imperial Russia*, Chapel Hill: University of North Carolina Press.

Rogger, Hans (1986), *Jewish Policies and Right-Wing Politics in Imperial Russia*, Basingstoke: Macmillan.

Roosa, Ruth A. (1983), 'Russian industrialists during World War 1: the interaction of economics and politics', in G. Guroff and F. Carstensen, eds, *Entrepreneurship in Imperial Russia and the Soviet Union*, Princeton: Princeton University Press, pp. 159–87.

Roosa, Ruth A. (1997), *Russian Industrialists in an Era of Revolution: The Association of Industry and Trade, 1906–1917*, New York: Armonk.

Rosenberg, William G. (1984a), 'The problem of market relations and the state in revolutionary Russia' *Comparative Studies in Society and History* 36 pp. 356–96.

Rosenberg, William G. (1984b), 'Social mediation and state construction(s) in revolutionary Russia' *Social History* 19 pp. 169–88.

Roshwald, Aviel (2001), *Ethnic Nationalism and the Fall of Empires: Central Europe, Russia and the Middle East, 1914–1923*, London: Routledge.

Roskies, David (1984), *Against the Apocalypse: Responses to Catastrophe in Modern Jewish Culture*, Cambridge, MA.: Harvard University Press.

Rozenfel'd, Ia.S., and K.I. Klimenko (1961), *Istoriia mashinostroeniia SSSR s pervoi poloviny XIX v. do nashikh dnei*, Moscow: Izdatel'stvo Akademii Nauk.

Rozentreter, B.A., ed. (1973), *Ocherki istorii tekhniki v Rossii (1861–1917)*, Moscow: Nauka.

Rudoi, Ia. (1925), *Gosudarstvennyi kapitalizm v Rossii vo vremia imperialisticheskoi voiny*, Leningrad: Priboi.

Sanborn, Joshua (2000), 'The mobilization of 1914 and the question of the Russian nation: a re-examination' *Slavic Review* 59 pp. 267–89.

Sanborn, Joshua (2003), *Drafting the Russian Nation: Military Conscription, Total War, and Mass Politics 1905–1925*, DeKalb: Northern Illinois University Press.

Saul, Norman (2001), *War and Revolution: The United States and Russia, 1914–1921*, Lawrence: University Press of Kansas.

Sayers, R.S. (1956), *Financial Policy 1939–1945*, London: HMSO.

Semennikov, V.P. (1927), *Monarkhiia pered krusheniem 1914–1917 gg.*, Moscow: Gosudarstvennoe izdatel'stvo.

Seniavskaia, E.S. (1997), 'Obraz vraga v soznanii uchastnikov pervoi mirovoi voiny' *Voprosy istorii* 3 pp. 140–45.

Seniavskaia, E.S. (1999), *Psikhologiia voiny v XX veke: istoricheskii opyt Rossii*, Moscow: Rosspen.

Senin, A.S. (1993), 'Russian army chaplains during World War 1' *Russian Studies in History* 32 pp. 43–52.

Senin, A.S. (2004), 'Zheleznye dorogi v marte-oktiabre 1917g.: ot krizisa k khaosu' *Voprosy istorii* 3 pp. 32–56.

Seregny, Scott (2000), 'Zemstvos, peasants, and citizenship: the Russian adult education movement and World War 1' *Slavic Review* 59 pp. 290–315.

Service, Robert, ed. (1992), *Society and Politics in the Russian Revolution*, Houndmills: Macmillan.

Sharyi, V.I. (1917), 'Dokhodnost' aktsionernykh predpriiatii za vremia voiny' *Vestnik finansov* 31 pp. 124–6; 33 pp. 190–91.

Shatsillo, K.F. (1963), 'Iz istorii ekonomicheskoi politiki tsarskogo pravitel'stva v gody pervoi mirovoi voiny', in A.L. Sidorov, ed., *Ob osobennostiakh imperializma v Rossii*, Moscow: Nauka, pp. 215–33.

Shatsillo, K.F. (1968), *Russkii imperializm i razvitie flota nakanune pervoi mirovoi voiny 1906–1914 gg.*, Moscow: Nauka.

Shebaldin, Iu.N. (1959), 'Gosudarstvennyi biudzhet tsarskoi Rossii v nachale XXv.' *Istoricheskie zapiski* 65 pp. 163–90.

Sheliakin, P. (1930), 'Voina i ugol'naia promyshlennost'', in *Voina i toplivo*, Moscow: Osoaviakhim, pp. 25–90.

Shepelev, L.E. (1963), 'Aktsionernye kommercheskie banki v gody pervoi mirovoi voiny' *Istoricheskie zapiski* 73 pp. 156–93.

Shepelev, L.E. (1969), 'Fondovaia birzha v Rossii v period pervoi mirovoi voiny' *Istoricheskie zapiski* 84 pp. 121–63.

Shepelev, L.E. (1973), *Aktsionernye kompanii v Rossii*, Leningrad: Nauka.

Shepelev, L.E. (1987), *Tsarizm i burzhuaziia v 1904–1914 gg.*, Leningrad: Nauka.

Shliapnikov, Alexander (1982), *On the Eve of 1917*, London: Allison and Busby.

Shumnaia, T.G. (1997), 'Ot fevral'skoi revoliutsii k Muzeiu revoliutsii', in P.V. Volobuev, ed., *1917 god v sud'bakh Rossii i mira: fevral'skaia revoliutsiia*, Moscow: RAN, pp. 218–24.

Sidorov, A.L. (1960), *Finansovoe polozhenie Rossii v gody pervoi mirovoi voiny*, Moscow: Nauka.

Sidorov, A.L., ed. (1968), *Pervaia mirovaia voina 1914–1918*, Moscow: Nauka.

Sidorov, A.L. (1973), *Ekonomicheskoe polozhenie Rossii v gody pervoi mirovoi voiny*, Moscow: Nauka.

Siegelbaum, Lewis H. (1983), *The Politics of Industrial Mobilization in Russia, 1914–1917: A Study of the War-Industries Committees*, London: Macmillan.

Smele, J.D. (1996), *Civil War in Siberia: The Anti-Bolshevik Government of Admiral Kolchak, 1918–1920*, Cambridge: Cambridge University Press.

Smirnov, N.N., ed. (1999), *Rossiia i pervaia mirovaia voina*, St Petersburg: Bulanin.

Smith, J.T. (2001), 'Russian military censorship during the First World War' *Revolutionary Russia* 14 (1) pp. 71–95.

Smith, S.A. (1983), *Red Petrograd: Revolution in the Factories, 1917–1918*, Cambridge: Cambridge University Press.

Sobolev, G.L. (1973), *Revoliutsionnoe soznanie rabochikh i soldat Petrograda v 1917g.*, Leningrad: Nauka.

Sokol, Edward (1954), *The Revolt of 1916 in Central Asia*, Baltimore: Johns Hopkins Press.

Solomon, Susan G and J.F. Hutchinson, eds (1990), *Health and Society in Revolutionary Russia*, Bloomington: Indiana University Press.

Somov, S.A. (1972), 'Poslednaia stranitsa istorii Osobogo soveshchaniia po oborone' *Istoricheskie zapiski* **90** pp. 78–108.

Somov, S.A. (1973), 'O 'maiskom' Osobom soveshchanii' *Istoriia SSSR* **3** pp. 112–23.

Sorin, N.V. (1916), *Zakon o podokhodnom naloge*, Petrograd: n.p.

Stanziani, Alessandro (1995), 'Spécialistes, bureaucrates et paysans: les approvisionnements agricoles pendant la première guerre mondiale, 1914–1917' *Cahiers du monde russe* **36** pp. 71–94.

Startsev, V.I. (1977), *Russkaia burzhuaziia i samoderzhavie v 1905–1917 gg.*, Leningrad: Nauka.

Steinberg, Mark D. (2001), *Voices of Revolution, 1917*, New Haven: Yale University Press.

Stockdale, Melissa K. (2004), 'My death for the motherland is happiness: women, patriotism, and soldiering in Russia's Great War, 1914–1917' *American Historical Review* **109** pp. 78–116.

Stone, Norman (1975), *The Eastern Front, 1914–1917*, London: Hodder & Stoughton.

Strachan, Hew (2001), *The First World War: Volume 1, To Arms*, Oxford: Oxford University Press.

Strakhov, V.V. (2003), 'Vnutrennie zaimy v Rossii v pervuiu mirovuiu voinu' *Voprosy istorii* **9** pp. 28–43.

Strumilin, S.G. (1958), *Statistiko-ekonomicheskie ocherki*, Moscow: Gosudarstvennoe statisticheskoe izdatel'stvo.

Strumilin, S.G. (1964a), *Problemy ekonomiki truda*, Moscow: Nauka.

Strumilin, S.G. (1964b), *Ocherki sotsialisticheskoi ekonomiki SSSR*, Moscow: Nauka.

Strumilin, S.G. (1966), *Ocherki ekonomicheskoi istorii Rossii i SSSR*, Moscow: Nauka.

Struve, P.B., K.I. Zaitsev, N.V. Dolinsky and S.S. Demosthenov (1930), *Food Supply in Russia during the War*, New Haven: Yale University Press.

Sviatlovskii, E.E. (1926), *Ekonomika voiny*, Moscow: Voennyi vestnik.

Swain, Geoffrey (1996), *The Origins of the Russian Civil War*, London: Longman.

Taniaev, A.P. (1927), *Rabochii klass Urala v gody voiny i revoliutsii*, n.p.

Tarnovskii, K.N. (1958), *Formirovanie gosudarstvenno-monopolisticheskogo kapitalizma v Rossii v gody pervoi mirovoi voiny*, Moscow: Izdatel'stvo MGU.

Tarnovskii, K.N. (1964), *Sovetskaia istoriografiia rossiiskogo imperializma*, Moscow: Nauka.

Tarnovskii, K.N. (1995), *Melkaia promyshlennost' Rossii v kontse XIX v nachale XXv.*, Moscow: Nauka.

Tereshkovich, A.M. (1924), 'Vliianie voiny i revoliutsii na psikhicheskuiu zabolevaemost' *Moskovskii meditsinskii zhurnal* 4 pp. 67–74.

Thurstan, Violetta (1915) *Field Hospital and Flying Column*, London: G.P. Putnam's Sons.

Thurstan, Violetta (1916), *The People Who Run*, New York and London: G.P. Putnam's Sons.

Tiutiukin, S.V. (1972), *Voina, mir, revoliutsiia: Rossii 1914–1917 gg.*, Moscow: Mysl'.

Tomsen, V.V. (1916), *Voenno-popribyl'nyi nalog i usilennaia amortizatsiia*, Petrograd: Soikina.

Trotsky, Leon D (1934), *History of the Russian Revolution*, London: Gollancz.

Tugan-Baranovskii, M.I. (1915), 'Vliianie voiny na narodnoe khoziaistvo Rossii, Anglii i Germanii', in idem, ed., *Voprosy mirovoi voiny*, Moscow: Pravo, pp. 269–324.

Tugan-Baranovskii, M.I., ed. (1917), *Voennye zaimy: sbornik statei*, Petrograd: Pravda.

Tverdokhlebov, V.N. (1915), 'Vliianie voiny na gorodskie i zemskie finansy', in M.I. Tugan-Baranovskii, ed., *Voprosy mirovoi voiny*, Moscow: Pravo, pp. 443–65.

Uribes, E. (1961), 'Koksobenzol'naia promyshlennost' Rossii v gody pervoi mirovoi voiny' *Istoricheskie zapiski* **69** pp. 46–72.

Vainshtein, A.L. (1960), *Narodnoe bogatstvo i narodnokhoziaistvennoe nakoplenie predrevoliutsionnoi Rossii*, Moscow: Gosstatizdat.

Vankov, S.N. (1921), 'O sostoianii nashei metalloobrabatyvaiushchei promyshlennosti k nachalu voiny 1914 g. i vo vremia voiny' *Nauchno-tekhnicheskii vestnik* **6** pp. 1–18.

Vasil'ev, N.A. (1939), *Transport Rossii v voine 1914–1918 gg.*, Moscow: Gosudarstvennoe voennoe izdatel'stvo.

Venediktov, A. (1917), *Voina i starye kontrakty*, Petrograd: Izdatel'stvo Vestnik finansov.

Viatkin, M.P., ed. (1959), *Iz istorii imperializma v Rossii*, Moscow–Leningrad: Nauka.

Vishnev, S. and V.Mikhailov (1928), 'Voennaia promyshlennost'', *Bol'shaia sovetskaia entsiklopediia*, first edition, Moscow: Sovetskaia entsiklopediia.

Volgyes, Ivan (1973), 'Hungarian prisoners of war in Russia, 1916–1919' *Cahiers du monde russe et soviétique* **14** pp. 54–85.

Volkov, E.Z. (1930), *Dinamika narodonaseleniia SSSR za vosem'desiat' let*, Moscow: Gosudarstvennoe izdatel'stvo.

Volobuev, P.V. (1962), *Ekonomicheskaia politika Vremennogo pravitel'stva*, Moscow: Izdatel'stvo Akademii nauk SSSR.

Vorob'ev, N.Ia. (1923), 'Izmeneniia v russkoi promyshlennosti v period voiny i revoliutsii' *Vestnik statistiki* **14** pp. 113–54.

Vorob'ev, N.Ia. (1961), *Ocherki po istorii promyshlennoi statistiki v dorevoliutsionnoi Rossii i v SSSR*, Moscow: Gosstatizdat.

Voronkova, S.V. (1965), 'Stroitel'stvo avtomobil'nykh zavodov v Rossii v gody pervoi mirovoi voiny 1914–1917 g.' *Istoricheskie zapiski* **75** pp. 147–69.

Voronkova, S.V. (1975), *Materialy Osobogo soveshchaniia po oborone gosudarstva*, Moscow: Izdatel'stvo Moskovskogo universiteta.

Wade, Rex (1969), *The Russian Search for Peace, February to October 1917*, Stanford: Stanford University Press.

Wade, Rex (2000), *The Russian Revolution, 1917*, Cambridge: Cambridge University Press.

Waldron, Peter (1995), 'States of emergency: autocracy and extraordinary legislation, 1881–1917' *Revolutionary Russia* 8 pp. 1–25.

Wheatcroft, S.G. (1980), 'Grain production and utilization in Russia and the USSR before collectivization', unpublished PhD dissertation, CREES, University of Birmingham.

White, Howard (1992), '1917 in the rear garrisons', in Linda Edmondson and Peter Waldron, eds, *Economy and Society in Russia and the Soviet Union 1860–1930*, Houndmills: Macmillan, pp. 152–68.

White, James D. (1994), *The Russian Revolution, 1917–1921: A Short History*, London: Edward Arnold.

Wildman, Allan K. (1980), *The End of the Russian Imperial Army: The Old Army and the Soldiers' Revolt, March–April 1917*, Princeton: Princeton University Press.

Wildman, Allan K. (1987) *The End of the Russian Imperial Army: The Road to Soviet Power and Peace*, Princeton: Princeton University Press.

Winter, Jay and Jean-Louis Robert, eds (1997), *Capital Cities at War: Paris, London, Berlin 1914–1919*, Cambridge: Cambridge University Press.

Wortman, Richard S. (2000), *Scenarios of Power: Myth and Ceremony in Russian Monarchy*, volume 2, Princeton: Princeton University Press.

Yaney, George (1982), *The Urge to Mobilize: Agrarian Reform in Russia, 1861–1930*, Urbana: Illinois University Press.

Zagorsky, S.O. (1928), *State Control of Industry in Russia during the War*, New Haven: Yale University Press.

Zalesskii, S.A. (1959), 'Mobilizatsiia gornozavodskoi promyshlennosti na Urale v gody pervoi mirovoi voiny' *Istoricheskie zapiski* 65 pp. 80–118.

Index